Investigative Journalism

Investigative Journalism

Sanoj Singh

RANDOM

RANDOM PUBLICATIONS

NEW DELHI (INDIA)

Investigative Journalism

ISBN 978-93-5111-956-2

Published in 2016 in India by

Reprint 2019

RANDOM PUBLICATIONS

4376-A/4B, Gali Murari Lal, Ansari Road
New Delhi-110 002
Phone : +9111-43580356, 011-23289044, 011-43142548
e-mail: sales@randompublications.com,
info@randompublications.com, randomexports@gmail.com

Type Setting by : Friends Media, Delhi-110089
Printed at : Mehra Printers, Delhi-110 092

Preface

Investigative Journalism explores the history, theory and practice of investigative journalism around the world.

Investigative journalism is a form of journalism in which reporters deeply investigate a single topic of interest, such as serious crimes, political corruption, or corporate wrongdoing. An investigative journalist may spend months or years researching and preparing a report. Investigative journalism is a primary source of information. Most investigative journalism is conducted by newspapers, wire services, and freelance journalists. Practitioners sometimes use the term "accountability reporting".

Investigative Journalism means the unveiling of matters that are concealed either deliberately by someone in a position of power, or accidentally, behind a chaotic mass of facts and circumstances - and the analysis and exposure of all relevant facts to the public. In this way investigative journalism crucially contributes to freedom of expression and media development.

In the service of the Public Interest, our purpose is to uncover corruption, injustice, maladministration and lies. As a duty to readers and viewers as well as self-protection in a hostile legal environment, investigative journalism seeks above all to tell the documented truth in depth and without fear or favour. It is to provide a voice for those without one and to hold the powerful to account. It's to comfort the afflicted and afflict the comfortable.

It is hoped that this book will provide new insights to the established journalists and the working journalists to develop practice in the field of investigative journalism. This book covers the whole syllabus of the students of journalism in various universities and it is hoped that the book will prove to be of immense value to the teachers, students, the journalists and the general public alike.

– Author

Contents

1

Introduction

Investigative journalism is a branch of journalism that usually concentrates on a very specific topic and typically requires a lot of work to yield results. It is an in-depth article or series of articles based on research and investigation, usually over a long period of time. The subject often involves legal or controversial issues, such as the mafia, the tobacco industry, now a days political controversies are forming a major part of investigation.

During the 1972 campaign for the White House, when Richard M. Nixon was seeking a second term in office, five persons, acting on orders, broke into the Democratic national offices in the Watergate complex in Washington and planted electronic eavesdropping devices. Their purpose remains unclear till date. Bob Woodward and Carl Bernstein, reporters with the Washington Post, became curious when a short news item appeared regarding a burglary at the Watergate office of the Democratic Party and began to make inquiries. Through their investigations, it was discovered that it was not a simple act of burglary but a case of political corruption and manipulation involving the highest office in the land.

Investigative journalism is a distinctive aspect of the work undertaken by the media. Essentially an information-gathering exercise, it looks for facts that are not easy to obtain by simple requests and searches, or those that are actively being concealed, suppressed or distorted. Where such investigative work involves the use of covert methods, it raises issues that tend to further blur the line between law and ethics. An informed citizenry – the bedrock of a democracy, holding the government accountable through voting and participation – requires investigative journalism. In many cases, the subjects of the reporting wish the matters under scrutiny to remain undisclosed. A healthy democracy cannot sustain itself on asymmetric dissemination of information. The political elite are ever sensitive to news; and news about economic or political wrongdoing can trigger judicial or quasi-judicial scrutiny.

Various methods are employed for their fact-finding – the study of often neglected sources like archives, phone records, address books, tax records and license records; anonymous sources; and going undercover. It is often suggested that anonymous sources are double-edged - on the one hand they may provide especially newsworthy information, such as classified or confidential information about current events, information about a previously unreported scandal, or the perspective of a particular group that may fear retribution for expressing certain opinions in the press; but the downside is that the condition of anonymity may make it difficult or impossible for the reporter to verify the source's statements. By going undercover, the reporter tries to infiltrate a community by posing as somebody friendly to that community.

The Bhagalpur Blindings provide a lesson in the crucial contribution that journalistic research can make in creating public awareness of human rights, more so in a society in which entrenched abuse is likely to be overlooked. Over three years, from 1979 to 1982, policemen blinded 33 criminals in Bhagalpur Jail using acid. Codenamed Operation Gangajal, a report carried by The Indian Express, the incident became a national scandal and 14 policemen were suspended. Of the 14 policemen, 13 were acquitted and reinstated in service. When The Indian Express brought the issue into national focus, the Supreme Court accepted it as a writ petition. In Bhagalpur, many people campaigned for the suspension of the policemen, arguing that such punishment deterred crime more effectively than protracted legal cases. It took a sustained campaign on the rights of prisoners along with the impact of the pictures of the blinded men to touch the public conscience.

A journalist once said, "News is something someone somewhere doesn't want to be published – all the rest is advertisement". That may be considered a far-fetched definition in today's media world which considers advertisements the lifeblood of journalism and a starlet delivering a baby more attractive news than a wave of suicides among exploited farmers.

However, any newsperson worth his/her salt knows that uncovering a hidden story is far more challenging and satisfying than covering a prime minister's foreign tour or hunting for Page 3 gossip in a celebrity party. Regrettably, this breed of committed reporters is fast vanishing, thanks to the bulldozing forces of the market that are converting the media profession in India into an enterprise like any other industry producing consumer goods.

Modern investigative journalism is a discipline, rigorous and demanding. Modern journalism, despite its many aberrations, is considered the most effective monitor and upholder of democratic values. And the powerful instrument to fulfill this obligation is investigative reporting. Democracy involves accountability of elected representatives and civil servants. There are many mechanisms for checks and balances, but these can be abused, circumvented, ignored or made ineffective. Investigative reporting steps into this vacuum to scrutinise and expose the wrong-doings of those in authority which hurt public interest and make them accountable to the people.

We rejoice at the robustness of our democracy. We celebrate the vibrancy of the sparkling free press of India. But we know that the constitutional instruments to make the establishment accountable are weakening or failing. The parallel democratic institutions, which are supposed to nourish these instruments, are not fully evolved. Leave alone the ordinary citizen, neither our political leaders nor the academicians and intellectuals have fully cultivated a democratic mindset and culture which should involve transparency, professional commitment and accountability. To that extent, our democracy is fragile and — to use an unpleasant word — underdeveloped.

The importance of the "organic" relationship, as described by Walter Lippman, between a healthy democracy and the free press need not be elaborated here. One cannot sustain without the other. Indian media is so intoxicated with its so-called freedom (freest press in the world, one might say) that it fails to understand that it is also equally underdeveloped and fragile, that freedom carries certain grave responsibilities and that as upholder of democratic values and freedom (not just another profit-making industry) it has some specific obligations and duties towards the society. It is so obsessed with itself that it does not realise that it is throwing to winds its credibility, respectability and power by not attending to its basic obligations.

For investigative reporting to flourish, what is required is: an independent and pluralistic media which is fearless, committed to democracy, universal human values, journalists with commitment who can identify problems and have the grit, perseverance, patience and skills to do research and owners and editors professionally non-partisan and without vested interests.

What goes under the name of investigative journalism (with some honourable exceptions) in India, can hardly be taught in a journalism school as classic investigative journalism. The so-called investigative reporting in India in the Bofors case, Fodder scam, Jain Diary Case, Petrol Pumps largesse scandal and even Satyendra Dubey's murder case have been either rankly partisan political exercises or half-hearted attempts to show off the fearlessness of those media units. Has anyone followed Satyendra Dubey's case to the end? Who are the murderers? Are they arrested? Who leaked Satyendra's confidential letter from the PMO? Is that person booked? And the mafia contractors of the Golden Quadrilateral? Has any paper or channel pursued them?

One remembers the sensation caused by Arun Shourie's series of 'investigative' stories on the then chief minister AR Antulay of Maharashtra in early 1980's. Shourie, then, was acknowledged as the pioneer of modern investigative journalism in India. One also remembers the first sentence of his first story. Paraphrased in memory, it ran something like this "...look at these political rats; how they run when cornered..." Now, any news editor worth his/her salt would spike that story. It broke all the tenets of not only investigative journalism, but also of ordinary reporting. Shourie's stories were written in a style that was blatantly partisan and spiteful. Moreover, he had not uncovered anything that had not been published earlier, that too, with much more detail, in local newspapers. Antulay's sins of omission and commission, his acceptance of cheques for his public trust in front of TV cameras, was public knowledge in the entire state of Maharashtra. But Shourie, instead of writing scathing comment pieces on the edit page, wrote 'investigative' news stories on the front pages of his newspaper!

POLITICAL EXPEDIENCE

Bofors, St.Kitts, none of the stories were followed thoroughly and with the rigour that investigative journalism demands. The pursuit was half-hearted; the stories tapered off occasionally, but were revived vigorously whenever a political occasion demanded.

No doubt, there have been laudable attempts at exposing some major scandals at local or state levels. But, often, the exposure is made in one sensational burst and then the press loses interest. The story tapers off or is not followed at all. Clearly, the Indian media has not nourished the discipline of classic investigative reporting. The political, economic and social scenario of India is so complex and rotten and the media's credibility, despite its enormous power, is so low that even conscientious bureaucrats do not dare to blow the whistle. One whistle-blower who dared was murdered. And the press has nearly forgotten him.

BASIC REQUIREMENTS OF INVESTIGATE JOURNALISM

For investigative reporting to flourish, what is required is: an independent and pluralistic media which is fearless, committed to democracy, universal human values, journalists with commitment who can identify problems and have the grit, perseverance, patience and skills to do research and owners and editors professionally non-partisan and without vested interests.

We have a fantastically free press, so free that it does not have a professional self-regulatory mechanism to monitor fundamental ethics of the press. Not even the journalists' associations, which are more interested in begging for more perks from the government and corporate bodies than in the health of their own profession. Many journalists may have the aptitude and skills for investigative journalism. But their owners and editors do not have the will, even if they have the resources, to encourage them. The owners and the editors too have multiple vested interests — in political parties, individual leaders, corporate bodies and so one.

Indian bureaucracy, notorious for its red-tapism, does not easily part with even ordinary information, never mind the information acts on the book, and, as mentioned earlier, those who really want expose the malefascence do not trust the press.

IMPRISONMENT AND CRIME RATES

At any one time, only a fraction of those committing crimes in society is apprehended and punished. Yet the public visibility of this process is held to act as a general deterrent for the remainder of the population, including those likely to offend. If general deterrence operates to an extent that justifies its central position in society, there should be some association between the activity of the criminal justice system and the total amount of crime. The broadest, though possibly weakest, kind of evidence pertaining to this comes from studies of the relationship between the numbers of persons incarcerated in a society and its general rate of recorded crime.

For example, where opportunities have been available to monitor recorded levels of crime across periods when rates of incarceration were steadily changing, no clear relationship materializes, even allowing for possible time-lags. This emerges particularly in studies of, and projections based upon, the increased use of incarceration in parts of the United States. Reviewing the evidence bearing on this point up to 1997, Nagin described the conceptual and other difficulties posed in researching this question, but could find no study that can be taken seriously as demonstrating a deterrence effect of imprisonment on general rates of crime. Furthermore, recent research has failed to establish any relationship, in a direction that would be predicted by deterrence theory, between lengths of prison sentences and rates of recidivism. Gendreau *et al.* have systematically reviewed this area in a report for the Solicitor General of Canada.

The research group reviewed 23 studies yielding 222 comparisons of groups of offenders who spent longer versus shorter periods in prison. The groups were similar on a series of five risk factors. Contrary to what would be predicted by deterrence theory, offenders who served longer sentences had slight increases in recidivism of between 2 and 3%; there was a small positive correlation between sentence length and subsequent rates of re-conviction. Incidentally, even Robert Martinson, in his widely cited and highly influential paper which gave 'very little reason to hope that we have in fact found a sure way of reducing recidivism through rehabilitation', also concluded that there was no evidence of an association between recidivism and sentence length. The foregoing review integrated information from many sources and was conducted on a mammoth scale. But smaller-scale research, for example on the comparative impact of fines and short jail sentences on rates of drinking and driving, have not unequivocally shown that the deterrence effect of the latter is necessarily any more powerful than that of the former.

Another frequently heard claim regarding deterrence is that it is more likely to work with 'white-collar' crimes, committed by mainly middle- or upper-class offenders. Weisburd and Chayet followed the criminal careers of 742 offenders convicted of such crimes. The sample, which was divided into those who received and those who did not receive prison sentences, was followed up for a total of more than ten years. There was no observable effect that could be attributed to specific deterrence.

ENHANCED PUNISHMENTS

During the 1970s, the proclaimed failure of education, training or psychotherapy to have their intended impact on criminal recidivism has been associated with a shift towards a more punitive stance in a number of legislatures. Particularly in the United States, from that decade onwards there was a progressive move towards harsher punishments and 'turning up the heat' on offenders. At an institutional level, such sentences included the use of boot camps and shock incarceration. In the community, intensive supervision, electronic surveillance, random drug testing, curfews and various permutations of each were tried and tested. Primary studies and evaluations of 'enhanced' and intermediate punishment therefore flourished during the 1980s and 1990s as the use of these types of sanction became more widespread. This created opportunities for controlled trials, in which more severe punishments were compared with standard punishments or 'business as usual' within the criminal justice system.

Participants in the stricter forms of treatment were sometimes allocated randomly, on other occasions selected on a voluntary basis. Analysis of outcomes in such studies is made difficult by the fact that although the harshness of punishment was intensified, in many cases additional elements of education, counselling and other types of rehabilitative activity were also introduced. Petersilia and Turner reported an evaluation of intensive supervision in probation and parole conducted in 14 American states. A sample of nearly 2,000 individuals across numerous sites was allocated randomly to experimental and control groups.

Follow-up evaluation found no impact of the more intensive and restrictive supervision, which in some agencies included close surveillance, electronic monitoring, random drug testing and other innovations, on recidivism. The only positive result along these lines to emerge was an association between clients' participation in drugs and alcohol counselling and subsequent reductions in re-offending rates of the order of 10–20%. However, the possibility that this was due to a selection effect could not be eliminated. Nevertheless, Petersilia was led to conclude that 'The empirical evidence regarding intermediate sanctions is decisive: Without a rehabilitation component, reductions in recidivism are elusive'. Examining this and other evaluations of intermediate punishment, Gendreau *et al.* concluded that none of the hoped-for goals of reduced prison numbers, reduced costs or reduced recidivism were delivered by these programmes. A more recent evaluation of the effectiveness of electronic monitoring in Canada, taking account of participants' risk levels, also drew negative conclusions. Bonta and his colleagues judged that the effectiveness of electronic monitoring 'as a true alternative to incarceration and reducing recidivism has yet to be demonstrated... If one is interested in reducing recidivism, then offender treatment, rather than sanctions, is the most promising approach'. For institutionally based sanctions, a similar large-scale evaluation was undertaken of the impact of shock incarceration or 'boot camps' for the US National Institute of Justice. Here, boot camp inmates were compared with other prisoners, prison parolees or probationers at a number of sites in eight states. Again, however, the results were not supportive of deterrence theory. The impact on recidivism was concluded to be 'at best, negligible... based on the totality of the evidence, boot camp programmes did not reduce offender recidivism'. This overall finding is very close to that obtained from evaluation of detention centres designed to deliver a 'short, sharp shock' in the United Kingdom in the early 1980s.

Evaluation of this initiative concluded that 'the introduction of the pilot project regimes had no discernible effect on the rate at which trainees were reconvicted. A number of ways in which effects on reconviction might have been masked were considered and discounted'. In a further test of deterrence effects, MacKenzie *et al.* have recently reported a review of 29 evaluative studies of correctional boot camps. The authors found that there was 'an almost equal odds of recidivating between the boot camps and comparison groups'. On the basis of their review, they therefore concluded that, 'in our overall metaanalysis of recidivism, we found no differences between the boot camp and comparison samples... the results of this systematic review and metaanalysis will be disappointing for many people... boot camps by themselves have little to offer as far as moving offenders away from criminal activities' is concerned. In both institutional and community settings, then, while the innovations being researched here were ones designed to impose stiffer penalties on offenders, no useful effect of this escalation in toughness was found. Where positive outcomes were observed, they were usually associated with an investment of time and effort in rehabilitative activities.

META-ANALYTIC REVIEWS

The findings from large-scale reviews of 'offender treatment' were surveyed. Some of the meta-analytic reviews described there included studies of criminal sanctions. We noted that the estimated 'grand mean' across all reviews, of the order of an approximately 10% reduction in recidivism levels, was probably diminished to some extent by the incorporation of studies that reported predominantly zero or negative effects. The average effect size was, in other words, dragged down by these particular results. Reviews that have examined criminal sanctions separately within a wide range of approaches to intervention have typically found deterrence-based programmes to have zero or negative effect sizes. One meta-analysis specifically designed to dissect the relevant literature on community-based intermediate punishments yielded negative conclusions regarding the impact of the initially much-lauded enhanced punishments. In their reviews of 135 outcome studies of surveillance, 'smart sentencing' and other measures of this type, Gendreau *et al.* found a mean effect size just below zero.

DETERRENCE ON TRIAL

The studies just discussed involved evaluation of changes in sentencing practices in criminal justice services where many other factors that were operating could not be easily or satisfactorily controlled. A possibly more robust approach is to examine deterrence effects when these have been directly manipulated, though published reviews of this field are hard to find. Sherman has reviewed studies in which the effect of deterrence practices has been evaluated using randomized designs. The use of randomization in this context clearly raises ethical issues. The focus here is upon those circumstances where it has been feasible to evaluate the use of criminal sanctioning because offenders were randomly allocated to experimental and control conditions.

Of 21 studies included in Sherman's review, 14 found no differences in recidivism between experimental and control samples. In five studies, increased severity of penalties resulted in increased recidivism. Only two studies showed any impact of punitive sanctions. In one, this effect was observed only in some sub-samples and not across the experimental group as a whole. The remaining report, by Sherman *et al.,* focused on the effect of arrest and brief incarceration on perpetrators of domestic violence in Minneapolis. However, subsequent extension and replications of this study at other sites obtained mixed results, so much so that the question of whether arrest should be mandatory for spousal abuse has been re-opened by other authors. For example, in another study responding to 1,200 cases of domestic violence in Milwaukee, criminal justice intervention in some cases precipitated further harm. Short-term arrest had an initial deterrence effect, but had a criminogenic effect in the following 12 months; full arrest with many more hours detention made no difference either way. On that basis, alongside other factors, it has been argued that the nature of legal decisions made should be tailored to the circumstances and demands of each individual case.

The most comprehensive attempt to catalogue the potential impact of punitive sanctions as specific deterrents was undertaken by Weisburd *et al.,* who compiled a 'Registry' of randomized experiments. The Registry provides details of a series of 68 studies published between 1951 and 1984 involving random allocation to different levels of criminal justice sanction. The definition of the word 'sanction' was very broad, and encompassed both heightened levels of strictness in terms of prison, probation or parole, as well as other experiments in which rehabilitative activities were included in traditional sanctioning procedures. Of the 68 studies available, 44 reported no differences between experimental and control samples. Only two showed apparently better outcomes for interventions that could be construed as more punitive. In neither case did the authors report statistical significance and the conclusions they drew were based solely on apparent trends in the data.

In the remaining 22 experiments, rates of recidivism, parole violation or other similar outcomes favoured experimental over control groups. However, in all the latter studies, the increased 'sanction' consisted of provision of individual counselling, participation in group treatments such as social skills training, or other forms of intervention that entailed sanctioning only in the respect that participation was non-voluntary. Though defined as sanctions for the purpose of the Registry, and involving some coercion in terms of limits on an offender's freedom, these interventions contained few if any elements that would ordinarily be considered directly punitive. In another context, that of work with substance-abusing offenders, coercion into treatment has been shown to have effects equivalent to voluntary participation, and the provision of services within such a framework may not be intrinsically punishing.

Another type of research though in a similar vein has more direct bearing on the question of general than of specific deterrence. Sherman reviewed a series of 18 studies of the impact of police 'crackdowns' on rates of crime. Crackdowns were defined as combinations of three tactical elements: increased police presence, greater use of sanctions and threats of increased sanction certainty, conveyed through the media. That is, the police announced to the public that they would be working more intensively on certain types of crime, that people were more likely to be arrested and would be more severely dealt with by the courts. In six of the studies, crackdowns were short-term and most of these experiments focused on illegal parking, drink-driving and other 'distinctly middle-class' vehicle-related offences. In five studies in this group, residual effects of deterrence were observed; in other words, the effect continued after police 'back-off' or lifting of the crackdown. The remaining experiments were longer-term, and focused on offences such as drug sales and trafficking. However, only two of the 12 studies in this category obtained residual effects. In another two studies, there was disturbing evidence that other kinds of crimes had increased.

SELF-REPORT SURVEYS

This category of evidence could be regarded as relatively weaker than some of the others discussed here, since it involves reliance on the verbal reports of people already convicted of crimes, some of whom may be dishonest, and indeed have convictions for offences involving dishonesty. However, there is no reason to believe that participants have anything to gain or lose just as to how they respond to questioners in research of this kind. Some investigators have focused on the reactions of individuals arrested and then punished for crimes, inviting them to comment on the extent to which their experience of the process might be likely to deter them from future offending. Other researchers have focused more closely on patterns in individuals' thinking in the period immediately before committing offences.

Some of this work has been based on interviews with offenders during which they have been asked to describe their offending behaviour in some detail. The types of offences committed by those taking part in these research studies varied considerably in seriousness, from shop theft and vehicle-taking to drug-trafficking and armed robbery. As suggested, return to these studies a little later in the stage. In a series of surveys, Klemke and his colleagues collected self-report information on shoplifting by teenagers. Young people were interviewed at two points several months apart. Researchers found little evidence of deterrence in preventing repeated acts of shoplifting by this age group. While only a small proportion of those arrested was apprehended a second time, a far higher proportion admitted to further acts of theft. Thus the experience of arrest appeared to have had little impact on their behaviour. Conversely, although we cannot rule out the possibility that another proportion was deterred, other factors such as increasing age and maturation could also have explained their desistance.

The impact of arrest has also been investigated in some of the longitudinal studies. In the Denver Youth Survey, Huizinga *et al.* collected data on the relationship between ongoing involvement in offending and experience of being arrested by the police. First, they found that the majority of offenders whatever their level of seriousness were not arrested at all. Second, for those who were, their delinquent behaviour did 'not appear to be well described by their arrests'. That is, the more serious offenders were rarely apprehended for their gravest offences: they were more likely to be detained for a fairly minor offence. Third, the majority of cases showed either no change in behaviour or an actual worsening of behaviour following arrest; and 'in only 8% of the cases was the serious offending rate of the arrested juvenile less than the matched control... being arrested is not a very strong deterrent against future delinquent behavior'.

THE DEATH PENALTY

Research on the most extreme of sanctions, capital punishment or 'judicial execution', self-evidently has no bearing on the question of specific deterrence, but may provide evidence on the effectiveness of this extreme measure as a general deterrent. The presumption that it is a deterrent is certainly invoked as a rationale for imposing it. Among the 71 countries that still retained its use up to the year 2001, 'the most common political justification is the belief that it has a unique general deterrent capacity to save further innocent lives or reduce significantly other capital offences'. Of course, the issue of the death penalty is a highly emotive one and attitudes towards it are primarily influenced by a range of ethical and political beliefs, rather than by evidence bearing on its outcomes. But as this evidence has nevertheless been collected and is relevant to the present discussion, it is included in this survey. Such research as is available has failed to find that the availability of the death penalty as a sentencing option has any clear suppressant effect on rates of the most serious crimes, such as homicide, including the murder of police or prison officers. Some researchers claimed to have found deterrence effects in the United States for the period 1935–1969, to the extent of calculating a ratio of executions to numbers of lives saved. But other researchers who have analysed the same data or attempted to replicate the analyses with other data sets have ultimately dismissed such claims.

In a global survey conducted on behalf of the United Nations, Hood compared different countries allotted to discrete categories just as to their pattern of usage of capital punishment over a 40-year period. Some countries or states were *retentionist*–they had retained the use of the sentence throughout that period. Others were *abolitionist*–they either had not used it throughout the same period, or had at some point halted its use. Others, most notably all states of the USA, had a period when execution was not used, but following which its use was reinstated. Analysis of the data for rates of serious crimes such as homicide under these different jurisdictions yielded no evidence that capital punishment was associated with reductions in their frequency. The assumed effects of capital punishment in suppressing rates of homicide or violent crime have proved similarly elusive even when side-by-side comparisons are made between roughly equivalent localities differing only in their usage of it.

They also fail to appear in other circumstances predicted by general deterrence theory, for example where effects might be amplified through the publicity given to executions. Even in the state of Texas, 'by far the most active death penalty state' analysis of crime statistics for the period 1984–1997 has found no relationship between the execution rate and the murder rate. One other kind of evidence might seem only tangentially relevant to the points at issue here but is nevertheless worth considering. Does the potential threat of sudden death at the hands of a fellow citizen dissuade individuals from committing crimes? McDowall *et al.* tested the widely held view that possession of lethal weapons acts as a general deterrent to crime. Such an argument is often forwarded in defence of widespread gun ownership in the United States. McDowall *et al.* analysed five sets of crime data covering periods before and after significant changes in levels of gun ownership.

In two of these cases, following an apparent upsurge in serious crimes, police forces offered training to citizens in the use of firearms, and levels of ownership increased. In one instance in the town of Kennesaw, Georgia, a law was passed making it a legal requirement for every household to maintain a firearm. In two other cases, new laws were passed in local communities prohibiting the sale or ownership of handguns. Extended time-series analysis of rates of the target offences showed no impact of these changes. This was despite widely publicized claims that guns made a difference; based, as McDowall and his colleagues showed, on misleading analyses of data over short and unrepresentative periods of time.

FAMOUS INDIAN INVESTIGATIVE JOURNALISTS

FEROZE GANDHI

Feroze Gandhi (born Feroze Sopariwala on 12 August 1912; died 8 September 1960) was an Indian politician and journalist of Parsi descent. He was the husband of Indira Gandhi, the former Prime Minister of India and daughter of Jawaharlal Nehru, the first Indian Prime Minister. He was educated at the City Anglo-Vernacular High School and Ewing Christian College, followed by the London School of Economics. He abandoned his studies in 1930 to join the struggle for Indian independence.

Feroze grew close to the Nehru family, especially Indira's mother Kamala Nehru and Indira herself. Feroze helped nurse the ailing Kamala, and briefly traveled with Nehru, Kamala and Indira to Europe.

Even before Kamala's death, Indira and Feroze had begun falling in love. There is some evidence that Kamala herself opposed the match, and although Nehru was personally averse to Feroze, he did not involve himself in opposing it. Indira and Feroze grew more close to each other in England. They married in 1942.

Arrested and jailed during the Quit India Movement less than six months after their marriage, he was imprisoned for a year in Allahabad's Naini Central Prison. Indira was also imprisoned. In 1944, she gave birth to Rajiv Gandhi, a future Prime Minister.

In 1946, Sanjay Gandhi, a major political influence on his mother when she was PM, was born. Indira and Feroze settled in Allahabad with their two young children, and Feroze became editor of *The National Herald*, a newspaper founded by his father-in-law. Feroze Gandhi contested elections to the Parliament of India in 1952, independent India's first general elections.

His wife served as his campaign organizer, and Gandhi won. But Feroze soon became a prominent force in his own right, criticizing the Government of his father-in-law and beginning a tirade against corruption.

His exposure of a scandal involving major insurance companies and the Finance Minister T.T. Krishnamachari caused the latter to resign, and Nehru major embarrassment. Feroze began building his own reputation and small coterie of supporters and advisors, and continued challenging the government.

He was re-elected in 1957. It should be noted that Indira did not envisage a personal future for herself in politics until the death of her husband. The marriage of Feroze and Indira was tumultuous, as Indira began living with her father, who was alone, and cared for him personally and often acted as his private secretary. When he became an MP, Feroze started living in his own house in Delhi, away from his father-in-law and wife.

This unwilling separation embittered Feroze, and it is speculated that he was having extra-marital affairs as a way of getting back on Indira.

Indira and Feroze were re-united in 1958, when Feroze suffered his first heart attack. Indira took him to recuperate in Kashmir, where with their young boys, they were together again. However, Feroze died in 1960 of a second heart attack.

ARUN SHOURIE

Born in 1941in Jalandhar, Punjab, India) is a prominent journalist, author and politician of India, he studied at St. Stephen's in Delhi. He is the son of Shri H. D. Shourie. He obtained his doctorate in Economics from Syracuse University in the United States.

He has been an economist with the World Bank, a consultant to the Planning Commission, India and editor of the Indian Express (a leading Indian newspaper).

In a series of exposés, many of which he wrote himself, Shourie and the Indian Express uncovered corruption in the highest echelons of the government and exposed several major scandals, including what has been dubbed "India's Watergate."

Shourie started a one-man crusade in 1981 against Abdul Rehman Antulay, the chief minister of Maharashtra State, who allegedly extorted millions of dollars from businesses dependent on state resources and put the money in a private trust named after Indira Gandhi. The story caused the eventual resignation of the state governor, the highest-ranking official in India ever forced from office by newspaper reporting, and great embarrassment to Gandhi and her ruling Congress Party.

Shourie's exposés resulted in a prolonged labour dispute at the Bombay offices of the Indian Express, where a labour organizer with ties to Antulay encouraged workers to strike for a minimum wage double than what was paid at any other newspaper in India. It also resulted in a government crackdown that included a host of legal cases launched against the Indian Express by various agencies. In 1982, the paper's owner Ramnath Goenka fired Shourie as a result of continued government pressure.

Between 1982 and 1986, Shourie wrote for various newspapers and magazines. He was appointed executive editor of the Times of India in 1986 but was lured back to the Indian Express by Goenka in 1987.

Shourie launched an attack on then prime minister Rajiv Gandhi over the Bofors howitzer gun purchase scandal. This contributed to Gandhi's defeat in the subsequent parliamentary elections.

Among the many battles Shourie fought for press freedom, perhaps the most famous was his crusade against the government's proposal in 1988 to introduce a defamation bill. It was widely perceived that the bill had been introduced with unusual speed in Parliament in an attempt to muzzle the Indian Express, and the entire media community joined Shourie and the Indian Express in condemning the move.

At one stage, there were 300 cases filed by the government against the Indian Express, and credit supply from banks was cut off. Shourie, however, continued his battle against government corruption until 1990, when differences on editorial policy forced him to resign from the Indian Express. The differences involved Shourie's opposition to the implementation of the Mandal Commission Report, set up reservations in government jobs for Other Backward Classes (OBCs) and were initiated by then Prime Minister V.P. Singh's government. After that, he devoted his energy to writing books and regular columns, which appeared in different languages in 30 newspapers across India.

Shourie is a member of the Bharatiya Janata Party (BJP). He has been a member of the Rajya Sabha and also held the office of the Minister of Divestment, Communication and Information Technology in the Government of India under Atal Bihari Vajpayee's prime ministership. As Disinvestment Minister, he led the sale of Maruti, VSNL, Hindustan Zinc among others. His position as Minister was a controversial one, but he and his secretary Pradip Baijal are much respected for kick-starting what people believe was a best-in-class process.

In a poll of India's top 100 CEOs in February 2004 he was ranked the most outstanding minister of Mr.Vajpayee's government. In his book Worshipping False Gods, Shourie criticized B.R. Ambedkar, the leader of Dalits for alleged complicity with the British and lust for power and wealth.

His writings have gained him a considerable following around the country, as well as several national and international honours.

Among these are the Padma Bhushan, the Magsaysay Award, the Dadabhai Naoroji Award, the Astor Award, the K.S. Hegde Award and the International Editor of the Year Award. The Federation of Indian Publishers recently conferred The Freedom to Publish Award on him.

M. J. AKBAR

Mubashar Jawed Akbar (b. 1951)is a leading Indian journalist and author. He's the founder and editor-in-chief of *The Asian Age*, a daily multi-edition Indian newspaper with a global perspective. He has written several books, including *Byline* (New Delhi: Chronicle Books, 2003), a biography of Jawaharlal Nehru titled 'Nehru: The Making of India', a book on Kashmir titled 'Kashmir: Behind the Vale', 'Riot After Riot' and 'India: The Siege Within'. He also authored 'The Shade of Swords', a cohesive history of Jihad.

M. J. Akbar is also the editor-in-chief of The Deccan Chronicle, a Hyderabad-based news daily. He is the only Indian Newspaper Editor who Blogs!.

He comes from Kashmiri Muslim ancestry. He attended Calcutta Boys' School when its principal was the legendary Clifford Hicks, and later Presidency College, Calcutta He belongs to the rare breed of journalists who have made a significant impact on Indian society by their writing as columnists and authors.

He revolutionized Indian journalism in the seventies and the eighties by successfully launching and establishing the weekly magazine Sunday and the daily newspaper, The Telegraph at the age of 28 years. He took a brief detour into politics with his election to the Indian Parliament in November 1989 but returned to his first passion, writing and editing, in 1993.

The books he has published have achieved great international acclaim: Riot after Riot; Nehru: The Making of India; India: The Siege Within and Kashmir: Behind the Vale, Byline and The Shade of Swords: Jihad and the Conflict Between Islam and Christianity, published in 2002, is perhaps his most influential and prophetic work.

N. RAM

N. Ram (Narasimhan Ram) (born May 4, 1945), is an Indian journalist, who is Editor-in-chief of *The Hindu* since June 27, 2003. Ram also heads the other publications of The Hindu Group, *Frontline*, The Hindu Business Line and *Sportstar*. He graduated from Loyola College, Chennai in arts in 1964, went on to get a masters degree in arts from Presidency College, Chennai in 1966 and later a M.S. in comparative journalism from the Columbia University Graduate School of Journalism.

Beginning his career in The Hindu as an Associate Editor in 1977, he was made the Washington Correspondent in 1980. N Ram's association with Frontline, dates back to 1984, when the magazine was started.A Padma Bhushan awardee, Ram has achieved several accolades such as, Asian Investigative Journalist of the Year (1990) Award conferred by the Press Foundation of Asia at the "One Asia Assembly", Manila, 1990 for "the courage and diligence which inspired him and his newspaper to continue searching for the truth in the now famous Bofors Case, the disciplined application of his journalistic idealism and the impact of his revelations on the Indian political scene"; B.D.

Goenka Award for Excellence in Journalism, 1989, shared with Chitra Subramaniam; National Citizen's Award, 1995, New Delhi (with the citation reading "for his brave and fearless writings in the interest of the nation") and XLRI's First JRD Tata Award for Business Ethics, awarded at this management institute's 46th Annual Convocation at Jamshedpur on March 23, 2002 for "following rigorously the canons of journalism and ethics" and making "this ethics part of a corporate philosophy"Prior to his present position he was Associate Editor until 1991 and then Editor of Frontline and Sportstar between 1991 and 2003. As a student activist, he was the vice-president of the Students Federation of India (SFI) (the students's wing of the Communist Party of India (Marxist) at the time of its.

SHEKHAR GUPTA

Shekhar Gupta is the Group CEO of the Indian Express Group of Publications and the Editor-in-Chief of The Indian Express, often touted as India's most independent national newspaper.

The paper that was traditionally identified with Journalism of Courage standing up to cynical commercialism and crude commodification of news. It has been claimed that the tradition flourished under Gupta and that he has affirmed that there is nothing contradictory about great journalism and good business.

Gupta's career has been marked by an unusual and unique combination in daily journalism: excellence as an individual with the highest professional and ethical standards in step with excellence as a leader who has brought about institutional changes in the profession and the industry.

In his years spent so far at the helm, The Indian Express, and its Sunday edition, The Sunday Express (which Gupta launched four years ago) are today at the forefront of investigative and public-affairs journalism.

Gupta has also been instrumental in taking Express journalism to cities and states left untouched by the national media. In 1996, at the height of the militant violence in Jammu and Kashmir, Gupta launched an edition of the paper in Jammu and Srinagar. The Express team in the state is now considered the best of any news organisation there, winning the highest number of national and international awards than any other news bureau in the state.

Under Gupta's leadership, The Indian Express and its journalists have won virtually every national award in journalism at every level of seniority.

The Express News Service is the largest network of reporters, editors and photographers in the country today, bringing together the best of talent and experience. Under Gupta's mentoring, many of the journalists have grown into positions of leadership in the Express and outside it in several newsrooms, print and broadcast across the country.

It is perhaps fitting, therefore, that it was at The Indian Express, where Gupta began his career as a reporter in 1977. Since then, Guptas byline has had an enduring association with the most important news events in India. In his first stint at the Express, Gupta, then 26, exposed a horrific massacre in Assam that marked a watershed in the regionÆs ethnic conflict (his work in

Assam won him several awards and formed the basis of his first book Assam: A Valley Divided, published in 1984) focusing national attention on a problem that continues to this day.

After six years at the Express, Gupta went to India Today, the countrys largest and premier newsmagazine. There, as Senior Editor, his investigative journalism covered the most important newsbreaks in the country in recent times, from the insurgency in Punjab that led to the assassination of Prime Minister Indira Gandhi to the war in Sri Lanka.

In 1984, Gupta exposed LTTE training camps in India (prompting many in the government to label him anti-national) and thereby showed how New Delhi's policy of appeasing terror was bound to backfire, which it did.

He nailed the lie of official intelligence agencies in a spy scandal that falsely implicated scientists of the Indian Space Research Organisation, a story that was vindicated by the court years later.

In an investigation, seven years before 9/11, Gupta travelled across Afghanistan, Pakistan, Germany, the US and the UK, to report extensively on the threat from pan-Islamic fundamentalism, including its links with Osama bin Laden. Not only was the piece prescient, it was the clearest foreshadow in journalism of what happened to the insurgency in Jammu and Kashmir.

Gupta's weekly column called National Interest, now in its ninth year, has become a touchstone for new ideas in politics, governance, society, business and sports. For two years, he has been the host of Walk the Talk on NDTV 24x7.

Gupta has been invited as a guest speaker by several universities and institutions in India and overseas. These include Stanford University, the John F Kennedy School of Government at Harvard, the Woodrow Wilson School of International Affairs at Princeton University, Infosys Technologies in Bangalore, the National Law Institute, Defence Services Staff Colleges (Army, Air Force, and Naval War Colleges) and several other institutions.

He is a regular guest and speaker at the World Economic Forum in Davos and its India summits.

Besides his book on Assam, Gupta has authored India Redefines Its Role, published by the Oxford University Press under the Adelphi Paper Series of the International Institute of Strategic Studies, London, where Gupta worked as a Research Associate. He was also a member of its council. Besides The Indian Express, Guptas writing has been featured in several newspapers and magazines in India and abroad, including The Wall Street Journal, International Herald Tribune, Newsweek and Le Monde.

Recently, Gupta became the first Indian journalist to insinuate the involvement of "Hindu fanatics" in the twin bomb blasts Delhi's Jama Masjid in an article in Newsweek International, while giving a clean chit to Islamic fundamentalists' involvement in the terror attacks in India which is widely documented. Because of this and other partisan work performed by him, he has been dubbed as the Wheeler Dealer Editor by a popular blog Spindian Express.

TARUN TEJPAL

Tarun Tejpal is CEO and editor-in-chief of tehelka, an Web-only news and literary site based in New Delhi — and one of India's most well-known editors. Since its founding in March 2000, two of the site's stories have brought it international attention: its investigation of a cricket match-fixing scandal and its sting operation that exposed corruption in the Indian defence establishment.

Till March 1, 2000, Tarun was the managing editor of Outlook, India's premier weekly newsmagazine. In an 18-year career, he has reported for The Indian Express and The Telegraph, and been an editor with the India Today and The Indian Express groups.

He is a co-founder of the publishing house IndiaInk, which first published Arundhati Roy's The God of Small Things. He has written for several international publications, including The Paris Review, The Guardian, The Financial Times, and Prospect. After Outlook and IndiaInk, tehelka.com is the third start-up project with which he is involved.

ANIRUDDHA BAHAL

Aniruddha Bahal is known for his operations to expose corruption at public places. His operations, aptly called *Sting Operations*, catches the culprits on camera by first luring them to accept bribes, asking favours etc.

Recently he has been involved in unearthing a cash for question scam which was named *Operation Duryodhan*. MPs from both Lok Sabha(House of People) and Rajya Sabha(House of Executives) were shown taking bribes for raising questions in the Indian Parliament.

2

The Ethics of the 'Sting' in Investigating Journalism

Most discussions about ethics in investigative journalism have focused on the methodology. What methods are valid to reveal wrongdoing? Is deception legitimate when the aim is to tell the truth? Is any method justifiable no matter the working conditions and the difficulties in getting information? Can television reporters use hidden cameras to get a story? Can journalists use false identities to gain access to information?

Operation Westend brought some particularly acute questions to the fore. Many argued that a vast gulf existed between 'snaring' or 'tempting' people into accepting 'gifts' or 'bribes'; and the exposure of corruption regarding specific deals. Is it ethical to hold someone responsible for a crime that would not have been committed if the undercover journalist had not encouraged the act? Also, how ethical was it to use prostitutes in order to expose corruption in defense deals? Tarun Tejpal, Tehelka editor, had justified the methods by saying that 'extraordinary circumstances justified the use of extraordinary methods'.

Clearly, there can be no consensus on the ethics of sting operations when the methods and objectives of each operation vary so vastly. In fact, the legal implications of reporters' actions are, by far, more clear-cut than the ethical issues involved. Ethics, dealing with distinguishing right and wrong, uses philosophical principles to justify a particular course of action. Any action can be judged ethical, depending on what framework is used to justify it, and what values are prioritized. Fortunately for this particular dilemma, the media's cherished values are not a matter of much debate. What journalists and editors need to determine is who will benefit as a result of the reporting. If journalism is committed to democratic accountability, then the question that needs to be asked is whether the public benefits as a result of specific investigative reports. Does the press fulfill its social responsibility in revealing wrongdoing? Whose interests are being affected? Whose rights are being invaded? Is the issue at stake a matter of legitimate public interest?

One can debate endlessly about the ethics of these issues, and not be any closer to resolution, except where motive is clear. Most people would consider the sting operation on Dilip Singh Judeo as unethical because it was motivated – not by concerns of informing the citizens, but for political one-upmanship. The 'reverse sting' on Ajit Jogi and his son falls in the same category.

At best, a case by case analysis may be undertaken to distinguish ethically right journalistic method from wrong. However, if one were to move beyond ethics and enter the realm of law, the determination of what is legally right method is easier. Such an enquiry is also apt in the context of the much-anticipated Broadcasting Bill. Undoubtedly, the starting point for any such discussion has to be the freedom of the press.

In such circumstances, what does a restless committed journalist do? He takes a hidden camera with him and broadcasts countrywide bulletins of responsible people accepting bribes. If documents, receipts, accounts, papers or files are not forthcoming as proof, here's how the journalist furnishes the proof. Live on screen. Tarun Tejpal and Tehelka's sting operation and subsequent imitations by others have raised a hornet's nest questioning the ethical propriety of this kind of journalism. A positive outcome indeed.

MEDIA CREDIBILITY

The press is losing credibility because of its blatant partisanship and rank commercialism. So take the camera and expose. Never mind, it is one-time exposure of a part. But the proof is there, clearly visible on the screen to make an impact on the minds of the people. This will at least shake the people and those who are concerned out of their slumber.

No, this is not investigative journalism. But it is the sting. An occasional sting operation made with professional commitment may serve the cause for the time being. But that is no alternative to investigative journalism. To build its credibility and ensure its freedom under democracy, the media in India will have to turn to serious investigative reporting.

The Tehelka style of investigative journalism has brought about a change in the way we look at news, amidst new notions of editorial freedom. Stirring stuff like the kind shown in 'stings' has a fair amount of shock value.

There is no denying the fact that a sting operation is by far the most effective way of exposing the truth. With a society and a system of governance that defies transparency, the doubting public demands credible proof. Being 'caught in an act' on camera leaves little scope for evasive answers by those who shamelessly manipulate the system for vested interests.

Public figures are often reminded that they have nothing to hide from the public, which has a right to know everything. The stinging truth however, is the easy conscience with which corruption is tolerated and allowed to plague the political system.

Operation West End

Newsgathering acquired a new meaning with Tehelka's 'Operation West End', which left the common man with deep revulsion for the political system and contempt for those in the defence establishment who are willing to trade national interest for vested interests.

It is not just governance but also other systems of everyday life, which if left unchecked spell disaster for the common man. Also the argument that it is virtually impossible to discover the real state of affairs through normal ways of investigation deserves a fair hearing.

The most explosive sting by Tehelka in recent times is the one, exposing the twists behind the Best Bakery case.Zaheera Sheikh, who has become a symbol of the Gujarat carnage has been continuously changing her testimony in the case. The Tehelka tapes allege that Zaheera was paid Rs 18 lakh by a BJP MLA.

The startling revelation has led the judiciary to now examine the possibility of a dubious deal. But whether the 'sting' is a legitimate weapon of the new media is an issue worth debating upon. Investigative journalism is synonymous with controversies. While it does reflect upon a vigilant media, it also allows the survival of a sensationalist press, which confuses cheap thrills with journalism.

To assume that a mere expose' can keep the audience hooked is the media's fatal error. Public opinion will eventually expose dumbed down journalism to sharp criticism.

Such exposures can thus stand the test of time only on account of credibility and veritable proof of the alleged facts. There are also occupational hazards to be battled when engaged in a sting operation. In the case of Tehelka, the associates were made to pay a heavy price, virtually grounding the organization operationally and financially.

But the fact remains that there is only so much that the press can endeavour to do. It cannot punish the guilty nor can it command accountability from those occupying positions of power.

Launched in 2000, Tehelka began as an on line news-views portal, unaligned of any of India's established media groups. Since then, it has become the sub continent's fastest growing independent weekly newspaper. Published by Tarun Tejpal, Tehelka's 2001 sting Operation West End captured several members of the then ruling party BJP - Bangaru Laxman accepting bribes to approve defence contracts. George Fernandes resigned after the tapes were made public. In the aftermath of these exposes, Tehelka drew the ire of the government and was at the receiving end of a destructive un-constitutional assault eventually forcing its closure. After a widespread public appeal to loyal readers, Tehelka re-launched in 2004 as a weekly newspaper, committed to free, fair and fearless journalism. Tehelka's reputation for ground- breaking investigations, tenacious public interest journalism, exposes of corruption, fiery reportage and fine writing, has earned it a strong national following and widespread international acclaim. Tehelka's in depth investigative stories on witness bribery in the Best Bakery Fire case, corruption over airline pilots' qualifications and child sex scandals in resort areas are among the many that have contributed to changing the fundamental nature of Indian media.

MEDIA THEORY AND ETHICS

In evaluating what media ethics has accomplished and assessing its academic status at present, theory is the most obvious place to begin. Ethics is a world of ideas. The mission of colleges and universities is critical thinking, creating new knowledge, building scientific models that are transferable and testable. Higher education is our home for teaching ethics, and the centerpiece of our vocation is ideas. Obviously, abundant things happen in media ethics, but we need to focus on its intellectual substance to ensure that it is equipped for the globalized 21st century. A crucial issue is whether our theorizing is adequate. What foundations undergird our enterprise? We find our pathway now and in the future conceptually. If we understand ethics as a world of ideas, our primary task is credible theory.

In the first half of the 1980s, the material was largely atheoretical, with media ethics typically defined as descriptive in character. Taking a complex professional arena seriously seemed to demand war stories rather than abstractions. The prominent text by John Hulteng, The Messenger's Motives: Ethical Problems of the Mass Media, first published in 1976 with a second edition in 1985, used ethics codes and accepted professional practice as the standards for how the media ought to operate. Hulteng's 1981 book was descriptive also, Playing It Straight: A Practical Discussion of the Ethical Principles of ASNE. Gene Goodwin's Groping for Ethics in Journalism examined a variety of issues such as conflict of interest and privacy in terms of interviews with quality professionals and codes of ethics. Tom Goldstein in The News at Any Cost: How Journalists Compromise Their Ethics to Shape the News focused on the techniques used by the press when dealing with plagiarism, money, accuracy, and so forth. The framework in Philip Meyer's Ethical Journalism was the First Amendment and written and unwritten codes of ethics.

While journalism values rather than ethical theory dominated the field as this period opened, John Merrill's work has been the exception and theoretically inclined from the beginning. The first anthology in media ethics, Ethics and the Press, edited by Merrill and Ralph Barney in 1975 includes a section on theoretical issues. His Philosophy and Journalism with Jack Odell in 1983 treats the substantive issues philosophically. And over the two-plus decades under review, the orientation of the field has changed in like fashion. On occasion, book-length studies in media ethics at present develop a philosophical framework. From journalistic morality or descriptive ethics or values in the early 1980s, normative ethics has become mandatory at present.

The major textbooks currently in use introduce students to philosophical ethics-classic and contemporary. Some examples are Philip Patterson and Lee Wilkins, Media Ethics: cases and Issues; Thomas Bivins, Mixed Media: Moral Distinctions in Advertising, Public Relations and Journalism; Louis Day, Ethics in Media Communications: cases and Commentaries; Richard Johannesen et al.'s Ethics in Human Communication; and Clifford Christians, Mark Fackler, Kathy McKee, Peggy Kreshel and Robert Woods, Media Ethics: cases and Moral Reasoning. The 2006 book Contemporary Media Ethics, by Mitchell Land and Bill Hornaday, is centered entirely around the debate in ethical theory between utilitarianism and communitarian philosophy, as Jay Black's Mixed News: The Public/Civic/Communitarian Journalism Debate was earlier in different form. Stephen Ward's The Invention of Journalism Ethics is rich in intellectual history. Christopher Meyers's anthology on journalism ethics, currently in development, and The Handbook of Mass Media Ethics edited by Lee Wilkins and Clifford Christians for Erlbaum both take ethical theory seriously. Jay Black has always welcomed theoretical ethics for the Journal of Mass Media Ethics, of which Chris Meyers's "Appreciating W. D. Ross: On Duties and Consequences" and Stephen Ward's "Philosophical Foundations for Global Journalism Ethics" are illustrative. In fact, a recent special issue of the Journal of Mass Media Ethics deals with ethical theory throughout.

The bi-annual "National Communication Ethics Conference"-originally at Gull Lake, Michigan, and now at Duquesne University-has featured theory over its 16 years, through scholars-in-residence, papers, and plenary sessions. "Colloquium 2000 in Applied Media Ethics," the brainchild of Jay Black and Ralph Barney to enrich the field through a series of annual workshops on critical issues, has produced some groundbreaking work in ethical theory. Ed Lambeth's week-long seminars on Teaching Journalism Ethics consistently had a theoretical component. The colloquium hosted at the University of Oregon by Tom Bivins focused on the ethics of care as a theory in addition to its application to media practice.

Several book-length treatments from university presses illustrate theories of communication ethics and present possible options for bringing the Summits' history to philosophical maturity. The four that follow develop normative models for communication as an enterprise in general or the press as a social institution in particular.

Ronald Arnett established the field of communication as a whole around Martin Buber and his legacy. In terms of the focus on media ethics in this Summit review, Edmund Lambeth's Committed Journalism: An Ethic for the Profession is the first of this genre. He advocates an ethical system of five principles: truthtelling, humanness, justice, freedom, and stewardship-derived from a combination of ethical theory, ideal institutional guidelines, and the "toughest minds and truest spirits in the field". Within this framework of prima facie obligations, journalists "become stewards of free expression".

John Merrill proposes a deontelic ethics that integrates theories of duty with those grounded in consequences. A synthesis of principles and consequences results from a dialectical process true to the dynamic world of journalism. In the existential moment, classical and neo-liberal antinomies, altruism and egoism, positive and negative freedom are reconciled. The foundation for Merrill's "organic unification of opposites" is the dialectical tradition from Heraclitus.

Good News: Social Ethics and the Press identifies individual autonomy as the axis of Enlightenment ethics and advocates a communitarian philosophy instead. The community is understood to be ontologically and axiologically prior to persons. Organizations in this model operate with the standard of mutuality rather than power pragmatism. Reporting facilitates public life and represents the moral landscape within which the human community is formed. Land and Hornaday (2006) apply communitarian theory to news, advertising, and public relations by contrasting its appeal to community values with an emphasis on individual liberty and consequences. The forthcoming Ethics for Public Communication by Fackler, Christians, and Ferré puts the communitarian model into textbook form, centered around those critical episodes in the world media that signal a democratic "tipping-point." The political communitarianism represented by Good News has been integrated with feminist ethics to establish it outside neo-conservative politics. Dialogic communitarianism is the most advanced version of the theory, ensuring its multiculturalism and gender inclusiveness.

The long-term future of the field depends on the common language of theory, not as an abstract authority, but to assist us in thinking more systematically about the major league issues. While academia is generally committed to theoretical media ethics as necessary for the complicated agenda at present, there are several issues in theory that need ongoing debate and resolution. Some are perennial issues requiring continual clarification, and others can be resolved.

THE CANONICITY PROBLEM

We ought to solve the canonicity issue rather than be immobilized by it. As the media ethics literature matures philosophically, its appeal to classical ethicists and contemporary intellectuals is soured by the savage attacks at present on Eurocentric paternalism within the liberal arts as a whole. Hostile students weary of learning about "the dead white guys" can be ignored if their exasperation is no more articulate than that. However, in astute and systematic terms the philosophically inclined in ethics are currently mounting an attack on canonical authority that is inescapable. Enlightenment notions of the good are now recognized as the morality of the dominant gender and ruling class. The canon of media ethics has been largely monocultural, and for all the achievements within it, the field must become multicultural, gender inclusive, and transnational instead.

The expanding and deepening work in feminist ethics is of particular importance in confronting the challenge of canonicity. Nel Noddings sets feminist ethics at odds with rule-based systems, that is, with the traditional Western trajectory grounded in prescriptions and norms external to society and professional practice. Formalist media ethics presumes autonomous moral agents who apply rules consistently and self-consciously to every choice. In Noddings's terms, an ethics of moral reasoning that "arranges principles hierarchically and derives conclusions logically" is "peripheral to or even alien to, many problems of moral action....Moral decisions are, after all, made in real situations; they are qualitatively different from the solution of geometry problems". The feminist ethics of Seyla Benhabib and the neo-Aristotelian social ethics of Martha Nussbaum are fundamentally restructuring ethical theory. Daryl Koehn supports the emphasis in feminist ethics on a relational order rather than individual selves adhering to formal codes. However, she opposes the feminist tradition of care and nurturance, and argues for a dialogic ethics that stitches feminist ethics into dialogic communication theory. Linda Steiner's work demonstrates, during the period under review, how feminist ethics establishes a politically and morally ambitious agenda for media institutions and practice.

On a broader level than feminist ethics, another approach is to reconceptualize the canonicity problem. Some issues do not disappear from our agenda. This is true about virtue, duty, and consequences. They are fundamental components of the moral life. We may reject the European formulation but the issues remain. Our prevailing theories need not be considered canonical-defined in this case as a body of self-evident truths without contradiction. The Greek Kanon means measuring stick, taxation table, or a blueprint. Canons do grant privilege to certain texts on the grounds that without boundaries there is only chaos, dissipated energies, "a babble of...complaints rather than a settled critique." Diversity arises out of unity; without a buffer zone, struggle is impossible. The canon "depends on who is teaching it how;...living in the same place does not mean living with the same history". We should go beyond the original without forgetting it. Socrates makes that point in the Crito-recognizing that the fact he criticizes, what he criticizes, and how he criticizes is made possible by the very city he is criticizing. Theorists are not abstract authorities, but enable us to think on our own.

In Aristotle, moral virtue is a middle state determined by practical wisdom. Of the four cardinal virtues, temperance is the capstone and gateway to the other three. In Confucius's golden mean, moral virtue is the appropriate location between two extremes. Islamic ethics is a version of virtue ethics. The majority of Islamicists consider it a virtue ethics system. In the 12th century, for example, wisdom, justice, and courage were considered the primary virtues, though here influenced by the Greeks through alGhazali, Islam's greatest philosopher. The feminist ethics of Edith Wyschogrod's Saints and Postmodernism is a version of virtue ethics too, in that moral principles are only conceivable in the context of good persons. In the tradition of Emmanuel Lévinas, but in terms distinctively her own, the saintly life is one in "which compassion for the Other, irrespective of the cost to the saint, is the primary trait". Reciprocal care and understanding, rooted in emotion and experience, and not in formal consensus, are the basis on which moral discourse is possible.

In addition, for solving the canonicity problem, we need to reconstruct the character of theorizing. Theories ought not be treated in static, scholastic terms. The Greek tradition of rational universals and the Enlightenment commitment to Cartesian non-contingency privilege the conceptual logos. Philosophical proclivity toward reason presumes an objective, ahistorical foundation of knowledge. However, theory should be redefined as meaningful portraits and not statistically precise formulations derived from artificially fixed conditions. Theorizing in these terms is not an examination of external events, but the power of the imagination to give us an inside perspective on reality. Thomas Kuhn calls this revolutionary sciencethe constructing of paradigms-rather than the normal science of verifying that propositions are externally and internally valid.

Theories are not ex nihilo. They are not conceptually immaculate, arising out of nothing. Theories are not abstract theorems, but oppositional claims about the world. We identify niches and inconsistencies and conundrums over against existing conventions and theorize how to start over intellectually. Moral Engagement in Public Life: Theorists for Contemporary Ethics meets the test of valid theory. Two classical thinkers are included, Aristotle and Confucius, and 10 contemporary thinkers crossculturally and internationally who are epistemologically legitimate but not gendered male, one-dimensional, and Western thinking is rooted in core beliefs rather than epistemic certainty, and in this way they give us ethical discourse for grounding professional practice.

RELATIVISM

Working on media ethics in 21st century terms, the most fundamental challenge is Friedrich Nietzsche's. In his totalizing attack on ethical rationalism, Nietzsche insisted that life can be justified only as aesthetic phenomena. In a world where God has died and everything lacks meaning, morality is appearance, even delusion. Since there is no transcendent answer to the why of human existence, we face the demise of moral interpretation altogether. In the era beyond good and evil, ethics has been replaced by aesthetics. Only aesthetic values matter. One can speak of beauty without implying that anything ought to be beautiful or that anyone ought to create something beautiful.

For Nietzsche, morality has reached the end of the line. In its contemporary version, defending a suprasensory good is not beneficent, but imperialism over the moral judgment of diverse communities. Popular culture gets caught up in the technological imperative, producing the visually interesting, creating programs at times of artistic wholeness, but driven by the conditions of aesthetic space rather than ethics.

Communications is one crucial laboratory for addressing this predicament. It is not a discipline per se with a discrete subject matter; communications is pervasive and integrative rather than specialized. And communications makes possible all cultural forms, all community life and socio-political institutions without being absorbed into any of them. Therefore, in today's wideranging assault on the foundations of knowledge, the communication infrastructure has no place to hide. Nietzsche was a philologist and today's conundrums typically come to a head at the nexus of language theory and theories of culture. Communication studies often bear the brunt of the attack-along with literature, philosophy, history, and theology.

Beyond epistemological relativism in the Nietzschean tradition, cultural relativity is unquestioned and celebrated-that is, the right and valid are only known in local space and native languages. A context that is intelligible, a proposition that is true, an argument that is legitimate, and judgments of right and wrong are accepted by such a culture's internal criteria. And therefore these concepts, propositions, arguments, and judgments are considered to have no validity elsewhere.

One could argue that relativism ultimately founders on Mannheim's paradox: "Relativists claim that truth is culture bound. But they cannot proclaim relativism without rising above it, and they cannot rise above it without giving it up." At least to me, Mannheim's argument appears unassailable. Deni Elliott casts it in empirical terms, demonstrating that without shared values, the practice of everyday journalism is impossible. Although reporters and editors are pluraliste, they are not relativists.

However, in addition to attacking relativism on the practical level, our constructive task is formulating a normative position that does not rest on first foundations and Newton's static universe. Appealing to unconditional a prions or a fixed human nature or philosophical prescriptions carry little resonance at present. But we can successfully embed norms within culture and history. In this intellectual strategy, transcendental criteria are shifted from a metaphysical, vertical, punctiliar plane to the horizon of community, world, and being, but compelling norms they remain nonetheless. As an indicator of our distinctiveness, the human species generates symbolic patterns along the boundaries between moral norms and actual behaviour, the deepest self and our collective roles, the intentional and the inevitable. Thomas Nagel's View from Nowhere documents those epiphanal moments coming with dynamic force from outside us, though not grounded a priori.

Refusing to fashion a normative framework on every level weakens our ethical agenda. How can we appeal to human dignity, to social change, to social responsibility in our media institutions without accepting a network of non-negotiable norms such as justice, compassion, and stewardship? Without norms that are more than contingent, we cannot finally condemn oppression except on the arbitrary grounds of personal preference. Without a defensible conception of the good, the by-product is moral agnosticism. In an ironic twist on conventional skepticism, normative claims are not a medieval remnant but the catalyst for innovation. Certainly no provocation will be as formidable over the long term as relativism. A viable media ethics of the future has a considerable stake in the outcome and an opportunity to contribute substantially.

UTILITARIANISM

Developing a credible normative ethics in media studies faces another major obstacle. Given the dual character of professional ethics, the morality of the practitioners' world interacts with the philosophical framework of academics. On one side of the equation, the conventions and guidelines of media practice are basically utilitarian. In print and broadcast journalism, public relations, advertising, and entertainment, the modus operandi is self-consciously or superficially determined by consequences. In news and editorial departments, advertising agencies, and media companies, the overarching appeal is to benefit the greatest public good with the least possible harm. In academic ethics, John Stuart Mill's treatise on political freedom in 1859, On Liberty, and his Utilitarianism in 1861 work in and through each other, as does the natural affinity today in democratic life toward determining the morally right alternative by the greatest balance of good over evil. Mill, in the legacy of Jeremy Bentham, contended that happiness was the sole end of human action and the test by which all conduct ought to be judged. With later utilitarians expanding the notion of pleasure, assessing Tightness or wrongness in terms of the total amount of value is a definitive guideline for aiding our ethical choices.

A utility calculus fits hand-in-glove with the press's zeal for the public's right to know, as well as with the commitment in public relations and advertising to provide clients with the maximum benefits at the least cost. For the entertainment industry, utility resonates with capitalism's supply-and demand principle and an institution's risk-benefit calculations. Moreover, the utility principle does not presume commands from heaven or a universe of natural laws and brings together disparate segments of a diverse society. The press's actions in Watergate, for instance, were considered appropriate by most people;

the public saw the pain inflicted on a few as proper because the overall consequences for the many were beneficent.

Although the utilitarian perspective is powerful, utilitarianism presents serious difficulties for theory formation in ethics at this Summit juncture. It depends on making accurate measurements of the consequences, when in everyday affairs, the results of our choices are often blurred, at least in the long term. In addition, utilitarians view society as a collection of individuals, all with their own desires and goals. Thus, institutions as structures are not analysed in a sophisticated manner, and an atomistic, procedural view of democracy is presumed. Moreover, the principle of the greatest public benefit applies only to societies in which certain nonutilitarian standards of decency prevail. And on a deeper level, there is mounting criticism of utilitarianism's commitment to an exceptionless norm as determining all ethical judgments. As a matter of fact, consequentialism in its various forms is intellectually appealing in the same way scientific theories are-a single principle constitutes all moral judgments. However, the exactness of this one-factor model represents a "semblance of validity by leaving out whatever cannot be calculated.

In some media situations, consequences are a reliable guide. But practitioners usually find themselves confronting more than one moral claim at the same time, and asking only what produces the most good is too limiting. In the full range of human relationships, we ordinarily recognize that fulfilling promises, preventing injury, providing equal distribution, and relieving distress are moral imperatives. But utilitarianism renders irrelevant other moral demands that conflict with its consequentialism. In some of the most crucial issues we face at present, utility is not an adequate guide-for understanding distributive justice, diversity in popular culture, violence in television and cinema, truth telling, conflict of interest, and so forth. We face the anomaly that the ethical system most entrenched in the media industry is not ideally suited for resolving its most persistent headaches.

A sophisticated model of utilitarianism emphasizing long-term consequences will eliminate many of the media's day-to-day quandaries and provide an important alternative to the quasi-utility that is typically invoked at present. However, based on a century of experience with utilitarian rationalism, it is arguable that an ethics of duty is a more compelling means of moral decision-making for the media professions. Duty recognizes that responsible actions are necessary to keep the human community humane. For Emmanuel Levinas, for instance, our duties to others are more fundamental to human identity than are individual rights. Oxford's W. David Ross developed the most influential critique of utilitarianism within philosophical circles and established prima facie duties as a compelling alternative, in which reparations, fidelity, justice, noninjury, gratitude, and self-improvement are given centrality. Therefore, in terms of the overall task of constructing a theoretically credible media ethics, the most promising direction is a deontological one. We face the challenge of moving particular problems (sexism, violence, hate speech, just distribution, for example) from their generally utilitarian orientation to duty ethics instead.

SOCIAL PHILOSOPHY

The emphasis since 1980 has been on professional morality, on the character of the news, on the values and structure of news organizations. While journalism has received primary attention, advertising as a media profession has been studied to some extent, and public relations too. The Hastings studies insisted on a narrow target. In credible versions of applied ethics, the professional worlds of medicine, business, law, engineering, and journalism would be taught from the inside out. Instead of generalizations and artifice, the classroom and research needed to represent the voice of the insider. Team teaching was considered the best method to ensure that both academia and the profession were represented effectively. If teaching and research were done by one person, he or she trained in one area should have at least legitimate competence and experience in the other. This serious attention to the profession as a bona fide entity is what made professional ethics a distinct enterprise.

Though called professional ethics, Hastings more accurately promoted professional morality.4 The agenda was to be set by the field, its struggles and problems as understood from the inside out and the bottom up. The Hastings monograph for journalism identified the content of ethics courses exactly in these terms: problems of daily newsgathering, reporters and sources, invasion of privacy, economic temptations, national security and government secrecy, photojournalism, free press/fair trial, and so forth. There has been substantial growth in free-standing media ethics courses since the first survey in 1978, though they have consistently maintained an ongoing orientation to the subject matter of the field.

The most dominant pedagogical technique, case studies, focuses on concrete problems. As the Hastings Report concluded, cases should be used "to draw out broader ethical principles," but recognized that "the sheer drama" of cases will tend "to overcome the more serious need for sobre analysis". Following generally the same trajectory, Sandra Borden provides a careful review of the pros and cons of case studies within the context of journalism education.

Jay Black, Robert Steele, and Ralph Barney bring the professional ethics strategy to its maturest level by developing a curriculum and teaching strategy for the classroom and professionals centered on the Society of Professional Journalists (SPJ) code of ethics. Dale Jacquette's entry in Prentice Hall's "Basic Ethics in Action Series," his Journalistic Ethics: Moral Responsibility in the Media, is a recent illustration of this tradition, based on 30 case studies from contemporary journalistic practice. Howard Good eschews "tired" and "watered-down philosophers" in favour of a series of eclectic lessons from and debates in the media such as hate speech, hip-hop music, and the Clinton-Lewinsky scandal. Bala Musa and Cindy Price broaden the analysis to include institutional issues such as ownership, public policy, advertising, and public relations. James Ettema and Theodore Glasser provide a sophisticated analysis of the values and moral ambiguities of investigative journalism built around open-ended conversations with newspaper and television reporters who are "designated by other journalists as among the best reporters doing the best reporting". Controversies in Media Ethics make a distinctive contribution to the literature by debating the issues and thereby stimulating thought engagement with them rather than superficiality. In what has become the authoritative empirical source, David Weaver and colleagues document the character and values of American journalism in credible social scientific terms.

GENERAL MORALITY

The rationale for this practitioner-centered genre is obvious. The complexity of the field and its changing dynamics require not only socio-cultural and political economic analyses but ongoing research in professional morality. However, our challenge at this stage is to ground media ethics education in the general morality, not first of all in professional ethics.

While the apparatus of professional ethics may be necessary logistically, our theoretical work ought to arise from and be accountable to the general morality. Rather than developing rules for experts, our preoccupation should be the moral dimension of everyday life. How the moral order works itself out in community formation must be the focus, not first of all what practitioners consider virtuous. The venerable issues of social ethics should determine the agenda-justice, truth telling, human dignity, for example, with the debates over journalistic practice understood in that larger context. The ultimate standard for media professionals is not role-specific ethical principles but the general morality.

Alan Goldman's critique is a mini-classic and inescapable. He argues in his Moral Foundations of Professional Ethics that the general morality is the ultimate framework for understanding professional norms. In his view, "the most fundamental question for professional ethics is whether those in professional roles require special norms and principles to guide their well-intentioned conduct". For practitioners in medicine, law, business, journalism, government, and so forth, we typically assume that their roles require principles or specially weighted norms. In fact, the standard approach is to define ethical codes as sharply as possible according to the peculiar demands each field entails-aggressive defence in law, for instance, the physician's responsibility to clients, journalists' obligation to sources, and the commitment of business executives to stockholders. Obviously, "special institutional obligations exist when their recognition has better moral consequences than would refusing to recognize them". Yet Goldman concluded: "The central problem in professional ethics as actually practiced is not that professionals often fail to live up to their unique official codes and professional principles; nor that they lack the will to enforce them. It is rather that they often assume without question that they ought to live up to them". The ultimate standard for professionals is not role-specific principles, but the general morality.

The mass media are institutions of power whose decisions and policies can be self-serving, and practitioners defensive when criticized. Competition and careerism often cloud the application of professional codes or ethical guidelines. For example, journalists may have an understanding with their sources that all information will be treated confidentially, but then change their mind when they come under pressure and conclude that the public has a right to know this privileged material after all. Whereas we agree in the general morality that we ought to keep our promises. In this case, canons of professional practice allow self-defined exceptions for the journalist as expert. A preoccupation with privilege and authority cuts journalism loose from the very public it is meant to serve. Rather than refining professional codes of ethics, the challenge for journalists is the moral life as a whole-no harm to innocents, truth telling, reparations for wrong actions, beneficence, gratitude, and honoring contracts. With this focus, reporters operate in the same arena as citizens themselves. After a detailed assessment of codes of ethics around the globe, Christians and Nordenstreng conclude that the compelling need today is a citizens' ethics rather than profession-based ethics per se.

Giving priority to the general morality and making professional ethics penultimate is the task, but it is not obvious how to do this effectively. Our challenge heretofore is working in concert on this re-orientation of our teaching and scholarship. The journal Philosophy and Public Affairs is suggestive in form and content. Colloquium 2003 opened up some avenues through political philosophy. Lee Wilkins and Renita Coleman have given us our deepest understanding to date of the ethical reasoning of journalists. They illustrate the approach the field needs at present by situating their analysis in moral development theory, which itself is linked to philosophical ethics. The explication by Louis Hodges and colleagues of accountability in journalism is situated broadly within the nature of the professions and social theory-through the latter distinguishing accountability and responsibility, for example.

DEMOCRACY AS CONTEXT

The Press opens the right pathway here. Democracy provides the framework for The Press's understanding of the structure and function of the news media. The press is considered "an institution of American democracy.... At the centre of this book is [the] question: What should a democracy expect of the press". Journalism is considered the means; "the end is democracy". The fourth section in the book deals with the journalistic enterprise, its practice, and performance, but section one frames the issues in the larger context of representative, constitutional democracy-its vitality and ongoing redefinitions. While the standard press-government relation is examined in section three-the first amendment, regulation, and public policy-The Press sees democracy philosophically and politically as the overriding concern. James Curran represents the flow of the argument with his chapter title, "What Democracy Requires of the Media". John Keane in coming to grips with global politics focuses on civil society rather than state institutions as he struggles with the question of whether "democracy [has] a chance of taking root in the emerging global order".

The intellectual strategy represented in The Press is analogous to the reorientation we need in media ethics. When we organize our teaching and research around the general morality rather than in terms of professional ethics per se, we participate in the debates over political philosophy and their implications for public communication. Ed Lambeth has demonstrated life-long leadership here on journalism and democracy since his early years as a Washington correspondent and then founding director of the Washington Reporting Programme for a decade. His Committed Journalism puts ethics in the context of civic life. He published a research essay on "The News Media and Democracy" in the Media Studies Journal and argued in the Journal of Mass Media Ethics that moral reasoning is an essential competence for democratic journalism. The Missouri School of Journalism adopted a capstone course in journalism and democracy for its news majors and Lambeth designed it.

Democratic entities are not merely political and economic arrangements but moral structures. As a matter of fact, democracy is inconceivable without ordering relations. A limited set of fundamental moral commitments such as tolerance are necessary for collective survival. Sissela Bok labels them minimalist values, and they provide a basis for political dialogue and negotiation but do not call for agreement as to their source or character. Without a broad acceptance of such common values, a viable democratic order is impossible. Without a framework broadly owned and understood, the resolution of practical issues is inconceivable.

In political philosophy we call it the common good, and the health of democratic life depends on its vitality. Aristotle's "common interest" is the basis for distinguishing constitutional governments in the people's interest from illegitimate ones on the ruler's behalf. Thomas Aquinas insists on the common good as the ultimate end of law and government. Rousseau understood the common good as the object of the general will and the end of the state, in contrast to "particular wills." Although philosophers have differed on the precise content of the common good and how to promote it, there is a core meaning that the welfare of all citizens should be served impartially, rather than the welfare of factions or special interests. Mass Media and the Moral Imagination argues for enlarging the moral sensibility as the arena in which the common good can be developed, and offers theological and philosophical reflections on how this expansion might be possible.

Democracy will not be successful unless the common good comes into its own conceptually. Citizenship, civic discourse, community activism, and grass-roots participation are only moralistic pleading unless they are grounded in a defensible notion of the common good. The common good is the axis around which communities and politics become a democratic organism. It is a normative principle, a fundamental concept of social morality, not just the majority results of voting or an opinion poll. Since our public life in democracy is not merely functional, but knit together by social values, the media are challenged to participate in a community's process of moral elucidation. If societies are moral orders, the various technologies of public communication ought to stimulate the moral imagination. From this perspective, the news media are obligated to appeal to democratic citizens about human values. News ought to further a community's ongoing values clarification by helping people penetrate through the political and economic surface to the moral dynamics underneath. Rather than merely provide readers and audiences with information, the press's aim is morally literate citizens.

In the tsunami disaster, December 2004, the news included the overwhelming acts of kindness around the world, and our moral imagination was invigorated. Historical documentaries on television relive human morality during the horrifies of the Holocaust and WWII-the benefactors hiding Anne Frank in the Netherlands, and the resistance of Dietrich Bonhoeffer. Out of the turmoil in the Middle East are the inspiring stories of Jews and Muslims working on water projects in Palestine, and teaching their children each other's religion. The great film Hotel Rwanda highlights the virtue of Paul Rusesabagina sheltering 1200 refugees, rather than raw bloodshed and human evil only. The moral dimension of the social order takes on life and inspiration.

Editorials have raised our consciousness of anti-Semitism and heightened our moral awareness of racism and gender discrimination. In the debates over war and worldwide trade in military arms, the moral issues in terms of just-war theory and pacifism have emerged at various times in news and commentary. Affirmative action, environmental protection, health, global warming, gun control, immigration policy, and welfare reform raise moral conflicts that journalists can help the public negotiate. Over time and across the media, one observes a redemptive glow on occasion in which the news and popular culture have facilitated moral discernment by their affirmation of democracy as a people's movement and their insight into humankind as a distinctive species. Along these lines we redeem the media as an agent of democratic formation. Building on its unique capacities as a genre, we are empowered toward moral literacy by reporters appealing to our conscience. Democratic life rests on moral principles. Communication ethics is the foundation of genuine democracy. In meeting this challenge, the media are accountable to the widely shared moral frameworks that orient the society in which they operate and give it meaning.

DIFFERENT TYPES OF STING OPERATION

HONEY TRAP

A honey trap is a form of sting operation, in which wrong doers are lured into revealing themselves to a policing organization. Where a sting operation targets a known or suspected individual and attempts to trap them committing a specific case of crime, a honey trap establishes a general lure to attract unknown criminals. So for example, the police might fit a bait car with hidden cameras and leave it in an area known for its problems with car crime as a honey trap. The expectation being that the car will eventually be stolen, recording the evidence in the process.

ESPIONAGE USAGE

In spy terminology honeypot (Espionage) has been used by Soviet, Cuban and Eastern European intelligence services defining a woman entrapping businessmen and officials from the West in sexual liasions to retrieve intelligence and to achieve subserviance.

The most well known case in this regard happened in the 1980s when the U.S. Marine Corps Sergeant Clayton J. Lonetree was entrapped by a female Soviet officer with revealing photographs. Consequently, the term is used in detective novels and espionage novels to describe a trap using some form of sexual enticement.

On the internet, the Honeynet Project attempts to attract and watch hackers breaking in to a number of network systems. In particular it monitors changes in routine and automated hacker activity, such as port scanning.

BADGER GAME

The Badger game is an extortion scheme, often perpetrated on married men, in which the victim or "mark" is deliberately coerced into a compromising position then threatened with public exposure of his acts unless blackmail money is paid. There are two competing explanations for the origin of the term *badger game*. One explanation is that the term originated in the practice of badger baiting.

Another says that it derives its name from the state of Wisconsin (the Badger State), where the con allegedly either originated or was popularized.

This con has been around since at least the early 19th century. There are several variations of the con, but the most common form goes something like this. A man, preferably a lonely, married man of some financial means from out of town, is marked by the con artists. An attractive woman who is part of the con goes up to him and begins flirting. The woman entices the man to a private place with the intent of coercing him into a compromising position, usually involving some sort of sexual act. An accomplice gathers evidence of the act by way of photographs, video, or some other means. The accomplice then goes to the mark and threatens to expose him unless blackmail money is paid.

The woman may also claim that the sexual encounter was non-consensual and threaten the victim with a rape charge. It can also involve such things as the threat of a sexual harassment charge which may endanger the victim's career.

In the days before photography or video, the accomplice would usually burst into the room in mid act and claim to be the woman's husband, father, older brother, etc., and demand justice. The con was particularly effective in the 19th and earlier 20th century when the social repercussions of adultery were much greater.

Variants of the con involve luring the mark with homosexual acts, underage girls, child pornography, bizarre sexual fetishes, or other activities deemed to have a particular social stigma.

Another form involves accusations of professional misconduct. In an example of this form of the con, a "sick" woman would visit a physician. The woman would describe symptoms that required her to disrobe for the examination, require the doctor to examine the genitals, or ensure similar scrutiny from the doctor. In the midst of the examination, an "outraged husband" or "outraged father" would enter the room and accuse the doctor of deviant misconduct. The "sick" woman, who is of course part of the con, takes the side of her accomplice and threatens the doctor with criminal charges or a lawsuit. The con is usually committed against married men but can also be used on married women, public figures, religious leaders, etc.

Non-sexual versions of this con also exist, particularly among ethnic or religious groups with strong social taboos. For example, enticing a Jew or Muslim to eat pork or coercing a Mormon to gamble or drink alcohol. The con-artist would then threaten to expose the mark's activity to the community. The Badger game has been featured in numerous books, movies, and television shows as a plot device.

BAIT CAR

A bait car is a generic term used for a vehicle used by a law enforcement agency to capture car thieves. The vehicles are specially modified, with features including GPS tracking, hidden cameras that record audio/video, time, and date, and the ability to remotely monitor a variety of vehicle sensors and to control a vehicle by disabling the engine and locking the doors. The practice does not violate entrapment laws, since suspects are not persuaded to steal the vehicle by any means other than its availability and their own motivation.

The bait car is a phenomenon in the study of criminal behaviour since it offers a rare glimpse into the actions and reactions of suspects before, during and after the crime. Unlike other crimes caught on surveillance cameras, suspects, at least initially, believe and react as if the crime has been wholly successful, until the bait car is apprehended by law enforcement personnel.

CALL GIRL

A call girl or escort is a prostitute who is not visible to the general public, like a street walker, and who does not usually belong to an institution like a brothel. One must summon her, usually by calling a telephone number—hence the name call girl. Often, call girls advertise their services in small ads in magazines, although an intermediary such as an escort agency, pimp or a pander may be involved.

Call girls can work either incall, where the client comes to them, or outcall, where they come to the client.

Call girls are commonly perceived to be elite amongst prostitutes, far more skilled, able to pick and choose amongst their potential clients and therefore demand higher prices for their services, and are more attractive, educated, well-groomed and youthful than street prostitutes. An escort service will not take on any woman that is unattractive, has a visible drug problem (such as needle marks from injecting drugs), or has an overly negative persona. Unless they specialize in tattooed women, escort services will usually not take on any women that have anything larger than a small tattoo.

Escort services seek to establish a reputation for offering desirable women and know that their customers only give them one chance. If an escort service sends an undesirable woman to a client, the client will very likely not use that service again. Also, many escort agencies do criminal background checks on applicants to weed out those that have been arrested for street prostitution or other types of crimes.

This weeding out is done to reduce the chances of being accused of being sellers of prostitution, trying not to draw the attention of law enforcement agencies. For these reasons, there is rarely any cross-over between call girls and street prostitutes.

Not all clients hire call girls for sex. Some simply do so to chat. This is most common in elderly rich men that simply enjoy the company of an attractive beautiful woman. Escort agencies try to determine if this is what a client wants and if it is, the agency will try to send their most educated and polite women to this type of customer. It is not unusual for these "chat" call girls to receive big tips or even bequests from clients. Another type of client who does not ask for sex is one who wants to impress others by having an attractive woman as his date, if not pretend to be their girlfriend or even wife. This is commonly done by men going to a high school or college class reunion or a social event at their office. Clients seeking this will tell the escort service that they want to hire someone for a class reunion. These clients often specify in detail what kind of woman to play this role. The client may have a meeting with the woman beforehand to evaluate the woman's level of intelligence, education, manners, speech and ability to execute the pretence as well as her to judge her appearance. They would go over his past, her past (often fake) and their deceptive relationship. This way she does not give away the truth when questions come.

Male celebrities and rich men commonly hire call girls for dates and usually sex afterwards simply to avoid what they view as hassles of dating women. For these men, call girls enable them to have fun without the fear of rejection and/ or commitment. Both parties understand their respective positions and do not go beyond them.

Some of these men are even open about what their date is to those they're partying with, though some call girls request they not be. These "dates" can include flying by private jet, staying in a luxury hotel suite, dining at the finest restaurants, dancing at the hottest nightclubs, and gambling at the casinos. Usually, the man will first hire the woman for a short date to determine if he wants to do longer ones (such as the one just mentioned) with her.

Here again, the woman's appearance, intelligence, manners, socialibility and education come into consideration. Interestingly, it is relatively common for these men to eventually develop romantic feelings for these call girls, but the feelings are rarely returned. In Europe, the system of City Tours is getting more and more popular, in cities such as Paris, Rome, Amsterdam or Zurich. Eastern European call girls, from countries such as Russia, Hungary, Romania or Ukraine, are brought by agencies for short stays not exceeding two weeks. The agencies book a room in a business hotel for them, where they receive customers all day long.

This system takes its toll on the call girls, who are relentlessly exploited during their short stay in Western Europe, and they rarely make more than three or four of them. For the customers, also called *punters*, this allows to have available an ever renewed supply of fresh girls.

Most call girl agencies and independent call girls are now online, and the Internet has become the main venue for a customer to find his match.

Generally, the picture of the girl is provided, and sometimes, the type of sexual services she is willing to offer. Some agencies also propose for a high fee people of special interest, such as twins, former porn stars, B-List models, prodommes or even submissives. The Internet is also used by punters/hobbyists to provide evaluation of the call girls they have met and rate them, on their aesthetics, behavior or sexual performances. For the readers of evaluation web sites, the rating of the call girls is often a determining factor in their selection.

This has led some customers to blackmail call girls by threatening of a bad rating in order to obtain more sexual services or a discount on the rate. Some call girls also cheat by logging stellar evaluations of themselves on these sites, although most of the sites try to identify and filter these "fake reviews".

Because offering sexual services in exchange for money is illegal in many areas, certain code words in the subculture of sex work have emerged to communicate in lieu of description of explicit acts.

For instance GFE, an acronym for "girlfriend experience" usually implies that an escort will have a warm personality, be willing to kiss the client, hold hands and be generally affectionate. This also includes an assumption that the girl will perform oral sex without a condom barrier. Usually this option would be explicitly stated as "Oral w/o" or "Oral without". Another codical term is "Greek." A call girl who is "Greek welcome" is willing to have anal sex with the client. This term is more commonly used in the USA. Other terms include DFK (Deep French Kissing - ie open mouth kissing with tongues).

Sometimes the police carry out a sting operation: a police officer, posing as a client, summons a call girl to a hired hotel room, or as a call girl, summons a prospective client. In the Netherlands, this has been done since 2004: although neither buying nor selling a call girl's services is illegal per se.

Until now, in half of the cases, the women have been foreigners illegally staying or working in the country.

The operation also serves to check the ages of the service provider and the receiver: if one of them is below 18, the escort agency breaks the law. To avoid entrapment allegations, the police do not specially ask for a foreign or very young call girl.

In India, this was done in May 2004: for the first time a prostitution ring using Internet to solicit customers was raided. A decoy client ordered two call girls to a hotel. Three pimps were arrested under the Prevention of Immoral Trafficking Act (PITA).

One thing that call girls have in their favour, as contrasted with street prostitutes, is that they're out of public sight. In some countries, the public dislikes seeing street prostitutes in or near their communities and usually actively campaigns for local law enforcement to arrest these women. Since call girls try not to draw attention to themselves and conduct their business beyond public view, the public seldom call for law enforcement action.

Those trying to legalize prostitution commonly use this sentiment to their advantage by telling the public that the best solution for street prostitution is to legalize prostitution arranged over the telephone and/or internet. This "out of sight, out of mind" argument carries the most weight with the public that opposes street prostitution due to it driving down the value of their real estate.

OPERATION PIN

Operation Pin is an initiative of the Virtual Global Taskforce, which consists of UK's National Crime Squad, the FBI, Interpol, the Royal Canadian Mounted Police and the Australian Hi-Tech Crime Centre/ Australian Federal Police (AFP).

Its stated aim is to identify pedophiles who are using the internet to access child pornography.

Announced on 18 December 2003, the operation is said to involve the creation and operation of a number of websites (so-called "honeypots") purporting to offer illegal images. While these websites will not contain child pornography images, they will be designed to look like the real thing so as to ensnare as many offenders as possible.

The websites will present visitors with a variety of options which, instead of leading to illegal images, lead to a law enforcement site that will inform them that their personal details have been recorded and that they have committed a crime. They will also be given details of appropriate helplines. It is unclear if the information recorded will be technical (for example, an IP address) or personal (for example, credit card details).

The stated purpose of Operation Pin is to cause people seeking out child pornography on the Internet to wonder whether they will find an illegal site or one operated by law enforcement agencies. It can thus be understood as a kind of deterrence.

It is also a controversial scheme. In the United Kingdom at least, it is an offence to advertise locations where indecent photographs of children are shown or distributed. If Operation Pin's websites do indeed "'look like the real thing", their operators would be committing a criminal offence under UK law.

ABSCAM

Abscam was an FBI sting operation run out of the FBI's Hauppauge, Long Island office which initially targeted trafficking in stolen property and thereafter was converted to a public corruption investigation. The investigation ultimately led to the conviction of a United States Senator, six members of the House of Representatives, the Mayor of Camden, New Jersey, members of the Philadelphia City Council, and an inspector for the Immigration and Naturalization Service.

The FBI set up "Abdul Enterprises, Ltd." in 1978 and FBI employees posed as Middle Eastern businessmen in videotaped talks with government officials, where they offered money in return for political favors to a non-existent sheik. A house (4407 W. St. NW, Washington, DC), along with a yacht in Florida and hotel rooms in Pennsylvania and New Jersey - was used to set up meetings between various public officials and a mysterious Arab sheik named Abdul. Much of the operation was directed by Melvin Weinberg, a convicted con artist who was hired by the FBI for that purpose. It was the first major operation by the FBI to trap corrupt public officials; up until 1970 only ten members of Congress had ever been convicted of accepting bribes.

On February 2, 1980 reports surfaced that FBI personnel were targeting members of Congress in a sting operation. The media dubbed the operation Abscam after the name of the company.

Of the thirty-one targeted officials, one senator, Harrison A. Williams (D-NJ), and five members of the House of Representatives (John Jenrette (D-SC), Richard Kelly (R-FL), Raymond Lederer (D-PA), Michael "Ozzie" Myers (D-PA) and Frank Thompson (D-NJ)) were convicted of bribery and conspiracy in separate trials in 1981.

Another, John M. Murphy (D-NY), was convicted of a lesser charge. While most of the politicians resigned, Myers had to be expelled and Williams did not resign until the vote on his expulsion was almost due. Five other government officials were convicted, including the mayor of Camden, New Jersey, Angelo Errichetti; members of the Philadelphia City Council; and an inspector for the Immigration and Naturalization Service.

Congressman Jack Murtha (D-PA) was indicted but not prosecuted because he gave evidence against Murphy and Thompson. The FBI videotaped Murtha as saying, "I'm not interested. I'm sorry... at this point."

CNSNews.com, a Division of the conservative Media Research Center, reports the full FBI video reveals Murtha later stating on the tape, "You know, we do business for a while, maybe I'll be interested, maybe I won't." Murtha has faced heavy criticism from conservative commentators since announcing his opposition to the war in Iraq in 2005. The Brattleboro Reformer also reported Murtha asked the fake sheik to consider investing some money in his hometown of Johnstown, Pennsylvania.

In November 1980, the Justice Department announced that Murtha would not face prosecution for his part in the scandal. In July 1981, the House ethics committee also chose not to file charges against Congressman Murtha, following a mostly party line vote, after which E. Barrett Prettyman, Jr., the panel's special counsel, abruptly resigned in protest. House ethics rules require members to immediately report any bribe offers to the FBI.

In 2002, one of the panel members, Rep. Don Bailey (who lost to Murtha in a primary challenge in 1982) released a public letter stating "I was, to be honest, critical about how you misled me about Abscam where you convinced me you had voluntarily told federal agents about the offer of money to you," Bailey wrote Murtha.

"I learned later, after I had successfully defeated the ethics charges against you, that you had merely manipulated the system to cooperate with federal agents to avoid prosecution," Bailey added- "The idea that somebody is going to trot out $50,000 in cash in front of you and you don't know that is wrong is pretty damn stupid to me," Bailey said. "What bankers or investors run around with $50,000 in cash?"

The FBI was accused of entrapment and in 1982 the conviction of Richard Kelly was overturned. However, an appeals court upheld the conviction and Kelly served 13 months in prison. (He had been memorably videotaped jamming $25,000 into his pockets. He then turned to one of the agents and asked "Does it show?") The FBI and the Department of Justice were also accused of having political motivations in the politicians they targeted. Only one lawmaker, US Senator Larry Pressler (R-SD), refused to take the bribe, saying at the time, "Wait a minute, what you are suggesting may be illegal." He immediately reported the incident to the FBI.

When Senator Pressler was told Walter Cronkite referred to him on the evening news as a "hero" he stated, "I do not consider myself a hero... what have we come to if turning down a bribe is 'heroic'?" Professor Alan Dershowitz of Harvard Law School frequently has cited Pressler as an example for his fellow Harvard Law graduates to follow.

When the investigation became public in early 1980, controversy centered on the use of the "sting" technique and Weinberg's involvement in selecting targets. Although Weinberg was found to have previously engaged in numerous felonious activities, he avoided a three-year prison sentence and was paid $150,000 in connection with the operation. Ultimately, all of the ABSCAM convictions were upheld on appeal, although some judges criticized the tactics used by the FBI and lapses in FBI and DOJ supervision.

In the wake of ABSCAM, Attorney General Civiletti issued "The Attorney General Guidelines for FBI Undercover Operations" ("Civiletti Undercover Guidelines") on January 5, 1981.

These were the first Attorney General Guidelines for undercover operations, and they formalized procedures necessary to conduct undercover operations.

Following the initial press accounts about the ABSCAM investigation, Congress held a series of hearings to examine FBI undercover operations and the new Civiletti Undercover Guidelines.

The House Subcommittee on Civil and Constitutional Rights began hearings on FBI undercover operations in March 1980 and concluded with a report in April 1984. Among the concerns expressed during the hearings were the undercover agents' involvement in illegal activity, the possibility of entrapping individuals, the prospect of damaging the reputations of innocent civilians, and the opportunity to undermine legitimate rights to privacy.

In March 1982, after the Senate debated a resolution to expel Senator Harrison A. Williams for his conduct in ABSCAM, the Senate established the Select Committee to Study Undercover Activities. In December 1982, the Committee issued its final report, which was generally supportive of the undercover technique but observed that its use "creates serious risks to citizens' property, privacy, and civil liberties, and may compromise law enforcement itself."

While nervous politicians encouraged public concern as to the danger and legality of the sting operations, FBI documents later disclosed in accordance with the Freedom of Information Act revealed that the American public had been overwhelmingly supportive of the operation.

A similar sting, known as Operation Tennessee Waltz was a sting operation set up by federal and state law enforcement agents, including the Federal Bureau of Investigation and Tennessee Bureau of Investigation. The operation led to the arrest of seven Tennessee state lawmakers and two men identified as "bagmen" in the indictment on the morning of May 26, 2005 on bribery charges. The FBI and TBI followed these arrests with an additional arrest of two county commissioners, one from Hamilton County, and the other a member of the prominent Hooks family, of Memphis. Investigators also arrested a former county administrator.

COPS IN SHOPS

Cops in Shops is an alcohol law enforcement program in the United States in which undercover police officers work with participating alcoholic beverage retailers. The purpose of the program is to discourage minors and adults under the age of 21 from buying alcohol. The program is funded by The Century Council, an organization that works to reduce underage drinking and drunk driving.

OPERATION CENTURY

Operation Century was the code name for a sting operation for investigating a triple murder at Rettendon (Essex, England) Essex Police Constabulary in 1995. It was assisted by Royal Ulster Constabulary Special Branch officers. The purpose of this operation was to bring pressure to bear on persons whom they suspected of having knowledge to disclose about the triple murder that would incriminate the suspects in question and/or others.

The operation produced no evidence leading to a criminal prosecution. The tactics deployed by Essex and Royal Ulster Constabulary Special Branch while Century was under way increasingly led to police voicing serious threats against the suspects in question.

The operation was also carefully timed to coincide with the London bombing of Canary Wharf on the evening of February 9 1996, which marked the ending of the previous mainland Republican bombing campaign cease fire.

One of the targeted Essex suspects received a call from Belfast within minutes of the Canary Wharf explosion. The Rettendon Triple Murders had no Irish connection with the bombing. There is a problem in trying to accurately portray what levels of threat and abuse Essex Police Special Branch descended to during the course of this operation - the language was extremely foul-mouthed and threatening.

On one such call on February 26, 1996 undercover Special Branch threatened: “I’ve got (expletive deleted) A levels... A levels in (expletive deleted) whacking (expletive deleted) people... “it’s time you did (expletive deleted) take these cacoincide with the London bombing of Canary Wharf on the evening of February 9 1996, which marked the ending of the previous mainland Republican bombing campaign cease fire.

One of the targeted Essex suspects received a call from Belfast within minutes of the Canary Wharf explosion. The Rettendon Triple Murders had no Irish connection with the bombing.

Transcripts of these calls exist and police eventually had to acknowledge that they were made by Belfast based Special Branch officers. These calls were repeatedly made to the Essex suspects from Ireland by RUC Special Branch posing as Republican drug runners making it clear that they could rely upon organisational back up.

The Rettendon Triple Murders had no Irish connection whatever. claiming that they had funded the criminal activities of one of the Rettenden murder victims who they were still demanding repayment from. This ruse failed to result in a meet with the suspects.

According to an article “Drug baron’s lover tell’s of IRA “terror”” in the ‘Basildon Evening Echo, 13 Oct. 1997, one of the suspects victimised in this manner was the common law wife of one of the murdered men by whom she had a young child.

She claims to have had no knowledge at the time that these threatening tactics were not being deployed by Belfast-based Republicans and so she sought the assistance of Essex Police who, after appearing to have investigated the matter, informed her that the calls were made from Belfast, there were Republican connections and that the latter had now crossed to mainland Britain where they had had since been lost track of by police. The effect of these torture tactics upon an already distraught and grieving mother has been deplored.

In addition an end of Rettendon trial Operation Century report by Ian Hepburn in The Sun newspaper “Cops Posed As Ira To Snare Hit Hitman” on January 28, 1998 judged it to have been “bizarre and intimidatory” for having “bombarded with death threat calls from Northern Ireland claiming they were owed money by one of the Rettendon victims”.

Details concerning this undercover police operation had came to light when persons were subsequently brought to trial towards the end of 1997 in connection with the Rettendon killings.

Dated timed tape recordings of the threatening police phone calls, recorded by one of the Operation Century “suspects” were produced in evidence by the defence counsel and were played in court. They clearly showed that the undercover police calls were increasingly threatening as Operation Cenby defencetury unravelled because the suspects were disbelieving that Belfast Republicans had ever funded Essex criminal enterprises and so did not conform as the undercover officers had hoped.

In order to be legal, compliance checks or sting operations must be conducted without entrapment. Basically, entrapment is inducing people to commit a crime they are not "predisposed" to commit and would not ordinarily commit.

To avoid losing cases because defendants successfully claim entrapment, the standard compliance check specifies that if a cashier asks for identification, the under age person assisting the sting operation is to immediately cease the attempt to purchase alcohol and leave the establishment. The under age person is not to present a false identification card, give an excuse for not having any I.D., produce an ID that shows the correct age, or otherwise try to obtain an illegal sale after being asked for identification.

Because of legal requirements, sting operations may not be as successful as we might hope. This is because clerks quickly learn how to avoid entrapment and under age purchasers learn how to demonstrate that they are not part of a sting operation. That is, an under age purchaser need only present a false I.D., make an excuse for not having an I.D., or even present his or her own legitimate I.D. The clerk then realizes that the sale can safely be made because the purchaser isn't involved in a sting operation.

Some law enforcement offices follow different policies to avoid charges of entrapment or might even cross the line and be guilty of illegal entrapment. In some cases, they may permit the under age operatives to offer an excuse or otherwise persist to some degree. However, underage purchasers and clerks quickly become aware of what is locally done in sting operations and adjust their actions accordingly.

In spite of their low effectiveness, sting operations are popular. They satisfy public desire to clamp down. They satisfy law enforcement desire to demonstrate that it's taking action and generates public and tax support. They satisfy parental desires to have community support in helping control and protect their young people. But what they don't do is satisfy is the need to significantly reduce the perceived problem.

Fortunately, there is an effective and inexpensive way to reduce the use and abuse of alcohol by young people. It's called social norms marketing and is based on the fact that most young people incorrectly think that most other young people are drinking and doing so frequently and heavily. Therefore, they feel pressured to engage in these behaviours to fit in. When credible surveys are conducted and the results widely promoted or marketed, young people no longer feel the need to consume alcohol or to consume it so frequently or heavily. Study after study has demonstrated the dramatic effectiveness of this technique.

Another advantage of using this approach is that it releases law enforcement officers to engage in other crime prevention and apprehension activities.

In India ever since Tehelka made news capturing corrupt politicians and army officers in the TV camera, sting operations by TV Channels seemed to be on the increase. The latest one is the sting operation involving the Hindi film actor, Villain in that, Shakthi Kapoor. The TV Channel India TV telecast the Kapoor expose where the greatest revelation was about the Casting Couch existing in Bollywood.

The term casting couch means, in simple term, taking a girl or a woman aspiring to become a film star to bed in return for the favour of giving her an opportunity to act in a film or for recommending the aspirant to film producers for a role.

It appears, the India TV Channel secretly filmed Shakthi Kapoor visiting a woman, who had posed herself as a Bollywood aspirant, at her hotel room late at night. After some alcohol, Kapoor became loquacious. As they say, when wine is in wit is out, more so, when there is only one woman in the room. Kapoor began to spill the beans saying unpleasant and untruth things about a number of famous Bollywood luminaries including Preity Zinta, Aishwarya Rai, Subhash Ghai and others.

Kapoor, also told the girl, "I want to make love to you", and started making amorous advances towards her and finally tried to embrace her. When she protested, unlike a Villain, and like a good boy, he returned to his seat and did not persist with his lustful desire. However, he told the reluctant girl the Bollywood truth.

According to Kapoor — that if one hopes to make it in Bollywood, then one should be ready to sleep with the benefactor.When the TV Channel telecast this sting operation, the viewers got the feeling that their long time film Villain on the screen is a loose talker in real life.

What was seen on the TV offended the members of his film fraternity so much that there was even a talk of boycotting him and to bring his film career, already on its last leg, to an abrupt and sad end. Fortunately for him, this has not happened.

Now the main controversy is about the existence or otherwise of the casting couch in Bollywood.

Be that as it may, Shakthi Kapoor has pleaded his innocence and justified his conduct in the given situation. It was a trap after all and he simply became a prey in front of the predator TV camera.

According to him, the girl had been telephoning him for months, making obscene suggestions and insisting that he visits her in her room. Well, if one is a man, one should move on. So, he moved on and did what came naturally to a man in such a situation, believing that he was offered sex for pleasure. He went along to her room. Once there, Kapoor says, the girl encouraged him by throwing coquettish looks at him and by using suggestive words rousing his libido and thus forcing him, through remote control, to go near her.

But sadly for Kapoor, the telecast version of this encounter had cut out moves of the temptress while showing only Kapoor's indecent behaviour. As for what he said of Preity Zinta, Subhash Ghai and others, he attributed it to manipulation by the camera and the audio (digital) technology.From what was seen on the TV and from what was heard from Kapoor's lips, it was clear that though he was sexually aroused he did not rape her nor did he make any serious effort to force himself on her. A gentleman Villain indeed! Apparently, he was ready for sex only if it was consensual. No wonder, many people seem to have sympathy for poor Kapoor.

However, this episode has brought to the fore certain legal and ethical questions relating to both print and electronic media. The question is: Should the media enter into the privacy of people who are not responsible or accountable to the people in general and where it is their own individual private matter, which does not harm, hurt or humiliate others?

A film actor, from his point of view, is different from a politician or a bureaucrat or even army men (who were exposed by Tehelka) because all these persons are responsible to the people and there is public interest involved in their conduct. Not so with the conduct of a film actor. Politicians, bureaucrats and army men are paid for their service from the taxpayers' money and, therefore, their conduct has a direct bearing on the peace, progress and order of the society. But a film actor is his own man. He is not responsible to you and me or the people in general unless he commits a criminal offence.

Kapoor may sleep with an aspiring film star with her consent; recommend her too for a film role. If she turns out to be a flop or a hit, it is purely the business of the producer. General public is in no way affected. Then why cry foul? It does not concern the public whether the producer went after the casting couch or not.

Therefore, what TV indulged in was just playing the role of a voyeur, a peeping tom. Now watch out your keyhole in the bedroom or look for hidden cameras if you are a VIP or a celebrity.

3

Investigative Reporting and Journalism

INVESTIGATIVE REPORTING

Undercover techniques used by journalists are increasingly coming under public scrutiny. Those targeted by investigative news operations are challenging the methods rather than the accuracy of the reporting - and often winning sympathy from the public. It is a trend that came into sharp focus in January 1997 when a twelve-member jury in North Carolina decided that ABC News should pay $5.5 million in damages to the Food Lion supermarket chain because ABC's reporters posed as employees and used hidden cameras to uncover alleged sales of spoiled meat at some of its stores. The jury found that network producers had trespassed and committed fraud when researching a Primetime Live segment in 1992 that accused the company of selling spoiled meat. Although Food Lion officials disputed the accuracy of the ABC report, they did not sue for libel. Rather, they accused ABC of fraud because it used techniques such as having producers submit fake resumes to get jobs in the meat department of company stores, and then used hidden cameras to film there.

Many journalists argue that hidden cameras and other undercover reporting techniques have long been necessary tools for exposing vital issues of public policy and health. The type of hidden-camera reporting ABC used to investigate Food Lion has become a staple of national and local TV news in recent years as cameras have become increasingly miniaturized. But some media critics say that TV producers have overused them in recent years in a push to create splashy shows and bolster ratings. In fact, the verdict against ABC may reflect a growing public sentiment against news organizations that are perceived as undisciplined and overly aggressive. Several jurors in the Food Lion case said, for example, that although they supported investigative reporting, they took issue with ABC's reporting methods.

In particular, they pointed to the use by producers of false resumes to gain jobs in Food Lion stores in South and North Carolina. In addition, the Food Lion case nicely illustrates the public's "schizophrenic" attitude toward the use of investigative reporting techniques such as hidden cameras. While many viewers seem to be uncomfortable with the growing amount of surreptitious taping, investigative TV shows have attracted a growing number of loyal viewers.

Despite the great public attention the Food Lion case attracted and the widespread speculations by the media about a possible backlash of this verdict on the future of investigative reporting, the overall impact of this particular case might have been overstated. A representative telephone survey of 1,001 American adults ages 18 and older conducted by the Roper Research Centre shortly after the verdict against ABC found that the majority (80 per cent) of those who had heard about the case said they thought ABC was not doing anything out of the ordinary in employing the reporting techniques. Of the 51 per cent who said they heard about the court case, half said they sided with ABC News, 21 per cent said they sided with the supermarket, and 27 per cent said they didn't know.

In view of these recent developments in public attitudes toward investigative reporting, this study compares past findings on perceived public importance of investigative reporting and the acceptability of different reporting methods with findings from a national telephone survey of 1,211 respondents conducted in February 1997 by Princeton Survey Research Associates for the Pew Research Centre for The People & The Press. In particular, results from five polls conducted between 1980 and 1997 are compared to track possible changes in public approval of investigative reporting techniques.

Additionally, the 1997 poll data is analysed for possible predictors of respondents' approval of investigative reporting techniques such as age, gender, education, income, and media use. While past studies have found only weak relationships between approval of investigative reporting and respondents' individual-level characteristics, the increased use of these techniques in popular TV shows and local evening news during the 1990s may have changed the previously found weak relationships, especially as more targeting of specific demographic groups by these programs has occurred. One goal of this study is to see if demographics are better predictors of opinions about investigative reporting in the late 1990s than in the 1980s.

RELATED STUDIES

Hidden cameras and other undercover reporting techniques have long been necessary tools for exposing vital issues of public policy and health. But despite the rising popularity of stories based on investigative reporting techniques and their more frequent use by TV shows such as 60 Minutes or Primetime Live, only scant attention has been paid to the question of how the audience perceives investigative reporting by the media. While some critics argue that the Food Lion verdict reflects overt hostility toward sensational TV news magazine reporting, others argue that Americans generally respect and are interested in the information generated by investigative reporting, including undercover techniques.

Both viewpoints might be only partially right. Two previous studies that analysed public attitudes toward investigative reporting found fairly consistent evidence for the hypothesis that people approve of investigative reporting in general, but are much less likely to support specific investigative reporting techniques such as the use of hidden cameras or microphones.

The first study, based on a representative telephone survey conducted by the Chicago Sun-Times in 1980, found strong support for the general concept of investigative reporting among 603 Chicago residents. More than three fourths of the respondents in this survey considered it "very important" for newspapers to do investigative reporting, and almost 78 per cent said that investigative reporting is worthwhile for a "problem to be exposed, no matter what happens later."

Specific investigative reporting techniques, however, received much less support, especially the so-called "checkbook journalism," which tolerates reporters paying for information or interviews (45 per cent approved). The study also found that the approval of investigative reporting was largely independent from respondents' demographic characteristics and media use habits, but interest in an ongoing investigative reporting series, "The Accident Swindlers," did predict perceived importance of investigative reporting (beta =.32).

Ten years later, a study by Daniels and Weaver9 compared the results of three opinion surveys that included questions on investigative reporting and were conducted throughout the 1980s with the results of the 1980 Chicago survey. Overall, compared to 1980, the level of public support for investigative reporting was found to be lower on a national and statewide level. However, throughout the 1980s, a large majority in all three surveys still thought that such reporting was at least "somewhat important." Daniels and Weaver also found that specific investigative reporting techniques received lower levels of public support than was found in the 1980 Chicago survey.

While a majority of respondents in the 1980 Chicago survey approved of most investigative reporting techniques ("hidden cameras & microphones," "reporters not identifying themselves," "use of anonymous sources," "paying for information" and "reporters paying for information"), the nationwide and statewide polls conducted later failed to find majority support for any of these techniques. The authors concluded that this might have been a result of the frequent use of such journalistic techniques over time in Chicago.

Similar to the findings obtained in the 1980 Chicago study, none of the respondents' demographic characteristics was significantly linked to the perceived importance of investigative reporting in the 1984/85 ASNE poll or the 1989 Indiana survey. However, weak relationships between support for investigative reporting and frequency of newspaper reading were found in the ASNE poll and the Indiana survey.

The purpose of this chapter is to update the findings of the two previous studies with data from the 1997 Pew Research Centre National Survey, which included a number of questions about the public's perception of investigative reporting originally used in the 1981 Gallup poll.

Such an update is important because, during the past ten years, significant changes have taken place in the public perception of the press. While surveys conducted a decade ago showed that many Americans criticized the press as inaccurate, unfair, and biased, these flaws have been traditionally overlooked by those who recognized the media's contributions to society as a political "watchdog" and information disseminator.

Today, those Americans who value the function of the press in society still judge the media more favorably than those who do not, but fewer Americans like the news product and many are less interested in the news in general. Moreover, while most people still trust the news, a growing minority "believes little or nothing of what they hear or read or has little or no trust in major news organizations."

Overall, public attitudes toward the press have worsened during the past decade, a trend which might eventually undermine the crucial support the media still receive as a democratic forum.

It is therefore imperative to identify the possible reasons for this negative trend in public perceptions of the media, especially as they relate to peoples' trust in the media. This study analyses one potential cause by comparing the public approval of investigative reporting in general with the approval of specific investigative reporting techniques.

To expand on previous studies, the analysis of possible predictors for approval of investigative reporting will be broadened to a series of questions that tap people's attitudes toward the function or role of the press in society, thus allowing a fresh look at why people like investigative reporting but dislike its journalistic techniques.

This most recent study is based on a representative telephone survey conducted by Princeton Research Survey Associates among a nationwide sample of 1,211 adults, 18 years of age or older, during the period of 20-23 February 1997.

Telephone numbers were selected by random digit dialing techniques, proportionally stratified by each county's share of telephone households in the United States. Within each contacted household, interviewers asked to speak either with the "youngest male 18 or older" or "the oldest woman 18 or older." The sampling error for this survey is plus or minus 3 percentage points at the 95% confidence level.

To evaluate the potential changes in public opinion about investigative reporting during the past years, the 1997 survey is compared with four national and state polls containing questions on investigative reporting that have been conducted between 1980 and 1989. All five surveys include a series of identically worded questions that ask respondents whether they approve or disapprove of specific investigative reporting techniques such as "using hidden cameras and microphones," "having reporters not identify themselves as reporters," "running stories that quote an unnamed source," or "paying informers for their information or testimony."

In addition, the 1981 Gallup survey and the 1997 Pew survey contain two questions that assess whether respondents "approve or disapprove of investigative reporting by the news media," and whether they would "like to see more of this type of reporting or less."

The findings of the most recent 1997 survey are discussed in light of respondents' demographic characteristics, media use patterns, and attitudes toward the press, and, where possible, compared to previous results. Demographic variables used from the 1997 survey are gender, age, education, race, party identification, and place of residence.

CHANGING PATTERNS OF REPORTING

Journalists reflect a pattern of access, credibility, and news practices across media content through the people they choose to quote or use in a television sound bite. Media scholars, journalists, and the communities they serve continue to debate the lack of source diversity, the level of expected diversity (which varies), and the path to achieving greater diversity since research on this subject began in the early 1970s. Source representation is a type of diversity most frequently studied by researchers who address this issue in ways that range from media channels and news structures to the diversity and affiliations of people represented in the news. If journalism is a reflection of the community, the quality of that reflected reality depends to some extent upon sources used.

During the past quarter century, only enterprise stories have shown promise for improving source diversity. Hansen found that such stories contained a greater diversity of sources. However, enterprise reporting is not common today, and there are no signs of improvement. One potential answer is civic journalism which assumes a stronger connection to non-traditional sources, leading to greater diversity of sources in news stories. This study tests a major assumption underlying civic journalism by asking whether civic journalism succeeds in moving television journalists toward more diverse sourcing patterns for race and gender.

Voakes, Kapfer, Kurpius, and Chern wrote: "Source diversity is a dispersion of the representation of affiliations and status position of sources to create a news product. The more even the dispersion of the representation among source affiliations, status, and proximity in a given story or medium, the greater the diversity." This study expands this definition to include the dispersion of representation of race and gender.

Reporters select sources for what they know, their position in an organization, and/or their status in society. Some selections are dependent on the form of media used. Newspaper and magazine stories reflect material through direct quotations or paraphrased statements by the reporter. For broadcast, it is the "direct voice of the quotee" or the quotee's words-restated by the reporter. This study uses these definitions.

Journalists gather information for their stories according to the norms and practices of their news organizations. Historically, the sources journalists turned to for information reflected a narrow section of society. Research shows sources are predominately white, male officials who are situated in proximity to the media organization and are easily regarded by journalists as providing credible information.

Some researchers focus on the governmental, business, and organizational affiliation and status of sources used. Others look at women and minorities as news sources. Still others analyse the structural elements that potentially alter source-selection patterns, including channels of news coverage, length and types of stories, and use of technological advances.

People of colour are generally missing from news coverage, unless it is coverage of crime or festivals. Grabe and Barnett found that 86 per cent of news sources in newsmagazine programs were Caucasians. Campell found underrepresentation of journalists and sources of colour in television news. "While news is not entirely white," he wrote, "the infrequent presence of journalists of colour and of minority news sources dictates an otherness that is compounded when the coverage that does exist perpetuates traditional racistnotions about minority life." Entman found that TV news used fewer black sources than white sources. Entman said, "The blacks received much less opportunity to convey their perspectives in their own voices and were much more likely than whites to be discussed by a police official not of their race."

Smith found that in both newspapers and television coverage of the San Francisco area, about 80 per cent of the sources used were white people. In television, black sources were used only 12 per cent of the time, and minority sources accounted for 19 per cent.

Several researchers found low gender diversity and a heavy reliance on elite male sources. Zoch and Turk found that 68 per cent of sources were male compared to 21 per cent female sources, but they attributed part of this to the heavy reliance on official sources who tended to be male. McShane found that women are underrepresented as sources in business magazines compared to their numbers in the labour force. Liebler and Smith's study of 159 network television news stories found journalists are more likely to choose males as sources and to present them in a professional capacity. Smith found that white men dominate news sourcing, but noted that minority women and men are used as sources in almost equal proportions.

Sigal argued in 1973 that routine news channels created efficiencies for journalists, who commonly rely on government officials and business leaders as primary sources. Today, marketplace forces dictate television journalistic practice more than beat routines. The FCC no longer requires television stations to assess their coverage of the communities in the local area of dominant influence. The lifting of this requirement, combined with the consolidation of ownership, has shifted the focus to demographically driven news based on advertisers' target audiences. Such marketplace emphasis creates a structure ripe for sponsor interference and these pressures are likely to continue or increase as larger ownership groups consolidate stations.

The federally mandated move to digital transmission standards also increased the financial burden stations face, resulting in increased airtime for news and therefore in journalists' workloads. Workload increases result in a greater reliance on non-local (feed) material and reapportionment of material (using the same story in multiple news programs). Sigal and others demonstrate that this leads to greater reliance on government officials as primary sources.

What works to improve source diversity? The answer is not much. Crisis coverage included much higher numbers of unaffiliated sources, but it is limited to a narrow type of coverage. One promising solution is enterprise reporting, a process through which journalists tend to use more diverse sources and fewer official sources than traditional news coverage, Hanson writes. However, enterprise reporting is costly because it takes time and effort to develop story angles and sources, and it is declining in use at television stations.

Civic journalism is an attempt by media organizations, print and broadcast, to link journalism and democracy to help public life go well. Friedland noted that the term "public" denotes three important associations: "public as government," "public as a collection of private opinions," and "citizens who argue and deliberate." Civic journalism is an effort to alter journalistic practices to improve the connection between journalists and the communities in news coverage. Civic journalism, in theory and practice, is a public discussion; thus there is no universally accepted definition. Jay Rosen, one of the founders of civic journalism, wrote that defining civic (or public) journalism "is something you're always doing as you try to figure out the shape the thing has." In his book, Rosen offered this definition:

Public journalism is an approach to the daily business of the craft that calls on journalists to (1) address people as citizens, potential participants in public affairs, rather than victims or spectators; (2) help the political community act upon, rather than just learn about, its problems; (3) improve the climate of public discussion, rather than simply watch it deteriorate; (4) help make public life go well, so that it earns its claim on our attention.

Civic journalism is designed to improve journalists' understanding of the community, its citizens, values, problems, issues, and aspirations. This deeper and more contextual understanding of the community is assumed to show through reporting as journalists identify alternative frames or angles for stories and focus more on developing enterprise reporting.

The definitions of civic journalism tend to avoid ties to the norms and routines of journalistic practice. Civic journalism specifically aims to improve connections to public life through development of new listening posts in non-traditional places (outside of government offices).

Civic journalists, therefore, must think differently about source choices. They identify people in the community who act as catalysts, connectors, and experts. Community catalysts are individuals who help initiate change and problem solving. Connectors are community members with a vantage point to see across community boundaries. Community experts are those people who hold the institutional memory for the community. Civic journalism also encourages reporting in five key layers of public life: official, quasi-official, third-place, incidental, and private. This is very different from the traditional conceptualization of source diversity, and while this would seem to dictate improved source diversity, no evidence exists that source diversity has in fact been altered at television stations where civic journalism is practiced.

In traditional journalistic practices, the value of a citizen source is often questioned. Charity wrote, "Many newspapers treat the printing of citizen voices as a kind of welfare system for the news-space impoverished-a service aimed much more at good community relations than at forwarding the debate on public issues-but public journalists think differently. They are perfectly comfortable drawing on citizens for ideas." Television journalists also tend to view citizen sources as simply storytelling elements that add emotion to the expert source's ideas.

While many newspapers have embraced civic journalism, the development of television forms of civic journalism has been less successful. Still, several shining examples of television attempts exist, including KRON's "About Race" project that spanned almost three years. But television civic journalism may be starting to develop. In the past two years, the number of entries to the Pew Centre for Civic Journalism Batten Awards has increased steadily, indicating a growing willingness to attempt this type of work.

Some evidence also exists that civic journalism improves source diversity in newspaper coverage. Kennamer and South compared election coverage in two newspapers, one civic and one traditional.

They found the civic journalism paper used a much greater percentage of unaffiliated sources (43 per cent vs. 12 per cent). Boynton found increased use of female sources in civic journalism work in her study of the Charlotte Observer, although female sources tended to be used less prominently. Boynton also found that male reporters were more likely to use female sources, but that many of these female sources were from the unaffiliated ranks.

Massey also found increased use of female sources in civic journalism newspaper stories. However, in his study the gender of the reporter was a confounding variable, because only female reporters increased their use of female sources.

This study builds on the previous research on source diversity. It asks whether a new form of journalistic practice that includes an emphasis on enterprise reporting and digging deep into community life does in fact improve diversity of source race and gender. Improved diversity might provide additional proof of the value of television forms of civic journalism. Lack of improvement will provide evidence of the limitations organizational norms and routines place on the practice of television journalism.

This study focuses on the diversity of sources presented in civic journalism television news reports. Because the number of television stations that practice civic journalism is limited, this study assumes that any station attempting civic journalism would be likely to submit a tape to the James K. Batten Awards contest. The Pew Centre for Civic Journalism has a history of encouraging stations to submit entries. Of primary interest is whether television civic journalists used greater diversity of sources-race and gender-compared to proportions in the 2000 U.S. Census. This leads to the following hypotheses for television coverage:

H1: Civic journalism will use minority sources in proportions equal to the U.S. Census.

H2: As part of an expected increase in minority sources in civic journalism stories, minority reporters will use a greater percentage of minority sources than non-minority reporters do.

H3: Civic journalism will use female sources in proportions equal to the U.S. Census.

H4: As part of an expected increase in female sources in civic journalism stories, female reporters will use a greater percentage of female sources than male reporters.

The data consist of a content analysis of all the television news stories on 184 entry tapes submitted for the James K. Batten Award from 1996 through 2001. This award is the premier recognition for civic journalism work in the United States. A total of 1,071 news sources was coded by three trained coders. The stations ranged in market size from the second largest to number 156. Stations were from all parts of the country. All the reports were original content created for the station by station employees. The Scott's pi intercoder reliability coefficient for each variable ranged from.84 to 1.0.41

News sources were defined as any person or group to which information was attributed. If a source appeared more than one time in a single story, the source was coded only once and the times for both appearances combined. The sources were coded for affiliation, race, and gender.

The first hypothesis predicted proportional use of minority sources when comparing civic journalism to U.S. Census data. This hypothesis was supported with some qualifications. Civic journalism used a higher percentage of minority sources (35.5%) than the actual population in the United States (24.9%). African-American sources (23%) were presented at a rate almost twice that of the population (12.3%). Asian-American sources (3.4%) were presented at a level almost equal to the Census (3.6%). Latinos were underrepresented compared to the Census (77% vs. 12.5%).

The second hypothesis, predicting that reporter race would be related to minority source selection, was also supported. African-American reporters were more likely to use African-American sources (38.2%) in their stories than non-minority (17.9%) or Latino reporters (18.6%). Latino reporters also were more likely to use Latino sources (33.9%) than non-minority (7.2%) or African-American reporters (2%). Minority reporters might simply hold a greater affinity for using minority sources, or they may be more likely to cover beats and communities with disproportionately more minorities.

The third hypothesis predicted parity use of female sources compared to U.S. Census data. In the civic journalism stories studied, women represented little more than 40% of the sources. Civic journalism did not reach the 50.9% census level. Thus the hypothesis was not supported. The fourth hypothesis predicted that female civic journalists would use a greater percentage of female sources. This hypothesis was supported. In fact, female reporters were significantly more likely than their male counterparts to include female sources in their stories. However, even in this case, female source representation does not rise to Census levels.

This study provides evidence that civic journalism alters the routines of coverage in a positive manner. While this research did not look at the nature of the portrayal of the sources, positive or negative, it does indicate that groups disproportionately left out of news coverage do gain access and an opportunity to express their views in a television civic journalism model.

Based on these results, it is possible to say that civic journalism produces a positive effect on the diversity of sources presented on television news. When compared to the literature on television sourcing, the difference is even more pronounced. Women and minorities are portrayed more often in civic journalism than in traditional journalism.

Civic journalism minority source use (35.5%) more than doubled Grabe and Barnett's findings of 13.6% minority source use in television magazine shows.43 In contrast with Smith's study of television news in one of the most diverse communities in the country, San Francisco, civic journalism was still higher than the 19% of minority sources reported. Minority sources in civic journalism exceed their proportion in the population. This is primarily explained by the high level of African— American sources used in civic journalism (23%)

compared to the African-American population reported in the Census (12.3%). However, both this study's and Smith's findings are significantly lower for Latinos compared to the Census data. People of Asian descent were reported at parity levels in all three versions.

At a basic level, it makes sense that journalists find it easier to locate sources most like themselves. Journalistic norms push journalists to cross racial and gender boundaries in search of diverse representations for their stories. Civic journalism tools help journalists effectively cross boundaries and understand unfamiliar communities in deeper and more meaningful ways. The findings in this study certainly indicate more work is needed, even within television civic journalism. African— American reporters over-compensated in their presentations of African— American sources compared to the Census. This is likely a response to less-than-equitable source use in stories covered by journalists of other races. Two important points maybe made here. One is that non-minority civic journalism reporters made progress in covering minority communities. The other is that civic journalism appears to give minority reporters the opportunity to draw minority sources into coverage. More research is needed to investigate how minority journalists use civic journalism tools within organizational routines to improve source diversity.

Television civic journalism's female sourcing is higher than the best gender diversity reported in the literature. For example, Zoch and Turk's study of 2,998 sources in the front and metro sections of daily newspapers found only 20.8% of sources were women. Liebler and Smith's analysis of 448 sources in 159 network television stories found even lower levels; women made up only 16.3% of all sources. Because the civic journalism entries studied here came from both networks and local stations, the percentages are not entirely comparable.

Unlike the sourcing by reporters of colour, female source use by female reporters did not reach the Census benchmark of 50.9%. Some might argue that a more fair comparison is with the level of female workers in the U.S. workforce. However, civic journalism is not simply covering the workforce. Also of note is that male civic journalists easily topped the best reported level of female source use in the literature (20.8%) by using 37.4% female sources in their work.

This replicates Boynton's finding that a civic journalism newspaper included a "significantly higher number of female sources than found in other studies where women comprise one-third or less of the identifiable sources." Grabe, Zhou, and Barnett's study of television news magazines found that "female reporters seek out more female sources (38.3%) than male reporters do (27.6%)." The current study replicates this finding but at higher levels. Of the sources selected by female television civic journalists, 44.5% were female. For male civic journalists, female sources accounted for 37.4% of all sources used. The enterprise nature of news magazines studied by Grabe, Zhou, and Barnett likely improved source diversity on these programs. Improved source diversity in civic journalism should not be surprising because it relies heavily on an enterprise model of coverage. In 1991, Hansen found that enterprise reporting improved source diversity. However, the civic journalism model goes well beyond simply developing an enterprise report. Civic journalism dictates that reporters spend time in communities gaining a greater depth and context of understanding. If it is true that reporters tend to use people they know and trust as primary sources, and if civic journalism creates a routine of getting to know and trust people in diverse communities, then it makes sense that civic journalism practices would improve the diversity of sources in race, gender, and affiliation.

The adoption rate of civic journalism among television stations remains low. While KRON-TV in San Francisco provided proof that television news is capable of doing high-quality civic journalism, Kurpius found that television forms of civic journalism were generally not sustainable in the current market-driven news model. While managers and journalists indicated a desire and a willingness to use a civic model for coverage, marketplace forces limited the potential for development without the now commonplace foundation financial support for this type of work.

The need for improved source diversity remains, even in civic journalism. Women and Latinos are still underrepresented. While the benchmark for improving gender diversity is a stable target, the Latino population is one of the fastest growing in the country. This will challenge journalists who make good faith efforts to accurately and effectively represent the communities they cover.

Another concern is that television stations are unlikely to see the gains found in this study because of the limited adoption of civic journalism techniques at stations across the country. This limits the potential for finally correcting an almost half-century-old problem in television's coverage: the lack of inclusion and accurate representation of minorities and women in news content. However, more work is needed. For instance, because there are differing levels of adoption of civic journalism practices among television stations, it is unclear at what level the tools start to produce improved diversity. In addition, a qualitative study of news workers within civic journalism television organizations might provide a better understanding of exactly how they altered their routines to improve diversity.

OVERALL APPROVAL OF INVESTIGATIVE REPORTING

A comparison of results from the 1997 Pew survey with results from the 1981 Gallup survey shows that the overall approval of investigative reporting has slightly increased during the past sixteen years. Even though the 1997 survey was conducted in the wake of the Food Lion case, which raised questions about news gathering techniques used by ABC News reporters, almost 84% of the respondents in 1997 said that they approved of the news media's practice of uncovering and reporting corruption and fraud in business, government agencies, and other organizations.

This compares to a similar, but smaller, majority of 79% that expressed support for investigative reporting in the 1981 Gallup survey. While support for investigative reporting in general has risen between 1981 and 1997, no difference is found in the level of demand for more investigative reporting stories. In 1997,64% of Americans said that they would like to see more of this type of reporting rather than less (29%), as compared to 66% who said they would like to see more of these stories in 1981 (19% less). Nevertheless, the data clearly show that most Americans still not only approve of investigative reporting in general, but that they would also like to see more investigative reporting by the news media.

APPROVAL OF INVESTIGATIVE REPORTING TECHNIQUES

Similar to previous findings, the 1997 survey shows that general approval of investigative reporting does not necessarily translate into approval of specific investigative reporting techniques. Approval of most investigative reporting techniques is only weakly correlated with approval of investigative reporting in general. Only about one-third of all respondents approve of reporters concealing their identity (33%) or paying informers for information (31%), while slightly more approve of news organizations' use of hidden cameras and microphones (46%), or running stories that quote unnamed sources (53%).

Thus, while an overwhelming majority of respondents approve of investigative reporting in general, almost as many respondents also disapprove of concrete investigative reporting practices. In fact, among those respondents who approve of investigative reporting in general, more than 15% do not approve of any of the four tested investigative reporting techniques, and only about 7% approve of all the techniques.

A comparison of national poll results between 1981 and 1997, indicates a moderate, national-level increase in approval for using hidden microphones and cameras (up 8%) and quoting unnamed sources (up 11%), but no increase in approval for reporters concealing their identity or paying for information. The observed increase in approval for the use of hidden cameras and microphones is notable in light of the fact that both techniques were used in ABC's Food Lion story.

IMPACT OF DEMOGRAPHICS

Results from the 1997 survey closely mirror the findings of previous studies that analysed the demographic profile of those people who are more likely to approve of investigative reporting in general. Consistently over the past sixteen years, it appears that especially the younger, more affluent, and better-educated respondents have a more positive view of investigative reporting by the media, although these relationships have been weak in strength.

To evaluate the potential impact of respondents' demographic characteristics on overall approval of investigative reporting and the specific reporting techniques, provides a demographic breakdown for both types of approval (general and specific) together with results from the question that asks whether respondents would like to see more or fewer investigative reporting stories.

In general, demographic characteristics do seem to have a distinct but weak influence on who approves of investigative reporting and whether someone is likely to want more investigative reporting stories. While respondents who are more educated are more likely to approve of investigative reporting and most of the investigative reporting techniques (except for quoting unnamed sources and paying informers), they are less likely to want more investigative reporting stories. The greatest support for investigative reporting is found among the 30- to 49-year-old respondents, but specific investigative reporting techniques find the most support among those under the age of 30.

Older respondents are especially skeptical of investigative reporting in general and tend to disapprove in particular of quoting unnamed sources and reporters paying for information. They are also less likely to want more investigative reporting stories. Familiar patterns are also observed for the relationship between income and approval of investigative reporting. The poorest respondents (less than $20,000 yearly income) are less likely to approve of investigative reporting, especially the use of hidden cameras and microphones and reporters concealing their identities, and these poorer people are also more likely to want fewer such stories.

Previous studies that looked at the rate of approval of investigative reporting in relation to place of residence found that rural respondents are less likely to approve of investigative reporting. The 1981 Gallup survey, for example, found that respondents from cities of more than 500,000 were more likely to approve (84%) than those from smaller cities. Results from the Pew survey indicate that this difference still exists in 1997. While the highest levels of approval for investigative reporting in 1997 can be found in the suburbs (88%), significantly less support is found in rural areas (78%). Rural residents, however, do not vary much from people living in suburbs or cities on whether there should be more or less investigative reporting.

In line with previous findings, party identification does not seem to influence whether respondents approve or disapprove of investigative reporting, although Republicans are less likely to approve of quoting unnamed sources. There is also little difference between African-American and white Americans in their approval of investigative reporting. However, the relatively few people of other races (predominantly Asians) are more likely to favour investigative reporting, especially the use of hidden cameras and microphones, concealing identity (going undercover), and, to a lesser extent, quoting unnamed sources.

These minorities are also more likely to ask for more investigative news stories. Somewhat more distinct differences are found between men and women. While men are less likely to approve of quoting unnamed sources (possibly because more men are Republicans than women), women are more likely to disapprove of the use of hidden cameras and microphones and paying for information, but are more likely than men to want more investigative reporting stories.

Statistical Analysis: Logistic Regression Analysis. In order to evaluate the individual contributions of respondents' demographic characteristics, media use, and attitudes toward the media on approval of investigative reporting, a series of logistic regression analyses are used. The logistic regression procedure allows us to examine the influence of multiple independent variables on dichotomous dependent variables. Compared to ordinary least squares (OLS) regression, which presents coefficients that result in the smallest squared distances between the observed and the predicted values of the dependent variables, in logistic regression those coefficients which make the model results most "likely" are selected.

However, because the logistic regression model is nonlinear, the interpretation of regression coefficients is not as straightforward as in OLS regression. Logistic regression coefficients (B) can be interpreted as the change in the ratio of approval versus disapproval of investigative reporting associated with a one-unit change in an independent variable while holding other independent variables constant. Thus a positive B indicates that an increase in the independent variable predicts an increase in the support for investigative reporting, whereas a negative B suggests that an increase in the independent variable predicts a decrease in support controlling for other independent variables. To assess the statistical significance of these coefficients, this study uses the Wald statistic.

Overall, six logistic regression models are used for the analysis of approval of investigative reporting. The first model predicts overall "approval of investigative reporting" in general, while the following models predict the approval of four investigative reporting techniques discussed above ("using hidden microphones and cameras," "reporters not identifying themselves," "quoting unnamed sources," "paying for information"). In line with the requirements for logistic regression models, all five dependent variables provide binominal answer categories (approve = 1; disapprove = 0; don't know = missing). The last regression model predicts whether people are more likely to want more or fewer investigative reporting stories (more = 1; fewer = 0; don't know = missing). Respondents' media use is assessed by a series of questions asking respondents to state on a 4-point scale (regularly = 4; never

= 1) how often they watched or read the following types of media products: the "nightly network news," the "local evening news," "CNN," "60 Minutes," "Dateline NBC," "TV news shows," "daily newspaper," and "tabloid papers."

Another important block of variables included in this study are measures of respondents' attitudes toward the role of the press in society. According to recent polls, the public's assessment of press performance has grown increasingly negative in recent years. A majority (56%) now say news stories and reports are often inaccurate, up more than 20 percentage points from 1985, when a similar majority (55%) said news organizations get the facts straight. The press is also attacked for its lack of fairness. Two-thirds (67%) say that in presenting news on political and social issues, news organizations tend to favour one side rather than dealing fairly with all sides. This negative view of the press is more prevalent now than it was twelve years ago, when a much smaller majority (53%) criticized news organizations for biased coverage of political and social news.

Attitudes toward media are measured with five dummy variables that assess respondents' attitudes toward the press by asking whether they believe that (1) "criticism by the press keeps political leaders from doing their job"; (2) "press coverage of the personal and ethical behaviour of political leaders is excessive"; (3) "press criticism of the policies and proposals of political leaders is excessive"; (4) "news stories are often inaccurate"; and (5) "news organizations tend to favour one side when reporting about political and social issues" (all coded: yes = 1, no = 0).

Control variables include measures of gender (male = 1; female = 0), age, education, race (two dummy variables: White and Black), party identification (two dummy variables: Republican and Democrat), income, and place of residence (rural = 1; small city, suburb, large city = 0).

FINDINGS FOR LOGISTIC REGRESSION MODELS

In line with previous findings, no significant links are observed between income, education, race, or political party identification on approval of investigative reporting. Older respondents, however, are less likely to approve of the use of hidden cameras and microphones (B = -.02) and of reporters not identifying themselves as reporters (B = -.02). Similar to the findings reported in 1982 and 1992, respondents living in rural areas of the country are less likely to approve of investigative reporting in general (B = -.50) and reporters not identifying themselves (B = -.44). Interestingly, male respondents are less likely to approve of quoting unnamed sources (B =-.30), but more likely to approve of paying for information (B =.35).

Media exposure to CNN is positively related to approval of quoting unnamed sources (B =.15), while those respondents who regularly watch Dateline NBC are more likely to approve of the use of hidden cameras and microphones (B =.25). Interestingly, those people who regularly watch tabloid-style TV shows such as Hard Copy or Inside Edition are less likely to approve of reporters not identifying themselves. None of the standard media exposure variables, such as frequency of reading the newspaper or watching TV news, was significantly related to any of the dependent approval measures, reinforcing the findings from the earlier studies that frequency of media use is less important than what one reads or views.

The most consistent predictors of respondents' approval of investigative reporting are attitudes toward the function of the press in society. Respondents are less likely to approve of investigative reporting when they believe that criticism by the press keeps political leaders from doing their job (B between -.34 and -1.01) or when they think that reports and stories by news organizations are often inaccurate (B between -.35 and -.89). Thus, those who are dubious about the media's watchdog role are more likely than others to say they want less, not more, investigative reporting.

The best predictors for respondents' willingness to see more investigative reporting stories in the media are age, place of residence, media exposure, and attitudes toward the media. Exposure to CNN (B =.15) and 60 Minutes (B =.20), on the other hand, boosts the likelihood of asking for more investigative news stories. Additionally, those who believe that the media are keeping politicians from doing their jobs are less likely to ask for more investigative news stories (B = -.47).

Overall, the findings reported here indicate that public opinion about investigative reporting did not change much during the past sixteen years. Similar to previous findings, a majority of respondents in the 1997 survey approve of investigative reporting in general, independent from such demographic factors as age, education, gender, or party identification. Compared to the findings reported in the 1981 Gallup survey, the percentage of respondents who approve of investigative reporting in 1997 has slightly increased to 84%. This indicates that a vast majority of people still favour a press that uncovers and reports on corruption and fraud in business and government, and that this support is increasing rather than diminishing over time.

Another important observation of this study is that the approval for investigative reporting remains much higher than the approval for specific investigative reporting techniques. Only about one-third of the respondents in 1981 and 1997, for example, approve of reporters working undercover or paying for information. Evidently, Americans do expect the media to take their role as a public watchdog seriously, but they also expect that the media do so with the greatest degree of openness possible.

Interestingly, during the past eight years, the public approval of hidden cameras or microphones and the use of anonymous sources in the news media also has slightly increased. This might possibly be a reflection of the more frequent employment of hidden cameras in news shows such as 60 Minutes and the increasingly routine use of anonymous news sources in political reporting. It is reasonable to assume that the repeated exposure to undercover news stories and source identifiers such as "a high-ranking government official" in regular news stories reinforces the impression that these techniques are standard journalistic practice. Asking respondents whether they approve of reporters not identifying themselves or actually paying for information, on the other hand, might create images of ethical misconduct on an individual level and thus could help to explain the lower approval ratings.

Overall, findings indicate that the best predictor for whether people approve or disapprove of investigative reporting is their general attitude toward the media's role in society. Those respondents who see the media as a force that undermines the work of politicians and those who believe that news stories are often inaccurate, are less likely to approve of investigative reporting in general and of most investigative reporting techniques.

Compared to the other observed relationships in the various logistic regression models which were tested here, attitudes toward the press proved to be the strongest and most consistent predictor for approval of investigative reporting. In light of the mostly insignificant relationships observed between media exposure and approval of investigative reporting, it appears that approval is primarily a function of attitudes toward the media, rather than increased exposure to investigative news stories.

It is somewhat alarming, though, that especially those who have a very negative view of the media's function in society are also more likely to disapprove of the very techniques that allow the media to operate as a political and social watchdog.

Because a vast majority of the people approve of investigative reporting in general, the explanation of this schizophrenic attitude is likely to be found in negative perceptions of specific investigative reporting techniques among most respondents, but especially among those who are critical of the press.

While the six regression models are fairly similar in total amount of variation predicted in approval of investigative reporting, it should be noted that the unexplained variance in all models is high, especially for the four models predicting approval of specific investigative reporting techniques (89 - 94%, based on Nagelkerke R2 estimates). This suggests that opinions about investigative reporting are related to other, unknown factors that were not included in this study or that they are fairly idiosyncratic, or both. The logistic regression model predicting approval of investigative reporting in general produced the highest Nagelkerke R^sup 2^, but most of the explained variance here is related to the above mentioned attitudes toward the role of the press in society and place of residence.

Future studies should search for other possible predictors to better explain why people are so much in favour of investigative reporting but, at the same time, disapprove of most techniques that make this kind of journalism possible. The findings of this study suggest that the focus at the individual level should be on attitudes and values rather than on respondents' demographic characteristics or their media use patterns. There are some hints here, however, that community-level characteristics, such as rural residence, may also play an important role in the formation of attitudes and opinions about investigative reporting, as suggested by the comparison of Chicago residents' opinions with those from national and Indiana samples in the 1980s.

More frequent exposure to investigative reporting projects that seem to be worthwhile revelations of wrongdoing is likely to influence public opinion about such reporting in general, as well as the specific methods used to carry it out. The key, though, seems to be whether the public perceives the use of ethically questionable reporting practices as justifying the exposure of wrongdoing, as in Chicago in 1980. And even there, levels of support for specific reporting methods were lower than support for investigative reporting in general, suggesting that such techniques should be used sparingly by news organizations that value public support, as Weaver and Daniels concluded in 1992.

4

Techniques in Public Journalism

Labels of elitism and egalitarianism are useless because there are elements of each in both objective and public journalism.

Each advocates a different level of constraint on the press. The past 50 years have witnessed much scholarship and debate regarding the practice of objective journalism. This discussion has been intensified with the advent of public journalism, whose advocates boldly assert that objective journalism is fundamentally flawed.

Not surprisingly, much heated debate has emerged in which proponents of either journalistic practice accuse the other of being negligent, misleading or culpable in the erosion of democracy. Of key concern to this chapter is the propensity for participants in this debate to talk past one another - to be too quick to judge and dismiss the other practice as intrinsically broken, and thus, something to be immediately recanted and forsaken.

The debate concerning objective and public journalism is flawed because it focuses almost exclusively on the final products of each approach, usually demonstrating how each fail to achieve desired goals. This is because there is no fair and standardized way to compare and contrast the processes of each approach.

The study of journalistic practices as techniques overcomes this problem. Analyzing objective and public journalism as techniques affords the opportunity to focus on the means, not simply the end results, of each approach. This is a necessary step in enriching the debate over objective and public journalism. Without this focus, debate will continue to produce more derision than deliberation.

FOCUS ON PROCESS

In discussing the impossibility of true objectivity, Denis McQuail asserts that objective journalism is more of "an approach... than an Achievement." Jorgen Westerstahl states that "maintaining objectivity in the dissemination of news can... most easily be defined as adherence to certain norms and standards. It is not a question of basing conclusions on some definition of the inherent nature of objectivity." Each of these scholars has emphasized the need to focus on objective reporting as a process rather than becoming distracted by the philosophical debate over the possibility of true objectivity.

Because public journalism is still very young, there is no single set of procedures which the approach advocates. However, using a series of case studies, some scholars have outlined how different organizations approach the practice of public journalism.

Other researchers have gone so far as to outline some common practices (i.e., public forums, public opinion polling, etc.) typical of public journalism projects and some urge the creation of a systematic approach for public journalism. Thus, while each public journalism project is unique, there remain some common practices which are consistently espoused. As a result, public journalism also yields itself to the study of technique.

STUDY OF TECHNIQUE

The study of technique is the study of process. Jacques Ellul states that the study of technique incorporates an examination of means, values and resources. First and foremost, the study of technique allows scholars to focus on the actual practices of any activity.

Second, technique examines how value structures dictate the practices of an activity. Finally, although Harold Lasswell alludes to the fact that the study of technique should involve the topic of resources, this study focuses exclusively on means and values.

FOCUS ON MEANS

Ellul asserts that "our civilization is first and foremost a civilization of means... the means, it would seem, are more important than the end." The means or practices of any activity are nothing more than steps taken to achieve a desired goal. Importantly, focusing on the means of an activity requires an examination of the efficiency of the means. Ellul claims that "technique is the totality of methods rationally arrived at and having absolute efficiency" and that techniques are designed to "search for the greatest efficiency." Clearly, the matter of efficiency is very important to the time-constrained world of journalism. Thus, in Ellul's terms, both objective and public journalists seek out the one best means to achieve their goals.

FOCUS ON VALUES

Lasswell stresses that a defined value structure is a necessary but not sufficient condition for the initiation of a given technique. Because value orientations necessitate the employment of a given technique, a complete analysis of a technique must entail a thorough explication of the goals and values that provoked the creation of any particular set of practices. Indeed, if an individual or organization does not have some set of values or desired goals in mind, then specific practices will not be generated.

Further, these goals and values must be conscious realizations of individuals or organizations. The conscious nature of these values brings a human element to the activity. Indeed, the study of technique "attempts to take human nature into account in order to keep man from being crushed by technique." It is not the technique that drives people, but the values constructed by people which initiates the process. People are not beholden to any one technique - any technique can be altered to suit changes in the value structure of an individual or organization. This gives technique a flexibility that allows for a more humanist approach to the study of human activities.

Objective Journalism

If you mean by objectivity, absence of convictions, willingness to let nature take its course, uncritical acceptance of things as they are... the hell with it. If you mean by objectivity a healthy respect for the ascertainable truth, a readiness to modify conclusions when new evidence comes in, a refusal to distort deliberately and for ulterior or concealed motives, a belief that the means shape the end, not that the end justifies the means, all well and good.

Opponents of objective journalism argue that pure objectivity is unobtainable and that the notion of objectivity is, at best, a shield devised by corporate America to insure a sanitized version of the truth, and at worst, an ideological weapon used to maintain the status quo. However, studying objective journalism as technique avoids this philosophical debate and concentrates on the means and values of the approach; instead, it is the practices employed to achieve this unobtainable goal which become most important. It is important to take note of the fact that objectivity is an ever-evolving term.

Richard Streckfuss makes this point clear in his tracing of the historical underpinnings of the term as it relates to the profession of journalism. Although objectivity is often treated as a synonym for neutrality by today's proponents of public journalism, its initial use was more closely associated with the growth of scientific naturalism in the 1920s than any notion of the need to remain neutral or detached. Objective journalism as a technique is based both on the original meaning as outlined by Walter Lippmann and the more recent practice of this form of newsgathering; studying each of these aspects is essential to understanding the values and means of this form of journalism.

Values of objective journalism Objective journalism is often seen as the successor to the sensationalistic journalism which was common in the 19th century. Wishing to avoid heavily skewed, sensational and propagandistic news, many journalists, most notably Lippmann, realized the need for a standard of journalism which would simultaneously ascribe credibility to the field and provide an intrinsically different news product.

This new standard took the form of objective journalism, a technique modeled after the social sciences. Its ultimate goal was to expunge the biases and ideologies that journalists bring to reporting. Objectivity, it was heralded, was a way to delineate facts from feelings, truths from opinions. Penultimately, it was hoped that the extraction of reporter biases would yield a more pure form of news reporting based singularly on facts - not absolute facts, but verified, consensual facts.

Further, it was believed that objective journalism would benefit the public by providing unembellished and unbiased presentations of facts from which people could formulate their own conclusions.

In short, the basic tenets of objective journalism are: To extract reporter biases from journalism; to present factual information in order to best inform the public; to protect the public from duplicitous or biased journalism; to eschew emotional or slanted reporting; and to raise the credibility of the profession of news reporting. Means of objective journalism It was Lippmann who best argued for the application of a systematic scientific study to journalism. He believed that “there is but one kind of unity possible in a world as diverse as ours.

It is unity of method, rather than of aim; the unity of the disciplined experiment.” Mirroring the social sciences, journalists like Lippmann devised rigorous procedures which, if followed, would consistently yield facts on which all reporters could agree. Herbert Gans writes, “like scientific method, journalistic method is validated by consensus. Equally important, the methods themselves are considered objective.”

Similarly, Everette Dennis states that objective reporting is possible if “procedures are followed providing for systematic decisions.” Thus, the values of objective journalism were translated into a technique meant to produce unprejudiced, evidence-based reporting. If the method is properly followed, objective reporting should allow 10 different reporters to reach similar conclusions from a set of consensually agreed-upon facts. Hence, “objectivity, in this sense, means that a person’s statements about the world can be trusted if they are submitted to established rules deemed legitimate by a professional community.”

The influence of scientific method is clearly seen in all introductory journalism textbooks. Students are taught to dogmatically follow procedures of fact verification. Melvin Mencher writes, “An objective report contains material that everyone would agree is based on fact.

Stories are objective when material in them is borne out by evidence.” As the basis of objective journalism, facts must be rigorously checked for validity, attribution, and accuracy. This is accomplished by checking every fact against multiple sources of information, including records, experts and other relevant information sources. Further, only after all the facts have been gathered should reporters comment upon them.

Gans states that reporters should "strive for opinions based on 'subjective reactions' which follow from gathered facts. Journalistic values are seen as reactions to the news rather than a priori judgments which determine what becomes newsworthy." Neophyte reporters are also admonished to gather as many facts as possible before conducting an interview to prevent news sources from using the media to disseminate mis- or disinformation; an informed reporter should be able to spot information discrepancies immediately and investigate them.

Further, students are told to strive for complete accuracy, which includes: Verifying the spelling of all names; understanding the information to be reported; avoiding unwarranted assumptions; placing the story in the most relevant context; and consistently seeking statements from all relevant parties in a story. The adherence to these practices is meant to mirror that of the scientist; reporters meticulously gather, question, verify and re-question information until they are convinced of its authenticity.

Only after this process is complete are reporters permitted to draw conclusions. In sum, objective journalism strives to use the scientific method of systematic fact-gathering and fact-verification to remove reporter biases from news coverage. Westerstahl succinctly expresses the need for objectivity when he comments, "objective news reporting is not accomplished without conscious will," and "when that will is missing, then the requirement of truth will occasionally be affected, but relevance decisions, balance between the parties in the conflict, and the presentations of the parties will always be affected."

TECHNICAL UTILITIES

In this section, we discuss the use of technical utilities for accomplishing research tasks. Some computer systems allow asynchronous communication interactions to be studied either by saving the individual messages, or archiving all postings for later perusal. Most of these have been around for some time. The ones we discuss here are electronic mail, news groups over Usenet, and list servers. Electronic mail is asynchronous (users generally are not communicating in realtime), quick (in terms of transmission and reply), text-based, and configured for dyadic or multiple connections (can be sent one-to-one, one-to-many, or many-to-many). Moreover, e-mail can be stored and manipulated. As Garton and Wellman noted in a recent review:

E-mail can be stored in external memory for future retrieval, searching, editing, and forwarding to others. People can edit their own or other's messages to change their meaning. The historical record of interaction may be used for surveillance of individual and group interactions, to review past decisions (as Oliver North belatedly learned), and to bring new members up to date. What makes this modality particularly suitable for ethnographic research are its personal-contact and archival functions.

For example, in his 9-month participant-observation study of "Zytech," a computer systems firm, Workman utilized e-mail in the following ways:

- Being placed on the company's various distribution lists, which on a daily basis delivered internal documents, minutes of meetings, meeting agendas, and announcements;
- Scheduling interviews;
- Accessing hundreds of BBS's, including Zytech correspondence going back several years;
- Communicating with informants, including follow-ups to FTF interviews.

Though the staggered progress of e-mail interviewing does not promote the same qualities of rapport or spontaneity as personal interviews, it does permit a more elastic time frame for both interviewer and participant to think carefully about the meanings of questions and replies. In another organizational study, special software was used to automatically save the headers (but not the message content) of all departmental e-mail to a designated file whenever a user read or transmitted a message, yielding a non-reactive means of learning who communicates with whom, when, and about what. For ethnographic purposes, the value of this procedure lies in its capacity to augment such methods as interviews or on-site observation.

However, the ability to retrieve and store this information without the users' permission (or below their conscious awareness, even when permission is granted) carries the potential for ethical abuse at worst, and suspicion on the part of participants at best. Usenet is a protocol that describes how groups of messages can be stored on and sent between computers, many of which lay outside of the Internet. In actuality, Usenet forms a "virtual forum" for the electronic community that is divided into a plethora of news groups dedicated to varied areas of interest. News group articles are read and written through programmes called newsreaders that keep track of articles that have been read, allow users to edit what has been read, and enable readers to reply to previously posted messages in the aforementioned study, Baym reported her participant-observation of a news group made up of soap opera aficionados.

Even though some Usenet sites can archive messages off-line, Baym herself saved the messages posted on the r.a.t.s group while she was an active member. Even working with a medium often described as low in social presence or media richness, she was able to develop a "thick" description of the personalities of this community based on features of their postings:

- Signature files (files automatically attached to postings containing identifying information about the sender),
- Humour in the messages,
- Self-disclosure,
- Comments made about personal lives.

By capitalizing on the features of Usenet news groups, variations of focus group interviewing become possible. During a two-month period of operating a public BBS, Myers set up a computer-mediated focus group "to determine what motivated frequent and active BBS use". As an alternative to a simple discussion, a focus group consisting of a theoretically interesting set of users could work on a virtual task. MacGregor and Morrison describe an editing-group protocol in which groups of people were given the opportunity to re-edit existing news reports (including video footage) in order to produce a more "ideal" version, thereby enabling them to understand viewers' journalistic values more concretely.

It is not difficult to see how this task could be adapted to computer news groups and the multimedia capabilities of high-end work stations, although techniques for training and monitoring the users in their editing-group activities would need to be developed. Listserv groups (managed by listserver software) are similar to news groups in that they are discussion groups, but they operate in a completely different way by using the Internet e-mail system to exchange messages. Once a person subscribes to a Listserv group (or Listproc group, as they are called on networks other than the early Bitnet), their name is added to a mailing list that receives postings from everyone else subscribed to the list. Many listservers offer features that allow users to search and retrieve files that are archived, and search the archives using keyword searches. Thus, anyone from a remote site can access archived messages for study from the host computer.

This capability raises interesting ethical issues: How does one receive consent to study the stored communications of users of a particular listserver? Is open access to a person's communications implied in the use of this service? Are the archived files considered the property of the individual subscribers, or are they "owned" in some form of fiduciary relationship by the listserv operator? Because the Internet has developed so rapidly, many such legal and ethical questions have yet to be resolved. The CMC technologies mentioned above have been in place for a while and are generally well known to most researchers. Most of the communication from these sources is asynchronous, *i.e.*, it is archived for later review and becomes an excellent database. However some of the newer systems allow for the actual observation of synchronous, or real-time, communication behaviour. It is to these we now turn.

Some of the more recent real-time technologies are:

- Internet Relay Chat (IRC) systems, or" chat lines";
- The entire gamut of multiple-user technologies, *e.g.*, MUDs (Multiple User Domains, formerly known as Multiple User Dungeons), MOOs (MUD Object-Oriented), and MUSHes (Multi-User Shared Hallucination);
- Groupware,

- Desktop videoconferencing over the Internet. All of these systems operate synchronously and as such more approximate face-to-face communication.

Internet Relay Chat (IRC) is a multi-user synchronous communication capability available worldwide to users with Internet accessibility.

These real time" chat lines" provide for mutithreaded conversations from more than two users in something very similar to an" electronic cocktail party". In these" chat rooms" users are able to don bogus" personas" (false identities) and communicate with interactants from all over the globe. These chat lines are very popular on commercial services like America Online and are now available through various web browsers (*e.g.*, students can" chat" with the president of a university via its Web site).

One step up from IRC is a whole family of computer programmes that allow more than just written conversation in real time. These are multi-user programmes that, in addition to providing text, allow the additional depiction of a physical environment. Multiple User programmes are designed to offer a pseudo-physical dimension via its object orientation. In MOOs, for examples, individuals" virtually" move through" rooms," interact with virtual" objects" such as chairs, doors, and the like, and have virtual conversations with others. As Reid has remarked, in MUDs," text replaces gesture and has even become gesture itself".

A third, more recent technology is found in a generation of software called" groupware." Unlike MUDs, MOOs, MUSHes, MUCKs, and the like that are used more for entertainment and amusement, groupware is being developed mainly for business and professional uses.

Most of the newer groupware programmes use Web-based technology and allow not only for sharing e-mail but for conducting synchronous multiuser conferencing. The promise for ethnographers in this technology lies in the" common thread" that runs through all these programmes--*i.e.*," the construction of shared memory" and recording of group discussions. In essence, groupware allows for observing the" virtual office," *i.e.*, electronic mail, conferencing, scheduling, shared documents, electronic" whiteboards," and so on, and recording these interactions.

All of this can function in real time or be archived for later study. Appearing now on the horizon is the capability to use the desktop computer for real time videoconferencing. Using fairly inexpensive video cameras attached to desktop computers, and software such as CU-SeeMe technology, mediated FTF interactions are now available for study. As soon as compression capabilities for full-motion video are perfected, these dispersed FTF interactions, mediated by the computer, can be recorded and used in data analysis.

When considering all these new technologies, the type of research done may have to be dictated by the characteristics of the medium. That is, for asynchronous media, the type of research conducted would be more akin to that for studying other forms of written communication, while synchronous media enable types of research more equivalent to naturalistic observation--*i.e.*, observing the unfolding of communicative events in real time.

It was inevitable that interpretive analysts would turn their attention to the profusion of common culture now moving through the Internet. Forms of ethnographic enquiry are being applied to many of the events that occur in virtual space, although questions remain about how well these approaches engage CMC phenomena. One such question is the appropriateness of" community" as a conceptual device. The conventional idea of community as a stable locus for the practice of ritual, custom, and moral obligation applies to cyberspace groups, albeit in the context of a shifting sense of commitment.

When members can easily come and go, when many" members" do not even post, and when identities cannot be verified beyond the current situation, the power of a community ethos may be weakened considerably. The structural properties of the Internet also raise questions about how far a user community extends. For example, can any array of Web sites found by a search term be considered a" community," and if not, what criteria do we use for including a site in the community set?

Finally, what is the relationship of computer-mediated action to local social networks? It has been suggested, for example, that the growing reliance on computer technology for communicating with distant others may undermine the vitality of public life in so-called real communities or play a role in their economic and social fragmentation. Answers to these and other important issues about virtual community await further and more inventive empirical studies.

If there is one theme that runs through the differences between FTF (embodied) and CIVIC (virtual) ethnography, it is the problem of participation. CIVIC ethnography moves us into questions of what it means to engage in and explain" experience" without being co-present with others. Screen-life is a social sphere of its own with vocabularies, motives, and expectations that increasingly re-interpret the meanings of off-screen-life (*e.g.*, mail becoming known as" snail mail").

Objectifications of life in the screen world are also a part of that world. Computer users do act as textual performers and analysts, and knowingly comment on the skills of other text-makers. The use of symbolic codes like" FOTFL" and the real-time deployment of a character in a MUD are operations that create the affect of participation for users, and it would be unusual for ethnographers; not to consider their situated usage.

However, the sites of semiotic action in CMC are not the texts, but the persons who produce them. The text-threads from a Usenet news group or a stack of e-mail messages exnominate the moments in which they were created and read, and the influences of local institutions on their users' action are seldom seen in the messages themselves. In the years ahead, ethnographers will be struggling with basic questions of what it means to" participate" in simulated worlds as well as with developing tactical ways to participate as researchers. Closely related to the problem of participation are issues of trust and ethical conduct to which we have alluded at various points in this chapter. These issues assume even more importance than usual in research practice due to the greater potential for engaging in covert surveillance of CIVIC social life and the still-unsettled distinctions between" public" and" private" behaviour across the range of cyberspace contexts.

The problem of the stable identifiability of persons who post in Usenet news groups, respond by e-mail, or visit a Web site may also confound the principle of informed consent as a precondition for engaging a human subject's participation. Generally, there is little debate about the need to provide as much disclosure as possible about research procedures to those who are asked to participate, and to shelter them from the possible harmful consequences of participation and subsequent publication.

However, as King notes, extremely wide ranges of" group accessibility" and" perceived privacy" exist on the Internet. The highest accessibility characterizes those public BBS groups that are unmoderated and unregulated, while the least accessible community is" a private, closed e-mail group where the subscription address is not published and there are enforced requirements to join".

Perceived privacy varies in terms of both the sensitivity of the information (in which, for example, a substance abuse support group would seek a very high level of privacy) and the need to disseminate information to the widest possible client group (the National Communication Association's CRTNET would seek a low measure of privacy). Yet a great many Internet conversations can in fact be monitored with relative ease, which complicates the understanding of what is permissible to study and whether observation is truly" covert" if no barriers are erected to keep one from observing.

Of course, it probably does matter to many virtual groups whether it is a naive visitor who is stopping briefly at their fora, or a person whose goal is to cast a long-term, analytic eye on their activities and publish the result. The conventional view holds that any research of on-line participants should" strive to obtain some degree of informed consent whenever possible.... Most importantly, researchers should negotiate their entry into electronic communities, beginning with the `owner' of the discussion, if one exists".

Preserving the dignity and empowerment of the persons being studied, even if their" real" identities and locations are unknown, demands that the researcher take steps to explain all of the elements of the study that may bear on their decision to participate voluntarily. Taking a different view, Jones argues that the highly elusive, evanescent presence and essentially unknowable identity of most of the subjects in cylberspace obviates the need in most cases for pursuing consent formally:" If the research does not involve identifiable subjects, there is no risk to subjects, and therefore the protection of these rights and interests no longer applies".

Jones goes on to argue that the strict application of conventional human subject protections would be especially detrimental to the study of cyberspace, which exists as an arena in which individuals can enjoy the freedom of withholding, revealing, and even fabricating information about themselves.

Somewhere between these positions is King, who states that" the perceived level of privacy with which most members of cyberspace forums post notes is the level that researchers are obligated to protect".

At the stage of publication, she advocates the removal from messages of all headers, signatures, references to the name and type of the group (e-mail, Usenet news group, etc.), and references to any person's name or pseudo-name. It may be that the evolving use of networked systems will alter the customs and arguments for what constitutes" privacy" and" autonomy," in turn informing the ethical practice of ethnography.

DIMENSIONS OF CIVIC JOURNALISM

The foregoing review of the literature and controversy concerning civic journalism displays recurrent themes that can be aptly transferred into dimensions of the variable concept "approval of civic journalism."

As we have seen, civic journalism involves journalistic initiative rather than reactive coverage; it involves an interest in moving toward solutions to community problems that takes journalism far beyond the detached reporting of the problems; it involves ongoing, long-term commitment to the betterment of the public life; and it involves not only the reporting of important public issues but also nonpublished efforts to probe citizens' concerns and engage them in the public life.

With the help of Ed Fouhy, former executive director of the Pew Centre for Civic Journalism, the research team for this project developed the following dimensions and indicators of civic journalism.

1. Enterprise. In the view of Merritt, Rosen, and others, civic journalism starts with the initiative of the journalists in reinvigorating the public life. It is rooted in the belief that journalists have a stake in the health of a community's public life, and that journalism stands uniquely poised to engage citizens. This enterprise not only discovers problems of common concern but continues to motivate citizens to seek out solutions. This is one of the aspects of civic journalism that has prompted the observation that it is no different from traditional enterprise reporting. That is true to some extent, but it is different in two basic ways: It begins with a consideration of what will improve

the public life, rather than what will make a good story, and it implies a commitment to solving community problems beyond the publication of one story or series.

2. Information for Decision Making. This dimension speaks to the development of what Charity has termed "public judgment. A principal role for the civic journalist is to enable citizens not only to communicate in a public arena but to be able to work toward solutions without necessarily being led by institutional policymakers. It requires journalists not only to listen to and synthesize public commentary but to present independent research on alternative public views, so that citizens can be informed in their public judgment. This also involves the journalists' close monitoring of official responses to the various alternatives. The effect, Charity states, is that the reporting can "foster a sense of drama and possibility" in the community.

Merritt also sees in this dimension an obligation of the civic journalist to identify shared ideas he calls "core values," to which all participants in the public discussion would adhere. The recognition of core values is often the critical first step in the assessment of alternative solutions.

3. Facilitation of Discourse. Critical to the success of public deliberation is that citizens feel they have an opportunity to discuss issues and concerns themselves in a public forum -not merely to read about them in the news media. The civic journalist does what is necessary to begin and sustain this public deliberation, even if it means taking nontraditional steps to convene participants. The most common practice in this dimension is the news media's hosting a "town meeting," usually to discuss a particular issue. Anderson, Dardenne, and Killenberg and Charity have written extensively about the news media's suitability for such a role, as they comprise one of the few institutions in American communities that regularly address a wide range of issues across economic, racial, and social boundaries. Public agencies and other private organizations have convened innumerable meetings, of course, but civic-journalism proponents cite the failure of current public life generally as an indication of the more traditional institutions' inability to kindle true public discourse.
4. Attention to Citizens' Concerns. This dimension of civic journalism refers to the rejection of agendas set by those in political and economic authority and the substitution of a citizens' agenda. Charity believes this aspect to be so strange to traditional journalists that retraining is needed, to enable them to elicit, understand, and represent the concerns of ordinary, unaffiliated speakers and to accord those concerns at least as much credulity as they do the concerns of those wielding power.

This dimension is the source of the critique that civic journalism relies mindlessly on focus groups and market research. Merritt and others respond that if such research is truly oriented toward news-consuming preferences, then it is indeed inappropriate as a tool of civic journalism. The value of seeking out public opinion is in setting an agenda for public discourse that reflects popular concerns regardless of political leaders' priorities. This understanding of public opinion resonates with the recent work of political scientist James Fishkin, who urges that public opinion research take place among small, representative groups of citizens who have been carefully informed of the issues under discussion.

The results would represent not an aggregation of individual Americans' uninformed hunches and heuristics but instead the "considered judgments of the public," which would elevate the utility of public opinion. Fishkin observes that this idea "builds on the movement toward public journalism."

As the final stage of the explication, indicators of each dimension were written for inclusion in the survey instrument. Respondents were asked "How do you feel about the following approaches to journalism?" The dimensions were represented by the following sentences:

1. (Enterprise) "A newspaper develops enterprise stories, supported with editorials, to focus public attention on a community problem and tries to help the community move toward a solution."
2. (Information for Decision Making) "A newspaper reports on alternative solutions to community problems, pointing out trade-offs that may be involved."
3. (Facilitation of Discourse) "A newspaper conducts town meetings to discover key issues in the community and follows up with stories focusing on these issues and some possible solutions."
4. (Attention to Citizens' Concerns) A newspaper polls the public to determine the most pressing community issues, then tries to get the candidates to focus on these issues."

While all four dimensions are meant to reflect basic conceptual changes in the way a news organization covers a community, the indicators represent two distinct degrees of departure from current norms. The Enterprise and Information dimensions' indicators represent modest departures from current reporting and editing practices, while the Discourse and Citizens' Concerns indicators represent bolder departures. The indicators were grouped as such in part of the data analysis.

Empirical Research on Civic Journalism

Because civic journalism is a relatively recent phenomenon, what little scholarly work has been done on the movement has been mostly evaluative and prescriptive, rather than empirical. Most of the empirical work has been concerned with the impact of civic journalism projects on political participation and community awareness.

For example, in a comprehensive, Pew— funded study of civic-journalism projects in four cities in 1996, Thorson et al. found that awareness of civic journalism projects was positively associated with citizens' attitudes that are known to bring about political participation.

Their overall conclusion was that civic journalism helps reconnect citizens to public life. In Pew's own report of the same study, 40 per cent of those surveyed in the four cities said the project had made them think more positively about their community.

Less work has been done about the journalists' attitudes and reactions to civic journalism. In a content analysis of the coverage of "The People Project" at Merritt's Wichita Eagle, Riede found that the journalists broke away from only a few traditional routines. He saw a reduction in the political reporting that focuses on personality and political strategy and an increase in substantive reporting of issues. He also noted an increase in stories that encouraged readers to become involved in community organizations and debates. He noted a tone of increased "engagement" and activism, as distinct from detached objectivity.

But he still saw widespread allegiance to experts and politically important people as sources for stories. Voices of "the people" were published more often, but usually superficially and episodically, in ways that could not facilitate discourse. "In fact, the project's doggedly nonadversarial stance, its avoidance of negativism and conflict and its faith in the efficacy of compromise and orderly voluntarism gave it a profoundly conservative tone."

In the Pew Center's own report of the four-city research project in 1996, reporters at the conclusion of the projects were portrayed generally as unimpressed with what they had done. Some thought their stories had been boring and had been read by only a few; others thought their work, focusing in-depth on a single issue, quickly had become repetitive. The Pew evaluators seemed to think that newsroom executives and middle managers were most supportive of the projects, and rank-and-file newsroom employees least supportive.

Webster University researchers surveyed editors and journalism educators to gauge levels of support for various aspects of civic journalism. They found that about half the editors approved the use of polls and focus groups to determine what stories the press should cover.

Majorities of the sample of editors also approved of the notions that journalists should see people not as news consumers but as players in the democratic process; that journalists should devote more attention to what affects ordinary citizens and less on the "major news events of the day;" and that political coverage should include more issue analysis and less "horse race" analysis.

The Webster project does offer a strong indication, however, that civic journalism is not as reviled as the popular, anecdotal accounts would have us believe. But the project surveyed only editors and educators, not rank-and file reporters, photographers, or copy editors-the foot soldiers of this campaign.

The most theoretically provocative finding is found in the most recent study of American journalists by Weaver and Wilhoit. In a replication of earlier analyses, the researchers used factor analysis to identify three "ideal types" of roles for journalism in society. In the analysis of their 1992 survey data, they found renewed evidence of identification with the roles of "disseminator" (whose priority is to deliver information factually and quickly); "interpreter" (whose priority is to provide analysis of complex problems), and "watchdog" (whose priority is to serve as adversary of government and business).

The analysis, however, also revealed a fourth, puzzling factor: journalists who identified with developing the cultural interests of the public, providing entertainment and relaxation, setting the political agenda, and letting ordinary people express their views. The last item suggested a dimension of civic journalism to the extent that Weaver and Wilhoit labeled this factor "populist mobilizer." Unfortunately, the "ordinary people" item had the weakest loading in the factor, but it obviously intrigued the researchers: "If our analysis is right, the new role ('populist mobilizer') is tantalizing evidence that the spirit of the 'public journalism' movement may have established a foothold among the core values of a tiny minority of journalists."

What sorts of journalists might embrace civic journalism? Another important goal of the current study was to develop a rough profile of the journalist who seems supportive of the indicators of civic journalism, based on a host of independent variables. In this regard the recent research literature provides some guidance. The Pew project's authors found qualitative evidence that younger journalists were less enthusiastic about what they were involved in, which the authors attributed to a sense of professional transience and a lack of commitment to the communities in which they worked.

The size and type of the news organization also may be a factor. In their investigation of the "populist mobilizer factor, Weaver and Wilhoit cautiously suggested that small-market journalists may have more favorable attitudes toward civic journalism than their metro-market counterparts. They found greater resonance for that factor-especially for the item "allowing ordinary people to express their views"-among journalists at radio stations, weekly newspapers, and small-sized dailies.

This is hardly surprising if civic journalism involves a commitment to local issues and community discourse-which are more likely staples in the news diet of small-market media. From the explication of the term civic journalism and from the suggestions of previous research, a set of hypotheses was developed:

H1: Majorities of the newspaper journalists will approve of each of the four indicators of civic journalism.

One goal of this project was to gauge journalists' approval of civic journalism without explicitly introducing the terms civic journalism or public journalism, thus keeping at bay the generally negative reaction that those terms seems to elicit, and thus keeping the focus of the survey on the concepts and practices of civic journalism rather than on labels. The expectation of approval stems from the findings of the Webster and Pew studies (in which editors, at least, approved of many aspects of civic journalism).

H2a: The smaller the journalist's newspaper, the more accepting he or she will be of these civic-journalism approaches.

This would verify the finding of Weaver and Wilhoit that the "populist mobilizers," few though they were, were more often in small-market media.

H2b: Newsroom managers will be more accepting of civic journalism approaches than will rank-and-file journalists such as reporters, copy editors, and photographers.

This would reflect the general sense of the Pew investigators who detailed the complaints of some of the reporters involved in civic journalism projects. It would also reflect Merritt's contention that support of civic journalism results from an understanding of its philosophical underpinnings. Because top editors are the most likely staff members to introduce and assign a civic journalism project, they are the journalists also most likely to have read and thought about civic journalism's purpose.

H2c: The younger the newspaper journalist the less accepting he or she will be of civic journalism approaches.

This last control variable would reflect the Pew authors' impression that younger journalists were less sympathetic to their projects' goals and practices.

H3: The association between identification with the "interpreter role of the media and approval of civic journalism will be stronger than the association between civic journalism and the "disseminator" and "watchdog" roles.

The disseminator and watchdog roles represent two traditional attitudes that Merritt and Rosen find somewhat incompatible with civic journalism.

The disseminator role implies a telling of the news without context or understanding, but rather a detached forwarding of information. The watchdog role implies a state of "adversariness" that delights in conflict and news that splits groups apart in a community. Rosen maintains that civic journalists constantly challenge elected leaders to heed the public discourse, but that bringing down public officials is not a goal of civic journalism.

H4: The stronger the feeling of the importance of neighborhood and community news, the stronger the approval of civic journalism.

Civic journalism focuses on the concept of community, and because community in journalism is often defined as a geographic community, it seems likely that civic journalism-friendly news people will also be highly interested in issues of local communities. Respondents were asked to rate the importance of "a number of things that newspapers the size of the one you work for do, or try to do, today," which included the item, "Cover community and neighborhood news." Respondents could choose a response from a fourpart scale ranging from "Extremely Important" to "Not Very Important."

H5a: Journalists who approve of a top editor's involvement in local civic organizations will be more likely to accept civic journalism than will journalists who disapprove of such activity.

H5b: Journalists who approve of rank-and-file staff members' joining civic organizations will be more likely to approve of civic journalism than will journalists who disapprove of such activity.

This set of hypotheses attempts to bring to a personal level the civic journalism tenet of involvement in one's community. One measure of a journalist's rejection of the traditional detachment from the people and issues that one covers would be the attitude toward personal involvement of the journalist in the community-not involvement in a particular faction or political cause, but in a nonpolitical civic organization.

If a journalist feels favorable toward making at least that modest personal connection to the community, he or she will endorse the connection for both the top editors and for rank-and-file staff members.

In the same vein, we might also expect journalists who themselves felt involved in their local communities-actually, not hypothetically-to share that attitude.

H5c: Journalists who describe themselves as involved in their local communities will be more likely to approve of civic journalism than will journalists who describe themselves as uninvolved.

The final set of hypotheses examines attitudes about the current state of journalism at one's newspaper. Proponents and observers alike seem to agree that civic journalism has grown out of a dissatisfaction with the role journalism has played lately, especially with journalism's inability to connect to citizens, and its inability to connect citizens to one another.

H6a: Journalists who feel their own papers do not connect well with readers will be more likely to approve of civic journalism than will those who feel well connected with readers.

H6b: Journalists who feel their own papers are getting worse in quality will be more likely to approve of civic journalism than will those who feel their paper is improving.

THE SURVEY METHOD

The survey was conducted in the fall of 1996 under the auspices of the Human Resources Committee of the American Society of Newspaper Editors.

A stratified probability sample of newspaper employees was constructed. From a list of the 1,487 newspapers in the United States, 61 were randomly selected, after measures had been taken to ensure proportionate representation from eight circulation categories. Three of the newspapers in the original group of 61 declined to participate; in these cases the research team randomly chose substitute newspapers from the same circulation groups.

The directing editor of each selected paper was asked to select randomly a sample of journalists from his or her staff. Only full-time employees who fit the categories of reporter, copy editor, photographer, artist, supervisor, or editorial writer were to be included. The number of participating employees depended on the size of the paper, again in order to maintain the validity of the stratified probability sampling procedure.

Each employee participating received a survey packet, which included the questionnaire with instructions and a computer-scannable answer sheet. Participants were assured, both in the written instructions and by the on-site survey coordinator, that responses would be entirely confidential. If an employee declined to participate, a substitute was to be chosen by use of the same "nth name" random process. Editors were asked to give the employees three days in which to complete and return the questionnaire, which in a pre-test in August 1996 had taken respondents about 30 minutes to complete.

Of the 61 newspapers that eventually agreed to participate, only 3 failed to return their questionnaires by the 15 October 1996 deadline. All 3 of these were below 25,000 in circulation. Thus of the 1,191 questionnaires sent, 1,037 were returned, for a response rate of 87.1%.

The four indicators resulting from the explication of civic journalism appeared as closed-ended items in the survey; respondents could choose the degree to which they approved or disapproved of each.

The two "modest" approaches to civic journalism appear first, and more than 90% of the respondents expressed some level of approval. The two "bolder" approaches, involving the polling of readers and the town meeting, appear next, each garnering more than 70% approval. The mean approval for all four measures is 81%, with only 19% on average expressing some degree of disapproval.

It cannot be known what the approval ratings would have been if this section of the instrument had been labeled "civic journalism," but clearly without the labeling these journalists seem to be comfortable with the approaches described in the four items.

It should also be noted that none of the four items cited any of the more controversial or radical examples of civic journalism, such as training editorial employees in mediation and conflict resolution, or having staff members register citizens to vote. This, of course, was in keeping with the explication of the concept, which was based in large measure on the work of the movement's two theoretical founders, Merritt and Rosen. The "strongly approve" rating for the modest approaches was, predictably, different from the "strongly approve" results for the two bolder measures: a mean of 60% compared to a mean of 28%. The results for "somewhat approve" were 10 percentage points higher for the bolder approaches, however.

The journalists seem to be implying support for town meetings and polling the public for agenda issues, but not as enthusiastically as doing enterprise stories and providing information on alternative solutions.

Survey respondents were asked to attach comments whenever they felt moved to supplement their closed-ended responses, and a few of these were directed to the items on civic journalism.

A staff member at a large East Coast paper wrote, again without using terms like "civic journalism," an eloquent explanation of the movement's rejection of detached objectivity: "Many papers, while remaining objective, led in some way the struggle for civil rights. Now, we do not lead as much as we try simply to report... Unless newspapers make people in their communities feel a part of them, as if they have a stake in them, they will disappear. Papers cannot be observers and reporters of a community. People no longer want to be merely observed. People want to be cared about."

A few others, however, voiced caution about the direction civic journalism may be taking. A journalist at a small paper in New England stated that there is only one place to be a catalyst for community discourse: "A newspaper and the stories it reports should reflect its surrounding communities and should always seek out the input of its readers. It is not a paper's role to 'lead' its readers, but to listen to its readers. There is plenty of room for our own agenda and suggestions of alternative solutions via the editorial and op-ed pages."

To test the remaining hypotheses, an index was created with the four civic journalism measures (Cronbach's alpha =.61) that enabled correlation and regression analysis using "civic journalism approval" as a dependent variable 46.

H2a is supported: the smaller the newspaper, the greater the support for the index of the four civic-journalism approaches. This association was especially pronounced for the two "bolder" forms of civic journalism. The influence of newspaper size remains significant throughout a multiple regression involving the variables with the strongest bivariate associations with the dependent variable.

Newsroom managers did indeed seem more receptive to civic journalism approaches than rank-and-file employees did (H2b), but the strength of this factor pales in the course of the regression. Age appears not to be a predictor of support for civic journalism. While it is likely that older, higher-ranking journalists may be the initiators of a civic journalism project at a paper, a three-way crosstab analysis also revealed that older reporters and copy editors are among the most skeptical about civic journalism. A few other personal variables were examined for possible correlations with support for civic journalism. Education seemed to make no difference, and while women seemed to approve of civic journalism more often than men do, the difference was never statistically significant.

The third hypothesis sought to learn whether conceptions of journalism's roles have any influence on attitudes toward civic journalism. But the connections seem flimsy.

The "interpreters" were neither less nor more supportive of civic journalism than others; the "watchdogs" and "disseminators" held no significant association with civic journalism either. H3 thus gets no support. It is worth noting, however, that "watchdogs" and "interpreters" both significantly influence approval of the "modest" approaches to civic journalism, but not the "bolder" approaches. Even that influence, however, lost its significance in a regression.

H4 predicted that journalists who accord respect to neighborhood and community news would applaud civic journalism approaches, and the data support the hypothesis. The influence is particularly strong when the two bolder approaches are considered.

Neighborhood and community news is one of the few independent variables to hold its influence throughout the regression. In a regression on only the bolder approaches, this variable had a higher beta coefficient than any other variable in the equation.

It was also predicted that journalists who were comfortable with their bosses' and colleagues' involvement with civic organizations would approve of civic journalism techniques, as would journalists who themselves felt "more involved than others" in the community. H5a and HSb, posing the hypothetical questions about staff involvement, both enjoyed strong positive correlations with civic-journalism support. The data suggest that those who approve of these civic-journalism approaches are also likely to approve of journalists at any level becoming personally involved in community organizations.

That approval does not extend to the respondents' personal lives, apparently. H5c enjoyed no support. Whether the respondents were involved in community activities themselves seemed not to make a difference in the attitude on civic journalism. This may suggest that journalists are more open to the personal dynamics of civic journalism in theory, but that there is no connection, at least not yet, between their own actual community involvement and their support for civic journalism. Perhaps they see journalists' personal lives as simply detached from whatever professional values they espouse.

The sixth set of hypotheses examined measures of dissatisfaction with the current state of journalism, but the data did not support either H6a or H6b. Whether the journalist felt his or her paper was connecting with readers was irrelevant to his or her feelings about civic journalism. The evaluation of the journalist's own paper, in fact, was significant in the direction opposite that of the hypothesis. It was expected that those who feel their own papers are deteriorating in quality would look to civic journalism as a means of rescue.

However, the data indicate that the higher the journalist's rating of his or her own paper, the more positive the reaction to civic journalism. And this influence held its significance throughout the regression. Apparently those who see their newspapers' quality eroding have no faith that civic journalism is the answer, and those who embrace civic journalism are journalists who think their paper is improving. Perhaps civic journalism will require a sense of collective confidence in the enterprise before it can win newsroom adherents.

Thus only a few independent variables remained, after a four-step regression, as significant influences on a journalist's approval of these four approaches to civic journalism: The smaller the newspaper, the greater the attention to neighborhood and community news, the greater the approval of journalists' joining community organizations, and the greater the sense that one's own paper is improving, then the more likely the approval of civic journalism.

It must be noted, however, that the regression equation accounted for only 14% of the variance of the dependent variable. Clearly other factors, not explored in this survey, also influence support for civic journalism.

One final piece of analysis was conducted: a factor analysis to follow up on Weaver and Wilhoit's earlier discovery of the "populist mobilizer." The data in the present study were gathered more than four years after the Weaver-Wilhoit survey.

Weaver and Wilhoit had included only one item that could be clearly identified as an indicator of civic journalism ("letting ordinary people express their views"). In a factor analysis of the present data, with a full mix of professional-role items including disseminator, interpreter and watchdog, the four civic-journalism items loaded onto their own separate factor (eigenvalue 1.88).

As the discussion above indicated, approval of civic journalism is correlated with some of the other, older role conceptions, but not robustly so. It could very well be that a new understanding of journalism's role in society has indeed begun to emerge, as Weaver and Wilhoit speculated in 1996, in which a newspaper's commitment to the public life, for at least some journalists in some situations, takes precedence over obligations of disseminating information quickly, analyzing events, or serving as adversary to powerful institutions.

Whether or not newspaper journalists scoff at the term "civic journalism," this much is clear: Many of them seem to approve of four specific manifestations of the movement's guiding principles. It would be inappropriate, however, to draw overarching conclusions about the future of civic journalism on the basis of this study alone. The survey's four approaches to civic journalism were referents of pillars of the movement's philosophical foundation, and while they represented a fundamentally different approach to journalism, not even the two "bolder" approaches seem revolutionary in form.

In fact, it might be argued that the two "modest" items are quite similar to longstanding normative understandings of strong local news coverage. Further research on journalists' conceptions of civic journalism is warranted, and it might begin with a broader selection of approaches and strategies, to see where journalists might finally "draw the line" and begin objecting to certain approaches. Because civic journalism projects increasingly involve broadcast and online media, further studies should include more than newspaper journalists.

Rosen has stated that the definition of civic journalism is phenomenological: Ultimately, it will be whatever journalists say it is.

For this reason it is important to measure not only what journalists think of a Merritt-Rosen— derived definition of civic journalism, as this study has done, but also to measure how journalists themselves would define the term.

If their definition emerges as similar to the explication of this study, then the future of civic journalism is more promising than even this study suggests. If, however, journalists define it in ways that cause Merritt, Rosen, Charity and others to howl with exasperation, it's more likely that the journalists will also disapprove. Then proponents of civic journalism will truly have their evangelistic work cut out for them.

The most influential independent variables have created a profile of sorts of the pro-civic-journalism practitioner. It suggests that civic journalism may enjoy greater success in smaller communities and in media outlets that are seen by their employees as improving.

But here, too, further inquiry is needed. In carefully steering away from respondents' preconceived notions of civic journalism, the survey instrument did not measure whether the respondent had read or discussed any materials regarding civic journalism, or had participated personally in a civic journalism project. These factors could be expected to influence a journalist's opinion of the movement and its practices.

Even with this early indication that a large proportion of the newspaper work force seems poised to approve of (at least this conception of) civic journalism, it is still unclear whether this will create any deep changes in journalism, or in the quality of civic life.

Riede's study of Merritt's own paper suggested that journalistic routines are extremely difficult to alter even in one of the pantheons of the movement.

Some scholars question whether civic journalism can survive within a liberal-economic media model like the United States'. Glasser and Craft, for example, suggest that civic journalism, if implemented consistently and seriously, might either risk losing its ratings appeal among advertisers or would challenge power structures in a way that would anger advertisers.

Rosen and Merritt, predictably, have pondered this concern and responded, but with different views. Rosen asserts that civic journalism, properly executed, can draw in a large audience of citizen— participants and thus more advertising revenue.

Merritt acknowledges that civic-journalism content may not compete for audience with the crossword puzzle or "Seinfeld" but that it doesn't have to. As long as it enjoys a permanent place in the mix of programming or editorial features that maximize an audience, it can continue to uplift the public life.

Judgment on the viability and desirability of civic journalism is beyond the scope of this study. Such considerations assume, of course, that civic journalism will indeed catch on among the majority of journalists.

This study suggests that at least one aspect of Weaver and Wilhoit's earlier notion of a "populist mobilizer" attitude toward journalism has taken hold among newspaper journalists.

There may still be only a few journalists actually waving "civic journalism" banners, but in terms of four specific activities that stem directly from the movement's philosophical roots, the movement is quietly finding acceptability. Civic journalism's ultimate reformative power— especially its ability to challenge powerful institutions on behalf of the public and "the public life"-will only be as strong as its support among its practitioners. That support seems to have made important initial strides.

PUBLIC JOURNALISM

By their [reporters'] actions, they should try to create the conditions in which the public can learn its business and find solutions to its problems. Public politics, public discussion, public involvement by public-minded citizens - these are the announced goals.

Values of public journalism Public journalism is an inchoate technique that has been steadily evolving over the last several years. Jay Rosen writes, "Public journalism is not a settled doctrine or a strict code of conduct but an unfolding philosophy about the place of the journalist in public life." Put less eloquently, public journalism "is ambiguous and messy work."

Charlotte Grimes comments that public journalism "aims to fix American public life and to fix American journalism, both of which it deems to be sadly, badly broken." Grimes is referring to the fact that the advent of public journalism was initiated by research highlighting that key American institutions are simultaneously eroding: newspapers' loss of readers, the decline in voting, the national loss of a sense of place, declining civic membership, the rising disgust with politics and the decay of public discourse were all speculated to be related in some way.

Several journalists and scholars assert that part of the problem stems from an objective press which has alienated itself from citizens by its code of detachment. The argument runs like this: People feel attachment to each other when they share certain core values; objective reporting champions itself as detached, thus implicitly claiming that it shares core values with no one; thus, citizens feel alienated from the news media, and this aids in the erosion of civic and political involvement.

For decades, journalists have worked under the assumption that credibility stemmed from an unwillingness to care about outcomes, and the result is a cynical, disempowered polity. Public journalists assert that credibility does not spring from detachment but from shared values and interests with their communities.

Necessarily, journalists must move beyond the simple telling of news and take a proactive stance on addressing problems and generating deliberative solutions to them. Arthur Charity writes, "Public journalism is nothing more than the conviction that journalism's business is about making citizenship work." Similarly, Monica Bowman asserts that public journalism "seeks to engage citizens in public discourse, foster civic responsibility, and encourage citizens to take ownership of community problems." Thus, the fundamental characteristic of public journalism is its emphasis on aiding the public in addressing and solving mutual problems.

Many public journalists have been inspired by Daniel Yankelovich's writings on generating public judgment. Public judgment is the outcome of informed citizens deliberating about social-political problems with the goal of creating viable, consensually-supported solutions. It stands in stark contrast to the term mass opinion and all of its cynical, negative connotations.

Yankelovich argues that there are three stages to reaching public judgment: Consciousness raising, working through and resolution. Public journalists realise that the news media are very good at accomplishing consciousness raising, as demonstrated by the numerous works on agenda-setting. However, to accomplish the second and third stages, public journalism "provides the information people need to engage in informed discussion of the items on that agenda" and it "moves beyond agenda setting by providing information relevant to the clarification of core values and organizing a discussion with that goal in mind."

The stage of working through assumes that journalism can assist people in making educated decisions on tough issues. Finally, once these decisions have been made, public journalists believe that it is the responsibility of journalism to champion these ideas to the public.

Bowman eloquently summarizes the stance of public journalism: "The goal of civic journalism is to provide citizens with the news and information they need to function fully as participants in our democratic society." According to public journalists, the accomplishment of these goals means going further than objectively supplying information to the public.

MEANS OF PUBLIC JOURNALISM

Currently, the practice of public journalism is just as nebulous and diverse as its philosophy. Nonetheless, there are several core practices which differentiate public journalism from objective reporting.

As Jay Rosen and Davis Merritt make clear, public journalism requires a fundamental change concerning the way that audiences are viewed. Rather than thinking of them as simply consumers or readers, public journalists attempt to think about the audience as a collection of citizens. Consequently, public journalists attempt to discover the core values shared by the community; these values will become the cornerstone of news coverage. As Richard Harwood points out, "the most fruitful insights from tapping into civic life emerge when journalists actively engage people in uncovering the essence of what they are thinking." This, of course, requires journalists to move beyond reporting and observing; they must adopt a pro-active and involved role in the community.

Most importantly, public journalism insists on a focus on solutions as opposed to problems. For instance, public journalists eschew the horse-race coverage discussed by Thomas Patterson, and they refuse to talk about politics in terms of tactics and machinations. Instead, they focus on the needs and concerns of the citizens, attempting to encourage discussions centered around the core values of the citizenry.

Merritt aptly points out that this requires "developing a new journalistic talent: the ability to understand and write clearly about the competing beliefs and priorities that underlie each public problem. Rosen and Merritt highlight four of the most intrinsic practices of public journalism: Sorting out the core values of citizens; encouraging constructive, deliberative citizen debates; providing in-depth reporting of particularly tough issues; and, reporting news stories which demonstrate the successes and potential of an active public.

Clearly, the above list is necessarily broad and vague; there are numerous ways to go about public journalism. In some communities, public journalism has taken the form of press-sponsored neighborhood round-table debates, while in other communities it has involved town hall meetings or mock legislatures.

But no matter how it manifests itself, the basic practice of public journalism always requires instigating citizens to confront and solve problems. Rosen states, "Public journalists thus try to challenge, cajole, and otherwise disturb the complacency of any community that has work to do, choices to make, opportunities to seize control of its future in a democratic manner."

It is important to emphasize that public journalists do not equate their breaking away from detachment with the breaking away from neutrality. Indeed, Rosen readily states that the pledge of neutrality is vital to public journalism because "it separates 'doing journalism' from 'doing politics'." Similarly, Ed Fouhy states that the essential values of traditional, objective journalism - accuracy, seriousness, context, and independence - are retained by public journalists.

Thus, the objective is to initially foment deliberation, after which the public journalist will allow the citizens to reach their own conclusions. However, due to the need for efficiency in journalism, it is difficult for journalists to emphasize simultaneously both thorough fact-verification and provocation of the public. Rather, journalists must decide which goal they wish to emphasize most, and this choice will fundamentally determine which style of journalism they embrace.

COMPARING AND CONTRASTING

It should be obvious that there is an intrinsic difference between objective and public journalism. The former places a premium on providing the most accurate and factual information possible.

It involves reporters quickly gathering and confirming facts and presenting them to the public in a detached manner. The latter places a premium on playing a pro-active role in communities.

It asks reporters to discover which issues concern the public and to then provide a forum in which these issues can be discussed, debated and resolved. These competing primary goals have led to the creation of the two distinct techniques marked by their own unique set of practices. Yet, recent debate reveals a fundamental lack of appreciation for what each technique offers to journalism.

ELITISM VERSUS EGALITARIANISM

One nuance of the debate between objective and public journalism entails the dichotomy of elitism and egalitarianism. While objective journalists have often been called elitists, public journalists herald themselves as egalitarians seeking to give the people a voice.

Placing labels on either of these forms of journalism is limiting and debilitates the debate over their relative merits. The study of technique allows the realization that both objective and public journalism contain elements of elitism and egalitarianism.

Public journalism strives "to re-engage readers, listeners and viewers with the public life of their communities" in order to encourage them into confronting issues. Further, public journalists are willing to actively promote public decision-making "even if journalists must create the public space where those decisions are discussed."

The fact that public journalists are attempting to force the creation of civic capital while simultaneously setting the conditions within which this capital can be exercised suggests elitist tendencies. William Woo, commenting on public journalism, states, "I think about the possibility of developing an elitism in which the non-voter, the non-participator, becomes not merely a second-class citizen but also a second-class reader."

Just as in the myth of Plato's cave where only those who apprehend the form of the good are fit to rule, public journalists are defining what a public good consists of and they are constructing the stage upon which the good is to be revealed. While this sort of issue prompting may be necessary, perhaps even beneficial, it still suggests elitism.

Clearly, the elitism/egalitarianism dichotomy is far too simplistic and misplaced to aid in the debate over objective and public journalism. The issue is not which approach is more egalitarian or elitist; the issue involves examining how each technique perceives its role in society.

THE ROLE OF CONSTRAINTS

The study of technique affords the opportunity to take note of an important difference between these forms of journalism; their varying notions of constraints. The practices developed in objective journalism were created out a perceived need for constraints to be placed on the press. Lippmann, criticizing the state of the press prior to the advent of objective journalism, states,

It [tabloid journalism] selects from events of the day those aspects which most immediately engage attention, and in place of the effort to see life steadily and whole it sees life dramatically, episodically, and from what is called, in the jargon of the craft, the angle of human interest.

For Lippmann, the only way for journalists to see life steadily and whole was to incorporate a set of constraints, mostly based on social scientific study. Thus, journalists do not utilize the technique of objectivity simply because it allows them to accurately gather facts; rather, they use objectivity because without it, they argue, no pure facts would exist. Conversely, proponents of public journalism are looking to break free of the constraints created by objective reporting.

Fouhy observes that "they [public journalists] are finding that some of the 'ancient' and 'sacred' practices of journalism are simply habits best done away with." It is very difficult for a reporter to disturb the complacency of a public or cajole the polity into making a decision while remaining detached, nor can a reporter urge action while remaining impartial. Charity points out that the ideals of detachment and impartiality have no sacred meaning or utility for journalists who wish to aggressively engage the public.

The study of these two journalistic practices as techniques has shed light on the fact that each form of journalism has a very different set of notions about the necessity of constraints. Objective journalism was conceived out of the desire to reel in a sensationalistic press whose sole focus was to create outrageous and attention-grabbing stories. It advocates the use of constraints to set the press apart from the public and social institutions in order to ensure fairness and detachment. In contrast, public journalism was born out of a perceived need to reinvigorate the polity. It advocates the breaking of prior constraints in order to directly engage and mobilize the public.

The first technique institutes constraints on reporters and news organizations in order to best serve society, and the other is looking to emancipate itself from those bonds in order to do the same. Any debate over the merits of these techniques must confront their divergent understandings of the role of constraints on the press.

CONTENT AND PUBLIC JOURNALISM

Studies have found that public journalism content has distinct characteristics. For example, McGregor, Comrie, and Fontaine studied coverage of a New Zealand election campaign, comparing papers that endorsed public journalism and papers that did not, and found the public journalism papers covered the race more constructively.

By comparing the Seattle Times Front Porch Forum Project coverage with the coverage by the Times in earlier years as well as content in the Seattle Post-Intelligencer, Blazier and Lemert found that among eleven public journalism traits, providing mobilizing information was the most distinguishing factor between the public journalism project and earlier coverage by the paper and coverage by the competition. Moscowitz also found mobilizing information in a study comparing coverage of homelessness in the Knight-Ridder-owned, civic journalism-oriented Charlotte Observer with the Gannett-owned, traditional journalism-oriented Indianapolis Star.

The Charlotte Observer was also less likely to use official sources and more likely to include solutions to problems in its coverage. seeking out citizen sources rather than relying solely on official sources has been identified as a characteristic of public journalism. By comparing two papers, one civic, the other not, Kennamer and South found the civic-affiliated paper had a much greater number of unaffiliated sources than the other. Kurpius also studied sources and found that local television news stories, employing public journalism techniques, used a larger percentage of African American sources than represented in the general population. Furthermore African American, Latino, and female journalists were more likely to use minority and female sources in their stories.

Rather than focus on the text of a story, Coleman compared the visual elements in public journalism and traditional journalism content. Although for the most part, visual elements did not distinguish public journalism and traditional journalism, Coleman did find that public journalism stories were significantly more likely than traditional journalism stories to include visual elements that facilitated contact of the media by the public. Because interactivity lends itself to citizen involvement and public journalism principles, Choi compared public journalism and traditional journalism newspapers in an online environment, expecting that online public journalism newspapers would exhibit more public journalism characteristics. Content analyses of online stories from the Rochester Democrat, Charlotte Observer, Orlando Sentinel, online versions of public journalism-oriented newspapers, and the Buffalo News, Winston-Salem Journal, Florida Times Union, online versions of traditional journalism-oriented newspapers, found little difference in the content of online newspapers that represented public journalism and traditional journalism newspapers.

Journalists and Public Journalism. Because a decision to practice public journalism usually rests with a senior editor or producer, Kurpius examined the relationship between management and content. In two separate examinations of local television news, Kurpius found that visionary managers were the key for the civic-model of successful issues coverage at local television stations, but he also discovered that market forces may hinder civic reporting efforts in local media in the long run. Factors that may influence journalists' attitudes toward public journalism were studied by scholars in New Mexico. After journalists at the Albuquerque Journal and Albuquerque Tribune and journalism students at the University of New Mexico completed self-administered questionnaires as part of a convenience sample, the results showed "a progression of socialization that begins with students supporting civic journalism."

Journalism students without newsroom experience appeared to be more supportive of civic journalism than practicing journalists and journalism students with newsroom experience. The authors suggested that civic journalism appeared to be inconsistent with autonomy, an attribute greatly valued by practicing journalists and journalism students with newsroom experience.

Indiana University scholars asked journalists directly about civic journalism in their most recent national survey. Although their previous national surveys of journalists, which were conducted in 1982 and 1992, had documented the backgrounds, attitudes, and values of journalists, the latest national study represented the first time that specific questions about public or civic journalism practices were asked. According to "The American Journalist in the 21st Century," 72% of journalists approved of giving ordinary people a chance to express their views on public affairs and 58% endorsed providing possible solutions to society's problems. Only 32% approved of convening meetings to discuss public issues.

Effects of Public Journalism on the Audience. The sixteen audience-centered studies identified in the Massey and Haas review examined the effects of civic journalism on the public rather than the public's expectations of journalism." For example, one study reviewed by Massey and Haas found evidence that public journalism produced positive results. In a study of broadcast and print media that included Wisconsin Public Television and Radio, WISC-TV, the Wisconsin State Journal, and the Wood Communications Group and their collaborative effort to provide a more civic-oriented approach toward election coverage, Denton and Thorson found respondents in Madison said the project made them more knowledgeable about the election, encouraged them to vote, and gave them useful tools to assess campaign information.

Although the literature found civic journalism practices improved public attitudes and increased knowledge of election issues, overall, the Massey and Haas review of public journalism studies found mixed audience effects. Public journalism was found to both increase and suppress voter turnout, to both increase participation in civic projects and have no impact on civic participation, and to produce both strong and weak agenda-setting effects. After reviewing forty-seven empirical studies, Massey and Haas criticized the public journalism literature for its lack of methodological rigor and for narrowly focusing on "jewel box" civic journalism projects that were conducted at the Wichita Eagle, Charlotte Observer, and Wisconsin State Journal.

Only one of the authors' six recommendations for future research involved the public and that was to conduct laboratory experiments that "could prove more useful for more convincingly identifying whatever causal factors may be behind any public-journalism influence on news audiences."

Surprisingly, none of the recommendations that resulted from this comprehensive review of public journalism studies focused on the public as an independent, active, and integral component of the communication process with opinions and expectations about a new type of journalism that ventures to re-engage the audience in the civic arena.

Although civic journalism has been discussed, practiced, debated, and studied for over a decade and a half, the public's perspective on civic journalism has not been studied empirically. Understanding the public's view of local news and civic journalism is important for the practice and business of journalism as well as society as a whole. Without an assessment of what the public expects of local news, it will be virtually impossible to identify journalism practices that may help reverse declining attention to news, restore dwindling public trust in news as a whole and journalists in particular, and bring back the vanishing participant in civic affairs. Unlike much of the research on public journalism, which has focused on the effects of specific public journalism projects on voting rates and other measures of civic participation, this study explores the public's views about journalism as well as the public's expectations of local news and the underlying dimensions of those expectations.

Specifically, the following research questions will be answered:

RQ1: What do survey respondents regard as the important attributes and roles of journalism and how does that compare with the norms of traditional and public journalism?

RQ2: How do survey respondents compare with journalists on the importance of practices and norms associated with traditional and civic journalism?

RQ3: What segments of survey respondents as defined by race or ethnicity, age, income, education, and gender are more likely to endorse civic journalism and traditional journalism norms?

RQ4: What are the underlying dimensions of survey respondents' expectations of local news?

As part of a research project for a local newspaper and local NPRaffiliated public radio station that was starting up a local news division to complement the national news broadcast from NPR, the authors worked with the radio station managers to design a research study that would ascertain public opinion about local news. A Pew Centre for Civic Journalism grant provided funding for the audience study. The radio station manager believed that understanding the public's expectations of local news was a prerequisite to building a radio news division that would report local news of importance and meet the public's needs.

The spring 2001 survey, conducted in a southwestern metropolitan area by a professional telephone survey unit, used random digit dialing to select the sample. Interviews were completed with 600 adults, representing a response rate of 62.2%. Calculation of the response rate was based upon the number of completed interviews (n=600) relative to the number of completed interviews plus refusals (n=286), incomplete interviews (n=37), and persons contacted but not interviewed due to illness, language barriers, or other impairments (n=36).

Answers to the four research questions were based on survey respondents' ratings of roles of local news media and characteristics of news coverage. Respondents were asked: What do you think is the most important role of local news media? Rate each on whether you think it's "extremely important," "somewhat important," or "not very important." The roles were (1) report the widest range of news; (2) concentrate on certain topics; (3) provide a forum for community views; (4) be a watchdog of powerful people and the government; (5) highlight interesting people and groups in the community; and (6) offer solutions to community problems. Respondents were also asked the following: What is the most important characteristic of news coverage you want? Rate each on whether you think it's "extremely important," "somewhat important," or "not very important." The characteristics were (1) accuracy; (2) rapid reporting; (3) understand the local community; (4) unbiased reporting; (5) care about your community; (6) be inclusive of different points of view; and (7) provide explanation of issues and trends.

To determine how survey respondents compare with journalists, the survey respondents' opinions about practices and norms associated with traditional and civic journalism were matched with journalists' opinions from "The

American Journalist in the 21st Century" national survey. Specifically, the opinions of survey respondents and journalists were compared in four areas: offering solutions, providing a community forum, being a watchdog, and rapid reporting. Although both studies used random sampling and "extremely" on the measurement scale, there were several methodological differences.

The question wording in the national survey of journalists differed on the four opinions that were compared. For offering solutions, the national survey asked journalists how important it was "to point people toward possible solutions to society's problems." For providing a community forum, the national survey asked journalists how important it was "to convene meetings of citizens and community leaders to discuss public issues." For being a watchdog, the national survey asked how important it was to "investigate claims and statements made by the government." For rapid reporting, the national survey asked journalists how important it was to " get information to the public quickly."

In addition to the difference in wording, the present study relied on a three-point scale to measure opinions about journalistic norms while the national survey of journalists relied on a four-point scale of "extremely," "quite," "somewhat," and "not really important." The difference in question wording and the number of points on the measurement may have affected the number of respondents that chose "extremely" as an option. The final methodological difference was that the present study was conducted in spring 2001 in one southwestern metropolitan area while the national survey of 1,149 journalists was conducted summer and fall of 2002. The survey questionnaire also included questions about socio-economic backgrounds and media use. Standard survey questions were asked to ascertain number of years lived in the area, marital status, level of education, income, age, and race or ethnicity. Respondents were also asked if they had children living at home and their gender was recorded.

To establish media use, respondents were asked if they read the primary daily newspaper 4-6 times a week, 1-3 times a week, less frequently, or never. Similarly, respondents were asked if they read the primary Sunday newspaper 3-4 times a month, 1-2 times a month, less frequently, or never. Respondents were also asked how often they heard news on the radio, which TV stations they watched for local news, and how often they obtained local news from the Internet. Bivariate analyses with appropriate statistics were used to determine if opinions about public and traditional journalism practices and norms differed by race or ethnicity, age, income, education, or gender. A factor analysis was used to identify underlying dimensions of survey respondents' attitudes about the roles and characteristics of public and traditional journalism.

SOCIO-ECONOMIC BACKGROUND AND MEDIA USE

Survey participants had established roots in this southwestern metropolitan area. The median number of years lived in the area was twelve; 55% were married and 42% had children at home. Although education was high, different educational levels were represented: 21% had a high school degree or less, 27% had some college, 28% were college graduates, and 24% completed at least some graduate school. Different income groups were also represented: 34% had a household income of less than $40,000; 31% had incomes between $40,000 and $69,000, and 35% had incomes of $70,000 or higher. Slightly more than one-third of the respondents were ages 18 to 39; 31% were ages 40 to 69; 35% were 70 years or older. Respondents were fairly diverse: 68% were white, 19%; were Latino, 7% were African American, and 5% were Asian American or other. The remaining 1% did not specify race or ethnicity.

When asked how many times a week they read the primary local newspaper, 30% said never or less frequently than 1-3 times a week, 25% said 1-3 times a week, and 44% said 4-6 times a week. Survey participants were more devoted to the Sunday newspaper with 64% reporting they read it 3-4 times a month. In addition to the newspaper, survey participants relied on other local news sources: 80% watched one of the five local TV news outlets, 59% often heard news on the radio, and 18% often turned to the Internet.

THE PUBLIC'S VIEWS ON JOURNALISTIC NORMS

The ratings of thirteen characteristics and roles of news coverage were examined to answer RQl (What do survey respondents regard as the important attributes and roles of journalism and how that compare with the norms of traditional and public journalism does?). The overwhelming majorities said that accuracy (94%) and unbiased reporting (84%) are extremely important, but two major tenets of traditional journalism did not receive strong endorsements. The traditional journalistic norm of being a watchdog of powerful people and the government was supported by only 49% of survey respondents and rapid reporting was endorsed by only 35%.

THE PUBLIC'S VIEWS ON THE ROLE OF LOCAL NEWS

Slightly more than half (51%) said offering solutions to community problems was extremely important, and 49% said providing a forum for community views was extremely important. To answer RQ2, these views were compared with journalists' views about civic journalism practices.

COMPARING THE PUBLIC AND JOURNALISTS

Although the survey of the public was conducted in a southwestern metropolitan area and the survey of journalists was conducted nationally, results from the two surveys were compared because both studies used random sampling techniques, included similar questions about characteristics of traditional and public journalism, and incorporated "extremely important" on the measurement scale. A difference in proportions test on independent random samples was used to determine if survey respondents were significantly different from journalists in their endorsement of two civic journalism norms and two traditional journalistic norms.

Even though the majority of survey respondents strongly endorsed the fundamental characteristics of journalism, accuracy and unbiased reporting, there was a statistically significant gap between survey respondents and journalists on two roles that are an integral part of traditional journalism: watchdog and rapid reporting. Only 49% of survey respondents said being a watchdog of powerful people and the government is extremely important, but 70% of journalists said that traditional journalism role is extremely important. Survey respondents were also significantly less likely than journalists to say that rapid reporting was extremely important (35% vs. 59%).

The roles and characteristics of traditional and civic journalism were analysed by five socio-economic characteristics (race or ethnicity, age, income, education, and gender) to better understand survey respondents' opinions about traditional and civic journalism roles and characteristics. Although there was no statistically significant difference between survey respondents and journalists in their endorsement of the civic journalism role of providing solutions to problems, there were significant differences when this civic journalism role was analysed by sub-segments of survey respondents.

SOLUTIONS

African Americans and Hispanics were significantly more likely than whites and Asian Americans to say that the civic journalism role of offering solutions to community problems was extremely important. Almost three quarters (72%) of African Americans and 64% of Hispanics said offering solutions was extremely important, but only 45% of whites and 47% of Asian Americans said this civic journalism role was extremely important.

Segments of survey respondents that made less money and had less education were more likely than wealthier and more educated segments to say offering solutions to community problems was extremely important. Almost three-fifths (59%) of adults who had incomes of less than $50,000 compared to 44% of adults with incomes of $50,000 or more said offering solutions was extremely important. This inverse relationship was also apparent when offering solutions to community problems was analysed by education. Adults with a high school education or less (68%) were more likely than adults with some college (54%) and adults with a college degree or higher (42%) to say offering solutions was extremely important.

Females were also more likely than males to attach greater value to the public journalism role of offering solutions with 56% of females compared to 44% of males saying it was extremely important for local news to offer solutions to community problems.

WATCHDOG AND RAPID REPORTING

The traditional journalism characteristics of watchdog and rapid reporting were also analysed by the five socio-economic variables and three were significantly related. The oldest age group (55+) was more likely than the youngest age groups to value the watchdog role of traditional journalism, with 62% of adults 55 or older compared to 47% of adults 35 to 54 and 45% of adults 18 to 34 saying being a watchdog of powerful people and the government was extremely important.

An inverse relationship emerged when the traditional journalistic characteristic of rapid reporting was analysed by education. Among adults with a high school degree or less, 47% said rapid reporting was extremely important; 30% of adults with a college degree or higher said rapid reporting was extremely important. Females attached greater value to rapid reporting than males. Among females, 40% said rapid reporting was extremely important but only 30% of males said this traditional journalistic practice was extremely important.

THE UNDERLYING DIMENSIONS OF THE PUBLIC'S EXPECTATIONS OF LOCAL NEWS

To better understand the underlying dimensions of survey respondents' expectations of local news reporting, researchers factor analysed the six roles of local news and seven characteristics of journalism. The good neighbour dimension that emerged included attributes of public journalism: caring about your community, highlighting interesting people and groups in the community, understanding the local community, and offering solutions to community problems.

The watchdog dimension was represented by four roles of local news including being a watchdog of powerful people and the government, concentrating on certain topics, providing a forum for community views, and providing explanations of issues and trends. The unbiased and accurate reporting dimension was defined by those two traditional characteristics of news; the fast dimension was represented by the traditional news characteristic, rapid reporting. Providing a wide range of news and being inclusive of different points of view did not load high on any one dimension. In fact, the inclusive factor loading was similar for the good neighbour, watchdog, and unbiased and accurate dimensions.

Although more than fifty empirical studies have been conducted on public or civic journalism, none of the studies has tried to gauge public opinion about this new approach to journalism practice. This study provided insight into a journalistic practice that developed over the past decade and a half in response to the vanishing newspaper reader and disappearing participant in civic affairs. Furthermore, this study provided insight into the public's views on traditional journalistic characteristics. At a time when newspaper readership, participation in civic life, and the credibility of journalism are at all-time lows, this study helped answer broader questions about journalism: Is traditional journalism meeting the public's expectations? Is the civic journalism movement on the right track? The results of this survey suggest that, in many cases, the public and the press, including traditional journalism and the civic journalism movement, are on separate tracks headed in different directions and unless something is done to better meet the public's expectations, civic participation, newspaper readership, and the credibility of the press may continue to decline.

While it is reassuring to know that the survey respondents overwhelmingly endorse accuracy and unbiased reporting, it is important to recognize that these same expectations can cause the public to turn away from the news. When Jayson Blair fabricates the news at the New York Times or star foreign correspondent Jack Kelley is accused of inventing parts of stories reported by USA Today, the public's trust in the news media is shaken and the reasons for reading the news are threatened.

It is also important to note that long-held norms of traditional journalism, being a watchdog and rapid reporting, are not strongly valued by a majority of the survey respondents. Only 49% said being a watchdog of powerful people and the government was extremely important, and 35% said rapid reporting was extremely important. But when the survey respondents were analysed by age, the press as watchdog was popular in the oldest age group. Over three-fifths of adults 55 years or older said the news media's traditional role of being a watchdog was extremely important.

Offering solutions to community problems, a characteristic of civic journalism, was strongly endorsed by only half of the survey participants as a whole, but when different segments were analysed, this public journalism practice was found to be more popular than first thought. The popularity of offering solutions is most evident among those who have traditionally been disenfranchised from the power sources of government and business: African Americans, Hispanics, adults with less income and education, and women. Perhaps these groups are looking to news media as a source for help.

Do the public's expectations of local news fit the traditional journalism model, the civic journalism movement, or some other ideal? The factor analysis of thirteen roles and characteristics of journalism revealed four dimensions with being a good neighbour-not watchdog, unbiased and accurate, or fast-representing the dominant expectation. Being a good neighbour included caring about your community, highlighting interesting people and groups in the community, understanding the local community, and offering solutions to community problems.

The expectation that the press should be a good neighbour may be related to declining trust in the news media and declining attention to news. If the public expects the press to be a good neighbour but the press fails in that role because it sees its professional responsibility as a watchdog, there is clearly a disconnect between the public's expectations and the press' expectations which civic journalism practices may not be able to fix.

Buzz Merritt and Maxwell McCombs argue for an expanded watchdog role of the press that is consonant with the good neighbour perspective:

News media need to be creative watchdogs and agenda setters scanning the horizon for the gaps in current public life. Part of this larger watchdog role is functioning as social radar, not just a chronicler of what government and other institutions are doing right now, whether good or bad. This means discovering the concerns of citizens and defining what the public needs to know in very expansive terms.

But for this expanded watchdog role to resonate with the public, the news media must educate the public and even persuade the public that in the role of watchdog, they are looking out for the public in the same way that a good neighbour would.

According to Andrew Kohut, director of the Pew Research Centre for the People and the Press, a decade and a half ago, which was about the time of the first civic journalism projects, the public thought the press was "too sensational, too pushy, too rude, too uncaring about people and the public." But most people saw journalists as moral, professional and caring about the interests of the country. Today, the public considers the news media even less professional, less accurate, less moral, less helpful to democracy, more sensational, more likely to cover up mistakes and more biased.

These are not exactly attributes of a good neighbour. Because this study represents only one metropolitan area in the Southwest, additional studies should be conducted in other parts of the country. Because different communities have different characteristics and needs, it is possible that they have different expectations of their local news. It is also possible that even with different community characteristics and needs, the public's expectations of local news are similar, regardless of community size or geographic location. Only by replicating this study in other communities can the public's expectations of local news be determined.

According to a 3 May 2005 New York Times article, the 1.9% drop in daily circulation and 2.5% decline in Sunday circulation reported by the Audit Bureau of Circulations represented the "largest circulation losses for the industry in more than a decade, and indicate an acceleration of the decline."

The magnitude of the circulation decline for 814 daily newspapers suggests that it is imperative that future studies determine how the public's expectations of local news relate to readership of newspapers and use of other news media. Future studies should also determine how participation in civic life is related to the public's expectations of local news. Finally, it is important for future studies to focus on the public's expectations of news with special attention paid to the concept of the press as a good neighbour. By gaining greater insight into the public's expectations of local news, it may be possible to initiate a dialogue between the public and the press. This dialogue may lead to a closing of the gap between the expectations of the public and the press that could, in the long run, reverse declining attention to news and waning participation in civic life.

DEFINING QUALITY JOURNALISM

Another issue of key importance involves the quality of news coverage. The examination of objective and public journalism as techniques reveals that each approach has a fundamentally different definition of a quality news product. Of primary importance to objective journalists is the presentation of reliable information. Conversely, public journalists place prime importance on presenting information that voters can find useful in making decisions important to their community.

This is not to say that objective journalists do not wish to provide useful information to the public or that public journalists do not strive to present reliable information, but that these two techniques vary in where they place these concerns along a continuum of importance. Again, time constraints force journalists to decide what is most important to them - extremely reliable information which may sacrifice some usefulness, or extremely useful information which may sacrifice some reliability.

These different ideals of quality are at the heart of much of the criticisms leveled against both forms of journalism. Objective journalism has been accused of making information useless by presenting it in a detached and aloof manner. The charge is that while objective reporting may indeed strive to provide accurate and unbiased news, this does not adequately assist the public in interpreting and using this information. Without such guidance, the argument runs, the public becomes disenchanted, disillusioned and cynical. Inherent to the criticisms is a belief in the primacy of making sure the information being provided spurs civic engagement.

Critics of public journalism question whether it is wise to allow the press to lose the detachment inherent to objective journalistic practices. Frankel claims that "the emphasis on 'solutions' and 'connections' will inevitably distort the news agenda, devalue problems for which no easy remedy is apparent, and end up compromising the newspaper and its independence." Further, he asserts that journalists should work harder at better reporting while leaving reform to the reformers. Dennis offers a similar sentiment when he claims that "journalists should cover the parade, not march in it" because community organizing must remain separate from journalism. Clearly, these criticisms stem from a deep-seeded belief in a need to keep the press detached.

The discussion of quality hints at tenuous assumptions made by each journalistic approach. Objective journalists assume that the public will make good use of the information provided to it. Merritt takes issue with this assumption, stating that "if journalists view their job as merely providing information - simply telling the news in a detached way - they will not be particularly helpful to public life." There is no guarantee that the public intrinsically knows what to do with all of the information it receives, which is why public journalists believe that information must be provided in a manner that is well-suited for the creation of a deliberative democracy. According to public journalists, detached news reporting does not provide the necessary assistance the public requires to understand its business.

Conversely, Michael Schudson points out that public dialogue does not ensure a healthy democratic process. He states, when we criticize the reality of the mass media, we do so by opposing it to an ideal of conversation which we are not inclined to examine.... We have developed a notion that all communication should be like a certain model of conversation, whether or not that model really exists or not. This is where public journalism has a problem: The ability of the public to generate a quality debate should not be treated as gospel.

Schudson points out that "there is an unspoken sense among students of the mass media [and the same can be said of public journalists] that the world of face-to-face communication is the world of rich and complicated interaction," but this idealized version of debate may not exist in the real world. In summary, both approaches to journalism rest on challengable assumptions.

This study of technique has afforded the opportunity to focus upon the means and values that are the driving forces behind both objective and public journalism. Rather than compare the final products of each approach with its self-professed goals - a comparison which is unproductive - this examines both through consideration of their values and means. As stated previously, a debate focused only on final products leads to a fruitless argument in which each side showers the opposition with labels, insinuations, and professional debasements. The study of technique, by focusing on the means and values of each form of journalism, has revealed some important points which need to be recognized in the debate over the relative (de)merits of each journalistic approach. Specifically, quibblings over elitism and egalitarianism must be replaced with discussions of constraints and quality.

THE IMPORTANCE OF UNDERSTANDING

Two final points of interest were revealed in the interviews when designers were asked whether they designed differently for public journalism than for non-public journalism. Designers at two papers said yes, public journalism design was different from non-public journalism design, and designers at the other two papers replied no, there was no difference. Interestingly, the no difference responses came from designers whose papers did not have training sessions on the concepts and techniques of public journalism, or who did not include visual journalists in those sessions.

Both affirmative responses came from newspapers whose designers did participate in public journalism education sessions. Understanding of public journalism principles was one of the explanations offered for some of the findings in this study, and the perception of designers regarding the difference in designing for public journalism reinforces such an explanation. Visual journalists who did not attend sessions aimed at explaining public journalism's goal and principles may not understand it as well as those who did and, therefore, may not consider ways to visually communicate those goals and principles.

Also, one of the designers interviewed complained that too many journalists at the paper felt like they had been ordered to do public journalism with no opportunity for discussion or input. This chapter did not offer training sessions in public journalism. "If they're really going to get people on board to do this and do this well, there has to be that discussion," said the designer, who asked to remain anonymous. "There are numerous ethical challenges in doing this, and they need to at least be explored, as do the possible pitfalls." Both these insights have implications for managing editors contemplating introducing public journalism into their newsrooms.

This study has used the emerging theory of public journalism, which claims a significantly different content than non-public journalism, and the theory of content-driven design, which says that visual meaning must reflect the written content, to examine the question prompted by these theories: If the content of stories generated through public journalism methods is different, and design is driven by content, shouldn't design for public journalism be different than design for non-public journalism?

The results from this study are mixed. Of six hypotheses that speak to the question of whether public journalism is visually different from non-public journalism, two showed significant differences among the newspaper issues sampled. Public journalism stories in this study used more visual devices to convey common ground and solutions, and ways to contact the media than did non-public journalism stories.. Four hypotheses showed no significant differences between public journalism and non-public journalism, but two had means in the direction hypothesized.

The public journalism issues sampled were more likely than non-public journalism to use fewer managed photo opportunities and more photos of real people than candidates or experts, but the differences were not significant These are signs that some of public journalism's goals may be beginning to be translated into practice by visual journalists, but that there are other goals that are not being addressed visually, at least in these newspapers.

The fact that the public journalism issues sampled were not significantly different from the non-public journalism issues in how they visually conveyed views of real people — one of the central tenets of public journalism — should be of concern. That the public journalism issues sampled visually communicated no more mobilizing information than the non-public journalism issues is less cause for worry because mobilizing information is not unique to public journalism the way the other characteristics can be. This study has also found that, in some cases, public journalism papers that have established new conventions in place of the old have found it easier to adhere consistently to public journalism principles; for instance, the development of standing graphics such as democracy boxes for mobilizing information.

One problem in the consistent communication of public journalism characteristics seems to be with journalists' fundamental understanding of public journalism. Confusion over and even unawareness of public journalism principles seems to be a basic, underlying reason why the practice of public journalism is not significantly different from non-public journalism in terms of visual communication. In addition, it appears that not all designers are practicing content-driven design. For instance, this research found stories which included views of real people in the text but not in the design. In conclusion, there appear to be some significant differences in this sample in the way public journalism is visually communicated compared with non-public journalism. However, there is not enough significance to say that it represents a radical departure from non-public journalism, at least in the issues studied here. It appears another researcher's conclusion regarding the content of public journalism may be correct for the visual display as well: "there is no overriding, core philosophy of public journalism at some of the papers practicing it; instead it has become a label used to name a variety of special projects."

CONCEPTUALIZING PUBLIC JOURNALISM

It was common among the evaluative studies either not to define the concept of "public journalism" or to define it in ways that did not show precisely how it differs from its putative adversary: traditional journalism. The result was that few of the studies were guided by clearly explicated conceptual or operational definitions of "public journalism." Indeed, more than a quarter of the works we reviewed conceded difficulties in defining the concept.

This is surprising and unfortunate, considering that some of public journalism's leading advocates have offered definitions that could have been used for inspiration. Many of the evaluative studies made a key assumption that the news organizations under investigation were practicing public journalism either because they participated in initiatives supported financially by such institutions as the Pew Centre for Civic Journalism, or because they themselves labeled their efforts as "public journalism."

Despite their sporadic efforts at theoretically guided definitions, many of the evaluative studies did appear to conceptualize "public journalism" generally as a journalistic movement whose primary goals are to increase civic commitment to and citizen participation in democratic processes. Still, the paucity of clearly and fully explicated definitions of "public journalism" could impose a number of limitations on attempts to evaluate the research that evaluates public journalism.

For one, the absence of such definitions would tend to frustrate efforts to determine if studies that inquired into journalists' affinity for public journalism actually measured the same underlying construct. It would do the same for efforts to determine if the "public" reporting projects under analysis shared particular distinguishing features. It also would tend to work against efforts to assess whether reported audience effects should be attributed to public-journalism content or noncontent factors.

To illustrate this critique, Bare scarcely explained the development of the belief-scale measures that served as the conceptual foundation of his work to identify characteristics that make a journalist a "public journalist." Jeffres et al. did not turn to the public-journalism literature in conceptualizing a press role they named "civic journalism/activist," nor did Weaver and Wilhoit in conceiving of a connection between public journalism and a "populist mobilizer" role that fit a handful of their journalist-respondents.

One also could argue the case that Meyer and Potter over-reached their conceptual framework by applying their measure of twenty newspapers' beforehand intentions of doing public-journalism election reporting to tests for audience effects from the newspapers' later, overt newswork behaviours. They reported finding statistical relationships between the "intention" variable and positive audience effects, but found no discernable audience effects for the newspapers' actual reporting.

This seems counter-intuitive, given that Meyer and Potter offered no explicit evidence that the newspapers had publicized their reporters' before-the-election, public-journalism intents. Absent that publicity, one would more logically expect audiences to be influenced by journalists' overt newswork behaviours-the publicly observable, physical manifestations of their privately held intents. Loomis and Meyer58 took up this conundrum in a follow-up study and reported this solution: journalists' prior "public" reporting intents are connected to subsequent audience effects through the extent to which the annual corporate-report messages of newspaper-chain CEOs emphasized social responsibility.

CONTENT ANALYSES

A key assumption of content analysis is that when coders assign content of interest to categories, they should be guided by "explicitly defined and accepted concept definitions. If the category definitions do not control [the] assignment of content, then human biases may be doing so... [and] findings are likely to be uninterpretable and unreplicable." Reliability is defined as the extent to which coders agree as they independently follow a study's coding protocols.

Coder reliability was not reported, however, in six of the studies that used content analysis. Another six underreported the extent to which their coders agreed, typically by providing an overall, simple-agreement coefficient that masks the reliability of individual variables by averaging all of them. Admittedly the constrained space of academic journals and books makes it difficult to fully detail how a study's variables were operationalized. But some accounting of this beyond merely listing category labels is important in judging a study's findings because variable definitions not only tell coders what content to assign where, they influence coder agreement as well.

Another issue in content analysis is who performs the coding. Three of the content studies were coded solely by their authors and one was coded by a lone research assistant. Reliability in these cases is of the weakest kind: intra-coder agreement, or "stability," a coder's agreement with himself or herself over time. Inter-coder reliability, or "reproducibility," is a better measure. It gauges the degree to which coding protocols yield similar results when applied by two or more coders and, ideally, none of them should be the researcher.

The idea is to demonstrate that the phenomenon being investigated exists independently-or outside the mind-of the researcher who designed the study. However, this was impossible to judge for eleven of the content analyses because they either made no mention of coders or did not make clear whether coding was done by the authors only, independent coders only, or the authors together with other coders. Three of the studies reported the authors and-others combination and although it is not the ideal scheme, it does lend itself to inter-coder reliability checks.

A chief goal of survey research is to generalize the responses of sample members back to the larger population that they are meant to represent. The accuracy of those estimates depends in part on how many sample members declined to respond and whether the nonresponders differed in fundamental ways from the population. The literature on survey methods notes that when people targeted as respondents have little to no specific interest in the research topic, they tend to not return mailed-out questionnaires or to decline telephone interviews.

"This means that mail [and other] surveys with low response rates almost invariably will be biased in significant ways that are related directly to the purposes of the research." Babbie advises that "a response rate of at least 50 per cent is adequate for analysis and reporting. A response of at least 60 per cent is good... [and] 70 per cent is very good [emphasis retained]."

All of the nonreporters were audience-effects studies. The rates for four of the journalist-attitude surveys fell below Babbie's standard for "adequate," which raises the probability of biased findings. One of the four-the APME et al.

survey-reported a miscalculated "very good" rate of 70 per cent, but when corrected, the rate falls well below "adequate."

There was a marked tendency among the survey studies to dwell exclusively on the responses of sample members. But a sample is only a tool for making population estimates, the more relevant "bigger picture" that is uncovered by generalizing sample responses back to the larger population of interest. Only three of the survey studies reported the margin-of-sampling-error rates required for making such estimates.

Also in the survey studies, information about the questions posed to sample members was largely sparse or absent. Poorly drafted survey questions can interject bias into the data they return, so knowing something of how the queries were worded is useful in assessing survey findings. Survey questions should be short and unambiguous, free of biased or ill-defined terms and words, and not written in ways that would make them "leading" or "double-barreled." A question is considered "leading" when it tends to guide respondents toward a particular answer. It is considered "double-barreled" when it asks two or more questions, typically indicated by the conjunction "and."

By way of illustration, Arant and Meyer posed this double-barreled, agree-disagree statement: "My newspaper has an obligation not just to point out community problems and explain alternative solutions, but also to set up meetings and organization programs to solve the problems." It holds one "sub-question" about pointing out problems, a second about explaining solutions, a third about setting up meetings, and a fourth about organizing programs.

The trouble is that a respondent could agree (or disagree) with one or two or three of the four dimensions, and disagree (or agree) with the rest. An "agree" or "disagree" response would not represent absolute agreement or disagreement with the question's overall, intended premise. The APME et al. survey offers another example. In it, newspaper editors were asked, "Do you use the tools and techniques of so-called civic or public journalism?"

The key terms "tools" and "techniques" were not defined, and that makes the question ambiguous and responses to it difficult to interpret. Among other methodological shortcomings, the survey studies were largely silent on how or whether measurement instruments were pre-tested. Also, none of the journalist-attitude studies and only one of the audience-effects studies attempted some form of controlled experiment, although a number of the audience-effects works were explicitly or implicitly arrayed as naturalistic experiments.

DATA INTERPRETATION

There was a tendency among many of the evaluative studies to generously interpret public-journalism performance data. This was particularly apparent in works that explored voter turnout as a key measure of the success of "public" election reporting. However, studies that claimed a causal connection between public journalism and voting failed to address adequately one of the two central assumptions of causality. Time-order admittedly was present: the public-journalism election projects under study occurred before Election Day.

It is a necessary but not sufficient condition for attributing causality. The second assumption is that one also must account for all other possible and knowable causal variables. On this, the audience studies that reported a public-journalism effect on voting did a generally poor job. Although it is probable that public-journalism election projects have had some (as yet undetermined) contributing effect on voter turnout, the complexity of voting behaviours makes it highly unlikely that they are solely or even mostly responsible for the observed increases in turnout.

To further illustrate this critique, Denton and Thorson credited the "We the People/Wisconsin" project with increasing respondents' self-reported interest in politics and knowledge of election-year issues important to state residents, even though both increases fell well within the margin of error they reported for their survey. Simmons did not account for contributing factors unrelated to public journalism when he concluded that a Florida newspaper's coverage of a controversial publicsafety office complex "ultimately set an agenda for public discussion about the... complex which had repercussions at the ballot box."

DISCUSSION AND SUGGESTIONS FOR FUTURE RESEARCH

Overall, empirical research on public journalism's effects on journalists and news audiences has focused on a handful of news organizations and reporting projects. Much of what is currently known about public journalism comes from studies of its use by primarily the Wichita Eagle, Charlotte Observer and Wisconsin State Journal, and the "We the People/Wisconsin" project. And that is to say that little is known about public journalism's performance beyond these "jewel box" examples. Even less may be known when a healthy dose of skepticism is aimed at studies with apparent methodological shortcomings.

Future research must evolve to capture a wider array of newsorganization experiments with public journalism. Researchers must redouble their efforts to ensure methodological rigor in the conceptualization, measurement, and interpretation of public journalism's performance. To not do so would risk the often-voiced criticisms that public journalism is no more than "just good (traditional) journalism" or little more than a misguided attempt to replace valuable, longstanding journalistic practices.

Many of forty-seven evaluative studies we reviewed could be reasonably interpreted as supporting the notion that public and traditional journalism are not that dramatically different in how journalists conceive of and apply their philosophies and practices, and how that influences news audiences. Public journalism, when seen in this light, is one point on a continuum of journalistic practices that range from the disappointing to the ideal. It is another tool in the journalist's kit, not a self-contained kit in and of itself.

To be fair, however, public journalism has had some effect on journalists, news content, and audiences, even when one considers the apparent methodological shortcomings. But the effect also seems to have been a kind of half-half proposition.

Journalists appear to have a generally pluralistic attitudinal approach to newswork and this was reflected in coverage that displayed some of the presumably signature features of public and traditional journalism. Why and how this approach develops is an area richly deserving of future research. While it also has been shown that publicjournalism election reporting differs in some important respects from traditional reporting, there is more to be known about why a shift in emphasis from political-process topics to citizen-agenda issues has not brought more ordinary people into the news as information sources. Perhaps the unexpectedly high numbers of "usual suspect" elite sources found in public-journalism election reporting reflects an economic concern among for-profit news organizations with keeping informationgathering costs low.

It certainly costs less in terms of reporters' time and energy to turn to the more accessible and quotable candidates, politicians, and experts. Or it could be that despite the strength of their commitment to public journalism's ideals, "public" news organizations still define their electoral responsibility in traditional terms: as top-down rather than bottom-up agenda setting. They may still see their role as one of informing news audiences of the views of candidates instead of as one of bringing issues of concern to the governed to the attention of those who would govern.

More work is needed on the audience effects of public journalism. These efforts could be fruitfully guided by the literature on persuasion and voting behaviour. Also, one lesson from the media-effects literature is that it is difficult to pin down causal, media content-audience effects relationships, especially under naturalistic conditions. Controlled laboratory experiments could prove more useful for more convincingly identifying whatever causal factors may be behind any public-journalism influence on news audiences.

On a related point, future research should consider looking at the kinds of communities in which public journalism is practiced. For example, is public journalism practiced primarily by news organizations that serve affluent or deprived communities? Or that serve socially homogenous or heterogeneous communities? Or that serve communities where civic participation already is high or low? The answers to these and other queries could illuminate whatever causal link may exist between "public" reporting and civic participation. They also could shed light on the potential and desirability of using public journalism to help a community work toward consensus on how to address and overcome public-policy problems. More work is needed, too, on understanding how the effects of public-journalism coverage are distributed within a given community. One could fruitfully ask whether public journalism helps reduce differences in political knowledge and participation among groups of high and low socio-economic status.

Or does it tend to stabilize, or perhaps even widen, any pre-existing differences? Researchers should consider as well the nature of community-problem solutions that public-journalism interventions seek explicitly or implicitly to move community residents toward.

Have solutions that are eventually enacted benefited everyone within a given community or have they tended to favour the interests of a community's most powerful segments? Have publicjournalism initiatives helped establish new community organizations or expand the missions of existing agencies? Have community agencies experienced measurable-and sustainable-increases in their membership or volunteer rolls as a direct or indirect result of "public" reporting?

The economics of public journalism's practice is another area deserving of future research. Leading public-journalism advocates have suggested that news organizations will find "public" newswork to be a profitable endeavor. We found no studies that attempted to systematically substantiate this claim. The literature is silent, too, on how news organizations plan and implement public-journalism initiatives. The success or failure of a project can depend on how it is designed and "sold" to rank-and-file journalists charged with enacting it. Public-journalism projects are similar to persuasive public-communication campaigns in terms of their ultimate objectives. But whether public journalists also are similarly as attentive in designing, executing, and following up on their efforts are questions deserving of scholarly attention.

In the end, it could be that public journalism's most unqualified success has been to keep "alive the soul-searching sparked by the poor coverage in the 1988 presidential campaign. It has helped revive [a] discussion about journalism's core values at a time when those values are under assault from the industry's profit motives." Its greatest impact may be more heuristic rather than practical. The idea of public journalism has prompted a much-needed discussion among scholars and practitioners about how to safeguard "journalism in the public interest" from an increasingly commercialized news-media system.

5

Effects in Investigating Synergy and Political Democracy

INTRODUCTION

Synergy, a marketing term, refers to the benefits derived from selling two or more compatible products simultaneously (*e.g.*, a blockbuster movie, the book on which the movie is based, the movie soundtrack, and action figures derived from the story), as well as the harnessing of relations between two or more elements of a media production and distribution process, including the repurposing of content created for one medium for distribution by another. In the context of this study, synergy refers to the possibility of two contiguous media behaviours-on air and online news consumption-having a greater impact on perceptions of media credibility than exposure to either medium by itself. Although telewebbing emerged as a mass phenomenon in the late 1990s, the effects of cross-platform media use remain underexamined and little understood.

In addition to examining synergy effects in a real-time setting, this study adds to a small but growing body of research that has applied the experimental method to questions of television news credibility.

The preponderance of studies on media credibility has been survey based, and most channel comparison studies have examined the credibility of television news in relation to newspapers. The survey approach to studying credibility allows researchers to track broad trends in public opinion about the media but the results of such surveys are limited in their ability to explain cause-and-effect relationships.

Survey research has established that use of a particular media channel correlates with high credibility ratings for that channel. But does media use lead to enhanced perceptions of credibility, or do people tend to use media they already consider credible? Survey studies, because they lack control and generally do not address the issue of temporal sequence, cannot effectively answer this question.

Surveys, moreover, are hampered in a data-gathering sense because they rely on reflections of past media use, an estimation process prone to distortion and social desirability biasing. Placing participants directly in different media settings (*e.g.*, telewebbing, television only, or Net news only) offers the opportunity to assess perceptions of credibility as they occur rather than relying on reflections of past media behaviour. The experimental situation also enables the researcher to control the sequence of presumed effects.

The documentation of synergy effects on perceptions of credibility could have important implications for the broadcast news industry, and network news organizations in particular, as audiences tend to pay more attention to and become more reliant on media they consider credible.

Perceptions of credibility have also been found to influence the processing of issue importance. When media are perceived as credible, acceptance of information veracity increases and agenda-setting effects-accepting issues given prominent media coverage as valid and important-are likely to occur. In an era of convergent media and twenty-four-hour news channels, when the future of the nightly newscast itself is being called into question, the networks are challenged with maximizing their believability, accuracy, fairness, and informational completeness across delivery platforms.

Media Credibility and Age Cohort. Studies of media credibility have consistently found an association between age and education with credibility assessments. In general, older, more educated audiences tend to be the most critical of media, while younger, less educated news consumers are more likely to be accepting of news coverage and to evaluate the media as credible. The youngest adults, 18-24 years old, are the most likely to rate news media highly believable. And it is network news, more than most other forms of media, that has been likely to elicit these demographic response patterns. Sophistication, life experience, and knowledge of the press-a type of news literacy-combine to make more seasoned audiences skeptical of the nightly news. Although displacement theory would suggest that a traditional medium such as television, besieged by new challengers and new communication technologies, would directly lose its audience to popular forms of new media, some studies conclude that the Internet supplements rather than replaces television viewing.

These findings are consistent with the idea that online sources provide what industry players like ABC-TV refer to as an "enhanced television" experience. Robinson and colleagues even found a positive relationship between computer use and television viewing.

Other researchers have argued, however, that television viewing is negatively affected by computer or Internet use. None of the aforementioned studies, however, explicitly considers telewebbing as a media behaviour that might influence the interpretation of these findings. In a time of rapid technological change and format experimentation, credibility remains central to understanding public perceptions of network news as well as encouraging acceptance of the Internet as a trusted source of news and information.

Documenting the potential contributions of online news operations to perceptions of network news credibility through experimental investigation may enhance industry and scholarly awareness of the nonmonetary value of the networks' online news operations beyond bottom-line issues of profitability and audience share.

If such effects are found, this will suggest to the industry that investments in online news operations may be justified not on the basis of economic considerations alone but on the grounds of enhancing public perceptions of network news through multiple media channels.

Research Questions

To assess whether cross-platform media use of online and on-air news has a greater impact on audience perceptions of media credibility than exposure to either medium in isolation, this study of synergy effects is guided by the following research questions:

- *RQ*1: Do different audiences for news, specifically younger and older age groups, rate the credibility of on-air and online news differently?
- *RQ*2: What influence does media channel have on audience evaluations of media credibility?
- *RQ*3: Is there a combined, or synergy, effect between on-air and online news sources that enhances perceptions of credibility over use of either medium in isolation?
- *RQ*4: Is there an interaction between media channel and age group resulting in different synergy effects for younger and older news audiences?

Method

Operationally, this study took the form of a 4 (media channel) × 2 (age group) between subjects, factorial experiment. The first factor, media channel, had four levels: television news, Net news, both TV and Net news, and no exposure (control group). The second factor, age group, had two levels: undergraduate students and older adults.

Student subjects consisted of 84 undergraduates enrolled in communications courses at a large Midwestern university and ranged in age from 18 to 25 (M = 20). Adult subjects consisted of 83 members of a local community group and ranged in age from 26 to 80 (M = 49).

A total of 167 subjects participated in the study, populating each cell of the design with a minimum of 20 subjects. Student subjects received extra credit for their participation, while adults received a small monetary incentive. Slightly more than half of the study participants (52.1 per cent, n = 87) were female, while just under half (47.9 per cent, n = 80) were male. Procedure. The study was conducted in the weeks immediately following the September 11 terrorist attacks. The news focus on terrorism remained prominent for the duration of the study, although the early emphasis on domestic security issues gradually gave way to a focus on the war in Afghanistan. Within each age group, subjects were randomly assigned to one of the four media channel conditions. To guard against primacy and recency effects, each condition had four randomized orders. At the beginning of the experiment, subjects completed a questionnaire asking about their media use, political attitudes and knowledge, and demographic information. Subjects assigned to the television condition were shown four, randomly ordered network news stories (from ABC, NBC, CBS, or MSNBC) about the World Trade Centre attacks and were asked to rate their responses. The stories were recorded off-air from network news coverage beginning on the day of the attacks and for several days thereafter. Each story consisted of an anchor lead-in, followed by a news report about the attacks or Bush administration response to the crisis and a direct presidential sound bite in reaction to the unfolding events. Altogether, there were eight unique stories in the stimulus material, two from each network. The average length of each story was just over 2 minutes (M = 125.75 seconds). After viewing each story, subjects completed a series of evaluative measures and open-ended questions designed to elicit any specific impressions prompted by the stories.

Subjects assigned to the Net news condition were instructed to visit two unaltered network news sites (among ABC, CBS, NBC with Tom Brokaw, or MSNBC with Brian Williams) and perform either an interactive or reading task for approximately 5 minutes.

The specific pages visited featured news stories, photos, graphics, and interactive features about the terrorist attacks, making the online content comparable with the broadcast news stories. The decision to not replicate the exact verbal content of the broadcast news stories and leave the Net news sites unaltered was made with the intention to maximize ecological validity and to deliberately test the effect of medium as opposed to modality. Consistent with previous channel studies, "news items were selected so that the same substantive information was included in each medium's version of the story, but the journalistic presentation varied as it actually does by medium."

After visiting each site, subjects completed a series of evaluative measures designed to elicit credibility assessments of the individual sites.

Subjects assigned to the cross-platform (synergy) condition, in randomly alternating order, first viewed four of the broadcast news stories and then visited two Net news sites. To guard against order effects, some subjects first viewed the broadcast news stories and then went online, while others went online first then viewed the stories. Again, after viewing each story and visiting each site, subjects completed a series of evaluative measures and open-ended questions.

At the end of each media condition, subjects completed a series of overall credibility measures separately for television and Net news. Media credibility, the focal concept of this study, was operationalized as the degree to which news consumers judge network newscasts and Web sites to be believable, fair, accurate, informative, and in-depth. Each item comprising the credibility construct was measured using a 7-point scale (1 = not at all; 7 = very). To determine the suitability of using the five items together in combined credibility indexes, a reliability analysis was performed for both TV news and Net news credibility. For both indexes the Cronbach's alpha coefficient was.89.

Subjects assigned to the control condition were not exposed to any media, but simply completed the experimental questionnaire and overall media credibility measures.

A between-subjects analysis of variance (ANOVA) was performed for the media channel and age group factors on the combined credibility indexes. For the age group factor, there were significant main effects for both the TV news index, eta-squared =.26, as well as the Net news index, eta-squared =.06. To reveal the contribution of individual items, a series of t-tests were run for each index separately.

Across all items, the younger age group rated TV news credibility significantly higher than the older age group, reserving its highest ratings for informativeness and believability. Interestingly, both age groups rated TV news lowest on its depth. On the bottom row of the table the combined index scores show that younger audience members evaluated TV news to be significantly more credible overall than older audience members.

Students were much more inclined to rate online news as informative and in-depth than adult subjects. As with TV news, adults also considered Net news significantly less fair than students. Again on the bottom row of the table the combined index scores show that younger audience members evaluated Net news to be significantly more credible overall than older audience members.

Although students' credibility ratings are higher overall than adults, within age groups adults rate Net news to be significantly more credible than TV news. Within the younger age group, the reverse occurs: students rate TV news more credible overall than Net news. Another difference between the TV and Net news credibility ratings is revealed by the fewer degrees of freedom in the t-tests for the older age group when compared to the younger group (76 versus 83). Several of the older adult participants said they had no online experience and declined to even rate Net news credibility for this reason.

In response to the first research question, then, different audiences do seem to rate the credibility of on-air and online news differently. Younger audience members are much more inclined to assign both news channels higher credibility ratings than older audience members. But within groups, adults consider Net news to be more fair, informative, and in-depth, and therefore more credible overall, than TV news. Students, on the other hand, give TV news higher marks than Net news on every item except in-depth and regard television as the more credible news source. Care should be taken not to read too much into these results, since these age-group differences do not take into account the unique effect of channel exposure, which is analysed next.

The second research question asked what influence media channel had on audience evaluations of credibility. Analysis of variance produced a significant main effect for media channel on the TV news credibility index. Across all subjects, exposure to television news resulted in the highest TV news index scores of any media channel. These scores were significantly higher than the control group, which was exposed to no media, and the Net news-only group, as determined by Tukey post-hoc comparisons. Media exposure did not have a significant effect on ratings of Net news credibility, which varied comparatively little regardless of channel used.

The columns representing exposure to TV news suggest an effect of channel congruence on credibility evaluations, where perceptions of credibility are enhanced when the channel used is consistent with the news source being evaluated. Simply put, television news viewing results in the highest evaluations of TV news credibility of any condition. Going online has the same effect on evaluations of Net news credibility for students, at a level significantly higher than the control group ratings, but not for adults. In three out of four cases, then, channel congruence enhances credibility evaluations. In response to the second research question, direct media exposure mostly enhances credibility evaluations when the channel is consistent with the news source being evaluated, resulting in what might be called a congruence effect. When the channel is inconsistent, direct exposure still results in higher evaluations than no exposure for students but lower evaluations for adults.

The third research question asked whether there is a synergy effect between on air and online news sources that enhances perceptions of credibility over use of either medium in isolation. Subjects exposed to both broadcast and online news in the same experimental session (telewebbing) rated TV and Net news credibility higher overall than any other condition except for the TV congruency case (TV exposure producing the highest TV credibility evaluations). For both students and adults, telewebbing has a small positive impact on TV news credibility beyond Net news use and no exposure, but these individual comparisons were not significant in Tukey post-hoc comparisons.

The fourth research question asked whether there is an interaction between media channel and age group resulting in different synergy effects for younger and older news audiences. When exposed to either TV or Net news, however, students and adults reacted quite differently (as indicated by the divergent upward and downward lines in the centre of the graph). For adults, exposure had a negative effect and evaluations of Net news credibility fell from the control group level. For students, exposure had a positive effect and evaluations rose. When adults were placed in the telewebbing condition (shown on the right side of the graph), with exposure to both TV and Net news, evaluations of Net news jumped to their highest levels.

For students, telewebbing caused perceptions of Net news to dip slightly. The interaction for media channel and age group for evaluations of TV news credibility was not significant.

To summarize these findings, when adults were placed in the telewebbing condition, with exposure to both TV and Net news, evaluations of Net news credibility jumped to their highest levels. Evaluations of TV news credibility also benefited from telewebbing, compared to the control group and to Web use alone. For students, telewebbing caused perceptions of TV and Net news credibility to increase in relation to the control group, but dip slightly or show no difference compared to other forms of media exposure. In answer to RQ4, then, telewebbing potentially results in greater synergy effects of Net news credibility for adults than students, but these results only approached significance.

Discussion

This study of synergy effects, which adds to the experimental literature of media credibility, found significant main effects for media channel on evaluations of TV news credibility and for age group on evaluations of both TV and Net news credibility.

The ANOVA model also produced a near-significant interaction for the two factors on evaluations of Net news credibility, which may have achieved significance had the group sizes been larger. Consistent with survey studies of media credibility, younger audience members evaluated both TV and Net news to be significantly more credible overall than older audience members.

In particular, students regarded both forms of network news as more informative than adults, while adults considered both forms of news to be significantly less fair than students. Both age groups rated TV news lowest for its depth. Within age groups, adults rated Net news to be significantly more credible than TV news, while students rated TV news more credible. These results are somewhat surprising, given that the audience for broadcast news tends to be older, while the online audience tends to be younger. Each age group evaluated the less familiar medium more generously.

Media channel also influenced credibility evaluations. The ratings for television news suggested a channel congruence effect, where perceptions of credibility are enhanced when the channel used is consistent with the source being evaluated. This was the case for both students and adults. The finding of a congruence effect in an experimental setting differs from the common survey finding that media audiences regard the medium on which they are most reliant as the most credible because the evaluations here were generated in response to direct exposure to a particular medium and not based on reflections of past media use. Nevertheless, similar to the association of media reliance with high credibility evaluations revealed by surveys, audiences seem to regard media they have just used more favourably than media to which they are not exposed.

Going online had the same congruence effect on evaluations of Net news credibility for students, but not adults. When the channel used is inconsistent, adults tend to evaluate the source less favourably compared to the control group. Adults were noticeably less inclined to view TV news as credible after exposure to the Web. For students, any media exposure had a positive impact and evaluations rose relative to the control group.

As for cross-platform media use, the results provided some initial evidence for the existence of a synergy effect. The magnitude of these effects, though relatively small, was greater for adults than for students, perhaps reflecting students' propensity to multitask.

A recent study of the gratifications obtained from new media found that students spend on average a total of 10.5 hours per day with a range of different media technologies.The telewebbing condition was arguably more novel for adults, and thus had a greater impact on their credibility evaluations. Overall, subjects exposed to the telewebbing condition rated TV and Net news credibility higher than the control group or subjects exposed only to Net news. The only exception was that TV exposure by itself elicited the highest evaluations of TV credibility.

The fact that several of the mean credibility ratings for telewebbing pointed to synergy effects but were not significantly different at the $p < .05$ level suggests that a larger number of subjects in this between-subjects experiment would have produced more significant results. Between-subjects experiments with 20 or fewer subjects per group, as was the case with this study, are notoriously underpowered. To overcome this classic problem without having to involve hundreds of subjects in a costly and time-consuming data collection process, future experimental research should take advantage of within-subjects, repeated measures designs, which provide greater statistical power with fewer subjects since each subject responds multiple times and serves as his or her own control.

When studying network news, the demographics of the audience are an essential consideration. Young adults who are wired, and therefore on a trajectory for the higher socioeconomic status that characterizes network news viewers, represent the future of the on-air news audience. Whether members of this audience will ever completely migrate online for their news and information seems doubtful, at least at this stage of the Web's development. Students in this study reported almost two nights of network news viewing per week-even as members of a residential campus environment that provides "cost free," high-bandwidth online access. What seems almost certain, however, is a continued tendency by younger audiences to teleweb and, beyond that, multitask with a variety of information and communication technologies simultan-eously.

The results of this study suggest that media exposure has differential effects on student and adult perceptions of news credibility. Future research should keep this finding in mind and not attempt to generalize about the news audience from a convenience sample of undergraduates. The experimental nature of this study, while desirable for the control it offered over the news channels subjects were exposed to, was limited in its ability to simulate actual viewing conditions.

Subjects in the telewebbing condition, for instance, either saw a series of newscasts first and then went online, or spent some time online first and then watched a series of broadcasts. At home (or in the office), news consumers who teleweb may use both media at the same time.

Follow-up studies should attempt to recreate a real-time telewebbing or "enhanced television"experience in as naturalistic a way as possible. In addition, other genres of media content associated with telewebbing, such as live sports coverage or news specials, should be studied. Satisfying these two conditions may lead to more pronounced findings for synergy effects.

With the growth of telewebbing and multitasking as routine audience activities, it will become increasingly important to understand and measure perceptions of news credibility under conditions of simultaneous media use.

Considering the potential contribution of synergy effects resulting from cross-platform media use could help recast the debate about media credibility so that the realities, rather than the hyperbole, of online developments are adequately taken into account. The networks have adapted to the online environment and are making gainful use of both delivery platforms. Moreover, most audience members do not stop using a source as heavily relied on as television just because a new medium arrives on the scene; instead, their media repertoire may become wider and more varied.

The rise of telewebbing and two-screen households presents media research with the challenge of understanding the impact of this new consumer behaviour on evaluations of news content. With technological convergence, the independence of different delivery platforms is eroding.

Even so, the stylistic differences between on-air and online news may persist, withbroadcast news retaining its trademark chronological narrative and online (text-based) news embracing the inverted pyramid style of print reporting. Although both forms of news are similar in that they are delivered through electronic telecommunications terminals, they may be processed and evaluated with vastly different criteria, as is the case for assessments of newspaper and television news credibility. From the perspective of the news audience, the ways in which television and the Web complement-and contravene-each other are only beginning to be understood. Research should investigate the different processing styles required for on-air and online news, with the aim of revealing the psychological mechanisms underlying credibility judgements.

Access to news making, that is, the chance to have our voices and experiences included in an influential public communication forum, is a critical political resource. Such access, especially the kind of serious voice routinely achieved by political elites, offers sources wide distribution for their ideas and the opportunity to significantly affect public debate.

Research suggests, for example, that news selections help set the public's issue agenda; that news constructions "prime"the audience in ways that affect evaluations of candidates and policies; and that journalists'framing choices can affect the audience's attribution of casuality and blame for social problems, and their tolerance for civil liberties. Consequently, the question of how news stories are created, and in particular whose voices are included in these constructions, has become a critical democratic question.

Access to the news is an especially important resource for social movement groups. For these groups, such as the women's or the environmental movement, communication is a central goal. They seek to change public attitudes and understandings on key social and cultural issues through the creation and communication of new information and new interpretive frameworks. To do so, however, they must reach mass audiences. Access to news media thus becomes an important mobilizing resource for such groups. In addition, as voices of political dissent and social change, social movements'ability to access news media provides a critical test of the media's ability to serve as a legitimate source of information in a democracy. But how open are news media to social movement communications? Can social change groups strategically access newsmaking processes? Can they achieve routine access to news? How have they done so and at what costs? This chapter investigates the media access strategies of the National Organization for Women (NOW), a central organization of the second wave of the U.S. women's movement. Using historical data gathered from NOW's archive and from a content analysis of New York Times coverage of NOW, it traces NOW's resource mobilization, strategy development, and media access during a fifteen year period, from its founding in 1966 to its institutionalization as a voice for women's issues by the 1980s.

NOW's ability to access news media in this period was the result of two key factors. First, NOW was able to mobilize the material resources-money, skills, technology, labour, organizational structure, and especially information-necessary to serve as a reliable and routine source for journalists. Second, the group was able to develop effective and reflexive media strategies by mobilizing its knowledge of the routines and discursive structures of news and using them in its own media communications. These two factors contributed significantly to NOW's public visibility over time and to the group's role in helping to create a public agenda for "women's issues"in the United States. A single case study approach to these questions has its limitations, of course. NOW is not typical of all social movement organizations. It is a mass-based organization with a national office and local chapters, not a local grassroots organization. Its longevity-more than thirty years-is also unusual for an advocacy organization. However, NOW is also an important organization in its own right. Though it has been seen as too "liberal"by some groups and too "radical"by others, there is widespread agreement in the women's movement that NOW played a central role as the public voice of feminism for many years. A recent history of the movement notes, "The fact is that if the National Organization for Women were to collapse and disappear, it would be taken as a signal of the end of this era of feminism."

Perhaps most critically for this analysis, though, NOW can be seen as something of a social movement "success story"in terms of media access. NOW has always been able to achieve at least some basic news access, and although early coverage was marginalizing, later news presented NOW as an important civil rights organization for women. In particular, around the Equal Rights Amendment (ERA) struggle of the late 1970s and early 1980s, NOW became a key source and definer of events for news media. Analyzing the resources and strategies that structured NOW's access, then, may help us understand the chances of other groups to access news media.

THE INDIAN MOVEMENT AND POLITICAL DEMOCRACY

This work investigates the implications of the Ecuadorian Indian movement for democratic politics. While its empirical questions focus on Ecuador's political processes, a key purpose is to offer a Latin American perspective on the broader debate on the "civil society argument"; namely, the proposition that civil association has intrinsically positive effects on democracy.

The assumption herein is that particularization is essential for appraising this wide-ranging claim. Civil society and democracy are knotty concepts because they refer to complex realities that can be approached from different points of view. To cut through the complexity, this study follows a strategy of double specification, concentrating on social movements as a distinct type of civil association and demarcating discrete functional terrains to observe their bearing on democracy.

Applied to the case at hand, this strategy provides a basis for a contextualized assessment of the putative democratic benefits of civil association and offers insights on the conditions of political engagement that social movements share with other kinds of civil society groups.

The pivotal claim of this study is that civil society actors may or may not contribute to democracy and that, in the particular case of social movements, the underlying tension between the participatory and insti- tutional dimensions of democracy may be expressed through a mixed bag of favorable and unfavorable effects on the different components of political democracy. The analysis of the Ecuadorian Indian movement demonstrates that to understand the varying impact of civil activism on democracy, scholars must adopt a nuanced, context-specific approach that does not lose sight of the particularistic orientations of civil associations and that pays close attention to their definition of means and ends, the institutional responses evoked by their initiatives, and the unintended consequences of their actions. The relevance of the case cannot be overstated. The Ecuadorian Indian movement is often cited as the best-organized and most influential indigenous movement in Latin America. Its origins date back to the rise of local and regional organizations that, in the 1980s, came together in CONAIE, the Confederation of Indigenous Nationalities of Ecuador.

The spectacular battles of the 1990s transformed the movement into a powerful force that, in addition to pressing indigenous demands, took up a leadership role in the wider resistance to the imposition of neo-liberal reforms.

By 1997 CONAIE had launched the party Pachakutik to take part in elections, and its political clout had been boosted by its role in the developments that led to the fall of president Abdalá Bucaram and the convening of a constitutional assembly. In January 2000, amid an economic and political crisis of unprecedented proportions, CONAIE joined a group of military officers led by Colonel Lucio Gutiérrez in a non-violent coup that toppled President Jamil Mahuad but failed to hold on to power.

Three years later, the same actors made another bid for power as an electoral coalition, which succeeded in winning the presidential elections. The presence of Indian leaders in the government was a high point for the movement, but it did not last long. After six months of conflicts over President Gutierrez's neo-liberal turn, CONAIE withdrew its support and Pachakutik's ministers abandoned the cabinet.

Clearly, this is a movement that has reached well beyond the bounds of a bid for indigenous rights. Much more has been at stake, including matters of national economic and social policy and issues that are directly related to the struggle for political power and the fate of Ecuadorian democracy. In the context of contemporary Latin America, then, this case is highly relevant to the discussion of the various types of impact that social movements can have on democracy.

This chapter lays the groundwork for the analysis with a conceptual discussion elucidating the notion of civil society, the specificity of social movements as a variant of civil association, and the paradoxical relationship between social movements and democracy. The factors behind the rise of Ecuador's Indian movement, the broadening of its struggles, and the saliency of its political protagonism are then reviewed. The enquiry is framed as a scrutiny of the movement's consequences for the participatory and institutional dimensions of democracy. After exploring the bases of CONAIE's support, the study examines the movement's two main modalities of political engagement: its efforts to influence government policies and its struggles to conquer positions of power. The appraisal of the effects on the democratic regime covers four areas: interest representation, control of state power, legitimacy, and political socialization. The conclusions assess the significance of the Indian movement for democracy, briefly rejoining the debate on the "civil society argument" and commenting on the present challenges for Ecuadorian indigenous activists.

CIVIL SOCIETY, SOCIAL MOVEMENTS, AND DEMOCRACY

This work adopts a modified version of Michael Walzer's definition of civil society, taking it to refer to the ensemble of social practices that generate a space of voluntary association and the sets of relational networks, or social actors, that occupy that space. Within this scope, the cast of civil society actors includes all voluntary groups formed for the sake of the common aspirations and concerns of its members. This formula is useful because it grasps civil society on its own terms, avoiding the pitfalls of definitions that imply assumptions about its relationships with the political institutions, such as the idea that civil society is necessarily autonomous from the state, necessarily opposed to the state, or necessarily good for democracy.

A good antidote to the mystifying sway of prescriptive definitions of civil society is to keep in mind that the realm of voluntary association is thoroughly marked by pluralism, particularism, and inequality.

Civil society is pluralistic because its practices are based on multiple forms of participation, express many social identities, and pursue a wide variety of goals.

Civil society is particularistic because its groups have their own norms and because, with rare exceptions, they restrict benefits to members and pursue goals that reflect their own priorities-even when, as often is the case, they claim to represent the public interest.

Moreover, civil society is tied up with inequality not only because different groups have different levels of opportunity to associate and further their ends, but also because a great deal of what associations do has consequences in terms of widening, maintaining, or narrowing existing social gaps.

Social movements are a particular form of civil association. They can be defined as organized drives to promote or resist change through collective practices that are embedded in a structure of conflict, involve episodes of mass participation, and challenge existing institutions.

The reference to conflict implies that social movements confront opponents in struggles over values and claims to resources, status, or power, a feature that sets them apart from civil associations that are not involved in such confrontations (*e.g.*, social clubs, churches, and charitable foundations). On the other hand, the emphasis on events in which large numbers of people engage in non-institutional forms of action foregrounds popular participation and defiance of prescribed rules, two elements that are absent in the case of associations whose activities are carried out by small circles of activists or professionals who follow" the proper institutional channels" (*e.g.*, interest groups and advocacy organizations). To understand movements, one must ascertain what is at stake in the conflicts in which they are involved. In empirical studies, the stakes can be inferred from their goals, their actions, and the context of their struggles.

The conceptual distinction between civil and political engagement is a useful tool for initiating that enquiry. In civil engagement, the conflict is located in civil society itself. There are two variants of this kind of engagement: construction of collective identity, in which movements seek to alter the self-consciousness of actual or potential followers; and cultural crusades, in which movements act on the general public to change dominant values or attitudes.

In political engagement, the conflict is played out through interactions with state actors or other agents from political society; that is, the arena of competition for control over the state apparatus and public policy. Here, the actions of movements are usually aimed at inducing policy changes. Sometimes, however, their struggles may turn into attempts to control the positions of power themselves.

Social movements are a modern form of participation that emerged with the changes related to the consolidation of capitalism, the national state, and liberal democracy. As a rule, movements have served as a medium for the participation of excluded groups and for the politicization of issues that the institutions are unwilling or unable to address.

By engaging in confrontational practices like marches, boycotts, and demonstrations, movements have shown that ordinary people can capitalize on numbers, unity, and determination to achieve goals against the will of the most adamant opponents or rulers. Movement practices, then, must be seen as practices of non-institutional power. Lacking other resources, excluded and powerless people use disruption. They generate might by withdrawing the tacit support that power holders derive from" business as usual," thus creating a political market in which they can trade the lifting of their sanctions for the changes they seek.

Some authors have argued that movements and revolutions are variants of contentious politics; namely, a particular kind of political activity in which challengers use non-institutional means in their interactions with elites and the state. By itself, though, the opposition of institutional and non-institutional means cannot capture the diversity that exists in civil society's political practices. In the view of this study, it should be combined with another distinction that, considering the actors' ends, marks the contrast between the politics of influence, which focus on swaying public policy decisions; and the politics of power, which are played as attempts to seize the positions from which the decisions are made. On the basis of the combinations of means and ends, identifies four alternative forms of civil society's political engagement.

As a static categorization, this matrix marks out the specificity of movements in regard to other forms of civil political involvement. But the framework can also serve as a dynamic referent for variants and transformations. Variants are relevant because movements often combine the use of non-institutional means with conventional modalities of action.

Transformations are also relevant because movements develop over time in a sequence of events that at some point is completed. At the peak of its cycle, a movement that initially focused on reforms may blend into a revolution, a sweeping challenge to the structure of power, which is usually violent and, if successful, involves dramatic changes in the organization and policies of the state. Far more frequent, however, is institutionalization, which takes partial forms when movements spawn lobbying agencies or political arms and final forms when they abandon the unconventional forms of action and reorganize themselves as interest groups or political parties.

What is the relationship between movements and democracy? To elucidate this, we must first dispel the myth that civil society activities are always beneficial to democracy. It is true that civil associations can assist democracy by disseminating its values, representing social interests, resisting state arbitrariness, and educating people for democratic participation. But although associations can fulfill these positive functions, they may not always do so.

Indeed, they may also harm democracy in various ways, such as upholding antidemocratic ideologies, using corruption to get privileges, and seeking co-optation as state clienteles. The key point is that civil society actors may or may not contribute to democracy; and in both cases, what they actually do may vary greatly.

The groups that are not helpful run the gamut from associations whose activities are devoid of political consequence to organizations that may be conspiring to subvert a democratic regime. When associations contribute to democracy, by contrast, they rarely do it by design, but as a byproduct or contingent result of their efforts to attain their own particularistic goals.

All the foregoing holds true for social movements, but with a special twist: their status in democratic polities is haunted by an intrinsic ambivalence.

Definitions of democracy can be broadly divided into procedural definitions, which view democracy as a regime based on electoral representation and guaranteed civil and political rights; and substantive definitions, which see it as a principle of participation that guides all political practices.

This counterpoint highlights a fundamental tension between two ingredients of democracy: the principle that" the people rule" and the institutional procedures that, at any given time, embody that principle. Generally speaking, institutions produce social order by imparting stability and meaning to behaviour.· In their domain, democratic institutions contribute to that order by protecting citizens' rights and providing means for their participation in politics. But institutions have a downside, aptly captured in Jean-Paul Sartre's assertion that they amount to" the systematic self-domestication of man by man". In dictating the acceptable ways of doing things, institutions foreclose alternatives, generating an effect of suppression that is magnified by their tendency to get entrenched in their own inertia.

The case of representative democracy is especially poignant because, for most citizens, the same institutions that enable them to choose their rulers also imply their exclusion from further participation. This tension underlies the paradox of social movements in democracies. As a form of political engagement that involves large numbers of normally excluded people, movements fulfill the principle of citizen participation. But their reliance on non-institutional means implies that they are often in breach of the rules that define how the polity works. What turns the inconsistency into a paradox is that it has not prevented the emergence of movements as a regular feature of political life. To the contrary, viewed from the side of democracy, the key element in the relationship is that political democracy is an open invitation to social movements. Democracy offers fertile ground because it guarantees the rights of expression and assembly and, perhaps more important, because its own claim to legitimacy, grounded as it is in a discourse of popular sovereignty, citizenship rights, and inclusion, lends legitimacy to the claims of those who do not feel represented and want changes in public policies, in the definition of rights, or in the democratic institutions themselves.

Viewed from the side of movements, however, the relationship cuts both ways. In positive outcomes, the paradox is resolved in the deepening of democracy; that is, in situations in which a movement helps make a polity more democratic by winning reforms that broaden citizenship rights and provide for greater citizen participation in politics. Europe and the United States offer many examples of movements that advanced democracy through struggles against slavery, for labor's freedom of association, for the enfranchisement of women and the poor, and for the civil rights of racial, ethnic, and religious minorities.

But there have been negative outcomes, too, including the Nazi and Fascist movements, which ushered in a catastrophic period when democratic institutions were wiped out, the political and civil rights of entire populations were revoked, slavery was reinstated, and genocide became state policy. Finally, there may also be cases in which a movement's impact is a mixed bag of favorable and unfavorable effects on different components of political democracy.

The paradox of social movements should give us pause. We cannot assume that movements always contribute to political democracy just because they involve popular participation. But it is also a mistake to think that movements automatically detract from democracy because they infringe on institutional rules. Mindful of the complexities, political philosophers have long been engaged in discussing the circumstances in which civil disobedience may be justified in democratic polities. For social analysts, the challenge is different. We must use the complications as pointers for trying to provide more nuanced answers to empirical questions about the origins of social movements, the sources of their power, and their consequences for democracy. These are the questions addressed in this work on the Ecuadorian Indian movement.

The Contentious Cycle of the 1990s

In 1979, Ecuador turned from military to civilian rule. By way of background, it is worth calling attention to three aspects of that transition. First, the Ecuadorian generals did not display the repressive and probusiness zeal that typified military rule elsewhere in Latin America. Instead, they pursued a nationalistic agenda focused on the development of oil exports, agrarian reform, and "inward-oriented" industrialization.

During the 1970s, the economy expanded, and there were ostensible improvements in the living standards of the popular sectors. This, and the absence of severe repression, fostered attitudes of support for the military regime. Second, the democratic transition was initiated and tightly controlled by the armed forces. The "handed down" democracy did not inspire the sense of commitment that could have existed if the political parties and civil society had played a greater role in wresting it from the military.

Because they had not been crafted through political compromises, moreover, the new institutions proved ill-suited for the resolution of conflict, which set the stage for relentless strife between the executive and congress, constitutional tampering in all branches of government, and a chronic exacerbation of party fragmentation, regionalism, and personalistic politics.

Third, the transition to democracy offered opportunities for the political involvement of the indigenous population. The 1979 Constitution eliminated the literacy requirement, which had excluded most Indians from the vote.

The process was boosted by the first civilian president, populist politician Jaime Roldós, who promoted the participation of Indian organizations in rural development and literacy programmes.

The downsizing of these initiatives under president Osvaldo Hurtado (from the centrist Christian Democratic party, 1981-84) and their elimination altogether by León Febres Cordero (from the conservative Social Christian party, 1984-88) provided an early rallying point for criticism and contentiousness among the Indian activists. These elements must be kept in mind to understand the developments of the 1990s. On the one hand, they draw a connection between the tumultuous nature of Ecuadorian politics and the reality that after a decade of civilian rule, Ecuador was still plagued by the flaws of its democratic institutions, the dubiousness of its politicians' allegiance to the rules of democracy, and the shallowness of its citizens' democratic political culture.

On the other hand they indicate that, by the late 1980s, favorable conditions for an Indian movement had appeared. The extension of political rights and the openings in government policy had stimulated indigenous organization. The subsequent withdrawal of state support, the policies of adjustment, and the downturn of the economy would provide strong motives for the Indian insurgency of the 1990s.

RISE OF THE INDIAN MOVEMENT

In the 2001 census, only 6.6 per cent of all Ecuadorians identified themselves as Indians. Including those who declared that they or their parents spoke indigenous languages, the proportion rises to 14.3 per cent, which is the best available approximation of the size of the indigenous population. The Quichuas of the Sierra account for about three-quarters of that population, with most of the rest distributed among smaller groups in the Amazon. Throughout Ecuador, the basic unit of Indian settlement is the community, which, despite variations, presents generic characteristics that will be discussed later.

The process of Indian organization was a classic example of bottomup networking based on local and regional associations of communities. In the Amazon, it came in response to the arrival of peasant colonists, oil companies, and state agencies. In the Sierra, the stimulus was the fight for the land, which peaked with the military's agrarian reform of the 1970s. With the return to democracy, the indigenous organizations continued to work for development and the defence of their culture and lands, coming together under umbrella federations in the Sierra and the Amazon and eventually under CONAIE, the Confederation of Indian Nationalities, in 1986.

Since its inception, CONAIE has combined livelihood goals and citizenship aspirations. The former have focused on economic improvements, education, health, and the protection of Indian lands; the latter on the redefinition of Ecuador as a plurinational state, the end of discrimination, territorial autonomy, representation in state institutions, control over education and development programmes, and official recognition and funding for the indigenous organizations.

CONAIE's first achievement came in 1988, when it negotiated with President Rodrigo Borja (the creation of a national programme of bilingual education, funded by the state and run by indigenous personnel connected with the Indian organizations. But the presentation of CONAIE's contentious credentials was the 1990 levantamiento (uprising), a huge mobilization that vented the frustrations of a rural population that had been severely punished by the adjustment policies and the long recession of the 1980s.

The uprising was a peaceful civic strike in which tens of thousands of highland Indians blocked highways and marched into cities to seize public offices. The protest continued for several days, until the government agreed to discuss the demands. There were measures to alleviate the situation in the rural areas and settle some pending land conflicts, but an issue that remained unsolved was the status of the ancestral lands in the lowlands. Two years later, CONAIE sponsored a large march from the Amazon. Once again, President Borja was forced to negotiate with the Indians, who stayed put in the capital until he agreed to demarcate and title their lands.

The Sierra uprising and the Amazon march revealed the depth of the Indians' discontent and opened the eyes of all Ecuadorians to their return as actors who could exert influence in national politics. The uprising, in particular, was a real shake-up. As a rural protest on a national scale, it had no precedent in the country's history. In most respects, it was a feat of collective creativity, the spontaneous invention of a new form of contention that turned into a blueprint for the string of mobilizations that would follow in the 1990s.

The Indian-Peasant Front

The 1992 election gave the presidency to Sixto Duran, a conservative independent candidate. His economic plan focused on deregulating trade and capital flows, reducing social spending, eliminating subsidies, and privatizing state enterprises and social security. But Durán lacked reliable support in the legislature, and his privatization initiative was also opposed by the military, which saw the state enterprises as an important legacy of the military regime. In addition, Durán encountered resistance in civil society. The main challenges came from the Indian movement, which, buoyed by its initial successes, was displacing the labour federations as the beacon of popular opposition.

The first confrontation took place in 1993, over the plan to cut the social security budget and liquidate the health service for rural areas. CONAIE and other peasant organizations supported the strike of the social security employees and a massive protest of the beneficiaries of the rural health service. After two days of blockades and demonstrations, Durán was compelled to restore the budget and reaffirm the continuity of the health service.

The success of this struggle proved that well-organized protests could thwart an antipopular policy. In addition, it was an important precedent of collaboration between the Indian movement, other peasant organizations, and the unions from the public sector.

Next came the battle over the government's Law of Agrarian Modernization. The bill sought to abolish the legal basis for land expropriation, concentrate state support on capitalist agriculture, eliminate communal property, and privatize irrigation water. CONAIE sponsored the formation of the Coordinadora Agraria Nacional (CAN), a coalition that included smaller

Indian and peasant organizations, such as FEINE (Indigenous Evangelical Federation) and FENOCIN (Federation of Peasant and Indigenous Organizations, influenced by the Socialist Party). CAN proposed its own bill and staged public debates on the issue.

In June 1994, the Coordinadora Agraria called an uprising that, once again, paralyzed the country for several days. Eventually, President Durán was forced to negotiate the bill. In its final version, the law defined peasant agriculture as deserving full state support, reaffirmed that water was a public resource, and recognized the legality of communal and cooperative forms of ownership.

The Popular Front

By 1995, CONAIE and its allies had participated in the formation of the Coordinadora de Movimientos Sociales, a broad coalition that included Indian and peasant organizations, unions from the public sector, and a large number of neighbourhood associations, feminist groups, and human rights activists.

Meanwhile, President Duran had called for a referendum that proposed constitutional reforms to strengthen the executive, weaken the unions, and allow the privatization of the state enterprises and social security.

While the business sector generously financed the "yes" advertising campaign, the Coordinadora de Movimientos Sociales and the labour federations mounted an intense grassroots effort to bring out the "no" vote. On the day of the referendum, the voters rejected all the reforms. The defeat closed the books on Durán's initiatives, leaving in place an empowered popular coalition.

The success of the "no" campaign reinforced the position of the activists who had been calling for electoral participation. In its December 1995 assembly, CONAIE launched a political party that was intended to be based on the Indian movement and its allies. The Pachakutik Movement of Plurinational Unity (Pachakutik means "time of resurgence" in Quichua) entered the scene in the elections of 1996, in alliance with an independent group led by television commentator Freddy Ehlers. Ehlers did not qualify for the second presidential round, but Pachakutik won 10 per cent of the congressional seats and significant representation in provincial legislatures, local councils, and mayoralties.

The victory of Abdalá Bucaram in the 1996 election opened a period of enhanced turbulence in Ecuador. This clownish politician led the Roldocista Party, a populist force with its main base of support in the suburbs of Guayaquil. As mayor of that city, Bucaram had earned a reputation for corruption, but he had also extended his clientelist networks. During the campaign he attacked "the oligarchy" and Durán's aborted reforms.

As president, however, he focused on dividing the Indian movement, creating a Ministry of Indigenous Affairs and trying to buy the support of some Indian leaders. At the same time, Bucaram stuffed the government with relatives and friends, and it soon became evident that the country was sinking to new depths of corruption. Bucaram's discourse had also changed. Now he spoke about promarket reforms, trying to ingratiate himself with the International Monetary Fund and inviting Domingo Cavallo, the architect of Argentina's neo-liberal programme, to be the consultant for his economic plan.

Bucaram announced that plan at the beginning of 1997, when the labour unions and CONAIE were preparing a rally opposing neo-liberal policies, corruption, and the Ministry of Indigenous Affairs. The measures included stiff budget cuts, higher electricity and gas rates, labour reforms, and a timetable to tie the currency to the dollar. The rally turned into a mobilization for the president's removal, and was supported by the main political parties.

As Quito swarmed with Indian demonstrators, Congress removed Bucaram on grounds of mental incompetence and named its speaker, Fabian Alarcón, as acting president. In the process, CONAIE and the other organizations extracted the promise that an assembly would be convened to reform the constitution. The 1997 elections for that assembly gave Pachakutik 10 per cent of the seats. Its delegates pushed through several reforms, including sections that defined Ecuador as a multicultural state and recognized social, cultural, and political rights for the indigenous peoples.

The next presidential election was won by Jamil Mahuad, from the Christian Democratic Party. The new president faced strong pressure from the IMF, which was vexed by the stagnation of Ecuador's reforms. At the same time, he confronted a popular coalition that rejected those reforms and had proven its oppositional power. To top it off, the economy sank into its worst recession since the 1930s.

The economic collapse of 1998-99 was triggered by the fall of oil prices and the devastation of the coast by the climatic phenomenon of El Niño. When the banana and shrimp exporters stopped repaying their loans, the banks plunged into crisis and, despite Mahuad's billion-dollar bailout programme, the financial system collapsed. A massive flight of capital ensued, the gross domestic product shrank by 7.1 per cent, and it became obvious that the country would not be able to pay its external debt.

Mahuad devalued the currency, froze bank accounts, and focused on securing the support of the Social Christian Party, traditional advocate of the coastal exporters and banks. But the IMF's conditions for a stabilization loan were tough: eliminate all subsidies, privatize public enterprises, raise taxes on income and rent, and refrain from saving the banks. Mahuad's situation became untenable. On the one hand, the popular opposition fought back against the cuts and privatization. In 1998 and 1999, Mahuad had to deal with three large mobilizations in which the popular front led by CONAIE broadened to include middle-class sectors, such as truckers, bus operators, and small and medium-sized entrepreneurs. On the other hand, the IMF's insistence on tax reform and forsaking the banks alienated the business sectors. When the Social

Christian Party pulled out of the negotiations, it became clear that Mahuad's presidency would not last long.

In the last days of 1999, Mahuad announced a plan to dollarize the economy and implement the IMF measures. Assisted by soldiers, Indian crowds flocked to Quito demanding his dismissal and occupying Congress and the Supreme Court.

On January 21, 2000, indigenous activists and young military officers cheered in Congress as Colonel Lucio Gutiérrez and CONAIE's president, Antonio Vargas, proclaimed a "government of national salvation." After frantic consultations among generals, politicians, and U.S. diplomats, however, the armed forces announced that they were restoring constitutional order by installing Vice President Gustavo Noboa as the new president.

Gutiérrez and the other officers involved in the coup were arrested, and the Indian leaders were forced to order the protestors to retreat.3 In the ensuing months, the detainees were granted amnesty and discharged from the army. While dollarization was maintained, the IMF negotiations were eventually abandoned without an agreement.

Much speculation has been offered about who manipulated whom in the military-Indian coup. In some versions, the conspirators appear as victims of a plot to get rid of a weakened president and proceed with dollarization. But the truth is that the colonels had been pressing their superiors for decisive action against Mahuad and that their contacts with the Indian leaders intensified after the Parlamento Popular, an assembly in which more that three hundred delegates of CONAIE and other groups called for Mahuad's removal and the formation of a popular government.

Thus it is unquestionable that the coup's organizers were acting on their own initiative. Their inability to hold on to power, however, proved that the whole enterprise had been utterly misguided.

Disillusionment and Demobilization

In preparation for the 2002 elections, Colonel Gutiérrez founded the Patriotic Society Party, PSP, which put forward his candidacy for president. After failed attempts to forge a centre-left coalition, CONAIE and Pachakutik decided to form an alliance with the PSP. Benefiting from the Indian vote and a fragmented field of 11 candidates, Gutiérrez won the first round with 20.4 per cent of the total. In the second round he defeated banana tycoon Alvaro Noboa, an independent conservative, by 9.6 per cent. Like previous presidents, Gutiérrez lacked majority support in Congress, where the PSP-Pachakutik alliance had won only 17 of the 100 seats.

After the coup, Gutiérrez had cultivated the image of a progressive populist. As the elections approached, however, he toned down his discourse and included business leaders among his advisers. He visited Washington to meet with IMF and U.S. officials and, immediately after his election, started to talk about austerity measures. The new attitude was reflected by the make-up of his cabinet. Although Gutiérrez appointed some Pachakutik ministers, the posts responsible for economic policy were assigned to the advisers who had been functioning as links with the business sectors and the IMF.

Gutierrez's priority task was a deal with the IMF, which wanted the fiscal deficit elminated. Knowing that an agreement would open the door to loans for social investment and development, Pachakutik's cabinet ministers went along with the austerity measures, doing their best to moderate them. The result was a salary freeze in the public sector and higher prices for fuel, transportation, and electricity. Many activists saw this as a betrayal. The Indian federation of the Sierra, Ecuarunari, demanded the resignation of the responsible ministers. CONAIE echoed Ecuarunari's reproofs, calling for a rectification of the government's economic policies.

By mid-2003, disagreements over several issues, including the government's handling of strikes by teachers and oil workers, had aggravated the tensions in the coalition. Gutierrez's intense proselytizing in rural areas irritated the indigenous activists, who decried it as a scheme to bypass CONAIE and form clientelist networks. While the cabinet was torn by mutual accusations, the "allies" maneuvered in opposite directions in Congress, where Pachakutik tried to form a centre-left block and the PSP courted the Social Christian Party. The alliance collapsed in August 2003, when Pachakutik refused to support a bill that modified labour contracts in the public sector and Gutiérrez dismissed its ministers.

With the end of the alliance, CONAIE's internal divisions rose to the surface. Amazon groups criticized the leaders for leaving the government, and radical sectors of the Sierra reproached their delay in breaking with Gutiérrez. Meanwhile, Gutiérrez went on the offensive to weaken CONAIE further, issuing a decree that allowed him unilaterally to appoint the personnel of the state agencies that dealt with indigenous issues. This ended the practice by which the officials were nominated by CONAIE and ratified by the president. The next step was the replacement of the agencies' staff with activists who had signed up with the PSP and leaders from FEINE and FENOCIN.

By the end of his first year in office, Gutiérrez was facing accusations of nepotism and corruption. He had not succeeded in winning support from the Social Christian Party (Notisur 2003d). CONAIE proposed a rally to demand his dismissal, but the Amazon groups opposed it, and the other organizations ignored the call. FEINE had chosen to back Gutiérrez in exchange for programmes for the Protestant indigenous communities, and some of CONAIE's own groups, particularly in the Amazon, were involved in similar dealings. Despite the warning signs, CONAIE staged a protest in February 2004. The Indian federation of the Amazon and the other organizations refused to participate; the grassroots response was decidedly weak; and by the end of the first day, the mobilization was called off. Four months later, CONAIE organized another protest. The outcome was the same, aggravated by the Amazon groups' public support of Gutiérrez, who had just appointed his former fellow coup leader, Antonio Vargas, minister of social welfare. Vargas, himself a Quichua from the Amazon, had left CONAIE in 2002, eventually joining FEINE and becoming a staunch supporter of Gutiérrez.

The failure of the 2004 protests exposed CONAIE's crisis. But Gutierrez's success in neutralizing the movement did not solve his problems in Congress. In November he barely survived an impeachment vote amid charges that he had bribed legislators and had secured the Roldocistas' support by promising the return of their exiled leader, Bucaram. Then Gutiérrez dismissed 27 of the 31 Supreme Court justices, installing docile judges who overturned Bucaram's corruption convictions. On April 15, 2005, after three months of constitutional upheaval, Gutiérrez declared a state of emergency and ordered the police to repress protesters in Quito. The move backfired when the radio stations opened their microphones to an outpouring of indignation against his attempts to assume dictatorial powers. Following a week of demonstrations, the military withdrew its support, Gutiérrez abandoned the presidential palace, and Congress replaced him with Vice President Alfredo Palacio.

Once again, an Ecuadorian president had been ousted on the crest of street protests. This time, however, the main protagonists had been the urban crowds of Quito. CONAIE's leaders were slow in deciding to join in the protests, and when they finally did, their calls brought few Indians to the capital. Ironically, the fall of Gutiérrez offered further evidence of the prostration of the indigenous movement.

The Indian Movement and Democracy

This section elucidates the implications of the Indian struggles from the point of view df democracy. First, it looks at participation as a source of power for the Indian movement. Next, it assesses the consequences, through separate enquiries into the politics of influence and the politics of power. The last part examines the various impacts on Ecuador's democratic institutions.

The Secret of the Indians' Power

The Indian movement became a significant force because it was able to compel governments to pay heed to its demands. It was a classicexpression of the power that grows out of the effective use of disruption. To determine the sources of that power would entail exploring many factors, including the geopolitical assets of the Indian groups (strategic location in places where they could block the main national highways), the functional capabilities of their activists and organizations, and the financial and logistical assistance of external allies, such as progressive sectors of the Catholic Church and a variety of domestic and foreign NGOs. Some of these elements were addressed in a previous study; therefore the focus here is on what can be considered the main source of the effectiveness of the mobilizations: at the grassroots level, people were willing and ready to participate in them.

Throughout Ecuador, the decisions to respond to CONAIE's mobilization calls were taken by the Indian communities. Legally recognized as rural neighbourhood associations, these communities have roots that go back to the colonial system of resguardos, or reservations. Their revitalization was boosted by the land struggles of the 1960s and 1970s, which, insofar as they involved appeals to primordial loyalties of extended kinship and reciprocity, reinforced the old community as the natural framework for these relationships. At the same time, the agrarian reforms diluted the landowners' power, creating spaces in which the communities, by taking up the representation of the Indian peasants, gained prominence as relevant actors in local and regional politics.

Today, Ecuador has about 2,100 Indian communities, functioning as self-regulated entities based on the authority of their asambleas (in which everybody participates) and cabildos (executive committees of five members). All important issues are discussed in the asambleas, where agreement is usually reached by consensus rather than by voting. The decisions are binding for all members, with formal and informal mechanisms to ensure compliance. Thus, joining in a mobilization is always the result of a decision of the community, which exerts its influence to make sure that the members join in the roadblocks and rallies.

The secret of CONAIE's power, then, lies in its ability to harness the resources for collective action that exist in the Indian communities. Pierre Bourdieu's concept of social capital helps elucidate this process. Bourdieu sees social capital as the aggregate of resources linked to the possession of a network of relationships of mutual acquaintance or recognition. Members of a group that, like the Indian community, is based on reciprocity and solidarity can claim access to the resources of their peers by virtue of belonging to the group. But the group as such can also use the resources embedded in the network. Indeed, the accumulation and use of social capital are always guided by contextual norms and institutions. This is particularly visible in communal groups, whose formal and informal rules define the available resources, the ways they can be claimed, and the sanctions that enforce delivery. The rules circumscribe and aggregate social capital, ensuring that its use is restricted to members and taking advantage of the effect of concentration to maximize benefits. In such circumstances, social capital is an asset that belongs to the group, which can institute itself as collective beneficiary in activities that benefit the group as a whole.

In practical terms, this means that a community that joins a mobilization is making a claim on its social capital, and that the members' readiness to participate is a resource that they owe to the community. As Alejandro Portes has shown, different motives may be at play when members contribute resources, including feelings of obligation (internalized norms), expectations of future repayment (norm of reciprocity), identification with the group (bounded solidarity), and fear of sanctions (enforceable trust). The same motives can explain the behaviour of each individual community within the networks of communities that make up the Indian movement. The general point is that the Ecuadorian Indian movement operates as a network of networks, whose activities can be analysed as a process of accumulation, concentration, and deployment of the social capital embedded in its grassroots community structures. By bringing that social capital to bear on the political system, CONAIE has been effecting its conversion into political capital; that is, into leverage that can be used to wrest concessions from governments or to compete for direct access to power.

The Politics of Influence

In the politics of influence, social movements seek changes in public policy decisions. We are interested, then, in these questions: On which issues did the Indian movement try to influence government policy? What was at stake in those issues? and How effective were the mobilizations in achieving their goals? Here, we should keep in mind that the issues changed with the evolution of the struggles. Initially, when the Indians were fighting alone, they focused on their own demands. Later on, CONAIE's coalition-building initiatives broadened the confrontation, incorporating issues that were relevant to the other rural groups and, eventually, to the popular sectors at large.

Through the issues we can discern the stakes. The Indians' demands focused on achieving the status of recognized ethnic groups with terri- torial rights and some degree of autonomy. This challenged the existing notions of nationhood and citizenship; the former by defying the assumption that white-mestizo identity was the foundation of Ecuadorian identity, and the latter by questioning the liberal axiom that citizen rights could only be individual, not collective rights. The Indian claims, then, sought changes in the existing conditions. By contrast, the struggles over agrarian and national economic policy matters were attempts to resist changes. The fights over the Seguro Campesino and the Agrarian Modernization Law focused on thwarting initiatives that would have worsened the situation of the rural population. Similarly, the national protests against neo-liberalism were defensive responses to attempts to unload the burdens of reform onto the shoulders of the popular sectors. The stakes, then, had to do with the distribution of the costs of adjusting the economy to the new conditions of global capitalist development.

Did the struggles achieve their goals? We may start with the opposition to the neo-liberal agenda, the results of which are trickier to appraise. Studies have shown that Ecuador ranks among the least effective reformers in Latin America. Clearly, the popular struggles played a role in this outcome, but their influence cannot be disentangled from the effects of the lack of political support and the hostility of the business sector to some reforms. Besides, we should not forget that neo-liberalism was never really defeated in Ecuador, as its setbacks were always followed by renewed attempts to enact its reforms. We can conclude, then, that in this area the struggles had limited success. Interacting with other factors, they delayed the reforms and, in some cases, mitigated their impact on the popular sectors; but they were unable decisively to vanquish the neo-liberal agenda.

On the rural-agrarian front, CONAIE and its peasant allies were much more effective. After soundly defeating the attempt to scrap the rural health service, they succeeded in influencing the new agrarian legislation to keep water in the public domain, secure the status of communal property, and restore the state's support to the peasant economy. Eventually, the 1998 constitutional reform enshrined all these attainments in the Ecuadorian charter.

Concerning Indian ethnic demands, the initial fights established CONAIE's contentious credentials and led to significant gains on the land rights front, particularly in the Amazon. Later, the confrontations over broader national policy issues became an effective means for attaining the particularistic goals of the Indian movement. In the give and take after the fall of Bucaram, for example, CONAIE won one of its most important achievements: the creation of CODENPE (Ecuadorian Council of Indian Nations and Peoples), the agency that now coordinates all support programmes for indigenous groups with participation of their own organizations. Further concessions were wrested from Mahuad in the battles of the late 1990s, including an investment fund for Indian areas, the legalization of traditional medicine, and budget increases for the state's indigenous agencies. On the whole, the movement was able to accumulate an uneven but substantial record of success in influencing government policies. One upshot was that CONAIE could reinvest political capital earned through the mobilizations in other forms of action and more ambitious goals. On the one hand, its lobbying drives yielded significant gains without having to resort to protests, including the creation of PRODEPINE (Development Programme for Indian and Black Populations, initiated in 1997 with World Bank funding), the establishment of a health programme for Indian communities, and the launching of CODENPE projects of infrastructural works, water and irrigation, soil improvement, rural housing, and organizational capacity building. On the other hand, the Indian movement took steps to establish itself as a contender in the struggle for political power.

The Politics of Power

In the politics of power, agents participate in contests to occupy the positions that control and direct public policymaking. The three main manifestations of the Indian movement's struggles for power were the fight for control over the state's agencies of indigenous affairs, Pachakutik' engagement in electoral politics, and CONAIE's involvement in the coup against Jamil Mahuad.

For the Indian movement, the agencies in charge of bilingual education and indigenous health; the council of indigenous peoples, CODENPE; the development programme PRODEPINE; and the indigenous investment fund constituted a first major arena of power contestation. Steered by the movement, the agencies of indigenous affairs could serve as a means to attain objectives while fulfilling the programmatic ambition of exercising autonomy. Controlled by governments, they could be turned into tools of clientelistic domination. In the heat of the struggles, CONAIE wrested from the government an informal deal whereby the officials were appointed on the basis of its nominations. Later, however, President Gutierrez's actions showed that, in a less favorable climate, CONAIE's grip could be easily broken. The situation was complicated by the rivalry among indigenous-peasant organizations. Under the initial arrangement, CONAIE monopolized the representation of the Indians; this had always been resented by smaller groups like FEINE and FENOCIN. Thus, Gutierrez's repeal of CONAIE's privileges was more than a step to exclude it from the agencies' resources. It was also a gambit aimed at luring the other organizations into a network of patronage and using their example to entice CONAIE's local and regional chapters onto the clientelistic bandwagon.

The second front in the struggle for power was electoral competition. Pachakutik was launched in 1996 as a party based on CONAIE and its closest allies. In practice, however, it has been the political arm of the Indian movement, which provides most of its candidates for office. The best indicator of Pachakutik's overall strength are the congressional elections, in which its candidates have won, on average, 7.5 per cent of the seats. While this falls short of the estimated size of the indigenous population, it can still be seen as a fair result for a new party. Moreover, the 2002 presidential election proved that Pachakutik's vote can be decisive, since Gutiérrez qualified for the second round by a margin of less than 5 per cent. But it is at local and regional levels where Pachakutik's results have been especially significant. In the 2000 elections it won 4 governorships, 17 mayorships, and substantial representation in the provincial, municipal, and parish councils of the Highlands and the Amazon. The party's performance was similar in 2004, with 3 governors and 20 majors elected. Thus, while Pachakutik has not yet fulfilled its potential, it is clear that it is serving as a vehicle for self-government in the main indigenous areas.

We do not have enough studies to draw a panoptic picture of Pachakutik's performance at the different levels of government. One area in which the outcome can be readily recognized is the country's charter. In the 1997 constitutional assembly, Pachakutik negotiated important provisions, including the definition of Ecuador as a multicultural state, the designation of the indigenous groups as peoples, and the recognition of their rights to preserve their culture and their forms of political organization and administration of justice. Together with other clauses about the creation of indigenous territorial entities, these rights offer a framework for some degree of autonomy. But implementation depends on further legislation by Congress, where Pachakutik's moves have been conditioned by its minority status and its role as an opposition party focused on undercutting initiatives coming from the executive.

In contrast to its adversarial role in Congress, Pachakutik's gains in local elections created real opportunities for exercising power. The initial research on these experiences has focused on counties with dense Indian populations or visibility as touristic or artisanal centers, including Guamote, Otavalo, Cotacachi, Saquisili, and Bolívar. The studies cast light on innovative efforts to encourage grassroots participation, establish practices that are free of corruption and clientelism, foster fairness in the distribution of resources, and promote multiculturalism by adapting traditional indigenous institutions. But they also show that the progress has been uneven and that, in some cases, Pachakutik's local authorities have been disappointing.

The third and by far the most dramatic incursion of the Indian movement into the politics of power was the January 2000 coup against Mahuad. In that episode, CONAIE conspired with military officers to overthrow the government and assume the powers of the state.

One way of coming to terms with the outcome is to look into the reasons for the coup's failure. In retrospective accounts, the Indian leaders have mentioned the generals' betrayal, the machinations of the elites and the U.S. embassy, the hostility of the press, the lack of popular response in the cities, and their own unpreparedness to take power. From this, one can conclude that the coup failed because it was marked by improvisation and, ultimately, because it reflected a gross misreading of the political scene.

Another way of assessing the coup's significance is to consider its repercussions for the Indian movement itself. The evidence indicates that there was public support for the removal of Mahuad but not for a military-Indian takeover. In the polls taken on the day of the coup, only 6 per cent believed that Mahuad could continue, 71 per cent approved the protests, and 79 per cent thought that Mahuad had to be replaced without breaking the constitutional order.

Two days later, the polls showed that 80 per cent were pleased that democracy had been maintained, 77 per cent supported the investiture of Vice President Noboa, and only 13 per cent would have preferred to keep the military-Indian junta. The overall pattern is clear. While CONAIE fulfilled a well-regarded role in expressing public discontent, its attempt to take power by force was rejected. The payoff for the Indian movement was also ambivalent. At the time, its image as a powerful player may have been boosted and its undemocratic behaviour may have been glossed over amid the general complacency with Mahuad's removal. But in the long run, CONAIE's collusion with the colonels put it on track for further blunders whose consequences would be far more damaging.

Recapitulating, what can we make of the Indian movement's involvement in these diverse forms of the politics of power? As we saw in the conceptual section, it is not rare for a movement to launch a party and combine protest with electoral participation. The juxtaposition of CONAIE's struggles over the indigenous agencies and Pachakutik's electoral ventures, then, are an example of what a movement undergoing institutionalization typically does.

The coup, though, was a very different matter. If we were dealing with a revolutionary group, we might think about the use of force as part of the strategy of" combining all forms of struggle." But CONAIE and Pachakutik have never claimed to be revolutionary organizations.

We are left, then, with the sense that the coup was an anomalous deviation from the path that the movement had been following.

To account for it, one could make allowances for the magnitude of the crisis, the intensity of the public's outrage, and the leaders' rashness and lack of vision. What is difficult to fathom is why, to this day, the activists have not conducted a real evaluation of those events and their fallout.

In the absence of soul searching, the naive opportunism that transpired in the coup kept haunting the Indian movement. Indeed, the leaders' decision to support Gutiérrez in the 2002 elections can only be seen as an attempt to cash in on whatever political capital they believed they had gained from the January 2000 adventure. Gutiérrez won the election, but the quick unraveling of the alliance showed that the move had been another serious mistake. The Indian movement could not stop Gutiérrez's neo-liberal turn, Pachakutik was forced to leave the government, and CONAIE was weakened by divisions. But the worst damage came from the disappointment at the grassroots, where Pachakutik's presence in the government had been hailed as an opportunity to access the resources that had been always denied to the Indians. Combined with the effects of Gutierrez's clientelist strategy, the loss of trust at base level became a major factor in the failure of CONAIE's latest mobilizations.

Impact on Democracy as a Political Regime

This assessment of the Indian movement's impact on the regime is grounded on elaborations of four ways that civil associations may impinge on democratic institutions.

The first of these is interest representation. In democratic regimes, political parties are the prescribed medium for representing citizen interests. Very often, however, party systems cannot express the diversity that exists in society. Civil associations can compensate for this deficit by conveying the interests of specific sectors to the political system. The Ecuadorian Indian movement exemplifies this function.

It gave voice to excluded groups, projected their concerns into the public agenda, and opened new areas for policymaking. Furthermore, its strategy of alliances was instrumental in aggregating and expressing the demands of all the rural groups and, eventually, the popular sectors at large.

To this we can add the creation of a party that incor-porated marginalized interests into the system and spurred indigenous participation in elections.

Interest representation by civil associations can help fulfill three principles of democratic governance: responsiveness (serving all sectors), consensus orientation (mediating among different interests), and equity (treating everyone equally). Realizing this potential, however, does not depend on the civil groups alone.

It also depends on the institutional actors' willingness to consider their views and adhere to democratic principles. In Ecuador, incumbent governments had many opportunities to hear what the indigenous and popular sectors wanted and to fulfill their side of the democratic governance bargain.

But those governments chose to ignore the input that came from below. Insisting on the imposition of unpopular reforms, they wasted the opportunities for building the kind of consensus that would have strengthened democratic governance.

This calls attention to a second function of civil associations: the control of state power. Liberal formulations emphasize the notion that citizens should protect themselves from state intrusion in private affairs and from violations of civil and political rights. Broader interpretations, however, include additional issues related to transparency and accountability. Once again, we find a connection with the principles of democratic governance, since the contribution of civil associations consists in holding governments responsible for fulfilling those principles.

In Ecuador, the popular opposition to neo-liberal governments repudiated the governments' insensitivity to the concerns of the majority, unwillingness to compromise, and unilateral commitment to the priorities of the business elites and the IMF. Thus, in the process of defending the interests of the popular sectors, the Indian movement and its allies were also fulfilling the watchdog role of trying to counterbalance what was widely seen as an unfair use of authority.

The foregoing interpretation leads to a third function: legitimation. In democratic polities, governments are acutely dependent on legitimacy because it is the people's support that justifies the right to exercise authority. Citizen groups can reaffirm legitimacy in two ways: explicitly, through actions that convey support; or tacitly, by doing nothing that might be construed as opposition.

The denial of support, however, must take the form of explicit oppositional action if it is to be understood as such. It is also worth noting that, in democracies, legitimation is rarely an all-or-nothing matter. The reason is that civil associations can legitimate or delegitimate authority at different levels.

Opposition to a policy does not necessarily imply disaffection with a government, and disaffection with a government does not necessarily entail rejection of the regime. Indeed, a common result of challenges at lower levels is the reinforcement of legitimacy at higher levels, as illustrated by cases in which a negotiated solution of a policy conflict boosts the image of a government, and situations in which the constitutional replacement of an unpopular government reaffirms the credibility of a democratic regime.

The legitimacy issue is particularly sensitive in the case of social movements because their motives are oppositional and their activities assume non-institutional forms. Still, taking into account the nuances of legitimation, there is much room for their fulfillment of this function.

The Ecuadorian Indian movement was certainly shoring up the political institutions when it created a party and urged its base to go to the polls. Beyond that, the routine challenges of the movement focused on policy matters that did not question the legitimacy of the governments or the regime as such. Through a different route we return to the point that, if the Ecuadorian governments had been more open to negotiation, the results could have enhanced their standing. Instead, their inflexibility became a factor in the escalation of conflict that led to their delegitimation. It was against this background that the Indian movement played an active role in the demise of two presidents. In the fall of Bucaram, the legitimacy of the regime was not at stake. The ousting of Mahuad was different because it involved a conspiracy to usurp power, which, had it succeeded, would have implied the breakdown of democracy. But the coup failed, and as a result, its actual impact on regime legitimacy is difficult to assess.

Intuitively, one would think that, by exposing the frailty of the institutions, the affair may have eroded their credibility. This inference, though, is not supported by the evidence. Over the last decade, the Latinobarómetro polls have shown a general softening of support for democracy, but the trend has been much less pronounced in Ecuador than in the rest of the Latin America.

Comparing the periods 1996-99 and 2000-2004 (before and after Ecuador's January 2000 coup), support for democracy declined by 12 per cent in the region as a whole but only by 6 per cent in Ecuador. One can speculate that, to some extent, Ecuadorians felt reassured that their democracy had survived the crisis.

Speculations aside, the movement's attempt to subvert the regime raises questions about a fourth function attributed to civil society: political socialization.

In one of the most prominent formulations of the "civil society argument," associations are presented as frameworks in which citizens acquire the values and dispositions that are needed for a workable democratic polity. This claim relies on two basic assumptions about political socialization: that it is a matter of the formation of individuals, and that its results can somehow "free-float" into the public sphere as a resource that can be readily harnessed for the benefit of democracy.

What these assumptions miss is the significance of the mediation of the group, which becomes a collective subject of its own socialization process, inculcates its particularistic norms along with the more general dispositions, and regulates the use of the resources that make up the network's social capital. In so doing, civil society groups invariably condition the impact their socialization may have on the political system.

Taking this into account, we can tackle what appears to be one of the most puzzling questions about the Ecuadorian Indian movement. This study has demonstrated that the movement's struggles have induced vast changes in the behaviour of the indigenous groups. Because those changes would not have been possible without processes of socialization, it is clear that the movement has been doing a massive job teaching people to work together, cultivating interest in policy issues, and providing knowledge and skills for participating in public activities, such as mobilizations and elections.

The seemingly puzzling question is how these contributions to political socialization, which, according to the celebrated claim, should be functional to democracy, square with the attempt to take power by force. The matter is less baffling if we keep in mind that movements do not socialize people to help the workings of democratic regimes; they do it to attain their goals. The real question, then, concerns the movement's lack of commitment to Ecuadorian democracy.

This lack of commitment can be traced to three sources. One is the conviction that Ecuador's democracy is a fraud. Time and again the Indian militants have decried what they view as a corrupt democracy, with institutions that are discriminatory and governments that benefit the elites at the expense of the common people. Another source is the disrespect of all the political players for the rules of democracy. Willy-nilly, the indigenous activists have "learned the ropes" of practical politics within a system of interactions in which the prevailing attitudes are not distinguished by reverence for constitutional conventions.

The third source is the tension between the principles that inspire the indigenous internal practices and the liberal notions of democracy. At one level, it is a matter of the contrast between direct and indirect democracy; the former embodied in the participation of all in communal decisionmaking, and the latter in the elected officials who decide for all citizens in the broader Ecuadorian polity. At another level, it is a contrast between two canons of representation. When the communities elect representatives to the associations, and when the associations elect representatives to the next-level federations, the elected persons function as delegates, whose powers are limited to specific mandates and whose authority can be revoked at will by those who elected them. In a liberal democracy, by contrast, elected officials operate as fiduciaries who use their discretion to interpret the interests of the represented and act on their behalf.

This raises the question of what the Indian movement's democratic ideals are, and whether these ideals and the standards of Ecuador's democracy are so incompatible as to justify the repudiation of the latter by the activists. In a political declaration approved in 1993, CONAIE called for a "plurinational communitarian democracy" based on equality, liberty, fraternity, and social peace. This goal would be achieved through a political reorganization aimed at guaranteeing the full participation of the Indian peoples and the other social sectors.

The platform adopted by the first congress of Pachakutik in 1999 was more specific, proposing a "radical democracy" based on a semiparliamentary system, decentralization, civil society representation in some state agencies, and direct participation through citizen initiatives, referenda, and recall of elected officials. These proposals could be easily integrated into an agenda to "deepen" the democratic character of existing institutions. The activists' lack of commitment, then, is not rooted in an unbridgeable programmatic rift.

Rather, it seems to result from a double ideological distortion: a view of Ecuadorian democracy that chooses to dwell on its deficiencies (ignoring that the conquest of indigenous rights and the Indian movement itself would hardly have been possible without it), and an exaggerated sense of the contradiction between the indigenous principles and those of the existing institutions.

This work has investigated the consequences of the Ecuadorian Indian movement for democracy. Its enquiry was based on conceptualizations that defined the specificity of movements as a form of civil society's political engagement and offered guidelines for studying their effects on the participatory and institutional dimensions of democracy. The analysis showed that the Indian movement had roots in communal mechanisms of direct democracy, that its multilayered structure had been built through bottom-up networking based on delegative representation, and that its protagonism in the contentious cycle of the 1990s marked a historic milestone for the involvement of the indigenous groups in Ecuador's public life.

The participatory breakthrough came on two fronts. Practicing the politics of influence, the movement forced new issues onto the public agenda, wrested concessions from governments, and led alliances that repeatedly hindered the imposition of neo-liberal reforms.

Engaging in the politics of power, it contested the control of the state's indigenous agencies and spawned a party that made strides in the electoral representation of the Indian groups, the procurement of their collective rights, and their progress towards self-government. These initiatives fulfilled important functions for Ecuador's democratic institutions. In the areas of interest representation and control of state power, the demands and protests provided ideas and contributions for improving the quality of democratic governance and imposed restraints on policies that were widely rejected by civil society. The launching of a new party was also significant as a development that upheld the legitimacy of the democratic regime.

It is unquestionable, then, that the Indian movement has made remarkable contributions to Ecuadorian democracy. Yet we have also seen that the swell of activism was not an unmitigated blessing for democratic politics. The critical drawback was the January 2000 attempt to subvert the constitutional order. At that point, CONAIE transgressed the threshold beyond which, in a democracy, an opposition becomes disloyal. The analysis here showed that the coup was inconsistent with the behavioural pattern of the Indian movement and that its negative impact was mitigated by its own failure and by the special conditions under which it happened. But the extenuating circumstances cannot absolve the movement of responsibility for threatening the democratic regime. Further scrutiny emphasized the reality that political socialization within the Indian movement had not fostered a sense of commitment to Ecuadorian democracy.

This evidence of contradictory consequences is consistent with the critique that the "civil society argument" plays up beneficial effects and ignores the possible downside. It also underscores that in Latin America, the study of the impact of civil associations on democracy cannot overlook three crucial points. The first is that the realization of the democratic potential of any civil society initiative depends on how the political institutions process it. Democratic governance is enhanced when decisionmakers take the concerns of civil associations into account. Conversely, democracy suffers when governments ignore citizen feedback, treat it perfunctorily, or demonstrate biases in their reactions to the bidding of different sectors.

The second point is that when civil associations mobilize broad support, the institutional responses to their functions of interest representation and control of state power can be highly consequential for regime legitimation. The legitimacy of democratic politics is strengthened when governments take notice of popular sentiment; but democratic regimes may fall into a tailspin of delegitimation when· the inputs from below are repeatedly rebuffed.

The third point is that it is a mistake to view civil society groups as neutral purveyors of citizens trained for democracy. Like other social capital resources, the results of political socialization remain embedded in the networks of interaction that produce them. As collective structures that constitute the primordial source of social capital, regulate its uses, and mediate between individuals and society, civil associations impart their particularistic slant to socialization and influence its fallout in the political system.

For Ecuador's indigenous activists, the stark contrast between the successes of the 1990s and the more recent frustrations underscores the urgency of rethinking their bearings.

To a large extent, their present predicament is a result of their own inability to respond to the complexities of the movement's institutionalization process. Two tasks in particular were sorely neglected. One was in the area of strategic development. To maintain coherence in situations of partial institutionalization, social movements must define a roadmap for combining protest with the use of prescribed means, and they must do it in such a manner that the two forms of action reinforce rather than interfere with each other.

The other neglected task was ideological elaboration. In the politics of influence, social movements can afford to condemn unstintingly the poverty of democracy. But in a democratic system, whatever its shortcomings, a movement that acts in the name of democracy cannot make the transition to the politics of power without taking a more constructive stance towards the existing institutions.

Essentially, it is a matter of reframing the movement's ideology by shifting the emphasis from antisystem representations to imageries of democratic renovation from within. In Ecuador, the lack of strategic guidelines and the shortsighted attitude towards the democratic institutions jumbled the responsibilities of CONAIE and Pachakutik, muddled their priorities, and paved the way for the missteps that weakened the Indian movement.

It may be a commonplace to say that a crisis can be turned into an opportunity, but that is precisely the challenge that the Ecuadorian indigenous activists face today. Whether or not they succeed will depend on their willingness to recognize that the time for reckoning and self-criticism is long overdue.

6

A New Direction for Journalism

It is foolish, I believe, to reject the idea of a new direction for journalism. Some, like Merrill, fear that new direction will eliminate what tradition sees as the proper role of journalism, to be a fourth branch of government, a watchdog, to keep its eye on those who really wield power--the government, those who make law and those who enforce law; the corporations, the churches--and without fear or favour to report what they see. Objectivity simply does not exist.

Even if it did exist, it would be wrong because objectivity always works on behalf of the status quo. It is true that the typical American journalist perceives this to be his highest calling: To get the facts and to lay out the facts for the reader, who may or may not act on those facts, as he or she sees fit. But objectivity is a mechanism for ensuring the status quo. It is an instrument to guarantee the preservation of institutions and the social order. It permits criticism of individuals but not of the fundamental system, political, economic, or social.

The state of impartiality is, in fact, defensive of the system. That in this model the press retains the potential to challenge the social order is the element that poses a threat to those who exercise power. Inasmuch as the press fails to live up to its potential, it is carrying out the political role that is desired of it by those in power. To the extent that the press endorses the idea that it is above politics it is serving the needs of power.

Isn't it the business of journalism to help the public understand? High up there among the reasons why I have been so murderously disappointed in today's press is, if you'll pardon the expression, its know-it-all-ness. The First Amendment was not written for the benefit of the press. It was written for the benefit of the people. Under the First Amendment, everybody has the right to be heard. It isn't only for people with the resources to own the newspapers and the broadcasting stations and the fibre-optic bitstreams.

Why are the media so unpopular? They always come in at the bottom in public opinion polls along with the politicians. I don't know all the reasons, but one of them, I'm sure, is their arrogance, their assumption outlined every day in the newspaper columns as well as on the Sunday TV shows where Sam Donaldson and George Will let us know every week how clever they are and how stupid we are.

When I was a journalist in my arrogant mode, I used to think down, too. In Washington, we always used to report movement: Who was up? Who was down? That's what the dumbbells wanted, we told each other. They didn't want to hear about issues, certainly not the complicated ones.... Well, don't let me go too far. We did do the complicated stories; we did try to report what the Hutchins Commission recommended, that is, the truth behind the facts. Some newspapers still do. Some TV reporters still do. But they are all losing ground--to tabloid papers and tabloid television. Or to USA Today and its many clones. Short and very spicy.

The Voice of Money

One of the ideas behind what we cheerfully speak of as the freest press in the world is that it gives voice to those among us who are the hardest to hear. Of course, I am talking about the poor, the homeless, the Black, the gay, the Native American.

Mainstream journalists need to listen to them, too. I think the Finnish Television Network did the right thing when its reporters went out into the community and asked ordinary people what they wanted to know more about. When they learned what it was, they went out and produced documentaries giving everybody a chance to be heard.

Unfortunately, it has dropped the programme. Even in Finland, I guess, it's very difficult to challenge the bottom line. But why not here? What have we got to lose, except--aha!--Money? It wins every time.

Giving up is not the answer. Money is for the most part indifferent to content. Audiences will likely be stimulated to pay attention to substantive news when they have participated in defining what it is. Definition is the key. Reporters can and should be devoting time to finding out what matters to audiences and then laying out the story for them with suggested solutions. This is what participatory journalism is all about. News is no longer defined in terms of the journalist's amorphous news judgment.

Permit me to raise yet another counter-cultural idea (I am using that phrase here to refer to something that runs counter to the standard culture of journalism). Is it in keeping with the idea of democracy for us to invoke the First Amendment just to avoid engaging a tough problem? Journalists could, with profit, devote more time to making our world a better place to live in than to roll eyeballs, scramble for high salaries, and insist rigidly on our rights under the First Amendment. Whatever we write or broadcast has consequences. Don't we have to pay attention to those consequences? We also have responsibilities, don't we?

Let me get into what I believe community journalism demands of journalists, certainly of reporters and editors; I hope we can include publishers and owners, but this means they must lower their financial expectations. Community journalism demands putting the public interest ahead of the maximization of profit. Think about that. But working stiffs, no matter how high, can't force this formula on the people or the corporations that pay their salaries. That's a weakness in community journalism.

Utopians hope that weakness will go away. In my new mood of guarded optimism (I love that phrase), I would like to try to persuade the bosses that by bringing the people into the process of journalism, they can continue to produce earnings while serving the needs of the people.

It isn't enough. The community journalist goes beyond the facts. Beyond them. I have come to respect the research and analytical insights of the English sociologist, John Burton, who wrote that if we are to have a stable society--and that means for the journalist, his or her boss, and all the people who live in the community--then everybody, all the people, all the social units, must have equal access to the community's resources and the skills they need if they are going to act within the rules of society. Those denied this kind of access, Burton said, will turn to "alienation behaviour". And that means going outside the norms of society to a life of what we, who have that access, call crime.

There is a special role for community journalists here, maybe the most important of all. They could become a third party to conflict. It's an idea that appeals to me, an idea that makes people in the media real mediators.

LET THE MEDIA PEOPLE MEDIATE

Best of all, however, the community journalist can and should bring the two sides together. Let the media people mediate. Most problems can be solved, or at least alleviated. Here is the classical third-party role. Study the background. Recognize that you can provide the data that shows the antagonists don't have to play the zero-sum game, where one wins and the other loses. The mediator finds the places where the antagonists are in agreement, no matter how small the area.

After all, most of us believe in our personal survival. And most of us believe in the survival of the community. That's a start. It may not be the journalist's job to bring the two sides together, but ask yourself: Who else is going to do it? You can be the *link* that facilitates communication and decision making by the actors. The journalist is not the one who comes up with a solution, but certainly a solution is what is meant to be the end product of the process.

This role is an extension of the First Amendment. It speaks not of our rights but of our responsibilities. It is the positive side of freedom. Why not be responsible to the community and for helping it solve its problems? There are risks. Very serious risks. That arrogance I have been talking about is one. We don't need journalists in the pulpit, but they can help the people in the pulpit, and that's no mean role to play. To carry this fearsome burden, reporters must be what they should be under any circumstances, well educated and learned in analysis. Here journalism really plays a part in what matters most and becomes a true fourth branch of government.

Journalistic objectivity and detachment may have been fine once upon a time, but that doesn't bring communities together. It may even drive them further apart. The apathy of the public is well known.

It is going to grow deeper and deeper if the public continues to see itself as separate and disconnected, uncared for and uncaring. People need to care if they are going to tune in to and read the news. An active community journalism has a chance to reverse that course.

When the United Nations *Human Development Report 1998* appeared, it revealed a somewhat damning picture of the UK as one of the most impoverished nations of the developed world: the UK was ranked fifteenth out of the seventeen countries included in the poverty index used by the report. In the UK one in seven of the population was below the poverty line, and the country contained about 30 per cent of Europe's children in poverty.

This was not the image conjured by the sparkling glitter of new Labour's 'cool Britannia', its millennium dome ascending symbolically skyward from reclaimed London mudflats, and consumer spending running riot on digital television sets in the homes of a population who were now all middle class.

Something was amiss, and as ever it was in the working and reworking of popular cultural narratives provided by the news media that explanations could be forged and framed. When the 'new Labour' government of Tony Blair came to power in 1997, one of its primary targets in the battle to 'modernise' the British state was the social security budget.

Social security minister Frank Field, with a reputation for an independent and tough approach in this area after an early career as a 'poverty lobbyist', and several years chairing the Commons Social Services Select Committee, was charged with 'thinking the unthinkable'.

But this task, as always, had to draw on public and deeply rooted mythology and understanding. In this chapter I briefly review how this process was worked out in the 1990s by examining news coverage of poverty and social security, and its consequences for public beliefs and policy.

SHIFTING GEAR IN THE RHETORICAL BATTLE

In earlier work I have argued that contemporary understanding of welfare is drawn from three roots-'efficiency, morality, and pathology: efficiency of the labour market and the economy; morality of the work ethic and self-sufficiency; and the pathology of individual inadequacy as the cause of poverty'. These three vary in intensity as conditions change. With rising structural unemployment, awareness of and familiarity with the circumstances and causes of unemployment became more diffuse through the population. But the increasing moralism of work as the only route out of poverty, and as the best cure for residual idleness, increasingly formed the core of a hardening set of political axioms arguing that duties as much as rights were the key to modern citizenship. This rhetoric became pivotal to the Blairite agenda, and to the welfare reforms the new Labour government began to pursue in office.

Samuel Smiles was back in favour. While the worthy toiled, 'Most wretched and ignoble lot, indeed, is the lot of the idlers'.

The intense 'scroungerphobia' evident in both press and public attitudes in the 1970s abates somewhat in this later period. But the rhetoric and vocabulary are by now set. Drawing on this three-part framework, news about social security now becomes merely a variant on the earlier period.

Within that a predictable and familiar set of motifs recur. First, the economic burden posed by social security expenditure, a restraint on growth and a punitive impost on the hard-working tax paying majority. Second, the need for control and punishment for illicit dependency on benefits, and especially for fraud.

Third, the clear and necessary boundary to be drawn between the deserving and undeserving poor, with single parents moving into greater prominence in the 1990s alongside the unemployed. Both receive vituperation as external to the social system, in association with the foreign or alien claimant. Fourth, the new moralism draws attention to the unduly pleasant 'lot of the idlers', when there is work to be done.

Tory Social Security Secretary Peter Lilley had the headline writers drooling in 1992 when yet another 'biggest crackdown ever against social security fraud' was launched at the party's annual conference. His gruesome adaptation of a Gilbert and Sullivan ditty ('I've got a little list/Of benefit offenders who I'll soon be rooting out/And who never would be missed…') had them rolling in the aisles and across the front pages.

As the *Mirror* warned of 'Dole scroungers facing new blitz', more simply in the *Daily Star* it was 'Stuff the spongers'. War was yet again declared on this outgroup of wasters, idlers, and loafers, a group set apart from the rest of society. The language of warfare underlines this imagery in two ways. First, battle is declared (as in the *Daily Mail* front-page spread, '£2bn blitz on dole cheats'.

Welfare claimants have endured more 'blitzes' than the Luftwaffe could ever have imagined possible. Second, readers are constantly reminded of their outgroup status by the recurrent and exemplary reporting of foreign spongers. In one brief period for example, from the *Mail* stable, we had 'A one man fraud factory', about a 'baby-faced 37-year-old' Nigerian who 'used Britain's benefits system like his own private bank' (*Mail on Sunday,* 21 September 1997); 'Thieving refugee sent benefit cash back home', about a Vietnamese caught shoplifting (*Daily Mail,* 25 July 1997); 'Irish fiddler takes British tax-payer for

£1 million' (*Mail on Sunday,* 20 July 1997); 'First family of fraud' about a Pakistani family being tried for social security fraud in a Dutch court (*Daily Mail,* 20 April 1998); and an 'exclusive' exposé of the 'scandal of the illegal immigrant benefits industry' (*Daily Mail,* 30 June 1997).

Scorned for this scandalous exploitation of our softness and generosity as a nation, scroungers are as excoriated as other objects of social contempt, as hinted at by headlines like 'Fraud-busters make a dawn swoop on welfare scroungers', the comparison with drug dealers or child abusers not far from the surface.

Social security fraud, as I demonstrate below, remains a staple of reporting of the benefits system. Yet the arithmetic of this area of criminal activity remains riddled with anomalies. Calculations of annual fraud figures depend on presumptions that short-term fraud would have continued if undetected.

This indeterminacy gets played out in media reporting by the eternal refrain that '£1.4 bn benefit fraud is tip of iceberg' (*Daily Telegraph,* 10 July 1995). Dee Cook has carefully contrasted the policy and ideological response to social security fraud with tax evasion, which, as she points out, is equally a cost to the public purse resulting from criminal fraud. By 1995/96 the Department of Social Security was undertaking over 10,000 prosecutions annually, compared with 192 by the Inland Revenue. In the same year, even assumed benefit 'savings' (which include payment 'irregularities') arising from this action amounted to £1.2 billion, compared with £5.2 billion actually accrued from imposing 'compliance' on would-be tax evaders.

Yet the latter remains veiled behind either total invisibility or humorous disregard for what is seen to be a victimless and innocent piece of mischief we would all engage in, given the opportunity.

Blurring the dividing line between welfare dependency and criminality fuels the sense that an unnecessary burden is being placed on the public purse by all this largesse. The day after disabled activists chained themselves to the railings at Number 10 in protest at threatened benefit cuts, that voice of middle England, the decade's most successful newspaper the *Daily Mail,* in its new conditional Blairite pose, argued that 'while those in genuine need will not be abandoned' the reforms would 'make sense of a welfare structure which creates a culture of dependency, fails to eradicate poverty, and yet imposes an ever-increasing burden on the economy'.

This was the welfare structure, as an earlier *Mail* lead article had pointed out, that 'has spawned a debilitating culture of welfare dependency, fecklessness, and fraud' (15 August 1997). The result, warned the *Sunday Times,* is that 'Benefit fraud is a way of life in Britain's sign-on society' (31 October 1993), a diagnosis echoed in the double page spread in the *Daily Mail* headed 'Sign up here for sick-note Britain' (14 April 1998). This fecklessness arises from the alleged luxury of the lifestyles endowed by social security benefits, and from the indolence and ease with which the system is exploited. My clippings files bulge with annual examples of the, invariably misleading, summertime accounts of social security enriched holiday-makers. The *Daily Express* front-page lead 'Dole cheat's sun holiday' ('A dole cheat soaked up the Caribbean sunshine while still claiming benefit in Britain'), catches the flavour (16 August 1995).

But towering over all such narratives are those of the 'super-scroungers'. Among the more prominent such bogey figures recently was 47-year-old former pig worker and invalidity beneficiary Paul Booth, who in 1998 found himself getting more column inches than the resigning social security minister Frank Field. The *Daily Mirror* gave a double-page spread to Mr Booth and his two-family, eleven-children household (8 April 1998).

By the following week further investigation enabled the headline 'Scrounger and a liar' to be printed (14 April 1998). Not to be outdone the *Sun* topped its story with a mock-up medal, 'S.O.B.

Order of Scroungers of Britain', and invited its readers to submit details if they knew 'a bigger parasite than Paul Booth? We're looking for one to win our Scroungers of Britain gong' (8 April 1998). As the paper editorialised, 'Wasters like Booth are a huge millstone round our necks...layabouts who do nothing but breed should be cut off without a penny.' And it added archly, and none too elliptically, 'Perhaps we should cut something else off too'.

The same allusion had informed the paper's front-page lead a month earlier that 'Blair snips Jack the dads' as absentee dads were to find that 'Their pay packets or benefits will be slashed in a massive crackdown on scroungers and cheats'. The notion that social security was a drag of enormous proportions on the motor of economic growth had become prominent in political orthodoxy again by the advent of the new Labour government.

The 1998 Green Paper on Social Security in which Frank Field unveiled his unthinkable thoughts was rapidly distilled by the press into two congruent themes. First it was another 'War on cheats', in which 'Welfare cheats face spot fines' *(Express)* as the 'Shake-up in welfare hits the workshy' *(The Times)*.

To help this policy along the *Sun* invited us to 'Shop a bad dad-Field war on spongers who cost us a fortune'. In fact criticised from left and right the Green Paper soon saw its two principal begetters, Field and Social Services Secretary Harriet Harman, both out of office, victims of hubris and the charge that 'Ministers fire welfare blanks'.

But the central message of modern welfare reform was well and truly forged. In a forceful front-page spread the *Express* shows a bewhiskered Field as Moses coming down from the burning bush, tablets in hand, alongside the divine full page headline 'Thou shalt not shirk'. The second theme continued to be the welfare burden which made all this necessary. As the *Mail* had explained a year earlier, 'Labour's radical social security reformer Frank Field yesterday pledged to cut the Government's £90 billion a year welfare bill' ('Field sharpens the axe for a purge on welfare'-5 May 1997). In fact, as many commentators have noted, UK welfare expenditure is relatively low by international standards. By 1995/96 UK expenditure on 'social protection' ranked ninth out of eleven in European comparisons, with only Italy and Portugal lower. Equally, as Hills points out, '...the UK is not a high tax country. Over the last twenty years the UK has moved from being slightly above the mid-point of the international range of tax as a share of national income to being clearly well below the international average'.

Nevertheless, the public rhetoric tells another story. Behind these 'unbearable' cost levels lies, of course, the excessive allocation of welfare generosity, not merely to too many recipients, but to quite clearly the wrong people. Maintaining a necessary cultural distinction between the deserving and undeserving poor remains one of the cardinal boundary sustaining functions of the public media, even though there are occasional shifts in the demographics of those two groups.

In the early 1990s, and occasionally thereafter, periodic out-bursts of puritanical outrage at single parents placed that large and rapidly growing group firmly in the firing line. Eventually the conclusion was clear: 'Lone parents are the biggest cheats: single mothers may be lying their way to £1 billion'. Not surprisingly, given both the popular and policy onslaught, we then find 'Fewer single mothers claiming benefit'. In contrast was the poignant tale of former legendary Liverpool soccer hard-man Tommy Smith, given a sympathetic treatment in his battle to regain his cancelled disability living allowance.

Equally sympathetic treatment is received by the 'genuinely' disabled, as in the case of an unambiguously 'deserving' woman whose plight was headlined in the *Sun* as 'No arms, no legs...but you're not disabled' (13 April 1998), in a story about a thalidomide victim whose Severe Disablement Allowance was stopped when the DSS found evidence of her selling puppies five years previously. By contrast our attention was drawn to the naivety and absurdity of Oxfam's venture into poverty in the UK. Real poverty is of course to be seen in the fly-encrusted faces of children lying helpless and starving on the dusty sun-baked ground of a far-away disaster zone.

As a *Daily Mail* feature, headlined 'Can you spot the difference', pointed out, 'generous people who wish to give to Oxfam are encouraged to do so by pictures of skeletal mothers and children in Africa'.

To help us understand the point, an accompanying photo of 'an African famine victim' is juxtaposed with a family snap of Paul Booth, the 'superscrounger', and his apparently rudely well-fed and voluminous family. This is not 'the poverty that means wearing rags or having no roof at night' (9 April 1998).

The durability of the deserving poor and the deeply-held foundational myths that sustain them enables a proud tradition of campaigning journalism to surface periodically. In December 1997 the *Mail on Sunday* claimed a success in its 'campaign' on the much-maligned Benefits Integrity Project, with 'Benefits U-turn ends disabled mother's order' (28 December 1997) in a story about a woman crippled by multiple sclerosis whose Income Support had been withdrawn.

Even more emotively signalling a nostalgic search for its heroic campaigning past, the *Daily Mirror* produced a three-page 'Poverty-shock report' feature on the 'virus' which is 'spreading at an alarming rate... The name of this virus is poverty' (30 October 1998), with a two-column photo spread of a three-year-old girl clutching her doll in the bleak passage of a 'grim Liverpool estate'.

Only the relegation of the feature to pages 33-35 signalled a very different set of priorities from the barnstorming polemics of the *Mirror* under Bartholomew and Cudlipp half a century earlier.

Powerful myths about poverty, public expenditure, and the moral economy of welfare remain immovably planted at the core of public understanding of policies related to social security.

Since the 1980s some of these myths have been severely tested by changing economic conditions, yet their potency seems largely undiminished. These exemplars, however, should not disguise the very limited nature of news coverage of pertinent areas of public policy, and it is to that wider, and more calculated picture, that I now turn.

SMALL BUT IMPERFECTLY FORMED: A MEASURE OF SOCIAL SECURITY NEWS

To obtain a measure of social security coverage in the media this section extracts relevant data from a larger study of policy news undertaken at the Communication Research Centre at Loughborough University. The data summarised here cover all national UK news media throughout the year October 1996 to September 1997.

The first and most obvious finding is how little coverage social security gets. In that period there were just twenty-four stories primarily about social security on the BBC's main evening television bulletin, eleven on ITN, and in broadsheet newspapers not many more (twenty-six in the *Guardian,* twelve in *The Times*).

Social Security is not big news, even compared with other social policy areas such as education, housing and health. Health is by far the most regularly reported, even dwarfing education in a period when all the main parties were ostensibly committed to that field as a priority.

Social security, like other areas of social policy, is first and foremost about politics. Poverty, benefits, and welfare are refracted through the legislative cycle and the machinery of government, or at least that fraction of it which surfaces in media exposure.

During the same period the Prime Minister appeared in roughly 15 per cent of all such social security news items and other government ministers in 60 per cent. Claimants and non-political actors of any kind made up just 12 per cent of the total actors appearing in these stories.

When social security minister Frank Field published his Green Paper it received high-profile coverage, but nothing so extended and close focused as his ill-tempered resignation saga some weeks later. One facet of this less than comprehensive account of social security and poverty in the major news media is a diminishing attention to social policy news of any kind.

In recent years frequent charges of 'tabloidisation', not least from within journalism, have argued that the major news media, most especially broadcasting and the serious newspapers 'of record' had abandoned their traditional and honourable role of serving citizens with the essential diet of information required to perform their democratic role, and were instead moving to a more diverse and diverting fare with aspirations to entertain more than inform.

I have examined the empirical foundation of this claim elsewhere. It shows a clear trend in both titles towards a much greater proportion of crime stories, and a rapidly diminishing proportion of both social policy stories and indeed of foreign news. With such a diminishing scope for news about poverty and social security it matters more than ever what aspects of these issues are given prominence or attention.

It is not altogether surprising, given the historic confusion in the British psyche between the iniquities of the criminally indigent and the lifestyles of the merely impoverished, that social security and crime news occupy close quarters in the journalistic corpus. In the period of our content analysis we examined both crime and social security stories.

Of all stories that were primarily about one or other of these topics, 27.1 per cent (in the tabloid press), 16.6 per cent (in the broadsheet press), and 11.7 per cent (in broadcast news) were about both-that is were about criminal activity associated with social security.

As I have noted above, it would be difficult to attribute this to the prevalence or scale of social security abuse, but it does certainly register a consistent association between the two areas of activity in the public mind, as we shall see shortly. My concern throughout this chapter has been, of course, primarily with the news media.

Nonetheless it would be remiss not to recognise that the welfare state in its various guises forms a luminous backcloth for the fictional lives of much popular drama, and no more so than in the working class sagas of the soap operas. In the lives and doings of these twenty-seven characters, and others like them, are embodied powerful and rich evocations of the understandings which imbue public perception of issues like social security. In *EastEnders,* for example, Irene (who claimed unemployment benefit despite living with her boyfriend Terry), fell foul of Susan (who also lives in the square but works for the Department of Social Security), leading to an inevitable showdown in the Queen Vic pub.

There can be little doubt, though evidence awaits, that in such constructions lie the source of much of the imagery and explication deployed by people in responding to news and experience of major social issues like poverty and social security.

Responding to the 'Wretched and Ignoble': Public attitudes

There is some evidence that public attitudes have, in recent years, softened and extended to suggest a broader understanding of the ways in which sections of the population are being cut adrift from 'comfortable Britain'. Despite that, the more severe responses which lie deep-rooted in our culture, and on which much of the media coverage illustrated here is based, seem entrenched.

If anything the same surveys show that hostile attitudes to those who do not avoid dependency on the state have hardened. Although such attitudes soften in periods of recession, animosity to presumed fraudsters remains consistent, a pattern that offers circumstantial evidence, though no more, for a contrast between the fluctuating direct experience of people in the wider economy and their more constant exposure to the punitive odium attached to social security 'abuse' in the mainstream media.

The sturdy beggar and his cousins, the 'wretched and ignoble', live on in pre-millennial Britain. In the 1990s, theories popularised by writers like Charles Murray argued that a section of the population in the USA, and in other countries like it, notably in the UK, had become detached from the mainstream of society, primarily by virtue of its distinct culture.

What separated this group from the majority was its 'deplorable behaviour', making them a quite separate 'underclass'. The term, and the imagery and mythology on which it drew, became deeply rooted in the policy aspirations of social security reformers across the political spectrum.

It was, of course, but a renaming of that multitude whose 'vicious habits and destitute circumstances make it certain that... they must hunger and sin, sin and hunger' till death in the 'darkest England' where General William Booth took his Salvation Army a century ago.

While an alternative and more recent language of 'social exclusion' expressed the structural forces preventing the entry of large numbers into the benefits and delights of late-twentieth century society, both rhetorics established symbolic barriers between the consumers of the social security and benefits system and the larger majority whose labours and diligence provided that system's resources. The discursive battle to understand and encapsulate the mystery of severe and extensive poverty within the affluent communities of late-twentieth century society takes place in the pages of the daily press, and on the screens of the nation's living rooms, as much as on the floor of the House of Commons. That battle seems as flourishing and as critical as it was in General Booth's time, and no less is at stake.

NEXT GENERATION OF JOURNALISTS FOR MEDIA

The news industry has been undergoing a fundamental paradigm shift since the end of last century. An increasing number of media companies around the United States, such as the Washington Post in Washington, DC, Media General in Virginia, the Tribune Company in Chicago, and New England Cable News, have taken solid steps to merge different media such as newspapers, television stations, radio stations, and online journalism companies to disseminate news content on multiple media platforms.

As a result, in a metropolitan area, one company would own print, TV, and online venues. Media call this industrial trend "media convergence," though the concept means much more than media mergers. Media convergence muddies the lines among broadcast journalism, print journalism, and online journalism, leaving college journalism educators to wonder whether traditional journalism programs have become dinosaurs.

After surveying 200 newspaper publishers worldwide, the World Association of Newspapers (WAN) found, "Despite a somewhat gloomy outlook for wholesale convergence in media companies worldwide in the near term, convergence is already being implemented with varying degrees of enthusiasm and speed among the world's media companies". The Innovation International Media Consulting Group estimates that at least 100 of the world's multiple media companies are planning and implementing integration strategies. South and Nicholson (2002) drew a sketch of a converged media company:

Daily journalists need to embrace the 24-hour news cycle, with continuous deadlines. And the story needs to be reported and produced for a multi-platform audience. That may mean delivering content first to the Web and cell phones, a streaming video broadcast later in the day, a TV talk-back interview still later, and a "second day" interpretive story for the next morning's newspaper.

Dominic Gates (2002) pointed out, "Convergence with broadcast and online media is the shape of things to come for newspapers." The trend remains controversial. Critics complain that such cross-ownership of both a television station and a newspaper in the same market is a threat to democracy because it limits the number of voices.

Delegates of the Communication Workers of America, a 60,000-member guild, passed a resolution in June of 2002 at the group's annual convention in Las Vegas, pledging to increase public awareness about the risks of ongoing media convergence. The delegates complained that shrinking media markets are a threat to editorial diversity and job security. In 1975, the Federal Communications Commission (FCC) ruled that no new broadcast licenses would be granted to companies that own a major daily newspaper and a local television station in the same city. Fairness & Accuracy In Reporting (FAIR) calls on the FCC to roll back limits on media consolidation.

The Newspaper Association of America (NAA), on the other hand, has asked the FCC to appeal the rule. On June 2, 2003, the FCC voted 3 to 2 to relax or eliminate some ownership restrictions, such as a rule barring media companies from owning television stations in markets where they publish daily newspapers. Although some lawmakers and advocacy groups are still fighting in the courts and on Capitol Hill to overturn the FCC's new media ownership rules, these rules will be likely to encourage cross-media ownership in the years to come.

The mergers have raised questions about whether they are good for the craft of journalism itself. Critics complain that by requiring journalists to be jacks of both trades, print and broadcast, the journalists will be masters of none. Robert J. Haiman, president emeritus of The Poynter Institute, compared the media convergence trend to an Amphicar, a cross between a boat and a car. The Amphicar, hawked in Florida during the 1950s, flopped. "It flopped because people quickly discovered that while it really was an ingenious combination of a car and a boat, it was a lousy car (because it also had to be a boat), and it was a lousy boat (because it also had to be a car)".

Willingly or unwillingly, many news practitioners' functions are gradually changing or are expected to change as media convergence rolls on. For a reporter in a converged media environment, knowing how to write is probably no longer enough. S/he could be expected to write the same story for different media in a timely manner.

Ideally, s/he can readily talk in front of a video camera. As a photographer, knowing how to tell a story both in video and in still images is more and more in demand. A designer should know how to prepare still graphics for print, moving graphics for television and dynamic graphics for the Web.

At the online version of the Chicago Tribune, for instance, staffers are supposed to cover stories, take pictures, operate video cameras, and create digital pages. The editors, too, need a wider variety of skills than the traditional paper editors. Along with infrastructure changes and the attempt to create synergy among the various media outlets, a new breed of journalists-digital or multimedia journalists-is expected.

As media jobs become more demanding, some news practitioners are beginning to team up to complete projects. At the same time, fear, confusion, and frustration from news practitioners are creeping into newsrooms. Carr (2002c) wrote: "Convergence frightens many people who wonder whether their current skill sets have prepared them for-or will even be needed in-that great undiscovered country, the future. This is probably the primary reason why I still find such great hostility to convergence among certain journalists."

Killebrew, a mass communications professor from the University of South Florida, suggested that "journalists must be prepared to either crosstrain themselves or seek training from other sources while management must be prepared to give them the opportunities and time to do so."

The 1999-2000 president of the Association for Schools of Journalism and Mass Communication (ASJMC), Shirley Staples Carter, questioned whether, in the midst of the "Internet revolution," programs are prepared to educate journalists of the future.

When specifically talking about writing, Keith Hartenberger, manager of news and programming for Tribune Regional Programming, said that journalism schools should make their students aware of the many ways to present the news. "It's a multimedia world out there," he said. "If you're just being prepared to write newspaper stories, you won't be prepared". "At some point, this [cross-media training] is something we're going to expect from everyone".

Media convergence, as a trend that is gradually shaping the landscape of the media industry in the new century, has called into question the conventional journalism school practice of having separate tracks-print, broadcast, etc. Journalism educators around the country also are trying to figure out what they should do, if anything, to better prepare students for the converged media.

For instance, should journalism educators consider merging different sequences such as magazine, newspaper, broadcast, and photojournalism, or still teach all such courses as if they were unrelated media? "Traditionally defined segments of the communications industry are less and less distinguishable for technological and market convergence," observed Moon (2001).

Are college journalism educators themselves both theoretically equipped and technologically prepared to teach their students for converged media? What do media companies expect from future news practitioners? What do current news practitioners in converged media feel is lacking? For both news practitioners and professors, the two most urgent questions cry for answers: Should journalism schools train specialists or fit for-all generalists? And how should college journalism education balance the teaching of critical thinking and technical skills?

Apart from all these education-related questions, we are also interested in finding out what are the driving forces behind the media mergers, who are regarded as the beneficiaries of this trend, and how people's political beliefs are related to their attitude toward teaching media convergence in colleges? These questions pertain closely to college journalism education, which has been the subject of debate and criticism for two decades.

A national survey was conducted among colleges, daily newspapers, and commercial television stations to explore the issue of how journalism schools should prepare students for the trend of media convergence from the perspectives of news editors, news professionals, and journalism professors. The study measured the level of general support for convergence education and determined if a new model of journalism education was called for.

If so, it examined whether consensus existed among the three groups on the direction educators should take when revisiting programme designs. Where consensus was not apparent, divisions among the sample of educators, editors, and reporters were defined. The goal of the study is to provide evidence that will help journalism educators make informed decisions about how to respond to media convergence in their curricula and courses and lay an empirical foundation for further discussions and conversations about media convergence.

The search results show that media convergence is a comparatively new topic in media research, though articles about it have inundated the Internet, magazines, and newspapers. Most research writings appeared no earlier than 1998. Articles about the relationship between media convergence and higher education are rare and have shown up more recently in trade magazines. A few research writings were found in academic conference (i.e., AEJMC) proceedings.

Many writings have addressed one of the toughest questions: What is media convergence? How to define "media convergence" had a direct bearing on how we conducted this study. Out of these writings, we identified four categories of media convergence that directly affect how journalism will be taught in colleges.

CONTENT CONVERGENCE

As Tremayne noted, decades ago, the term media convergence referred to the content convergence between competing newspapers and even among newspapers, magazines, and television. Today, pure content convergence continues on the Internet. For instance, the St. Petersburg Times has incorporated local Channel 10's TV news into its online newspaper though they are independent business entities. In other words, media convergence may not necessarily be tied to media merger. Form convergence (or technological convergence). Around the mid-1990s, as Tremayne and Wurtz (2000) noted, computer technology and Internet technology made possible the convergence of all forms of mediated communications including video, audio, data, text, still photo, and graphic art for "on-demand" audiences.

Using these different forms to tell news stories on the World Wide Web has been widely regarded as the future of mass communication regardless of the fact that most online news sites have had a hard time making ends meet, let alone making a profit. Form convergence, often called technological convergence, has been a fundamental force to guide and lead convergence in the market, industry, and regulation.

CORPORATE CONVERGENCE

Since the late 1990s, media convergence has been escalated to the level of media mergers. The News Centre located in Tampa, Florida, owned by Media General, and the Tribune Interactive, owned by the Tribune Company, for instance, are the products of media mergers. In The News Centre, WFLA-TV, The Tampa Tribune, and Tampa Bay Online operate out of the same building.

They share daily tips and information, spot news, photography, enterprise reporting, franchises, events, and public service. Each of the three entities in The News Centre has its own independent newsroom, but they issued a joint statement of coverage principles, titled "News Centre Pledge".

The Tribune Interactive has brought together the interactive functions of the company's four newspapers and more than a score of television stations including WGN-TV and CLTV. The individual media outlets have their own newsgathering staff, but their coverage is enhanced by their multimedia desks in the Chicago Tribune newsroom and the Tribune Media Centre in Washington.

"A synergy-team of print editors and TV news veterans at the Chicago Tribune work together to manage resource sharing and the relationship". Media merger has made both content convergence and form convergence handy. Corporate convergence via vertical and horizontal integration, mergers, alliances, and acquisitions will make traditionally defined segments of the communications industry less and less distinguishable.

ROLE CONVERGENCE

Russial identified several examples of role convergence in newsrooms. For instance, the roles of reporter and librarian, the roles of copyeditor and compositor, the roles of graphic artist and Web designer, and the roles of photo editor, darkroom technician, and photographer are all converging in different media.

In more recent years, content convergence, form convergence, and especially corporate convergence have sparked more in-depth role convergence among news practitioners. For instance, Victoria Lim from The News Centre in Tampa revealed at a February 2002 conference on media convergence at the University of Florida that she primarily works as a television reporter for WFLA-TV, but she also has to write for the company's newspaper, The Tampa Tribune, as a senior consumer investigative reporter and for the Web company TBO.com on a daily basis; at the time of the conference, she was working on 31 stories.

A newspaper reporter may also produce a newspaper in QuarkXPress or serve as a TV news anchor, while a newspaper photographer may shoot video stories or produce interactive online stories in Flash. Role convergence requires that both reporters and editors re-equip themselves both journalistically and technologically.

Of the four types of convergence, role convergence has the most direct effect on future journalism education. Within the media industry, there are serious doubts about whether training cross-media journalists are possible or desirable. When asked whether reporters of the future must be equally skilled in print, TV, and online, Forrest Carr, news director of WFLA-TV at The News Centre in Tampa, said no. He said he believed that there would always be areas of specialization and students may still choose specialties, but said that it no longer makes any sense to pretend print journalists and electronic journalists are in different professions.

On the other hand, he said that journalists who have skills in TV, print, and online media certainly will be more valuable to their employers; and he emphasized that prospective employees must be willing to work in an environment where reporters cooperate across platforms. In most cases currently, he said, cooperating across platforms simply comes down to the sharing of tips and information.

Charles Kravetz, the vice president for news and station manager of New England Cable News (NECN), the largest regional news network in America, concurs with Forrest Carr. When asked "Do you see a time when all journalists will have to be able to file stories on all platforms (print, TV, radio, online)?" Kravetz said: "I am not sure that is the way it is going to work out.

This notion we had that one-journalist-fits-all-media is perhaps not that realistic. ... There are very few people we will talk about in the future that are TV/newspaper/internet reporters". Gates agreed, "The 'backpack journalist'-a superhack master of multimedia who can do it all and who routinely packs a laptop and a video camera along with the tape recorder and steno notebook-may be the subject of avant-garde j-school courses, but it's not likely to become the norm."

Some other media executives have tried to define the extent to which role convergence is expected. Gil Thelen, executive editor and senior vice president of The Tampa Tribune, for instance, gave suggestions to journalism educators based on his two years of experience in The News Centre.

"The fully formed, all-purpose, multiplatform, gadget-laden journalism grad is NOT what we're looking to hire. ... Journalism schools must continue to produce graduates who are competent in one craft area: reporting, design, producing, directing, editing." However, Thelen encouraged journalism schools to train writers to write for print, online, and broadcast and train print photographers to learn how to shoot and produce TV packages. Thelen said that cultural resistance is the biggest hurdle for converging newsrooms, and that employees or current journalism students need to learn to cooperate and collaborate across newsrooms.

What is unclear is whether these media administrators' predictions are limited by the status quo of the current generation of news practitioners who might not be very well prepared for convergence or who might even resist the notion of media convergence. At Brigham Young University, students with multiple skills are more valued and feel more comfortable in the converged media environment. In addition, sharing tips and information does not entail convergence. Reporters have been doing this for decades. It seems that keeping convergence only on the level of sharing tips and information can hardly justify the high cost of rebuilding infrastructures like The News Centre. We are interested in finding out what expectations media companies have for future journalists. From news professionals' self-evaluations of their preparedness for media convergence, we should also be able to infer what is most desirable in the media industry nowadays.

In the face of increasing demand for technically skilled journalists-conversant with QuarkXPress, Photoshop, Avid, and Dreamweaver and able to crunch statistics using spreadsheets and other statistical methods in order to uncover the hidden story-should longstanding staples such as ethics, law, and theory remain at the heart of journalism curricula? Or should such materials, commonly grouped together as "critical thinking", share equal hilling with technology or "skills" training?

In other words, how should journalism schools balance the teaching of professional skills and that of critical thinking in an era when technology penetrates every facet of news gathering, preparation, editing, production, and delivery.

Convergence further complicates this age-old battle in journalism education.9 Abraham noticed that the goal of most restructuring in journalism institutions is to provide an integrated skills environment where students would get the chance to practice the skills of multimedia production. Abraham argued: "The role of journalism academy should be very different from that of the industry. Its role should not simply be to inculcate skills that will help students to flag down jobs.

They should aim to provide a scholarly background for a deeper intellectual understanding of our lives, media forms and of communication in general". The dean of the University of Nevada at Reno thinks the ability to use multiple media skills is essential. Brigham Young University, which has built a working converged newsroom into its curriculum, expects students to graduate with multiple skills.

University News Director, Dean Paynter, said, "We expect our students to more than anchor, more than report, and more than produce. The best ones can do it all, including write for the newspaper". Mitchell Stephens, professor of journalism and mass communications at New York University, holds up the other end.

"In a world where corporate pressures on 'content providers' seem to be increasing and civic affairs decreasing, the argument for emphasizing the basics does have much to recommend it." Thomas Kunkel (2002), dean of the Philip Merrill College of Journalism at the University of Maryland, sums it up: "Today's journalists, first and foremost, must be strong critical thinkers who know enough about geography, history and the human condition to understand why events play out as they do. They must be intellectually curious. They should speak a second language. They should read something other than Jim Romenesko's MediaNews site. They ought to have a world view."

A controversy in late 2002 at Columbia University demonstrates how volatile the argument is currently. The debate arose when the graduate school of journalism at Columbia University halted its search for a dean. The new university president, Lee Bollinger, wanted to re-evaluate the school's mix of craft versus theory, and the move created a flurry of opinion about the journalism school's existing curriculum.

This critical curriculum question is often reflected in the questions of whether and how new technology classes should be included in the existing curriculum and how they should be taught. Some journalism schools are preparing to embrace the wave of media convergence in their new curricula by converging print and electronic media sequences to adapt to the industrial trends and the new technological environment.

Blanchard and Christ warn that universities with limited resources will no longer tolerate duplicating specializations with separate courses such as writing for television, writing for newspapers, writing for public relations, and writing for advertising. Blanchard and Christ add that the communications revolution (the media's convergence and related trends) is making journalism and mass communication's traditional sequences obsolete. Actually, Blanchard and Christ's opinion is not something new. Early in 1972, the University of Iowa School of Journalism already eliminated its sequences but at the expense of being denied reaccreditation by ACEJMC. About thirty years later, their decision seemed to be finding more sympathy.

Many schools are still exploring where to go. In October 2001, seventeen professors and leaders of new media from thirteen journalism programs across the country gathered in Berkeley, California, and had a discussion about new media in journalism education. The University of Nevada, Reno, offered several different elective courses in new media, but it did not have a special sequence.

It was struggling with how to incorporate them in other classes.

The University of Florida had a concentration in online media, which was equivalent to other concentrations such as reporting and editing and photojournalism. Students who were not in that concentration couldn't always squeeze in the online media courses because they did not have any leftover électives they could take in the school.

American University had three divisions, journalism, public communication, and visual media, but they did not work together very well most of the time. The University of South Carolina was restructuring its graduate masters programme in newspaper leadership and was focusing it on convergence. The University of Maryland had an online curriculum, but it was not formally structured as such. Northwestern University had an introductory New Media course at the undergraduate and graduate level, which was offered as an elective. It was packed with everything from new skills training to wrestling with the business issues of new media to actual production. After three admission cycles, enrollment declined.

The University of Minnesota established the Institute for New Media Studies, which merged broadcast journalism and print journalism programs to make them a concentration with the idea that future journalists would work in a multi-channel environment and should know how to operate within all those channels.

Although editors and academics sometimes agree on the qualifications a journalism student needs, an ideal curriculum doesn't always include convergence preparedness courses. In a 2000 poll, editors and educators agreed "on the same five of 14 types of knowledge considered most necessary for journalism graduates and listed them in the same order of importance".

Technical skills were not mentioned in the top five, surpassed instead by "understanding of a journalist's responsibility to the public, understanding of the ethics of journalism, knowledge of current events, broad general knowledge, and knowledge of government".

With so much variance across universities, we are interested in finding out how many journalism schools have revamped their curricula to prepare students for the trend of media convergence, what professors' attitudes are toward teaching critical thinking vs. teaching technical skills and training generalists vs. training specialists, and what editors' and news professionals' attitudes are toward the same issues. In this regard, several scholars and news practitioners have tried to give advice to journalism professors and students in the context of media convergence.

In 2002, David Bulla from the University of Florida presented his "Media convergence: Industry practices and implications for education" to the AEJMC annual conference in Miami. This is the first research writing of its kind. The theme of the paper is the closest to that of this study. Bulla's study looked at the changing nature of contemporary mass communications practices, focusing on multimedia or converged journalism.

It described what scholastic journalism scholars are doing to prepare their students for these changes and provided recommendations to educators about how to update curricula to account for convergence. The research questions for that study were: (1) what are journalism educators currently doing to incorporate convergence into their curricula; and (2) what abilities, skills, and attitudes do professional journalists expect from their newest employees? Media convergence in Bulla's study was defined as multimedia journalism, which means reporting, writing, and disseminating content in two or more media platforms.

Because of the controversy about media mergers, Bulla tried to find answers to some hot issues concerning democracy including: Does corporate media merging reduce public discourse and hinder democracy? Will it ultimately mean the need for fewer and fewer reporters, as the development of other technology has meant a decline in the number of employees in other areas of the production process? All these questions pertain to our study.

Bulla obtained a sample of 114 news practitioners working at newspapers, television stations, wire services, magazines, radio stations, and online publications in the United States. The sample was randomly selected from Editor & Publisher and Yahoo lists of media companies in the U.S. Media Web sites. With a response rate of 36 per cent, Bulla interviewed 41 news practitioners. Bulla also interviewed college educators, but he did not state how he sampled them.

What is unclear is the extent to which the Yahoo list and Editor & Publisher list overlap each other and if a sample from two potentially overlapping lists is any longer a random sample. In addition, since Bulla's questions were almost all unstructured, that is, he conducted interviews, he did not really need a random sample.

Researchers strive for depth rather than breadth and don't mean to claim external validity in the statistical sense by conducting interviews. Finally, if he did need a random sample, a sample of 114 people with a 36 per cent response rate could be statistically defective because of big statistical errors. Bulla needed a better research design to make his study valid and reliable.

Some scholars doubt whether journalism school professors are theoretically and especially technologically prepared to teach media convergence. In an article written for Journalism Education magazine, John Irby, a professor from Washington State University and a veteran newspaper editor and publisher, for instance, was concerned about the disconnection between the newsroom and the classroom. Irby (2000) asked:

Are universities and educators effectively preparing students for the work force? Do educators understand what newspapers are looking for in future reporters and editors? Does the newspaper industry have a responsibility in the division between educators and professionals? Are journalism educators "discounted" by professionals who believe those who teach couldn't succeed in newspapers?

Irby said older generations of newspaper reporters also appeared on radio and television periodically though they had no training; they never even felt like it was part of their job and thus did not take it very seriously. But now, he continued, print journalists do need to take it seriously; journalism educators need to re-evaluate, and probably modify, the separatetrack approach in training print and broadcast journalists. Irby believed that there is still a need for specialization, but he told students to take both broadcast and print courses and told them that computer literacy is as crucial as the old-fashioned kind.

In October 2001, seventeen professors and leaders of new media from thirteen journalism programs across the country gathered in Berkeley, California, and had a discussion about new media in journalism education. The University of Nevada, Reno, offered several different elective courses in new media, but it did not have a special sequence. It was struggling with how to incorporate them in other classes.

"Critical thinking can result in a new way of approaching significant issues in one's life or a deeper understanding of the basis for one's actions. Or it might result in political activity".

Along the similar line as Kurfiss's critical thinking theory and unlike Allan Bloom, who condemns the introduction of non-Western materials into the university curricula so as to protect the curriculum from the contamination of ideological conflict, Jerry Herron also highly promotes the teaching of critical thinking by calling on faculty to bring their conflicting ideologies into open engagement so that students can discover what is at stake in different ideas and can see their representational meaning.

The questions are whether universities should totally give up the teaching of skills today and how the needs of the job market and the goal of college education can be in harmony. In other words, can the teaching of common traditional content and the teaching of higher order skills join forces? Patracia Graham, ex-dean of the Harvard Graduate School of Education, argues that we need both commonality and flexibility in American education and there is no reason we cannot have both at once.

The question of training specialists vs. generalists is an extension of a larger conversation about reforming the fragmented curricula in higher education. Often classified as "cultural right," Ernest Boyer, Allan Bloom, and E. D. Hirsch share similar views about the problems in higher education. They point out that the university now is anarchistic. There is no vision of what an educated human being is. The curriculum is disjointed and disciplines are fragmented into smaller pieces.

Undergraduates find it hard to see patterns in their courses and relate what they learn to life. Careerism conflicts with the liberal arts. And finally, schools have failed to thoroughly carry out the educational goal of promoting mature literacy for all our citizens. They all agree that an educational reform is needed to teach more common traditional content apart from the higher-order skills that are commonly emphasized.

Boyer calls for a balance between individual interests and shared concerns while the actual priority is given to the latter. To promote a liberal education, Boyer advocates the "integrated core" or "enriched major"-a programme of general education that introduces students not only to essential knowledge, but also to connections across the disciplines, and, in the end, to the application of knowledge to life beyond the campus. Boyer points out, knowledge becomes important only when we use it and apply it to humane ends; therefore, the undergraduate experience should not only generate new knowledge, but channel that knowledge to the service of the society. It is a matter of invigorating "the claims of community while protecting with full vigour the dignity and origins of each individual," to use Boyer and Kaplan's words.

In a similar vein, Bloom calls on teachers to look toward the goal of human completeness and to provide students a liberal education, in which learning is both synoptic and precise. To Bloom, liberal education feeds the student's love of truth and passion to live a good life. It also requires that a student's whole life be radically changed by it. Bloom offers an ivory tower vision of the university-"the good old Great Book approach"-undergraduate students spend four years reading certain generally recognized classic texts for answers to philosophical questions of personal and human identity and aspirations. Bloom thinks that man may live more truly and fully in reading Plato and Shakespeare than at any other time because then they are participating in essential being and are forgetting their accidental lives.

In accordance with Boyer's and Bloom's points of view, Hirsch argues that "the greatest human individuality is developed in response to a tradition, not in response to disorderly, uncertain, and fragmented education" and "only by accumulating shared symbols, and the shared information the symbols represent can we learn to communicate effectively with one another in our national community". However, Hirsch places emphasis more on the content of education, ensuring that students acquire all the "right" elements of knowledge that will enable them to get along in the Real World.

He believes that neither the content-neutral curriculum of Rousseau and Dewey nor the narrowly specified curriculum of Plato is adequate to the needs of a modern nation. Hirsch calls for a curriculum, including extensive curriculum and intensive curriculum with an emphasis on the former, which is traditional in content and provides students with a common core of cultural information. "The conception of a two-part curriculum avoids the idea that all children should study identical materials" Hirsch says.

Based on our literature review, media convergence in our study is defined as the assimilation of media content for multiple media platforms. Media convergence may involve any combination of the convergences of media contents, media forms, media companies, and roles of news practitioners.

Our general research question is how college professors should prepare students to cope with media convergence. To be specific, should college professors prepare generalists who can competently work in multiple media platforms or prepare specialists who know inside out how to work for one particular medium platform? And how should journalism schools balance the teaching of critical thinking and technical skills? Corresponding to these two questions, we also would like to find out if college journalism educators themselves are both theoretically equipped and technologically prepared to teach their students about media convergence. The study serves both as an attitude finder and a fact finder.

We believe that professors, editors, and news professionals are the best candidates to answer these questions. Editors represent the media companies to hire news staffers with news reporting abilities desired by the company. News professionals work in the forefront of news reporting and know best about what news reporting abilities they need.

The attitudes of the editors and the current generation of news professionals toward media convergence will have a great implication on future journalism education. Professors run journalism schools, and they have the final say about where their schools are going. Their attitudes toward journalism education in terms of media convergence will have the most direct influence on the kind of education journalism students will receive and how the students will perform in tomorrow's media.

Editors include daily newspaper editors in charge of newsroom operations or online news operations and news directors in charge of newsroom operations in a commercial TV station with news content, both in the United States. News professionals refer to non-management news staff, such as reporters, anchors, photographers, designers, producers, Web staff, etc., working in American media companies.

Journalism professors are defined as full-time instructors with any academic rankings who teach journalism courses in a U.S. journalism school, department, programme, or division which could be administratively affiliated with an institution with a name like College of Communications or Department of Communications Studies.

To obtain opinions about media convergence, we could have targeted our survey only at those editors and news professionals in a converged media environment. The opinions obtained from those editors and news professionals, however, could be biased. Those media companies that have not gone through convergence must have a reason for not doing so. We also wanted to find out what they are doing about convergence. Balanced views both from the converged and un-converged media companies will better assist colleges in their strategic planning.

We conducted a national survey among editors, news professionals, and journalism professors with three different versions of online survey questionnaires posted on a school Web site. Respondents were asked to fill out the questionnaire online and submit answers online as well. The answers went through a commercial form handler and reached the primary investigator's email address. By doing so, the primary investigator had no way to detect who answered the questionnaire unless the respondent voluntarily revealed his/her email address to request the findings from the study. There were twenty-two questions in each of these three questionnaires. Almost all questions were close-ended. About half of the questions used a 5-point Likert Scale from "Strongly Agree" to "Strongly Disagree." Some questions across the three questionnaires shared similarity, so that comparisons could be made when analyzing data. A text field was created for respondents to provide feedback to the survey freely.

The textual answers in the text field will be reported along with the statistics to illustrate and explain the quantitative findings. All questionnaires went through pilot tests. The unit of analysis was each participant.

In order to conduct a systematic random sampling of editors and news professionals, we needed a list of newspaper editors and TV news directors in the United States and a list of newspaper and TV news staffers. We found that such lists did not exist, though lists of newspapers and lists of TV stations did exist in multiple places online like Editor & Publisher Yearbook and Broadcasting Sr Cable Yearbook. Therefore, we decided to construct our own. To do so, we went through two steps. First, we constructed a combined list of daily newspapers and TV stations so that we could sample these news institutions. Second, we visited the Web sites of all sampled news institutions to find the email of the editor/news director and the email of one news professional randomly chosen.

In total, 1,190 U.S. daily newspapers with a valid URL were listed alphabetically by state. We sampled one out of every four dailies. Then, we visited each of those Web sites to find the email address of the managing editor, chief editor, online editor, or equivalent in each of those dailies and sent out a survey invitation email to him/her. If an individual email address was not available, we replaced it with a generic email address listed on their Web site and specified that the email was for the editor.

From the list, we removed PBS network companies, which mostly did not provide staff information, companies that did not generate news content such as WB network companies and UPN network companies, religious TV stations, and foreign language stations. In total, we extracted 674 TV stations with a valid URL. Since this population is smaller than that of the newspapers, we over-sampled it. Instead of sampling every other four, we sampled every other station.

Then, we visited each of those Web sites to find the email address of the news director or equivalent in each of those TV stations and sent out a survey invitation email to him/her. If an individual email address was not available, we replaced it with a generic email address and specified that the email was for the news director. In total, we successfully sent out invitation emails to 523 newspaper editors and TV news directors as our sample.

We also sampled one news professional out of each of the sampled U.S. dailies and TV stations for the survey. Since there was always more than one professional in a company, we simply randomly clicked on one name and picked him/her and made sure that s/he was on the news staff. Then, we sent him/her a survey invitation email. If an individual email address was not available, we replaced it with a generic email address and specified whom the email was for. S/he was asked to fill out a questionnaire that was worded in a slightly different manner. In total, we successfully sent out invitation emails to 398 news professionals.

We also needed to conduct a systematic random sampling of college journalism professors, but we were disappointed that all lists we found had many J-schools, even major ones, missing. In total, the new list contains 205 alphabetically ordered U.S. J-schools that contain 2,194 journalism professors.

We sampled one out of every four professors from the virtually running list of all journalism professors across the schools. For instance, if a school had six journalism professors, we picked the fourth one; then, the second journalism professor from next school was picked. We sent an invitation email to every professor in the sample. In total, we successfully sent out 500 emails.

The three samples of editors, news professionals, and professors included 1,421 cases.

We understood that nonresponse had been a serious problem with online surveys in recent years. In order to counter possible low response rates in our survey, we created three samples for editors, news professionals, and professors containing roughly 500 people for each group, which were much larger than the sample sizes for populations recommended by Mildred Patten (2000) in her book Understanding Research Methods: An Overview of the Essentials so that, if low response rates occurred, we could base our confidence limits on the actual number of responses themselves. We also sent out one reminder email to the samples, which drastically boosted the response rates, especially for professors and news professionals.

After two weeks of online data collecting in November 2002, we received 223 responses from professors (a 44% response rate), 151 responses from editors (a 29% response rate), and 142 responses from news professionals (a 35% response rate). The overall response rate is 36%. As Singletary (1994) notes, returns of 30% to 40% are common in mail surveys.

The response rates of this online survey seem typical. However, the response rates are still comparatively low. A response bias is potentially present. Many respondents (41%) left textual answers to explain and illustrate their answers to the close-ended questions and/or made comments on the topic.

1. What is the status quo of media convergence in the industry?

By the end of 2002, 19% of the newspapers and commercial television stations with news content in the United States had gone through media mergers. Being merged or not has to do with the size of a company. Larger companies tend to have been merged while smaller ones have not. Roughly half of the news professionals surveyed (48%) reported that they produced news content for multiple media platforms on a routine basis; that was true both in merged media (50%) and non-merged media (48%).

In other words, media merger is not the precondition for practicing news for multiple media platforms. The pressure on news professionals to learn to produce multimedia content is also felt in many non-merged media companies. This finding confirms that media convergence is not necessarily related to media merger.

A typical editor or news director was a man (71%) between 36-45 years old (42%) with a bachelor's degree (76%) who had worked for at least two media (57%) for more than 20 years (53%). A typical news professional was either a man (52%) or woman (48%) between 26-35 years old (43%) with a bachelor's degree (84%) who had worked for at least two media (60%) less than ten years (62%).

Editors had generally worked for more years than news professionals, but they did not have more multiplatform experience than news professionals. As more news companies are practicing cross-media reporting with or without their companies being merged, it is important that editors with multi-platforrn experiences are chosen to direct newsroom businesses. Many editors need cross-media training more urgently than news professionals do if the news company they work for produces news contents for multiple media platforms on a daily basis.

2. Should J-schools train specialists or generalists?

Gil Thelen (2002) said that writers should learn how to write for multimedia and still photographers should learn how to shoot videos, but he was not interested in hiring people with multiple sets of skills. We designed four questions to test how popular Thelen's opinion was.

The majority of the respondents (84%) agreed or strongly agreed with Thelen that journalism students should learn how to write for multiple media platforms. One-way ANOVA shows significant difference among the means for professors, professionals, and editors.

Tukey HSD post hoc tests show that professors were more positive on this statement than editors and professionals, while no significant difference existed between editors and professionals.

A similar number of respondents (85%) agreed or strongly agreed with Thelen that journalism students with a visual emphasis should learn how to produce and edit photos, videos, and online interactive images. One-way ANOVA shows significant difference among the means for professors, professionals, and editors. Tukey HSD post hoc tests show that professors were more positive on this statement than professionals, while professionals were more positive than editors. Most respondents (78%) agreed or strongly agreed that all journalism majors should learn multiple sets of skills, such as writing, editing, TV production, digital photography, newspaper design, and Web publishing.

Oneway ANOVA shows significant differences among the means for professionals, editors, and professors. Tukey HSD post hoc tests show that news professionals who worked in the forefront of news production felt this need more deeply than other respondents. Editors also had such an expectation for them. There is no significant difference between editors and professors.

These findings support the growing evidence that news professionals are being asked to wear multiple hats. The findings also indicate that Thelen's view has its market at this moment when news professionals with multiple sets of skills are highly desirable but not easy to find. Such a view may change as more journalism graduates equipped with multiple sets of skills enter the job market.

The professors' textual answers show that some of the difficulties J-schools have come across include the lack of a friendly curriculum, lack of credit hours to include the components of convergence content, lack of willing cooperation among faculty from different sequences, and lack of expertise, interest, or even time for some professors to develop new courses on convergence.

When asked whether journalism students should still have a specialization, such as writing, photojournalism, broadcasting, and new media, over half (63%) of the respondents agreed or strongly agreed. Over a quarter of the respondents (28%) were negative and 9% were not sure. One-way ANOVA mean comparisons show no significant difference of attitude among professionals, editors, and professors.

Comparing the support rate for this question to those for the first three questions, it is fair to argue that editors, news professionals, and professors emphasized the importance of cross-media training more than that of specialization, though they believed that specialization should not be neglected either.

Currently, students in many J-schools specialize in one area by subscribing to a sequence such as news-editorial, magazine, photojournalism, and broadcast. When asked whether sequences should be reorganized considering the trend of media-platforms merging in the industry, 56% of the professors agreed or strongly agreed, 22% were not sure, and another 22% disagreed or strongly disagreed. The concept of sequences is being shaken among professors though it is still being accepted as a legitimate means of training students in various specialization areas in some J-schools. Speaking on behalf of herself and her colleagues, Professor #93 offered some special insight on this issue:

We can't teach for the "now." We have to prepare students for when they graduate...which in most instances is now five years out. And, we feel a commitment to expose them to all types of writing in all platforms so they can be flexible about their career choice at the front end of their academics. Then, they can apply the skills to a specialty area where they are totally proficient.

"Flexible" is a key term repeatedly seen in editors' and news professionals' textual answers as a suggestion for future journalists. Editors statement is typical:

Our job descriptions are open ended and new hires understand that they are being hired for their skills. They may be hired today to cover the city beat. In six months or in two weeks, if necessary, a person with Quark skills may be asked to fill in or shift duties to include pagination of a particular section. It is important that hires stay flexible.

The new hires, wrote Editor, "need to understand that the information they gather and process can have many different uses, audiences and shelf lives. They need to understand the complexities of the audience mix and be able to respond."

"Those unwilling to be flexible may find themselves in a difficult scenario later in their careers". From a different perspective, Professional concurred: "Students must be flexible, have a vigorous skill set and be prepared to get laid off and move around in the changing media arena." In short, "young journalists must be prepared to fill a variety of roles if they hope to succeed". "The most successful journalists are those that take on assignments willingly, can learn and want to learn".

Specialization in journalistic jobs is still honored, but is losing its favour to cross-media capability in converged media. Today, professionals with different specializations team together to work on multiple media projects. Tomorrow, it is likely that one-man bands will be more and more desired in newsrooms.

3. How should J-schools balance the teaching of critical thinking and that of technical skills?

Most respondents (93%), especially professors, agreed or strongly agreed that journalism students should both learn technical skills, such as online information search and Web design, while learning critical thinking skills in media law, ethics, etc. One-way ANOVA shows significant difference among the means for professionals, editors, and professors. Tukey HSD post hoc tests show that professors were more positive on this point than editors and professionals, while no significant difference existed between editors and professionals.

But, should journalism students spend more time on learning critical thinking skills than on technical skills? Opinions were divided. More than half of the respondents (62%) believed that should be the case, but 19% of the respondents were not sure and another 19% of them did not agree. Oneway ANOVA shows significant difference among the means for professors, professionals, and editors. Tukey HSD post hoc tests show that editors were more positive on this point than professionals, and professionals were more positive than professors. Throughout all the answers from the three groups of respondents, critical thinking was highly regarded as being more important than technical skills. Editors, news professionals, and professors all liked to see good stories, and good stories come from good thinking ability. An editor said: "Journalism graduates need to have a broad, well-rounded education; be critical thinkers; have the ability to write clearly; have a serious work ethic; and know computer basics - in that order".

"You can teach a monkey to type," echoes a writer. Therefore, he strongly suggested that J-schools "get more critical thinking skills pounded into the skulls of the students". While highly emphasizing the importance of critical thinking ability, editors did not mean to neglect the importance of teaching technical skills in schools. We will develop this point when we discuss the next question. Comparing the professors' highest mean for the first question and their lowest mean for the second question, it is clear that professors saw critical thinking as highly important, but preferred a comparatively balanced approach for the teaching of the two sets of knowledge. One professor's comment illustrated this observation:

Knowing technical skill alone will not make you a "good" journalist. Critical thinking is vital not just to a career but to life itself. Without developing your ability to discern and evaluate, you will become "the prey" of society. Next, a technical skill is critical to a career in journalism today. Even print Journalism is very high tech these days and all electronic media require extensive computer knowledge as well as other technical skills. I would place critical thinking skills first on your list of things to do because a developed mind will make it that much easier to develop a creative and technically sound understanding of the technical side of the business.

From a holistic view, there was no substantial disagreement between classrooms and newsrooms when we examine the issue of teaching critical thinking vs. teaching technical skills. Compared to Terry's 2000 poll, this study shows that professors gave a higher status to technical skills in journalism curricula in 2002 than they did in 2000. This is a period during which media convergence garnered its momentum. In short, all respondents generally agreed that J-schools should place emphasis on teaching critical thinking, but at the same time, should not neglect teaching technical skills.

4. Should technical skills be learned at work or in school?

News professionals were asked, "If you wish to possess the technical skills you don't have now, do you prefer to learn them at work or wish you had learned in school?" Editors were given the same question with a slightly different wording.

Chi-Square test shows that the difference between editors and news professionals is significant. This finding well supplements the findings from the preceding questions. It suggests that editors not only looked at future journalists' critical thinking ability, but also hoped that future journalists would already possess the skills needed in a converged newsroom when they are hired.

On the other hand, most professionals preferred that they spend most of their school time on gaining critical thinking ability and learn skills largely at work. The professionals' general preference, to some extent, also reflected their need for technological update at their current positions, so that they can better qualify for multimedia productions.

Many editors and reporters said that school is the best place for journalism students to explore every facet of the media and acquire basic technical skills, though some advanced skills can only be learned on the job. Learning skills while in school, they said, can build confidence and an expansive and broad understanding of the entire field and help with damage control and communication in newsrooms. "If editing and the technical skills were more prevalent in college courses," wrote a multi-tasking editor, "I think I could stave off a lot of headaches when the students become professionals."

An internship was the news professionals' and editors' most recommended venue for enhancing and learning more technical skills and gaining other practical experience. Reporter said: "While I value my college education, my internship and first job provided me with the most valuable skills today." Another reporter said: "While education is great, students who work in media while in school fare much better in the real world."

Some editors had complaints about graduates with a 3.5 GPA but no practical experience and no published news work. An anchor/reporter said that it is important even "for a freshman or sophomore in college to visit a newsroom and shadow someone. So many students wait until they are juniors and seniors to do this and then they realise they made a mistake in selecting their major. You will learn more by watching and doing". One reporter said, "To remain competitive, education must continue throughout a career".

The implication of the discrepancy from this finding suggests that Jschools should place emphasis on teaching critical thinking, expose students to new technology, and design a comprehensive internship programme for students to gain real-world knowledge and further develop their crossmedia technical skills.

5. What skills do news professionals need to learn most at their current positions?

Both editors and news professionals were given this unstructured question with slightly different wordings. We read through all the answers, and categorized them into the following nine facets in random order:

Multimedia production: producing and editing news stories on video, for the Web, and for print; re-purposing the same story for different media. Editors and news professionals both believed that it is not very important for a newspaper reporter to learn how to talk like an anchor in front of a video camera. This skill was even regarded as being less important than knowing how to speak a second language.

Some editors and news professionals also mentioned learning how to manage time for producing multimedia news stories. Editor hoped that journalists in a converged environment would learn to avoid "extra" work by working "smarter" and with greater awareness of the requirements of the different publishing media.

This finding, again, shows that editors valued critical thinking ability more than news professionals did. Editors wanted news professionals to be good thinkers first, and the latter wanted most to learn how to express their thinking in different media.

6. If news professionals have to re-purpose their work for multiple media platforms, will the quality of their work suffer?

Since some authors such as Haiman expressed the concern about the possible decline of work quality if news professionals have to "re-purpose" stories for multiple media platforms, we tried to find out to what extent this concern was shared by editors and news professionals.

Opinions split. Thirty-eight per cent of the editors and professionals agreed or strongly agreed that the quality would deteriorate, 40% disagreed or strongly disagreed, and the other 22% were not sure. Editors and professionals showed no significant difference on this attitude T-test. Such a concern was not prevalent in the news industry.

In response to such concerns, the news director from a converged media company wrote: "When reporters do cross platforms we give them the time to finish the project for all three platforms.

Quality does not suffer. If we were to try to force reporters to cross platforms while operating under daily deadlines then quality could suffer depending on the nature of the story and the extra time consumed".

Another editor summed up this issue: "Some employees can capably handle multiple media and tell stories effectively. Others cannot. Certainly strong technical skills and training can help, but it's not just dependent on that; it depends more on the attitude and aptitude of the journalist".

Quality multimedia work also involves a solid understanding of different cultures in different media. Editors both for and against media convergence noted the difficulty of merging different media with different cultures, and editors in those merged media called for flexibility in aptitude and willingness to cooperate across platforms. For instance, Editor wrote:

Clarity of what convergence means to the news organization is vital and often lacking. This causes unneeded anxiety. Managers have to realise that each medium has its own culture, language, skill set and timetable and is naturally skeptical of anything unfamiliar. It is also true that these same journalists' stock in trade is learning a new culture, language, skill set and timetable-on a daily basis. Therein lies the hope for an efficient news operation running on all cylinders and an effective -maybe even happy-staff.

If most editors and news professionals are not concerned about the quality of the work prepared for multiple media platforms and if news professionals are given enough time to complete their cross-media work, there is little reason to worry that future journalists, if well trained both theoretically and technologically for multiple media platforms, will produce work of poorer quality. Training students to practice news in multiple media platforms will help bridge newsroom cultures from different media and eventually erase such differences.

We have noticed that no significant statistical differences existed between the editors and news professionals from the converged media companies and their counterparts from the not-yet-converged media companies when they answered the questions reported above.

7. How are J-schools coping with media convergence?

From 1998 to 2002, about 60% of the J-schools in the United States redesigned their curricula or developed new courses to prepare students for practicing news in multiple media platforms.

A typical journalism professor was a man (71%) between 46-55 years old (42%) with a doctoral degree (63%) who worked in news media for one to ten years (48%), may still be practicing news (45%) in one way or another, and conducted academic research (66%).

More professors claimed that they were theoretically equipped (81%) than technologically prepared (53%) to teach students how to report news in multiple media platforms. More than half of the professors (57%) had not taught any journalism courses in the last five years where skill sets were beyond their own expertise; 25% of the professors taught one such course and 11% taught two. Nevertheless, the majority of the professors (84%) added content about media convergence either to their existing courses or to new courses or participated in cross-media team-teaching in the last five years.

Worries, concerns, and, sometimes, misconceptions about media convergence appeared in professors' textual answers. For instance, a professor from Montana said: "convergence is not happening". A professor who no longer practiced news said, "In my judgment, the writing portion of preparing news for print and for the Web is exactly the same". Another professor maintained that it was not necessary to teach cross-media news practicing because "few 'want ads' for newspaper reporter and editor positions specifically listed multimedia platform skills as required or preferred experience for new hires".

Many professors worried that media mergers would restrict the number of voices in a community. They regarded media mergers as a grand experiment in the profession and waited for the FCC's ruling on the cross-ownership of different media in the same market.

Wait-and-see-that was the strategy some universities took for teaching media convergence. One professor said that he needed to see the substantive contribution media convergence could make before he would be more serious about this phenomenon. He said that J-schools should be cautious about embracing convergence. Some other universities didn't have the time and resources to teach convergence courses or make major curriculum changes.

Most professors, however, did believe that media convergence was a reality; and "anybody serious about practicing media needs at minimal an acquaintance with various media and at best multiple competencies," as Professor said. Many professors (and editors and news professionals as well) had a clear opinion as to which comes first, teaching critical thinking or teaching technical skills.

While acknowledging the need for incorporating media convergence content in curricula, especially the technological components, professors cautioned against sacrificing conceptual and theoretical courses such as law, ethics, history, cultural studies, critical perspectives, etc. Professor analogized critical thinking as meat and potatoes and technical skills as dessert and side dishes and argued that "the meat and potatoes need to come before one begins to worry about the dessert and side dishes (or side shows)." This viewpoint was popular. Professor wrote:

It's the message, not the medium, that is of paramount importance. If students cannot understand and appreciate the underlying concepts, principles and ethics of journalism, then they cannot produce the type of content that will be of value to a free society. A thorough grounding in journalism must come before any training in tools. The tools are means to an end, not the end in and of themselves.

Incidentally, a reporter had similar thoughts:

- The medium isn't the message, the message is the message. In short, the fundamental analytic and synthetic skills of the news writer are paramount to the message. The medium does not alter the reporter's craft of interpreting news events in the context of the society in a way that will make sense for the receiver of the information. ... Additional skills may be desirable, but for the most parFinally, my answer on merging media companies... reflects my disdain for the corporatization and concentration of control in the media. I think we ought to train mass communicators for a converged world, but as professors we ought to fight like hell against media mergers.

Very few respondents (19%) believed that media mergers benefit all three parties, the general public, news professionals, and media companies, but about one third of the respondents (35%) believed that media companies are the only beneficiaries to such a practice.

These 35% respondents, who were almost equally proportionally found in editors, news professionals, and professors groups, could be regarded as the most critical toward media mergers. We compared these 35% respondents with the rest of the sample and found no significant difference in their answers concerning the necessity of teaching journalism students cross-media writing and visuals and teaching multiple sets of skills. Always, more respondents believed that professors should teach all those things. In short, the respondents' political view was not directly tied to their views of teaching students cross-media practices.

As an experimental industrial trend, media convergence in the sense of media mergers is still in its formative stage. Whether it will sustain its momentum to reach popularity in the nation and how its advantages balance against disadvantages are yet to be seen. While there seems to be a good deal of support for cross-media education, on some questions, professors are more gung-ho than editors and news professionals about the trend. The legitimacy of media mergers needs repeated tests before such mergers can be truly accepted as a healthy development and a full-force education of media convergence can be seen in many in J-schools.

Media convergence, however, is not tied to media mergers. Media convergence, initiated and made possible by digital technology, is more than media mergers propelled largely by financial considerations. More pervasive is the media convergence in the senses of content convergence, technological convergence, and especially role convergence, which have occurred not only in merged media companies but also more in non-merged ones. No matter whether media mergers will continue, the other three forms of media convergence, which are not subject to the FCC regulations, are likely to continue to develop.

Most editors and news professionals in this survey are not from merged media companies. Many editors, news professionals, and professors do not yet see media mergers as beneficial to the general public and news professionals. But, their backgrounds and political views do not prevent them from sharing with other respondents with different backgrounds and political views many opinions regarding where future college journalism should go. Such common understanding is shaping a force to push forward the education of media convergence in campuses nationwide.

To better direct newsroom businesses in a converged media environment, many editors need cross-media training. Many opportunities are out there for news companies and universities to work together to explore the issue of media convergence and provide mid-career professionals and editors cross-media technological training. It seems sensible that opportunities for learning multimedia skills should be made available both on campus and through off-site continuing education programs that are geared for midcareer news professionals as technological developments continue to evolve.

Multi-dimensional news reporting in multiple media platforms will be tomorrow's way news is presented. Therefore, dealing with media convergence in college journalism education is an urgent necessity. The wait-and-see strategy will place a Jschool in a disadvantaged position over the long run. These findings tell us that J-schools do need to provide cross-media knowledge and experience to their students, so that the latter can better qualify for cross-media jobs in the future. Media convergence poses both challenge and opportunity to J-schools for them to reconsider their current curriculum design, sequence setting, faculty composition, teaching methods, and internship approaches.

Many professors, editors, and news professionals have expressed concern that media mergers will eliminate voices in a community, thus potentially eroding democracy. However, media mergers did not start only these days. As a TV reporter wrote in the textual answer, when she first went to Philadelphia years ago, there were five daily papers. Now, there are two; and they are both published by the same company.

Philadelphia is not alone in such media reduction. The question is whether the general public feels that it is less well-informed than it was thirty or forty years ago and that democracy has been eroded by such media reduction prior to media convergence. This is a topic for another study. Nevertheless, students should be exposed to such a legitimate concern and learn to take a critical look at the phenomenon of media mergers.

J-schools should continue to teach critical thinking courses and meld critical thinking components into the teaching of all courses. Critical thinking is the cornerstone of journalism education. However, technology courses or course components should also be given the status they deserve. In other words, there should be a balanced curriculum to include both kinds of courses, and many cross-media related courses should contain both components. An ideal curriculum should balance the load of technical skill-based courses and critical thinking courses, weighting toward the latter.

Critical thinking and technical skills can go hand in hand rather than being competitors for class time. A balanced curriculum can help students better gather, produce, edit, and deliver quality news; more creatively and professionally materialize their ideas; and make them better fit into the market, especially in an economic downturn.

University of Florida professor Melinda McAdams, one of the Washington Post's first online editors, told colleagues that if colleges don't teach journalists the technical skills they will need, no one else is likely to take on the responsibility. "[T]he reality they'll face in the world is they'll have to teach themselves". The classroom should be the first stop for students to at least get exposed to and get familiar with the technology for cross-media practices, though they can become more proficient with such technology through internship and their future jobs.

With all that said, technology courses should not dominate journalism students' education, and technology should not be taught for the sake of technology. Technology must serve the purposes of doing good journalism.

Apart from teaching students multimedia productions, new technology, and computer-assisted reporting, J-schools still need to place good writing-the very basics of being a journalist-as the top priority for all journalism students regardless of sequences or specializations.

Many respondents point out that the teaching of technology should not be at the expense of the teaching of critical thinking. Many J-schools have no more elective hours for students to learn cross-media technology within the existing parameter of curriculum. For such schools, curriculum redesign is a necessity.

Though some J-schools such as Indiana University School of Journalism have eliminated sequences to provide a comprehensive education to all journalism students, we expect that sequences will continue to exist for some time in some other J-schools. However, it has become increasingly important to encourage students from all sequences to learn technology and reporting skills from other platforms. Sequences in many J-schools are regarded as dinosaurs because it no longer makes sense to teach broadcast and newspaper, for instance, as two unrelated bodies of knowledge in the era of media convergence and students can opt for a specialization without sequences but with professors' advice.

Most respondents expect that future journalists will be competent in producing news in multiple media platforms while being particularly strong in one area. It appears that students will be prudent to opt to specialize in either print or television and take several electives in a secondary platform, either radio or online journalism. Versatility and specialization should be equally important.

The majority of the editors do expect that future writers will be able to and willing to write for multiple media platforms, and photographers and designers will create multimedia visuals, though such expectations will not be converted into requirements in job ads for a while because "too many newsroom dinosaurs have to die off first," as Editor put it. But chances are they will, as Nelson (2002) predicted. Most editors even expect that new hires will possess multiple sets of skills to become "superhack masters of multimedia," to use Gates's term.

The needs are out there, but whether the training of such superhack masters will become the norm, as Gates questioned, largely depends on whether J-schools are willing and able to develop those "avant-garde" courses. Apart from the technological aspect, students also need to learn to cooperate and collaborate across newsrooms so as to bridge different newsroom-cultures. Students need to be both theoretically and technically prepared for media convergence.

The findings from this study show that more than half of the J-schools in the United States have redesigned their curricula or developed new courses to cope with media convergence, but professors need to be better prepared technologically. Team-teaching is one approach to solve the problem, but will the teaching of media convergence be more effective if a professor at least knows as much as a student in a convergence class will learn? Does the Gestalt psychological principle "the whole is more than the sum of its parts" also apply in such a context? Professors normally learned little or no technical skills while studying in a J-school doctoral programme.

Their technical knowledge inherited from their previous media experience is easily dated. More than half of the professors (54%) no longer practiced news after they began to teach, as we found out in this study. In some cases, professors know less technical knowledge than their students do.

Therefore, in the middle of heavy teaching and research, updating and learning more technical knowledge for teaching convergence is a big challenge for many professors. Learning from each other during team-teaching is, of course, a good way of learning, but professors also need to find time to do self-teaching to gain more in-depth knowledge. J-schools should provide financial support for professors to attend new technology workshops. Being exposed to or involved in community news reporting in a multiple-media-platform environment, if possible, is an even better way of learning new technology for professors.

Attitude and aptitude, together with time management ability, will be the key to producing quality work in newsrooms. Since editors and news professionals are not prevalently concerned about the quality of work currently re-purposed for multiple media platforms, there is no reason for them or professors to be concerned that students being trained on multiple media platforms will be jacks of all trades but masters of none.

Students need to learn how to re-purpose their work in a timely manner and control the quality of their work in a professional manner. One editor said it best: "To sum things up, journalists need to be prepared to hit the workplace running. With limited resources and cutbacks across the country, the new hire will be the person who is the most skilled, coupled with energy and willing to be flexible as needed."

Media convergence is a comprehensive topic. Many sub-topics related to this study are yet to be explored. For instance, how can the general public benefit from media convergence? Does the general public in markets where media are converged think that they are less well-informed and that democracy has suffered in their areas? How can news professionals benefit from media convergence? What are the typical differences between the career lives of the news professionals in converged media and the career lives the same news professionals led before the media were converged? We call on mass communication scholars to continue to study media convergence to shed more light on this phenomenon that will affect every one of us.

7

Sting Operation and Investigative Journalism

Setting a trap to nab wrong doers is no doubt an accepted facet of a criminal investigative process. In corruption cases, apprehending the bribe-taker in the act is accepted as a clinching evidence of his culpability.

But catching someone on camera engaged in the sex act does not necessarily establish any. If a sting operation of the kind set up by the private channel suggests anything at all it is the tendency of some officials and politicians to misuse their positions.

That is neither proof of past misconduct or the certainty of such behaviour in future. In the novelty of catching some action on camera, one should not make the mistake of viewing a tendency towards criminality as proof of actual wrongdoing.

However the following norms should be looked into carefully before going for any kind of sting operation:

- Sting operations are to be mounted only on persons against whom some evidence of criminality exists and a sting operation is considered necessary for getting conclusive evidence.
- Permission for sting operations must be obtained from appropriate courts or the attorney general. This safeguard has been laid down since those who mount a sting operation themselves commit the offence of impersonation, criminal trespass and making a person commit an offence. (Remember that 'Cheating by Impersonation' is a crime under Section 416 of the Indian Penal Code.)
- 'Where there is evidence of editing of tapes and films, there is an automatic presumption that the recording is probably not authentic. '
- 'There must be a concurrent record in writing of the various stages of the sting operation.

Sting journalism is not new to India. Years ago, an operation by an online news site called Tehelka caught top politicians and army officers taking bribes from journalists posing as businessmen. It was widely praised as investigative journalism carried out in the public interest. Today, almost all television news channels in India routinely use spy cameras to expose corruption.

But in a society that remains more buttoned up than those in the United States or Europe, the Indian news media have been reluctant to report on the private lives of public figures. In the land that gave the world the Kama Sutra, the ancient guide to carnal relations, public displays of affection by couples are discouraged. Bollywood movies showed their first on-screen kiss only a decade ago, and television remains strictly controlled.

STING OPERATIONS IN INDIAN CONTEXT

Today, television media has more or less taken the lead. Among the most popular programmes in India, are those reporting on corruption and misdeeds of politicians and government officials. 'Candid camera,' as it is called here in the US, has taken hold in India.

It reports with hidden camera the many true stories of the day — the bribe that the police inspector extracts from the victim of a crime before agreeing to investigate, the 'fee' that the government officer charges for his giving the order to make an electric connection, and the 'contribution' that a company pays a member of Parliament before bringing up a legislative concern in the Lok Sabha.

These stories are now part of the family entertainment offered by many television stations, and, believe it or not, those in power are a lot more careful today.

As many new television channels enter the market, there is even greater competition for viewers. These stations will have to offer something better and more informative than the ordinary.

With foreign media joining forces with Indian operators, these stations have the financial backing to produce better programmes. Sure, there will be some weeds, but overall the flowers will brighten up the garden. The nation will benefit immensely. Unfortunately, the print media, especially the daily newspapers, are still monopolised by a few proprietors. Foreign media is not allowed to have more than 26 per cent of the total ownership. Consequently, many newspapers do not have the financial strength to take on today's major players in the market. When this last bastion of power in the media is removed from the few proprietors, we can expect vigourous competition in search of truth. The power of the pen shall prevail. Neither the politician nor the judiciary will be able to deny the people's right to information – the truth about ourselves and our rulers.It is the best time for Indian media.

There are so many television news channels around which were utterly unimaginable even 10 years ago. Many of them many not be there a few years hence. The "shaking out" process will take care of that. But if you had thought that plenty meant diversity, then you are in for great disappointment. Almost all of the channels want to do the same thing better than the others, outwitting each other in terms of deafening loudness and numbing triviality. It would be dishonest not to say that some of that "trash" is indeed delightful. The dozens of channels do not give dozens of perspectives or views. Plenty does not translate into intelligent choice for the viewer.

Viewers of A and B might feel that C may have miscalculated in choosing news anchors with the élan of models, and that D is too belligerent. But there is no simple polarisation. It is hard to ignore the wimpy liberalism of A, with anchors wanting to convert the tragedy of October 8 earthquake to solve the problem of the two Kashmirs.

The channel clearly supports economic liberalisation in the most unintelligent way, that only English-educated, muddled Indian middle class can do. The reporters and anchors of this channel are only too ready to jump at the poor communists every time they raise pertinent objections to the Manmohan Singh government's woolly-headed ideas about privatisation.

They perceive the poor and marginalised people of India's cities and villages in the same way that socialite socialists did in the 1960s and 1970s. Forget the countless other inanities of this channel and those of others. They may improve in time. At the moment they are wallowing in their callowness.

In between this a sting of the "Operation Duryodhan" kind comes as a whiff of fresh air in this hothouse atmosphere of news channels. And that is the danger. A sting operation should not be considered journalism as such because of the many ambivalences and ambiguities involved in its modus operandi. It is guerrilla journalism at its worst.

And the best is based on naïve assumption contained in the assertion often made by those who carry out a sting like that of "Operation West End" and "Operation Duryodhan" that they are exposing the corruption embedded in the polity. Of course, there is also the "art for art's sake" aspect to it.

"We are interested in the story. We are not really concerned about its implications or its fallout" they say. The aestheticism implied in this chimes well with the spirit of guerrilla journalism.

A sting is problematic because it is a curious mixture of fact and fiction. The companies that are floated to entrap the corrupt politicians do not exist. The transactions truly belong to the virtual world because no real transaction is done despite money changing hands.

In "Operation West End", no arms were purchased as is the case in corrupt defence deals. Similarly, in "Operation Duryodhan", no real business interests benefited by those few members of parliament raising those questions. Yes, it shows the system is full of holes. But that is not good enough in journalism.

As in the case of the 1951 case of HG Mudgal, who was shown to have raised questions on receiving money from the Bullion Merchants Association, where both parties to the transaction are real, what is missing in a sting is a real instance of corruption. Sting is, on the one hand, a prank, a serious one. Like a good joke which has an undeniable element of truth, sting-as-prank does have its element of truth but it does not have a greater status than that. Sting journalism is not an alternative to opiate journalism of the news channels of the moment.

Television channels face terrible limitations. They cannot ever show the whole picture, but only a part of it. They cannot debate the pros and cons except in the manner of sophomores, either supporting or opposing a motion in a college debating society.

The intellectual disability that the channels display can be overcome, but no one wants to and the commercial motives are not always the only ones for not doing so. Unfortunately, debate, the essence of democracy, can only be carried out in and through the print media.

It is in the traditional print media that we see the present-day distortions much more clearly than even in the television channels. We need to look at the English language newspapers, though they represent a minority section of the reading public in the country, to get the full flavour.

Excepting an obdurately left-leaning English language newspaper, all the others are blindly pro-economic liberalisation. It is, of course, no sin to champion the cause of a free market economy. The curious part is that the English newspapers display a herd mentality. There are no individual voices.

There is no dissent. They do not even differ among themselves that there can be many kinds of market economy, and that the Manmohan Singh- P Chidambaram version need not be the only one. It is hilarious to hear young and serious editors citing the not-always-reliable planning commission statistics to say that poverty in India has declined.

Not just liberalisation, the English-language papers are gung ho about Bush and his regime. The president and his men would blush at the unstinting support they get from the India's English-language newspapers. While the Americans are having second thoughts about the wisdom of the war in Iraq, foreign policy pundits in these papers speak the language of the US State Department.

At the time of the invasion of Iraq, when the Bush team brushed aside the need to obtain a United Nations mandate, India's strategic affairs experts in the media pooh-poohed the spineless UN. When the Bush administration recognised the need for getting the UN backing to legitimise its presence in Iraq, there was silence on the Indian front.

It seemed that our school dropout politicians had a better sense of reality than the "erudite" writers on foreign affairs. One of the editors has been described as "pathologically pro-American", which is true of many others in the newspapers as well. And even when something is true about the American view, you suspect it when it is published in these papers. On the other hand, the habitually vocal anti-Americans stance does not enjoy credence even when what it says is true.

It is a good thing that biases hang so openly all round and they are being flaunted proudly. It is better than dull and monotonous objectivity of the past.

But the problem with the Indian English newspapers is that there is nothing much more than uninformed biases.

In the United States, the Nation and the National Review stand at the opposite ends of the ideological spectrum and they are as loud as anyone in India. But they engage with the opponent, and argue out their positions. That is missing in India.

There is a need to get back to this liberalisation phenomenon, and the starry-eyed gaping of the Indian editors and reporters. The implosion of Enron was nearly a "non-event" in the Indian newspapers despite the fact that the swindling executive team of Enron, many of whom have been punished by the US courts, played their dirty games, going out of their way to woo the politicians in the country when they got the Dabhol project.

No one raised questions about the inequitable power-purchase agreements (PPA) made with Enron, which was the main cause of the debt burden of the Dabhol project. But the whole of the Indian media went hammer and tongs about the Volcker report, which had no substantial truth in it. The report was an attempt by the Americans to make the case against the UN as a den of corruption. The Indian journalists were so overwhelmed by their pro-American bias that they went into action over something that does not affect India's interests in a big way.

It is hard to imagine Indian newspapers doing critical and sharp stories against the Reliance group of companies the way many of the American newspapers did over Microsoft. Bill Gates did not enjoy any media immunity being the richest person in the world. Indian corporate honchos will never face the heat in the media. Even with regard to an angel company like the Infosys, the media would not write a critical story about the company.

Narayanan Murthy and Nandan Nilekani are fully aware of the limitations of Infosys, and about what little it can do to solve the problems facing the Indian people and the Indian economy. But the media dare not say anything about it. Indian reporters failed to pursue anything resembling investigative and independent journalism, and the media was generally prepared to go along with the government's view of things.

Corruption in both the government and private sector and the cynicism on the part of almost everyone towards the possibility of any positive change, in this context a free and independent media in India is the country's best hope. Until the Indian media is prepared to uncover and report on the corruption and misuse of power by politicians, government officials and private companies, the country will not be able to achieve its full developmental potential in an equal and fair society. Without transparency in governance, it would be difficult, if not impossible, to formulate sound policies.

It is hard not to quote an interesting report that Amy Waldman of the New York Times did for her paper. She travelled to the outskirts of Vishakhapatnam and Bangalore, and described the ironies and contradictions of liberalisation. She showed how many in the Indian middle class are getting into credit card debt trap, like their counterparts in the US. The report revealed the vulgarity of money power. It was published on December 5, 2005.

The Hindu was the only paper to have reprinted the report though many other newspapers too subscribe to the NYT Syndicate. It is the kind of story that will not be written or published in the Indian newspapers of today. And thereby hangs a tale of the state of the Indian media.

Can things be better than this in the media? It would not be right to draw up utopian scenarios where everything is right in the business. It will never be so. The alternative to a media chasing the market is not the altruistic dreamland of non-governmental organisations and the myopic idealism of those who lead them.

As they say of democracy that the cure of the ills of democracy is more democracy, it is so in the case of media as well. There is need for more voices in the India media. Monopoly in the information sector is not only unhealthy but also dangerous as well. One of the advantages of a market economy is that it is possible for many people to enter the arena, start newspapers and magazines, set up radio and television stations.

What is needed then is for social entrepreneurs to enter the media, and contribute to the apparently cacophonous chorus. It is then possible for people to have access to different points of view. There is a need to craft a media policy by discerning individuals, and chart the necessary legislation, to enable people with limited budgets to start radio and television stations.

The big houses should not be allowed to swamp the sector. The persistence with which advocates of right to information have been able to get through the necessary legislation should serve as a model to those who want keep the media scene free and vibrant. Private monopoly and governmental controls have to be fought constantly to safeguard media, the effective channel for the inalienable and natural rights to freedom of speech and expression.

There is section of people who firmly support the opinion that to expose corruption in the high places, both the media and legal community are justified to use the sting operations as an instrument of exposure where gathering normal evidence under the normal provisions of the Indian Evidence Act is made impossible by the men and women in exalted positions.

The discussion with the eminent legal luminary was triggered off by a series of media exposure, both by the print media and TV channels, ranging from the Judeo affair, the Telgi affair, the operation against former Chief Minister of Chhattisgargh Ajit Jogi and the JMM bribery case against former Prime Minister P.V. Narasimha Rao, in which he had been finally acquitted after years of trial and litigations. The Tehelka and Hawala cases too hovered in the background. Think "If a Prime Minister, a Home Minister or a Chief Minister is corrupt, how does one gather dependable information against them which can be cited in courts of law as reliable evidence?

In such case the media, often with the support and collaboration of the legal profession, had resorted to sting operations. British court in a sensational sting operation against a top British leader involved in bribery and sex scandal to expose corruption in high places, the media was justified in using sting operations. Since the Indian law is mostly based on the English law, the implementation is obvious.

Corruption had infiltrated into the judiciary too, political corruption, increasing by leaps and bounds of this country, in this scenario bribe-taker is of course, guilty of corruption but the bribe-giver should also be held guilty of equal corruption. Actually sting is good if it is done with ethics and for public interest. In India There was a lot of fine investigative journalism. Indian Express under Arun Shourie was taking on Rajiv Gandhi's government. But no, there were no hidden camera stings, and the few who were taking on the government were some exceptionally brave souls. Actually they are thoroughly professional and understand the true ethics of investigative journalism.

STING OPERATION AND INDIAN LEGAL SYSTEM

A succession of recent sting operations reinforced the public's worst fears about India's politicians. Three such events damned the reputation of Parliament itself. First, there was the sting operation that captured on camera MPs accepting bribes to put questions in the House.

Never mind how severe the punishment meted out to the erring legislators, the damage in terms of public perception has left an indelible mark. People no longer need rumour to convince them about corruption in politics. They have seen it with their own eyes on TV. They now know that most, if not all, politicians are corrupt.

Quick on the heels of the cash-for-questions scam was another sting operation that targeted MPs. It captured some of them on camera accepting cuts from the money they sanctioned for projects under the Local Area Development Scheme.

Several politicians questioned why the scheme should be criticized due to its misuse by a few. It will take more time and harder knocks before our honourable MPs get around to focusing on the more fundamental question: Why should those elected to make and protect laws be empowered to spend official funds for development work? That should be strictly under purview of the executive, whether at the national, state or local levels. The mere fact that legislators have encroached in executive functioning exposes the gross distortions that have crept into our system.

The final blow to Parliament came when two MPS, with other criminal cases pending against them, provided false information to a foreign embassy for obtaining visas. This created international embarrassment. An earlier sting operation was telecast to show innumerable local officials accepting bribes. The government itself was impelled to move in court against 90 of them. Another ongoing crisis regarding buildings illegally erected escalated after the court ordered their demolition. This has exposed the rotten state of governance inflicted on citizens for five decades. The nation is caught in a dilemma.

To demolish some and spare others equally guilty violates a fundamental principle of justice – of providing equality under law. But if all the guilty are to be punished almost whole cities would have to be demolished. Over five decades of permissive sanction of law violation have wrecked the system. The beneficiaries of the original corruption that connived at illegal construction are in many cases dead and gone. With vengeance the piled up crimes against the system are now confronting the nation.

Critics have questioned the morality of sting operations carried out by journalists. At the micro level there is much to question this brand of journalism. The motives of the journalists may be questionable. The degree of entrapment practiced on the victims to fulfill a preconceived script raises serious questions about the extent of real guilt of those caught on camera. For instance, in the earlier *Tehelka* sting operation there were serious lapses that made the exercise spurious. Out of 100 hours of tape only select portions suiting the political agenda of the journalists or their unseen mentors were shown.

One Tehelka reporter involved in the sting, Mr Mathew Samuel, said there were tapes implicating Mr L. K. Advani, then home minister, for having received kickbacks in the Rs 1,300 crore Indo-Israeli deal to provide border fencing and communication systems.

Immediately the *Tehelka* chief contradicted him and cabled the home minister giving assurance there would be no release of any such tape. So, which *Tehelka* activist spoke the truth? Why couldn't all the 100 hours of tape be made available to the public? The less said about the commission of inquiry that went into the matter the better.

There was deliberate effort to persuade people on camera to take names, and if names were taken, to treat such hearsay as evidence. Thus two of those interviewed on tape, Mr RK Gupta and Mr RK Jain, volunteered imprecatory information to their questioners. Mr Aniruddha Bahal, a senior operative in the sting operations later told the press: "Jain and Gupta talked to Mathew first.

Then they replicated these things which are on tape to me. Jain cooked up something while talking to Samuel, then he was trying to recook the story for me. " What was he need to replicate a story? Or was it simply rehearsal before going on camera? When Mr RK Jain was threatened for defamation by Mr Yashwant Sinha for remarks made on camera, he quickly apologized and admitted he had lied!

Was it mere coincidence that the two major victims of the *Tehelka* episode were at that time the main rivals of Mr LK Advani, then home minister? Mr Fernandes was the high-powered NDA coalition chief and Mr Bangaru Laxman was the first Dalit president of the BJP. The sting operation implicating the cash-for questions MPs was also masterminded by Mr Aniruddha Bahal. Learning from experience perhaps, this time there was a lesser degree of entrapment. Although one of the MPs did at first say that there was no need to make payment. Should his level of guilt be equated with the others who considered cash-for-questions to be their right? It is for parliament to consider this.

Spurred on by the power of camera and the impact of TV, the police exposed their grotesque perception of what makes good democracy. A lady officer in Meerut actually invited TV channels to capture on camera her colleagues and herself visiting a park that was a rendezvous for young couples. The police slapped and beat up unsuspecting and innocent young couples.

The cops actually thought they were doing a great job that deserved exposure on national TV! They administered their version of quick justice.

If this is how the police perceive their role as guardians of law, what kind of democracy do we have? TV also reported several other cases of police bestiality as they tortured and thrashed victims who they thought were guilty. In one case the police thrashed one of their own colleagues and harassed his school going children!

Irate politicians say there should be sting operations against media too. All strength to them! There must be plenty of corruption in the media. Much of what the media does merits serious questioning. But all this is at the micro level. We may deify or damn what individual politicians, officials or media persons may do. It is the macro effect that deserves consideration. If all the thieves in society fall out and start demolishing each other for motives entirely unworthy, it is nonetheless good. An unintended cleansing process would have begun. Public cynicism generated by such exposures could damage the system. That would be even more welcome. The system needs some destruction before it will be repaired. As the year ends, the destruction seems to have begun. If the human instinct for survival asserts itself, those who sit at the commanding heights of society will wake up and undertake serious systemic reform. To accelerate the process just one catalytic event is required. The final Supreme Court judgement on the unconstitutional dissolution of the Bihar assembly should be delivered early next year. It could be the necessary catalyst. Or it could be new revelations in the Volcker probe. 2006 may well be the year in which India starts to reform itself.

SETTING A TRAP

Sting Operation asThe Exposure of sordid truths is not just a duty of the media, but a public expectation. The 'sting' is a legitimate though often contentious adopted by both the electronic and print media. Now a days sting operations undercover police work that sets up a situation to catch criminals in the act an undercover police operation in which police pose as criminals to trap law violators. Originally Sting means "to cheat or swindle".

Act of stinging means "carefully planned theft or robbery". The word "sting" derives its origin from 1930's American slang, meaning an act of theft or fraud, especially one that was carefully planned in advance and swiftly executed. In this sense the term is best known as the title of a Hollywood film. The term then evolved in 1970's American usage to mean a police undercover operation designed to ensnare criminals. In this latter sense, "sting" is therefore a synonym for the expression "set a trap to catch a crook".

In law enforcement, a sting operation is an operation designed to catch a person committing a crime by means of deception. A typical sting will have a law-enforcement officer or cooperative member of the public play a role as criminal partner or potential victim and go along with a suspect's actions to gather evidence of the suspect's wrongdoing.

TRIAL BY MEDIA AN ETHICAL PROBLEM

There is the classic ethical problem that haunts all sting operations: can you hold somebody responsible for a crime that he would not have committed if you hadn't encouraged him? The essence of all entrapment is that you promise a man a reward for breaking the law and then, apprehend him when he takes the bait.

Tehelka's journalists wore wigs, pasted on false moustaches and affected strange accents. To be able to do all this requires skills that most of us simply do not possess. To be sure, there are exceptions. In the UK, *The News of the World* a sensationalist newspaper often referred to as The Screws of the World has a Pakistani investigative reporter whose specialty requires him to dress up as an Arab and fool important Brits into believing that he will give them lots of money if they are indiscreet or unethical. Once notable victim of such a sting operations has been Sophie Wessex, the wife of Prince Edward.

But no senior British newspaper would go as far as The News of The World. Most journalists take the line that acting and all that it implies – lying, dressing-up, making-up stories, fabricating identities – involve non-journalistic activities and therefore will have nothing to do with stings.

Trial by media is a phrase popular in the late 20th century and early 21st century to describe the impact of television and newspaper coverage on a person's reputation by creating a widespread perception of guilt regardless of any verdict in a court of law.

One of the first celebrities in the 20th century to be arguably tried by media was Fatty Arbuckle who was acquitted by the courts but nevertheless lost his career and reputation and ultimately his life due to the media coverage.

Along similar lines to the Fattle Arbuckle example is the case of Michael Jackson, whose career has been severely negatively affected by the media circus surrounding various accusations of child abuse. Although acquitted by the courts, Jackson's reputation and career has been diminished to a certain extent.

Parallels can be drawn between these cases and the trial of O. J. Simpson. The connection is less about guilt or innocence but about the promotion of the media coverage in the public mind above the status of the court. Another interesting case in the US was the Rodney King incident and subsequent trial of the police officers involved. Once again an acquittal is challenged by the media reporting with violent consequences.

What makes this case particularly important historically is the fact that it was amateur video footage which provided the key evidence of perceived guilt. As video cameras and their digital successors and CCTV become more wide spread, this type of 'caught on camera' incident become more and more common (another case of alleged police brutality has come to light in Manchester in February 2004.) This can pose real problems for the legal system as the evidence they provide may be inadmissible for technical reasons (e. g. not being able to pinpoint exact times) but they give very strong images for the media (and public) to seize upon and the potential to manipulate by editing.

Even where a criminal court finds somebody guilty the media can still appear to sit in judgement over their sentence. Examples include Myra Hindley whose proposed release from prison after thirty years was widely condemned by the British press (the argument became moot when she died in 2002); Maxine Carr who, having served her sentence, has been released and is, according to some commentators being "demonised by the press".

One case popularized by the media between 1980 and 1982 was the murder trial of Lindy Chamberlain in Australia who was convicted of killing her baby, but later released in 1986 on new evidence showing that a dingo had in fact committed the act as was originally claimed by Chamberlain. The motion picture *A Cry in the Dark* depicted Chamberlain, as played by actress Merry Streep, caught in a "trial by media" which fed the publics, and subsequently the jury's false conviction of her.

While often the coverage in the press can be said to reflect the views of the person in the street. However, more credibility is generally given to printed material than water cooler gossip. The responsibility of the press to confirm reports and leaks about individuals being tried has come under increasing scrutiny and journalists are calling for higher standards. There was much debate over U. S President Bill Clinton's Impeachment Trial and prosecutor Kenneth Starr's investigation and how the media handled the trial by reporting commentary from Lawyers which influenced public opinion.

Another example was the investigation into Biologist Dr. Steven Hatfill allegedly sending anthrax through the U. S. mail as a terrorist attack, which resulted in no conviction, but Hatfill went on to sue as his reputation was severely tarnished and career destroyed.

Families and friends of convicted criminals have apparently successfully used the power of the media to reopen cases, such as the Stephen Downing case in Derbyshire where a campaign by a local newspaper editor resulted in a successful appeal and his release after twenty seven years in prison.

In India, between September 2004 and March 2005, the media - print, audio and visual all wrote about His Holiness Sri Jayendra Saraswathi, the revered Hindu religious leader, suggesting his guilt in a murder case, but the High Courts of Madras and Andhra Pradesh and the Supreme Court of India repeatedly found that there was no material evidence to find him guilty and came down heavily on the media and the Government of Tamilnadu for misuse of Government Machinery.

Tejpal may still be a hero (judging by the manner in which ordinary, middle class citizens react to him) but he is a hero who is deeply in debt. Of his targets, George Fernandes is back as Defence Minister and acts as though Tehelka never happened. Bangaru Laxman has yet to get back his party post but seems rehabilitated in all other respects. He appears regularly on TV as a legitimate political spokesman to remind us that he believes he was set-up.

Tehelka itself has closed down. After the government targeted two of its investors and destroyed their lives, nobody with money would touch Tehelka. Its offices were raided and its journalists arrested.

The Commission set up to investigate the revelations that emerged from Operation West End was also charged with investigating Tehelka's antecedents (an act that is unprecedented in the history of investigative journalism anywhere in the world). Such were the demands of the Commission that Tehelka spent more time on finding files and writing legal responses than it did on journalism.

For a while, Tejpal kept it going by borrowing money from friends. Eventually, he called his staff and said that he simply couldn't borrow any more.

The web-site closed down. So, that's the second paradox. Everybody in politics (though not the service officers who have been court-martialled) indicted by Tehelka has flourished, but Tehelka and its backers have been finished.

In any sting operation, the motives of those who conduct the operation are as important as (or even more important) than the results of the sting.

Tehelka team's work is now baptised as "cowboy journalism". Sting operations carried out by Tehelka which exposed certain Members of Parliament who were accepting cash from interested parties finally became a mere farce. In the sting operations, the motive was not bribery for the sake of getting questions asked but for checking out the susceptibility of elected representatives.

If these gentlemen are willing to sell their souls for a penny, shouldn't they be exposed? And how else, may one ask, can they be exposed? Would those inclined to accept bribes admit to their weakness to the media in an act of bravura? If MPs have for years been accustomed to play in tandem with interested parties for some compensation should they not be exposed in public interest? Admittedly two wrongs do not make a right, but what about the public? Should it not have the right to know what is going on behind its back?

Let us admit that a string operation is, ipso facto, illegal and unethical. Can the media indulge in illegal and unethical means to achieve a noble end? Isn't it time that the entire nation addresses itself to this question? We live, alas, in a corrupt world. Should the media accept it as just one of those things and devote itself to 'Page three journalism' ignoring life in the raw? What sort of media would that be? Whether one likes it or not, the string operations recently carried out have shown human nature at its lowest.

And, but for those operations, one would never have known how some MPs conduct themselves. If reports are to be believed, the string operators sold the result of their operation for Rs 58 lakh. The idea, obviously, was do make the information gathered to as large an audience as is possible in the circumstances.

Can one blame the string operators? In this matter there are many rights and wrongs. One can take a high and mighty attitude towards the sting operators and charge them with immorality. But should not one also be grateful to them for exposing those who were elected in good faith and have proved by their action that they do not deserve public respect and are best deprived of their status?

MEDIA BIAS

Media bias is a term used to describe a real or perceived bias of journalists and news producers within the mass media, in the selection of which events will be reported and how they are covered.

The term "media bias" usually refers to a pervasive or widespread bias contravening the standards of journalism, rather than the perspective of an individual journalist or article. Sting Operations is one of the best part of modern media revolution. It just uncovers the real face of people whether it is Page3 Audience, Politicians, Bureaucrats and even the Mob.

Things used to happen before as well, but perhaps we weren't too well equipped with the right technology to catch them red handed. Sting operations leave no scope of negotiation.

They leave no questions unanswered. An *NDTV* sting operation exposed trucks carrying foodgrains from the Food Corporation of India godown ending upin private warehouses, instead of the ration shops in the capital.

For a country of couch potatoes, the 'casting couch' story about the seamier side of the glamour world, or the soft underbelly of Bollywood, is simply one more item for entertainment. But there's more to sting than meets the eye or hits one's ears on the cocktail circuit. Bruce Hay of Harvard Law School writes in his working paper titled, "Sting operations, undercover agents, and entrapment",that sting operations are "a common but controversial law-enforcement technique — controversial because the police participate in, or even orchestrate, the very crime for which the defendant is convicted".

The defining feature of a sting operation, says Hay, is that through covert means the authorities create, or facilitate, the offence.

"Normally this is done by having an undercover agent hold out some sort of bait, or opportunity, to commit a crime, and then punishing the person who takes the bait.

The obvious advantage of this technique is that the crime can be caught on tape, thus eliminating many of the evidentiary difficulties of ordinary law enforcement. It is this `manufactured' quality of the offence that makes sting operations so troubling," explains the author. That's something applicable to stings by the media too.

"Injustice is relatively easy to bear; what stings is justice," said H. L. Mencken. Adapting it, protagonists of sting may sing its praise thus, "Injustice is not easy to bear!

So, what's just is to sting!" Yet, when sting ends up merely tickling rather than ensuring enough evidence for an open-and-shut case, its venom fails to deliver its full potency.

UNDERCOVER OPERATIONS EXPOSED

New information has confirmed that the undercover British soldier who shot and seriously wounded an RUC man in North Belfast on 14 January was carrying out surveillance on Ardoyne republicans.

TWO STING OPERATIONS RAISE DISTURBING QUESTIONS ABOUT US TERROR ALERT

Two "sting" operations involving the US and Pakistan have raised disturbing new questions about the latest terror alert, and the so-called "war on terrorism" as a whole.

The first was a major international operation against the Al Qaeda network, involving intelligence agencies in a number of different countries, including the US, Britain and Pakistan. The second was strictly a US trap sprung by the FBI against immigrants in Albany, New York.

Taken together, these two operations provide fresh confirmation that the first priority of the US "war on terrorism" is to terrorise the American people in order to achieve political ends, even at the cost of aiding and abetting real acts of terror. The major sting operation centred on the figure of Mohammad Naeem Noor Khan, the 25-year-old computer expert arrested by Pakistani security forces in Lahore. A top Bush administration official released his name, claiming that he was the principal source of the information that led to raising of the terror alert level from yellow to orange in New York City, Washington, D. C., and Newark, New Jersey. The officials described his computer as a "treasure trove" of data on Al Qaeda's operations and potential US targets of terrorist attacks.

It was subsequently revealed that information on the computer pointing to the surveillance of financial institutions in the US was several years old, predating the September 11, 2001, attacks on New York and Washington, and that there was no intelligence pointing to any imminent threat or terrorist plot. The media lavished coverage on official government warnings and unsubstantiated claims given by unidentified intelligence officials that other undisclosed intelligence pointed to a pending attack.

While helping to stoke an atmosphere of hysteria, the major news outlets largely ignored what was undoubtedly the most substantive story to come out of the official fear campaign and police-state security measures mounted by Washington. Mohammed Naeem Noor Khan, whose name the White House first leaked to the *New York Times*, was at the time working for Pakistani intelligence as a covert agent.

After his capture, he agreed to continue functioning as a key communications link between far-flung Al Qaeda operatives. Using encrypted e-mail, he was luring senior Al Qaeda officials into the open so that they could be arrested by Pakistani, US and British intelligence agents.

By publicizing his name, the Bush administration exposed the secret anti-terrorist operation.

Pakistani government officials reported that the disclosure of Khan's month-old arrest had alerted Al Qaeda to the sting and allowed several top figures in the organization to escape.

This intelligence leak jeopardized the plan and some Al Qaeda suspects ran away. British intelligence officials were also reportedly furious over the White House leak. The disclosure of Khan's name forced them to terminate an ongoing investigation of alleged Al Qaeda suspects in England with whom Khan was in communication, and hastily organize their arrests.

Press reports, five suspects eluded capture after the operation was blown, and British officials fear they may not have enough evidence to hold 13 who were rounded up. Writing an opinion column in the *Observer*, British Home Secretary David Blunkett criticized Washington's handling of its terror alerts in remarkably caustic and blunt terms. Citing media complaints in Britain "that we don't say enough... we don't sufficiently raise the profile, and therefore the concern about terrorism," In the United States there is often high-profile comment followed, as in the most current case, by detailed scrutiny, with the potential risk of inviting ridicule.

Is that really the job of a senior cabinet minister in charge of counter-terrorism? To feed the media? To increase concern? To have something to say, whatever it is, in order to satisfy the insatiable desire to hear somebody saying something.

Anyone familiar with the methods employed by the media and their government sources knows that "on background" means the information may be published, but the identity of the source must be withheld.

The second "sting" operation uncovered was on a much smaller scale. It involved two Muslim immigrant residents of Albany, New York, who were lured by an FBI informant into a convoluted scheme that allegedly involved talk of purchasing a rocket-propelled grenade launcher to assassinate the Pakistani ambassador to the United Nations.

No real plot ever existed—it was entirely an invention of the FBI. A Pakistani immigrant was arrested by the FBI on charges of helping other non-English-speaking immigrants obtain driver's licenses by accompanying them to their written tests and feeding them the right answers. Charged with document fraud, he was promised that he would not be deported if he served as an informer, spying on a local mosque.

When a member of the mosque, a Bangladeshi immigrant, approached him for a loan to bail out his failing pizzeria, the FBI sprung its trap. The indictment, the informer enticed the Bangladeshi, Mohammed Mosharref Hossain, and an Iraqi Kurdish refugee, Yassin Muhiddin Aref, into agreeing to launder money from the supposed sale of the grenade launcher. In return, they were to receive $5,000.

To bolster its flimsy case, the government has accused the Bangladeshi of saying that he supported Jamaat-e-Islami, which it described as a "terrorist organization. " In fact, it is a political party and a partner in the country's coalition government.

The Justice Department has also claimed that the Kurdish refugee's name was found by US troops in a notebook in northern Iraq.

The "terrorist plot," which, as one defence lawyer pointed out, existed only "in the imagination of the government," was trumpeted by the media. Initial reports went so far as to claim that the Kurdish background of one of the defendants revealed the presence in the US of a cell run by the alleged mastermind of Islamic fundamentalist attacks in Iraq, Abu Musaab al-Zarqawi.

The FBI sting in Albany was sharply condemned by the Pakistani government. A spokesman for the Pakistani Foreign Office described the FBI entrapment of immigrants in an invented scheme to assassinate a Pakistani diplomat as "mind-boggling" and a "bizarre mission. " He said that his government had filed a formal diplomatic protest with Washington.

"This has increased our ambassador's and our mission's vulnerability. This technique and methodology are tantamount to auto-suggestion and could have endangered the life of our ambassador," the spokesman added. It is revealing that, in the midst of a terror alert in three major cities and a nationwide attempt by the government and media to whip up fear and hysteria, the only significant arrests conducted in the US are of people lured into a phony plot invented by the government itself.

MEDIA AND STING

These are the days of sting operations in media. Using hidden cameras, TV channels and newspapers/magazines are coming up with exposes of various kinds. These sensational disclosures generally achieve the desired objective of attracting a lot of public attention. It is quite another matter how many of these actually serve any public interest.

In a society plagued with high levels of corruption, glaring violations of democratic norms and ethical behaviour in public affairs, the use of the hidden camera to expose serious irregularities has a legitimate role to play but only if the public interest of such efforts can be firmly established. Secondly, those who carry out such sting operations must themselves function in a transparent way so that their motives as well as source of funds can be easily identified.

Without these safeguards, the outcome of hidden cameras will be reduced to sheer sensationalism and voyeurism. What is even worse, there will be a possibility of using sting journalism for blackmail. Hence, what is promoted in the name of curbing corruption may actually be used to increase corruption and crime.

BLACKMAIL AND EXTORTION

This is not to deny that hidden cameras and related techniques have been used at times with great courage and foresight for very clear public interests. Such efforts deserve our applause. But these rare causes should not prevent us from being critical of the more frequent 'sting operations' of a highly dubious nature.

In some cases, even the identity of those who carried out the sting operation is not known, even though the contents of the videotapes make headlines all over media. In other cases, entirely unsubstantiated, incidental allegations made about people, not at all involved in the sting operation, are also splashed around indiscriminately. The debate on various aspects of sting operations may be quite intense today, but actually it is only a small part of the much wider, increasingly urgent debate on the relevance, credibility and ethics of media. In the modern, globalised world, the reach of media is so wide (and getting wider) that its importance in mirroring as well as shaping our daily lives and views is not questioned many more.

CAN YOU TRUST THE MEDIA'S INFORMATION?

To give a recent example, the USA Presidential election last year was clearly a very important event for the entire world as millions of people in many countries, not just the USA, could draw a link between how this electoral choice could impact their own lives in important ways.

It was equally clear that the debate carried out in the media, particularly on TV, played a very important role in shaping the views of a very large number of voters. It was even stated at one time that a single documentary on the 9/11 terrorist attack could play a decisive role, although this was probably exaggerated.

On the whole, while the importance of the role of media cannot be denied, questions of great urgency need to be raised about how ethical this role is. With the media reaching out to an increasing number of people and claiming more of their time, can we rest assured that people are now better informed about important events and issues?

In the recent American Presidential election, the 9/11 terrorist attack and Iraq were obviously two very important issues. In this context two key points of the debate were — Did any significant WMDs, more specifically nuclear weapons, exist in Iraq prior to the invasion of Iraq by the USA and its allies?

Did any evidence exist to establish a close link (or for that matter, any link) between the Al Queda and the Saddam Hussain regime? All available evidence indicated negative answers to both these questions. But at the same time, several surveys and polls indicated that a significant number of American citizens believed the answers to be positive.

How could such a situation emerge that widely known facts regarding crucial election issues could not reach American voters when the election campaign was so extensively covered by the media? Why did American voters remain misinformed about some of the most crucial issues when they had access to several TV channels, radio news, newspapers, journalists and Internet?

One reason may be that several leading politicians made false statements on these crucial issues and these were prominently splashed in media, often without any adverse editorial comment. One strategy is to confuse the ordinary people with some prominently displayed statements by well-known persons so that they remain confused.

MEDIA DISTORTION OF NEWS

Thus even in a country like the USA where freedom of the press is so persistently emphasised at least at the surface level, it is possible for the media to present facts in such a distorted way that a large number of people, perhaps even a majority, remain misinformed on some of the most crucial issues, even at election-time.

It is complex but also fascinating to try to understand how despite the apparent freedom to publish a very diverse range of facts and opinions, vested interests eventually succeed in ensuring that it is their viewpoint that eventually reaches the majority of people.

Today, the world faces several threats of such a serious nature that we should start worrying about a crisis of survival. These threats include climate change, the accumulation of WMDs and the highly accelerated rate of loss of many species of life. But the media has by and large failed to accord adequate importance to such issues or to present these in a proper perspective. More specifically, only technological solutions are presented for problems, which require basic changes in the way we think, live and organise our world.

At the same time, the media has created its own world of glamour, sex and sensation, which has played an important role in distracting attention from the real issues of our times. This aspect of the media has played an important role in the rise of crimes (including sexual crimes) and commodification of women.

The media has also contributed to the trivialisation of human sensitivities, which makes violence and injustice more acceptable. Media has promoted consumerism and glamour to the exclusion of the most essential concerns of our difficult times. The occasional sting operations try to create a mistaken public impression of a crusading role of media, but there is no doubt that very basic changes are needed before the real potential of the media in effectively tackling the most important issues of our time can be realised.

HOW EFFECTIVE ARE STING OPERATIONS?

Sting operations are becoming familiar day by day. The grainy, curiously distorted images, the awkward camera angles, the unclear audio and the anchors promising startling revelations. They're sting operations; the exposés conducted by journalists in much the same manner as investigative agencies conduct undercover operations. And what's more, they're flourishing: Indeed, the era could be called as the era of the sting operation.

INVESTIGATION AND STING OPERATIONS BY INDIAN MEDIA

Tehelka has been at the forefront of investigative journalism for some time. The impact they had in the long run is debatable but they surely broke some sensational stories. Here is a list of some important sting Operations by Indian media-

1971 NAGARWALA SCANDAL

On May 24, 1971, Rs 60 lakh was withdrawn from the State Bank of India and given to a "man from Bangladesh" after the chief cashier at the Parliament Street branch in New Delhi got a call purportedly from Indira Gandhi then Prime Minister of India asking him to do so.

Later it was found out Rustom Sohrab Nagarwala, a former Indian intelligence agent got the money from Chief Cashier Ved Prakash Malhotra by "mimicking the voice of Mrs. Indira Gandhi". The opposition parties suspected that either money belonged to Indira Gandhi.They also alleged that it was not an isolated case.

The investigating officer, D. K. Kashyap, investiging the case was killed in a car attack. Rustom Sohrab Nagarwala died in prision. A Commission of Inquiry was set up under Justice P. Jaganmohan Reddy on June 9, 1977, to probe into the Nagarwala case.

Justice Jaganmohan Reddy listed four "incontrovertible facts" - one of them being the fact that Indira Gandhi did not have any account in that branch - but concluded that they were not sufficient to hold that the money belonged to her. "There were several lacunae," he said, and listed them.

"To supply an answer to these (lacunae) would force me to leave the safe haven of facts which required to be established by evidence and enter the realm of conjectures and speculation."

SURESH SUSHMA SEX SCANDAL

Sushma Chaudhary was the daughter of a person who arranged for the procurement of wood at Nigambodh Ghat. Beautiful but not very bright, Sushma used to work at the Payal cinema at Naraina. It was widely known that she was having an affair with the two Sikh brothers who were the then proprietors of Payal cinema.

Sushma was not of a very sound character herself. And from the very beginning was hand in glove with Jagjivan Rams opposing camp which consisted of Chaudhary Charan Singh. KC Tyagi and Om Pal Singh. Charan Singh' s camp conspired to set a relationship going between Suresh Ram and Sushma Chaudhary. Suresh Ram did not have a happy married, which helped to support their plan. Suresh was married to Kamaljit Kaur, older to him by around 7-8 years and a senior of his at Delhi University. By temperament, Kamaljit Kaur was extremely erratic. Very often when Suresh Ram would be sitting in a restaurant or at a public place, she would land up there and simply start abusing him! Suresh would very often frequent Maqsood Pur, an MP putting up at Western Court. Maqsood pur was an old friend of Jagjivan Ram's family.

And the opposing camp planned to place Sushma in a job with the MP so that Sushma and Suresh would be able to meet. And that is how the relationship began. Suresh was a bright boy but perverted. He was in the habit of capturing his sexual exploits on camera. And Sushma was aware of this. Suresh had captured the intimate and uninhibited moments of the sexual dalliance between Sushma and him on camera too.

All along Sushma was aware of the events. On that fateful day, August 20, 1978, Suresh as usual went to pick up Sushma from her Nigambodh Ghat residence. But before they could leave Sushma had a request: She wanted to see the pictures of their intimate moments spent together. Suresh tried to wave it off to a later date but Sushma insisted. Suresh was forced to go back to his residence and get the pics in his Mercedes. This entire routine was a plot hatched by Sushma in connivance with the Charan Sngh camp. It was meant to besmirch Jagjivan Ram's name. The goal: To put an end to Jagjivan Ram's career who was widely tipped then to be the next prime minister.

The method: To smear his name by exposing his sons perversion. As Suresh sped away with his ladylove Sushma, unknown to Suresh, around 10 - 11 young men, jats, in three taxis were on his trail. Soon they overpowered him, forced open the car and started roughing up Suresh. But this was just a cover operation. All along they knew that the porn pictures were in the car. Their motive was laying a hand on the pics. Once they obtained the pictures, they lost no time in making thousands of copies of the same and distributing it all over the town.

The incident broke Jagjivan Ram's heart. It broke him mentally and physically and was a big factor in the downslide of his career. A year later, in 1979, Jagjivan Ram passed away. Around 40 years old in 1978, Suresh Ram was the philandering son of the then Defence Minister Jagjivan Ram and is belived to have made the maximum use of his fathers political connections. Suresh Ram died at the age of 46 of a heart attack.

PEOPLE INVOLED IN THIS SCANDLE

- *Sushma Chaudhary*: A student of Satyawati College, she belonged to a lower middle class Jat family. Her father handled the procurement of wood at Nigambodh Ghat. According to Sushma, she married Suresh Ram and stayed with him till he died in 1986. After his death, says Sushma she was not treated by the family as she would have desired and considered it best to leave
- *KC Tyagi*: General Secretary, Yuva Janata in 1978 and considered to be Choudhary Charan Singh's man. He was one of the main accused in the Suresh Ram abduction case but was later granted bail by the judge as there were glaring contradictions in the charges against him. Delhi High Court judge RN Aggarwal who stated that the FIR had been lodged after inordinate delay (Aug 23) and the photographs were not taken under duress.He was also among those who got the photos distributed in all the media offices and all over the town. In 1978 KC Tyagi was a young man of 27 trying to make a place for him in politics. He was the general secretary of the Yuva Janata Party and a close ally of Chaudhary Charan Singh.
- *Om Pal Singh*: He was the office secretary of the Kisan Sammelan in 1978. A close aide of Chaudhary Charan Singh he originally belonged to Huseri, Meerut. He was among the prime accused in abducting Suresh Ram. Along with KC Tyagi he also helped in the distribution of the photographs.
- *AP Singh*: Among the three main people who assaulted Suresh Ram,

he turned a court witness later. He has a house in Varanasi and Patna.

- *SP Chibber*: He was an arms agent with several armament firms of repute in 1978. He was also the agent for the supersonic deep strike Jaguar aircraft which was being considered by the Government then. The Mercedes Benz, which Suresh Ram flaunted around and careened in with Sushma Chaudhary was a luxury granted to him by SP Chibber.
- *OP Arora*: He was Jagjivan Ram's trusted secretary from 1959 till Jagjivan Ram passed away in 1979. In 1978, when the Suresh-Sushma scandal broke out, OP Chibber made a thousand calls to prevent the pictures from getting published. He requested, pleaded and threatened many to stall the publication of the magazine but to no avail. Even today, OP Arora maintains that Sushma Chaudhary had been planted by the Charan Singh camp to besmirch JRs name.
- *Maneka Gandhi*: She was the daughter-in-law of Indira Gandhi. She was married to Sanjay Gandhi in 1974. According to Khushwant Singh, Maneka was making heavy demands on Sanjay Gandhi's time and he suggested that she run a magazine and was hugely helped by Khushwant Singh in her maiden and only journalistic venture, the Surya magazine.In 1978, it was under her editorial command that the lurid pictures were splashed as a centrespread in the magazine along with interviews of Kamaljit Kaur, Suresh Ram's wife.
- *Churhat Lottery case*: Arjun Singh was accused of corruption in what was called by some the Churhat Lottery case in the 1980s, in which allegations, never proved, were levelled that he had helped set up a phony state lottery. He has built the Karwa Dam palace. The palace has been differently assessed between 10 to 20 crore although he claims that it cost him only forty lakhs.
  Arjun Singh was the Chief Minister of Madhya Pradesh when the Bhopal gas leak occurred in 1984. There have been allegations since that the state administration did not do enough for the victims of the fatal gas leak..
- *Bofors Scandal*: Bofors Scam was a major corruption scandal in India in the 1980s; several Indian politicians, including then Prime Minister Rajiv Gandhi, were accused of receiving kickbacks from Bofors AB for winning a bid to supply India's 155 mm field howitzer. The scale of the corruption was far worse than any that India had seen before, and directly led to the defeat of Gandhi's ruling Indian National Congress party in the November 1989 general elections. Following his withdrawal from the Government, Rajiv Gandhi's security detail was reduced. He was subsequently assassinated on May 21, 1991. On February 5, 2004 the Delhi High Court exonerated Rajiv Gandhi of any involvement in the scandal.

The name of the middleman associated with the scandal was Ottavio Quattrocchi, an Italian business man who lived in India for over 20 years. He became a very powerful broker in the 1980's between big business and the Indian government. He allegedly used his closeness to Indian government officials including Prime Minister Rajiv Gandhi to swing an arms deal for purchasing anti-aircraft guns in the favor of Bofors. Although this was investigated by the Indian government, acting as a middleman in itself was (and is not today) illegal. He was wanted by the Delhi court that was conducting hearings about the scandal but has been exonerated in any illegal activities in the scandal. On May 31, 2005, the High court of Delhi dismissed the Bofors case allegations against the British business brothers, Shrichand, Gopichand and Prakash Hinduja.

On January 11, 2006 the high Court in London ordered the defreezing of the two British bank accounts of Ottavio Quattrocchi on the grounds of insufficient evidence to link these accounts to the Bofors payoff. The two accounts, containing □ 3 million and $1 million, had been frozen in 2003 by a high court order by request of the Indian government (when the (now) opposition party BJP was in power). On January 16, the Indian Supreme Court directed the Indian government to ensure that Ottavio Quattrocchi did not withdraw money from the two bank accounts in London. The CBI (Central Bureau Of Investigation), the Indian Federal law enforcement agency, on January 23, 2006 admitted that roughly Rs 21 crore, about USD $4.6 million, in the two accounts have already been withdrawn. The British Government released the funds based on a request by the Indian Government.

- *St. Kitts Forgery Case*: The St. Kitts forgery case was one of the three cases of corruption registered against former Prime Minister P.V. Narasimha Rao after he demitted office in 1996, following the Congress' rout in the general elections that year; the other two were the Jharkhand Mukthi Morcha (JMM) bribery case and the Lakhubhai Pathak cheating case. Together these cases had symbolised the erosion of ethical values in the polity during Narasimha Rao's five-year rule.

As such, the legal course these cases took after the end of Narasimha Rao's term in office evoked considerable public interest. For the first time, a former Prime Minister was being prosecuted for offences allegedly committed by him while in office, and therefore it reinforced people's confidence in the rule of law.

In the JMM bribery case, Narasimha Rao was convicted by the trial court but acquitted by the Delhi High Court. Both in the Lakhubhai Pathak cheating case and in the St. Kitts case, the trial court acquitted Narasimha Rao and his associates; in the St. Kitts case even the Supreme Court upheld his acquittal.

The St. Kitts case (St. Kitts is a small island in the Caribbean) had its origin in 1989, during the run-up to the general elections to be held later that year. V.P. Singh, who had quit as Finance Minister in the Rajiv Gandhi Cabinet following the Bofors expose and had emerged as the force that rallied the Opposition parties, was Rajiv's main challenger. From November 1988 to October 1989, Narasimha Rao was the External Affairs Minister in the Rajiv Gandhi government, and K.K.

Tewary was his Minister of State. Chandraswami was Narasimha Rao's spiritual guru and also an associate, as he had been to several other political leaders. K.N. Aggarwal alias Mamaji was Chandraswami's private secretary. All the four, along with a few other key persons, were accused of forging documents against Ajeya Singh, son of V.P. Singh, to show that he had opened a bank account in First Trust Corporation Bank in St. Kitts and deposited $21 million in it, making V.P. Singh its beneficiary.

The story first hit the headlines in the Indian media, following a report in the Kuwait-based *Arab Times* newspaper, in August 1989. The Rajiv Gandhi government asked the Enforcement Directorate (E.D.) to probe the matter. In October 1989, the E.D.'s Deputy Director, A.P. Nandy, visited St. Kitts and later presented a report to Parliament.

It was only after V.P. Singh became Prime Minister in December 1989 that the CBI registered criminal cases against Enforcement Director K.L. Verma, Chandraswami, K.N. Aggarwal, arms dealer and Chandraswami's associate Adnan Kashoggi's son-in-law Larry J. Kolb, and First Trust Corporation's managing director George McLean. According to the case, it was Kolb who managed to insert the news item in *Arab Times* on August 20, 1989, which was reproduced by sections of the Indian media. Kolb, with Chandraswami, also arranged the visit of Nandy to St. Kitts in a private plane.

In St. Kitts, Nandy obtained letters and documents showing the details of the bank account allegedly opened by Ajeya Singh, from McLean. Nandy then got these documents, which allegedly carried the signatures of Ajeya Singh and V.P. Singh, attested by R.K. Rai, then Consul-General of India in the United States, and Deepak Sen Gupta, Deputy Consul-General in the U.S., the CBI said.

Both Ajeya Singh and V.P. Singh soon denied any connection with the account. The CBI sent these documents to the handwriting experts at the Central Forensic Science Laboratory, New Delhi, and on the basis of their report, concluded that the signatures of Ajeya Singh and V.P. Singh in the documents were forged, on the model of their signatures found in their passport applications, which Tewary managed to secure through official influence. Narasimha Rao's role was allegedly confined to asking R.K. Rai to attest the forged documents. The case, first registered by the CBI in May 1990, dragged on until the People's Union for Civil Liberties moved the Supreme Court in February 1996 seeking disclosure of the CBI's findings. It was only after Narasimha Rao demitted office that the CBI, under directions from the Supreme Court, pressed for Narasimha Rao's prosecution in the case.

Fodder Scam: Fodder Scam is a scam related to Animal Husbandry Department of Government of Bihar in which irregularities of nearly Rs. 950 crores were detected.

The scam was unearthed in 1996 during the regime of chief minister Lalu Prasad Yadav but it goes back to 80s and had started during tenure of Jagannath Mishra. Lalu had ordered probe into these massive irregularities in accounts by constituting a committee.

However motives of these people were questioned by a Public Interest Litigation and Supreme Court of India handed over the case to CBI. Many people who were in this probe committe themselves became accused. Charges were filed against Yadav too and later on Mishra was also framed. Developments of the case has been the deciding factors in political situations both at state and national level.

CBI filed 69 different cases related to this scam 31 of which has been in Jharkhand and remaining in Bihar. Political situation of 1996 was the main factor in deciding the fate of the case.

The then Prime Minister H D Deve Gowda who was dependant on allies and saw Yadav as his potential threat for the coveted post is said to have connived with CBI Director Joginder Singh who got a free hand in the case and broke established norms to file charges against Yadav. Because of his unfair handling of the case he was given a technical promotion to be shunted from the hot seat by succeeding Prime Minister I K Gujral who too depended on Yadav for support.

However the cat had already gone out of the bag and Yadav was soon convicted in record breaking numbers of cases booked under conspiracy angle involving him,his family,beureaucrats and many other politicians.

The charges were framed under sections 420 and 120 (b) of the Indian Penal Code and section 13 (b) of the Prevention of Corruption Act. There are a total of 76 accused, of whom three have died and three turned state witnesses.Charges were also framed against former Bihar chief minister Jagannath Mishra, former MP Rajo Singh, former Bihar animal husbandry minister Vidyasagar Nishad, former central minister Chandradeo Prasad Verma, four bureaucrats of the Indian Administrative Service, veterinary doctors and other government officials. There are 20 truckloads of documents in the case.

It was only after Special Investigation Team(SIT) under U N Biswas was constituted that investigation started at a brisk rate. Soon many heads started rolling and Yadav and members of his party had to loose their ministreal berths both at centre and state facing corruption charges. Under these pretext began the post-mortem of one of India's greatest financial irregularities after indipendence. In the years to follow Fodder Scam became the most talked about topic in state and national level politics involving nearly whole generation for the kind of impact it had on Government and State. In fact because of this case only Lalu Prasad Yadav has the distinction of being the only person ever on whom Lok Sabha debated for whole session as official agenda The then Member and ex-Prime Minister Chandra Shekhar had severely criticised the move adopted by Lok Sabha and called it unfortunate event.

Match Fixing: Expose that shaken the cricket world, the Crime Branch of the Delhi Police charged South African cricket captain Hansie Cronje and three of his team mates, Herschelle Gibbs, Nicky Boje and Pieter Strydom on the count of accepting money to "fix " matches in five-match limited overs series against India.

Also charged were two Delhi-based businessmen, Sanjay Chawla and Rajesh Kalra. The charges were made on the basis of recorded telephone conversations Cronje reportedly held with Chawla. The South African captain was named as one of the prime accused along with Chawla and Kalra in the Delhi Police charge sheet.

According to details available, the charges were filed on the basis of telephone conversations Cronje reportedly had with Chawla. While Chawla is based in Delhi, he spoke to Cronje only from London, where he is apparently a frequent visitor.

Excerpts from the transcripts indicated that Cronje was alleged to have taken money to decide on the course of the first two matches, both of which, incidentally, India won. In the transcripts, Chawla is reported to have asked Cronje to tell Gibbs, South Africa's key batsman in teh one-day series, to go slow in chasing Indian scores.

The dashing Gibbs was one of the most successful batsmen for South Africa during their Test and one-day series against India which ended in late March.

Operaion westend: It all started with Senior Section Officer Sashi Menon, in the Ministry of Defence, wanting to make some money from arms dealers. *Tehelka.com* floated a fictitious arms manufacturing company, based in London, called West End International.

Tehelka was in search of a product whose indent existed in the Indian Army and also wanted to get an entry into the lowest end of the defence chain. Here Sashi Menon, after getting a monetary incentive, takes *Tehelka* to Brigadier Anil Sehgal's house in New Delhi. Sehgal is the deputy director in DGOS, a crucial army procurement post. Brigadier Sehgal and Sashi Menon give *Tehelka* the two things - a defence product and an entry into the gravy train.

As a matter of fact, Sashi himself was setting up different channels for *Tehelka* that would take *Tehelka journalists* right upto Defence Minister George

Fernandes and the then Minister of State for Defence, Harin Pathak. He was using state party functionaries of the BJP and Shiv Sena for lobbying with the politicians.

For army officials and bureaucrats, he used their personal secretaries. Towards the end, Sashi's channels hit a roadblock. In the meantime, Tehelka had already opened two-three independent channels of own which started bearing fruit. One such operator they tapped was Colonel Sayal (Retd). He was *Tehelka* conduit to many officers concerned with procurement. Here, Sayal has fixed a meeting with his old colleague Brigadier Iqbal Singh, PPO, Prospective Procurement Officer, a crucial post under the Master General Ordnance (MGO). Here is an excerpt from Brigadier Iqbal Singh's first meeting with Tehelka at his home.

After many stages of talks and meeting with several defence personals Tehelka reached at that point where additional Secretary L.M. Mehta issued a letter to Major General Choudhary in the second week of January. He asked for Rs 2 lakh in cash. He was paid Rs 50,000 by Major General Murgai as advance in his office and the rest was promised upon receipt of the letter. *Tehelka* planned to collect the letter and run.

Major General Choudary issued a trial evaluation order in the third week of January. It was a 26-page order. General Murgai collected it for Tehelka. Mehta's dilemma was that he couldn't organize an evaluation letter just for West End and had to include 3-4 more companies. He did that.

In the meantime around January 10 Tehelka cover had already blown with Samta Party treasurer R.K. Jain and BJP President Bangaru Laxman Both had been expecting money and were desperately looking for West End representatives. Tehelka waited that cover remained with General Murgai for some more time.

But it was not to be. Tehelka delayed by 24 hours to visit to General Murgai to collect the letter. And cover blew. For three days *Tehelka* tried to ambush General Murgai at his home.

On each of those ocassions the cars of Surendra Singh and General Choudhary were parked outside. The trio has been in constant consultation to plan a damage limitation exercise. It's been nearly two months since the letter was issued. *Tehelka* was told they have doctored the files. But truth is, if the Military Intelligence interrogates the office staff of General Choudhary they shall have the truth.

Dilip singh jodev: Dilip singh jodev was the Indian Minister of State for Environment and Forests in Prime Minister Atal Bihari Vajpayee's Bharatiya Janata Party led coalition government. In November 2003 he was accused of accepting a bribe from an Australian company in exchange for mining rights in Chhattisgarh. The accusation was made by *The Sunday Express* newspaper, which had received a video of the bribe taking place.He rejected initial calls for his resignation, however he did resign on November 17, 2003. Judeo claimed that he had been set up by "Christian missionaries" and/or by his Congress Party rival for the post of Chief Minister in Chhattisgarh, Ajit Jogi. Ajit Jogi used this incident to further the aims of Christian Missionaries in creating a "Christstan" in the tribal belt.

In 2005, the Central Bureau of Investigation told the Indian Supreme Court that the bribe exposé was planned by Amit Jogi, the son of the Chief Minister of Chhattisgarh, Ajit Jogi, as a means to *derive political mileage in favour of Ajit Jogi* in upcoming elections.

Operation Duryodhana: Operation Duryodhana "expose" showing 11 MPs "accepting" cash for asking questions in Parliament was carried out by a Cobrapost-Aaj Tak team through a sting operation codenamed "Operation Duryodhana."

A COBRAPOST-AAJ TAK investigation entitled Operation Duryodhana unearths 11 members of the Parliament accepting cash for asking questions in the Indian Parliament. Spread over eight months, Operation Duryodhana logged more than 56 video and 70 audiotapes besides recording more than 900 phone calls.

Posing as representatives of a fictitious lobbying organisation called the North Indian Small Manufacturer's Assosciation (NISMA), journalists Aniruddha Bahal and Suhasini Raj penetrated the nexus operating between MPs and their middlemen and succeeded in having MPs, across party lines, submit more than 60 questions in the rigorous question balloting system of the Indian Parliament, out of which 25 (at last count) were selected.

Sometimes, the same set of questions were put in by more than one MP.

Names of MPs taking cash for asking questions in the Indian Parliament are:

Anna Saheb M.K. Patil (BJP, Erandol, Maharastra)	₹ 45,000	Manoj Kumar
(RJD, Palamau, Jharkhand)	₹ 110,000	Narendra Kumar
Kushwaha (BSP, Mirzapur, UP)	₹ 55,000	
Y.G. Mahajan (BJP, Jalgaon Maharsahtra)	₹ 35,000	
Suresh Chandel (BJP, Hamirpur, Himachal Pradesh)	₹ 30,000	
Lal Chandra Kol (BSP, Robertsganj, UP)	₹ 35,000	
Chhatrapal Singh Lodha, Rajya Sabha (BJP, Orissa)	₹ 15,000	
Pradeep Gandhi (BJP, Rajnandgaon, Chhattisgarh)	₹ 55,000	
Raja Ram Pal (BSP, Bilhaur, Uttar Pradesh)	₹ 35,000	
Chandra Pratap Singh (BJP, Sidhi, Uttar Pradesh)	₹ 35,000	
Ramsevak Singh (Congress, Gwalior Madhya Pradesh)	₹ 50,000	

While the bulk of the questions given to the MPs related to the welfare of the Small Scale Industrial (SSI) units, there were several public interest questions also handed over to them, for instance, on non-performing assets, the SEBI inquiry into the 2004 stock market crash and a few others. For submitting all these questions MPs took money ranging between Rs 15,000 and Rs 110,000. Several MPs also wanted an "annual fee" of Rs 5-6 lakh from NISMA for the organisation to put in as many proxy questions as it wanted, through the MPs concerned, in the Indian Parliament.

Spread over eight months — April to November — the "investigation" logged more than 56 video and 70 audiotapes, besides recording over 900 phone calls, Cobrapost.com said. Posing as representatives of a fictitious lobbying organisation "North Indian Small Manufacturers Association," journalists Aniruddha Bahal and Suhasini Raj penetrated the nexus between MPs and their middlemen and succeeded in having MPs, across party lines, submit more than 60 questions in Parliament's rigorous question balloting system, the portal claimed.

Out of this, at last count, 25 were selected. Sometimes, the same set of questions was put in by more than one MP, it said.

Though the bulk of the questions given to the MPs related to the welfare of small industrial units, there were also several public interest questions, such as non-performing assets and the SEBI inquiry into the 2004 stock market crash, the portal said.

For submitting all these questions, MPs allegedly took money ranging between Rs. 15,000 and Rs. 1,10,000. Some of them wanted an "annual fee" of Rs. 5 to Rs. 6 lakh for the Association to put in as many proxy questions as it wanted through the MPs concerned in Parliament, it alleged.

Casting Couch: India TV sent a woman reporter posing as a struggling actor to trap Shakti Kapoor and Aman Verma to prove the prevalence of the casting couch in Bollywood. A LEADING Bollywood actor was embroiled in a sex scandal last night after being filmed apparently offering to promote the career of an aspiring actress if she slept with him.

An Indian television station broadcast footage of Shakti Kapoor, famous for playing movie villains, in a Mumbai hotel room propositioning an undercover reporter who was posing as the actress. Kapoor was also filmed naming Bollywood stars who he claimed had slept their way to success.

In the video clip, the actor said: "I want to make love to you... and if you want to come in this line [of business] you have to do what I am telling [you] to do."

Kapoor has accused the television channel behind the sting of setting him up and denied any wrongdoing.

Bollywood, the Mumbai-based Hindi film industry, reacted to the scandal with a mix of faux outrage and weary resignation. While some demanded a boycott of Kapoor, others suggested his behaviour was commonplace in the Indian film industry.

Kapoor certainly seems to think so - in the video clip he names three leading actresses and claims they have had sex with top producers and directors to clinch roles. "So you have to do it just once," he told the undercover reporter.

Mahesh Bhatt, a producer, described sex for screen-time as "Bollywood's best-known secret" and suggested Kapoor should be fined for his actions. "The rot is within us," he said. "The casting couch is a reality. It is a power thing, to which vulnerable girls who want to join the industry fall prey."

But Kapoor, who has performed in more than 300 films and is best known for his portrayal of villains, insisted he had neither solicited sex nor made allegations against other celebrities. He said the video had been tampered with by India television and threatened to sue the channel. "The tapes have been doctored," he said after the first clips were broadcast. "I never touched her."

The woman had pestered him for months for a film role and he only went to the hotel to meet her when she threatened to commit suicide, he said. Despite his denial, India's Film and Television Producers' Guild urged its members to boycott Kapoor. "Kapoor has been completely irresponsible in his behaviour and utterances and must publicly apologise to all those whom he has insulted and slandered," it said in a statement.

"The guild is advising its members not to engage Shakti Kapoor in any work in any of their productions."

Preity Zinta, a leading actress who was one of those named by Kapoor, said: "The comment is made in very poor taste. He is truly a real-life villain and deserves to be banned from our film industry." But many directors and producers preferred to condemn the way the channel had got the story.

Pehlaj Nihlani, the president of the Association of Motion Picture and Television Programme Producers, said: "The way the meeting was set up makes the media equally guilty. It was a well laid-out plan. It was a planned conspiracy to defame him." In India, showbiz gossip revolves almost exclusively around Bollywood actors. Newspapers and television stations devote whole sections and programmes to celebrity tittle-tattle, a subject area known as. Kapoor seems determined to fight to restore his reputation. As for his career, according to anonymous Bollywood insiders quoted in the Indian press, it may already have been over.

Operation Chakravyuh: 'Operation Chakravyuh' by *Star News*-Detective Intelligence Guild (DIG) showed a former Congress Goa Chief Minister and Lok Sabha member Churchil Alemao, former Union Minister and BJP MP Fagan Singh Kulaste and one Samajwadi Party MP and another supported by it involved in corruption in allotting work for the MPLAD (Member of Parliament Local Area Development) Scheme.

The *Star News* released the transcripts and event descriptions of the meeting with MPs. It said that one Samajwadi Party MP Toofani Saroj was honest and refused to disscuss or accept any commission.

Alemao, a Congress MP from South Goa, who discusses commisson in two meetings, is shown in the third meeting asking the DIG reporters to open a bag full of money as commission for a project to popularise Konkani language.

The former Chief Minister demands an advance of Rs. Two lakh, but on suspicion threatens to check the bags of the reporters at which team scrambled out.

The sting operation also shows Yuvraj Siingh, Personal Secretary of Fagan Singh Kulaste, a former Union Minister, taking money on behalf of BJP MP Chandra Pratap Singh, who was also exposed in the cash-on-camera 'Operation Duryodhan' last week. Yuvraj Singh was again shown accepting money for Kulaste, a Lok Sabha member, who signs the recommendation letter for a particular scheme. Others shown in the sting operation are Ramswaroop Koli (BJP), Paras Nath Yadav (SP), Sakshi Maharaj (Rashtriya Kranti Dal supported by SP), and Isan Singh (BSP).

Operation Water Rat: CNN-IBN smuggled explosives into Mumbai to show gaping holes in the security apparatus. Mumbai On March 12, 1993, Dawood and his men carried out the worst ever terror strike on India. Led by Abu Salem, the gangsters brought in as much as 7000 kg of explosives from the sea.

March 12, 1993: Mumbai city rocked by serial bomb blasts at 13 places. It was the most destructive ever terror attack on India.Key Targets: Mumbai Stock Exchange at Colaba, the Air-India Building at Nariman Point, Shiv Sena Bhavan at Dadar, Zaveri Bazaar at Girgaum and the Passport Office at Worli.Casualty: 257 killed and 1,400 injured.

CNN-IBN Special Investigation Team tried to smuggle in a cargo of three crates, which could well have contained over 100 kg of RDX, to Mumbai from the international waters right past the Navy and the Coast Guard. And it did succeed, not once, not twice, but thrice at a stretch - without a single roadblock.As the SIT re-enacted the terror attacks of 1993 as part of its Operation Water Rat, it exposed, in the process, an explosive conclusion - that Mumbai is still a sitting duck for a terrorist attack.

CNN-IBN Special Investigation Team Another Expose:Petrol adulteration in Uttar Pradesh is a business and the mafia running it has no fear of the law. A CNN-IBN Special Investigation found that the area around the Mathura Oil Refinery is a hub for adulteration which begins as soon as oil tankers roll out of the refinery gates.

"This is our business and we have been in this for ages," says a mafia leader. The Mathura refinery is one of the six owned by the Indian Oil Corporation.

The petrol adulteration mafia stalks the area around this refinery and both the local administration and law enforcement authorities look the other way. There is a reason for that: Mafia members allege that they regularly give bribes to officials. "We are not scared of administration at all, they get their quota," says the mafia leader. The CNN-IBN Special Investigation Team has on camera caught the mafia siphoning and adulterating petrol from an oil tanker just a few hundred metres away from the refinery.

When the CNN-IBN crew spotted near the refinery, goons on motorcycles chased us. "As soon a truck comes out of the refinery, we take it directly to our store.

In the store we swap the oil. We have setting an understanding with drivers. The trade is well organised and every one gets their cut. There is no confusion between the administration and us," says the mafia leader. Indian Oil Corporation officer S Manjunath was murdered in Lakhimpur Kheri last year after he warned a petrol pump against selling adulterated petrol.

UNDERCOVER OPERATIONS

An undercover operation is an investigative technique in which an operative either an undercover agent who assumes a covert identity or purpose, or a confidential informant who takes action to gain evidence or information which would be unavailable but for the target's reliance on the operative's covert role. The undercover technique may be used in relation to criminal violations enforceable under the investigative jurisdiction of the IRS.

The use of undercover operations is an essential technique in the detection and investigation of criminal activity involving tax and money laundering offences. Undercover does not include the temporary assumption of a pretext identity for the purpose of protecting the integrity of surveillance.

The FBI may use undercover activities and conduct undercover operations, pursuant to these Guidelines, that are appropriate to carry out its law enforcement responsibilities. These guidelines do not apply to investigations utilizing confidential informants, cooperating witnesses or cooperating subjects, unless the investigation also utilizes an undercover employee.

The FBI, through the development of internal policy, may choose to apply these Guidelines to certain confidential informant, cooperating witness, and cooperating subject operations by referring such matters to the Undercover Review Committee pursuant to Section IV, Paragraph (D)(6).

Under this authority, the FBI may participate in joint undercover activities with other law enforcement agencies and may operate a proprietary to the extent necessary to maintain an operation's cover or effectiveness.

All joint undercover operations are to be conducted pursuant to these Guidelines.

Undercover activities are classified as either Group I or Group II. All Group I undercover operations must be approved by the Chief, Criminal Investigation (CI). Group II undercover operations are approved by the Director, Field Operations

AUTHORIZATION OF UNDERCOVER OPERATIONS

Any official considering approval or authorization of a proposed undercover application shall weigh the risks and benefits of the operation, giving careful consideration to the following factors:

- The risk of personal injury to individuals, property damage, financial loss to persons or businesses, damage to reputation, or other harm to persons;
- The risk of civil liability or other loss to the Government;
- The risk of invasion of privacy or interference with privileged or confidential relationships;
- The risk that individuals engaged in undercover operations may become involved in illegal conduct restricted in paragraph IV.
- The suitability of Government participation in the type of activity that is expected to occur during the operation.

Undercover Operations Which May be Authorized by the Special Agent:

- The establishment, extension, or renewal of all undercover operations to be supervised by a given field office must be approved by the SAC. If the undercover operation does not involve any of the factors listed in paragraph IV. C.
  - Initiation of investigative activity regarding the alleged criminal conduct or criminal enterprise is warranted under any applicable departmental guidelines;
  - The proposed undercover operation appears to be an effective means of obtaining evidence or necessary information. This finding should include a statement of what prior investigation has been conducted and what chance the operation has of obtaining evidence or necessary information concerning the alleged criminal conduct or criminal enterprise;
  - The undercover operation will be conducted with minimal intrusion consistent with the need to collect the evidence or information in a timely and effective manner;
  - Approval for the use of any informant or confidential source has been obtained as required by the Attorney General's Guidelines on Use of Informants and Confidential Sources;
  - Any foreseeable participation by an undercover employee in illegal activity that can be approved by the SAC on his or her own authority is justified by the factors noted in paragraph H;
  - If there is no present expectation of the occurrence of any of the sensitive or fiscal circumstances listed in paragraph C, a statement to that effect.
- Undercover operations may be authorized pursuant to this subsection for up to six months and continued upon renewal for an additional six-month period, for a total of no more than one year. Undercover operations initiated pursuant to this subsection may not involve the expenditure of more than $40,000 ($100,000 in drug cases of which a maximum of $40,000 is for operational expenses)

- The SAC may delegate the responsibility to authorize the establishment, extension, or renewal of undercover operations to designated Assistant Special Agents in Charge. The delegation of this responsibility by the SAC should be in writing and maintained in the appropriate field office.

SENSITIVE CIRCUMSTANCES

In all undercover operations involving any sensitive circumstances the SAC shall submit an application. The application shall be reviewed by appropriate supervisory personnel, if favourably recommended, sent to the Undercover Review Committee for consideration. The application shall then be forwarded to the Director or a designated Assistant Director, who may approve or disapprove the application.

For purposes of these Guidelines, sensitive circumstances are involved if there is a reasonable expectation that the undercover operation will involve:

- An investigation of possible criminal conduct by any elected or appointed official, or political candidate, for a *judicial-*, *legislative-*, *management-*, or *executive-*level position of trust in a Federal, state, or local governmental entity or political subdivision thereof;
- An investigation of *any* public official at the Federal, state, or local level in any matter involving systemic corruption of any governmental function;
- An investigation of possible criminal conduct by any foreign official or government, religious organization, political organization, or the news media;
- Engaging in activity having a significant effect on or constituting a significant intrusion into the legitimate operation of a Federal, state, or local governmental entity;
- Establishing, acquiring, or using a proprietary;
- Providing goods or services which are essential to the commission of a crime, which goods and services are reasonably unavailable to a subject of the investigation except from the Government;
- Activity that is proscribed by local law as a felony or that is otherwise a serious crime — but not including the purchase of stolen or contraband goods; the delivery or sale by the Government of stolen property whose ownership cannot be determined; the controlled delivery of drugs which will not enter commerce; the payments of bribes which are not included in the other sensitive circumstances; or the making of false representations to third parties in concealment of personal identity or the true ownership of a proprietary (this exemption does not include any statement under oath or the penalties of perjury).

- A significant risk that a person participating in an undercover operation will be arrested or will supply falsely sworn testimony or false documentation in any legal or administrative proceeding:
- Attendance at a meeting or participation in communications between any individual and his or her lawyer;
- A significant risk that a third party will enter into a professional or confidential relationship with a person participating in an undercover operation who is acting as an attorney, physician, clergyman, or member of the news media:
- A request to an attorney, physician, member of the clergy, or other person for information that would ordinarily be privileged or to a member of the news media concerning an individual with whom the news person is known to have a professional or confidential relationship;
- Participation in the activities of a group under investigation as part of a Domestic Security Investigation or recruiting a person from within such a group as an informant;
- A significant risk of violence or physical injury to individuals or a significant risk of financial loss;
- Activities which could result in significant claims against the United States arising in tort, contract, or for compensation for the "taking" of property;
- Untrue representations by a person participating in the undercover operation concerning the activities or involvement of any third person without that individual's knowledge or consent.

VIOLATION OF LAW AND STING OPERATION

Sting operations have raised many questions relating to citizen's privacy or violation of existing laws. Thanks to technology explosion, in the coming years India besides making progress in several fields will also be entering the age of sting operations and phone tapping. At the rate at which politicians are vying with each other in claiming that their phones are being tapped, a time may come when anyone whose phone is not being tapped will probably feel deprived or convinced that he needs to do something drastic to get his phone tapped or become a victim of sting operations.

The feeling of being deprived and not being considered important enough to be target of a sting operation or telephone tapping may put you into a category of a second class citizen and force many to seek different ways to become a VIP who is a target of telephone tapping and sting operation. If one were to believe all the stories floating around, one will have to reach a cease that every second person in our cities is working for a detective agency or some state organization in the profession of telephone tapping for a fee.

As for the sting operations every channel is competing to undertake such operations to improve their ratings or viewership despite recent disclosures that such operations have not added many in numbers.

But as sting operations have become a fashion, no channel would like to be left behind. This has raised many important questions relating to citizen's privacy or violation of existing laws. There is no doubt that new technology which can be obtained for a measly sum of few lakhs of rupees has made these operations easy and simple.

The Government which was quick to act in case of cyber law by enacting legislation on the subject to prevent its misuse has not acted promptly enough in case of sting operations or telephone tapping.

This requires action as these sensitive areas are no more the monopoly of public sector and many private players have entered the field. As indicated in a recent case the network run by a private company was involved in phone tapping case. As such the need for having proper legislation to make the process fullproof and to discourage its misuse.

On the issue of phone tapping, Parliament must draft a law to lay down rules under which such operations can be undertaken. The authority which can authorize such operations must be specified and the reasons for ordering such a probe specified.

The private agencies should be debarred from indulging in the same and stiff punishments including closure of their operations should be made mandatory in case they are found guilty of undertaking such activities. It is strange that the mushroom growth of detective agencies, security agencies, indulging in illegal methods to recover bank loans are being allowed without any legislation to govern their working.

Even the highest court in the country has commented on the misuse of data released by telephone companies which is used by many institutions including banks to harass the subscribers by making calls soliciting business at all odd hours and harassing them. This activity has neither been curtailed nor regulated despite observations by the Supreme Court on the subject.

Telephone companies which allow the release of data for small gains probably could also be guilty of allowing tapping for considerations. The effective way to check this menace will be to ask agencies investigating such cases to also suggest legal amendments to safeguard the users of telephones. As for sting operations a time has come when media organizations like the Press Council of India should step forward and regulate this activity.

In case they fail to do so, the job of censorship or regulating TV channels will fall on Government which will be worse than the original crime as it would give them power to introduce censorship through the backdoor. In this entire debate one must keep in mind the fact that as new technologies develop they will provide many new benefits but will also open doors for their misuse by unscrupulous agencies in public as well as private sector. The Government and media organizations must remain vigilant and deal with all such activities before they get out of control. The possibilities of invading the privacy of individuals have become very easy with new aids available so the temptations to use them for short-term gains will remain strong unless the regulators are equally alert. Recently the controversy on these issues instead of trying to resolve the problems has become a part of political upmanship with ridiculous demands being made to suggest that an inquiry be conducted by Chief Ministers.

The leaders occupying such offices may have many qualities but are by no stretch of imagination capable of conducting inquiry or doing so professionally. This work must be done by professionals.

The politicians who by misusing official agencies create doubts about their bonafides are also the first to cry foul when they are at the receiving end. Solution is more active role by agencies like Election Commission and courts to preserve the independence of agencies who are expected to do such work as per our Constitution and laws of the country.

PLANNING AND IMPLEMENTATION OF STING

Sting operations are not conducted by the media and law-enforcement agencies alone. The Satara-based CSO, Dalit Mahila Vikas Mandal, has nabbed seven doctors red-handed for violating the Pre-Conception and Pre-Natal Diagnostic Techniques Act and revealing the sex of foetuses.

The relevant provision that may be used for countering the "sting operations" is section 72(3) that reads: 'Whoever intentionally captures or broadcasts an image of a private area of an individual without his consent, and knowingly does so under circumstances violating the privacy of that individual, shall be liable to pay compensation not exceeding Rs. 25 lakhs to the person so affected, and shall also be liable for imprisonment for a term not exceeding one year or with fine not exceeding Rs 2 Lakhs, or with both on the complaint of the person so affected. '

However, section 72(4) bars the courts from taking cognizance of any offence punishable under sub-section (3) except upon a complaint filed by the aggrieved person in writing before a Magistrate.

Article 21 of the constitution confers the right to privacy. This is not expressly mentioned in it but the same has been enunciated by way of judicial interpretation by the Supreme Court.

It is personal in nature and only the concerned person has a right to control it subject to the restrictions imposed by the law.

In Kharak Singh v. state of UP (1963) *justice Subba Rao*, while expressing the minority view, laid down the foundations for the development of law of privacy in India and observed that the concept of 'liberty' in article 21 was comprehensive enough to include privacy.

In Gobind v. State of MP (1975) the Supreme Court observed that 'right to privacy' must encompass and protect the personal intimacies of the home, the family, marriage, motherhood, procreation and child bearing.

In R. Rajagopal v. State of TN (1994) the Supreme Court held that the right to privacy is a 'right to be let alone'. None can publish anything concerning the above matters without his consent, whether truthful or otherwise and whether laudatory or critical. If he does so, he would be violating the right to privacy of the person concerned and would be liable in an action for damages.

In another verdict the Supreme Court held that the right to privacy may, apart from contract, also arise out of a particular specific relationship, which may be commercial, matrimonial or even political. Public disclosure of even true private facts may amount to an invasion of the right to privacy. In this background the legality of sting operations must be judged.

LEGALITY OF STING OPERATIONS UNDER IT ACT, 2000

The proposed analysis will be made by answering certain queries: What are the provisions that are likely to have an impact, implicitly or explicitly, on "sting operations"?

Section 72(3) of the proposed IT Act amendments may "impliedly" cover a "sting operation" that is "vulgar" in nature. It cannot be applied to any other sting operation.

Does the proposed amendments take into account that "sting operations" justify invasion of privacy for a larger public interest? No. The proposed IT Act Amendment is not considering that aspect either expressly or impliedly. That, however, cannot be excluded since the Constitution of India warrants such inclusion.

If the amendments are passed, and a TV channel conducts an operation, would the courts be able to take the "public interest journalism" issue into account? Yes. The court will take the "public interest journalism" into consideration except where that is used for "adventure", "news making", "vulgar reporting", etc.

If national interest is being compromised in the comfort of privacy, would the invasion of privacy be justifiable under the provisions of the act and/or before a court of law? If national interest is involved then there cannot be a question of either invasion or violation of privacy right.

What prompted the government to introduce this provision in the proposed IT Act amendments?

The secret video recording that is frequently found these days is the real reason for this provision and it should be strictly confined to that aspect only.

The sting operations must be excluded from the ambit of this provision unless where they were used for "adventure", "news making", "vulgar reporting", etc. Will it cover "sting operation" not involving capturing of private parts? The proposed amendments can never include sting operation not covering "vulgar recordings".

CEASE

In short, the traditional sting operations are not covered by the proposed amendments and only "vulgar recording" is covered. Further, every recording involving 'private parts" is not per se vulgar and it depends upon the facts and circumstances of each case.

If the reporting is "predominantly" meant for some other "purpose", including making public an "offence or contravention", then merely because some private parts were also recorded should not make it an offence under this provision.

However, the media must take "precautions" and "avoid" showing the actual facts and details as they are. These facts and details must be kept for the appraisal of the court only and media must not make them public unless anonymity is maintained in all its aspects. Otherwise, it may find itself in trouble.

8

Journalistic Practice

In order to make some generalized comparisons of journalists and journalistic practice in the United States, in English-speaking Canada, and in French-speaking Canada, it is necessary to indulge in some oversimplifications about groups which, in themselves, tend to be rather complex and diverse. Lysiane Gagnon, in her discussion of "Journalism and Ideologies in Quebec," offers a useful starting point in her review of the classic work by Siebert, Peterson, and Schramm on The Four Theories of the Press, which provides a framework for generalizing about differences between these three groups of journalists and for beginning to identify the French, English, and American influences on the practice of journalism in North America.

While the so-called "social responsibility" theory of the press grew out of the 1947 report of the Hutchins Commission on Freedom of the Press in the United States, American journalists have tended not to accept its basic premise, which calls for government intervention when and if the media fail to act responsibly.

For the most part, they continue to subscribe to the more libertarian view and its imperative that the press be free from government control and influence. However, the most recent national survey of journalists in the United States reveals a shift in the perceived functions of journalism favoring some of the original recommendations of the Hutchins Commission.

As Weaver and Wilhoit explain, "most journalists in 1992 appeared to have a `belief system' that reflected the Commission's goal of investigating `the truth about the fact[s]' and providing `a context which gives them meaning.'" Concerning the appropriate role for government, journalists in English Canada, who share British traditions allowing for more government secrecy and control of information and the reporting of information, are more tolerant than their American counterparts of government intervention and control.

And by further comparison, journalists on French-language media in Quebec subscribe even more to the tenets of the social-responsibility theory and are willing to accept an even greater role for government involvement in media matters to assure the public's right to information. According to Fulford,

English-Canadian journalists have inherited most of their techniques from Britain and the United States, except for the extensive foreign correspondence of British journalism and the investigative reporting in the United States.

Further, and perhaps more important, is his observation that English-Canadian newspapers tend to mix elements of British and American heritage and share the ideal which involves truth, completeness, and justice. Explaining that English-Canadian journalists seek "to report the truth," Fulford quotes publisher Stuart Keate who wrote that "Any publisher, editor or reporter worth his salt recognizes that he has only one basic duty to perform: to dig for the truth; to write it in language people can understand; and to resist all impediments to its publication."

While changes in English-Canadian journalism during this century have paralleled similar changes in the United States, journalism in Quebec has been more influenced by French models that include government distribution agencies, newspapers with more readily identifiable political leanings, and greater acceptance of government intervention in media affairs.

The latter is linked to the basic tenet of the social-responsibility theory of the press which, according to Gagnon, has become more accepted by journalists in the province of Quebec than anywhere else in North America. One of the recent presidents of Quebec's federation of professional journalists, Real Barnabe, supported this observation by writing: "Now that they have acquired the conditions under which they may practice their profession with dignity, never have they [Quebec journalists] been so preoccupied by their responsibilities."

Gagnon further explains that the notion of freedom of the press, which was widely accepted by Quebec journalists in the 1940s and 1950s, has given way to a more complex concept of the public's "right to know," and that this has enjoyed considerable success in Quebec, certainly more than it has in English Canada and, with even more reason, the United States.

Part of the explanation for this has to do with the French traditions and perspectives which place a greater value on collectivism over individualism. As Siebert, Peterson, and Schramm explain in their classic work, the social responsibility theory is "in closer harmony with a collectivist theory of society than with the individualistic theory from which the libertarian system sprang."

Other ways in which the French tradition has contributed to differences between French and English journalism and journalists in Canada include: the emphasis on analysis over simple reporting of facts; the tendency to treat matters conceptually rather than in terms of people and events; the need to rationalize; and a greater personalization of articles and editorials. This is not to say that Quebec journalists are less committed to the facts and to being factual. A recent study by Pritchard and Sauvageau, for example, found that Quebec journalists are more likely than other Canadian journalists to think that it is important to accurately report comments from news sources. Similarly, an earlier study by Langlois and Sauvageau, which also documented this commitment to the facts, found there to be considerable variation among newspaper journalists in Quebec.

Concerning the greater personalization of articles and editorials, mentioned above, Siegel found in his study of the coverage of the FLQ crisis in 1970 that the French-language papers tended to project an image of self-importance in a variety of ways including "frequent reference to media and journalists; personalized coverage which, at times, included the raising of rhetorical questions which they then proceeded to answer; and editorials written in the first person."

Another conclusion he reached point to still another important difference between journalism in English and French Canada. Following a comparison of coverage of several major issues or events, as well as a comparison of French and English broadcasting, Siegel found a homogeneity of outlook in the French press system.

"Of particular interest is the leadership role in French-Canadian society in which French-language journalists see them-selves. The articulation of a clearly defined value system is evident in French-language journalism, a practice that goes back a long time."

He found no such uniformity of outlook on the part of the English press, which he termed "fragmented." His conclusion is reinforced by David Thomas, an English-speaking journalist from Quebec: "Unity of thought was, and remains, infinitely more obvious in Quebec's French-language media—a phenomenon implicitly recognized by politicians and journalists who repeatedly point to the harsher treatment accorded the government by the English media."

Dominque Clift, a Montreal author and free-lance journalist who worked for major Canadian newspapers in both French and English Canada, characterized this uniformity of French-language journalists in a different way: the way in which they viewed themselves and their role in Quebec society.

In his article, "Solidarity on a Pedestal: French Journalism in Quebec," he charged that "French journalists see for themselves a much more exalted role in society than do their English-speaking counterparts," adding that: "It is in the actual practice of journalism that French and English writers differ in the most pronounced manner.

It has to do with the way in which journalists look upon themselves, their profession, their public, as well as on their employers." But Florian Sauvageau, in his more systematic study of journalists on French-language dailies in Quebec, could find no such homogeneity in Quebec's journalistic circles.

Instead, he found changes in Quebec media to parallel those in the modern corporate media of North America. Those include: the tendency to view newspapers as, first and foremost, businesses and journalists as "news workers"; journalists talking not so much in terms of "news" but of the "product"; and business and marketing functions gradually replacing the news function.

Journalists are far from all being those radicals trying to control the news, as depicted a few years ago with some help from the pronouncements of the most militant of them. There are some, of course, who still turn for inspiration to the theses of the news as a driving force, and journalism as a tool for development, seeing themselves as agents of change and keeping up with the rhetoric of the 1960s and 1970s.

However, a good number are content simply to report the remarks of the dignitaries they meet, or to get the news out as quickly as possible. The result, he said, is that the work of journalists is becoming more and more routine and fairly unfulfilling, and that this is partly due to the rigid application of certain clauses in collective agreements between journalists and management.

In summary, this brief review of research and commentary on journalists and journalism in the United States, English Canada, and Quebec provides some insight into how the practice of journalism in these different settings has been influenced in a variety of ways by English, French, and American traditions.

Our concern, however, is in how these different traditions or perspectives may have resulted in journalistic practices that vary in their tendencies to promote individualism or to serve the community or broader societal interests.

ANECDOTAL EVIDENCE

Despite the growing body of literature from systematic studies of journalists in Canada and the United States, most of the "evidence" about how journalists and journalistic practices differ between the two countries tends to be anecdotal rather than the result of formal research. There are some exceptions, of course.

For example, we already reported how the most recent national survey of journalists in the United States shows a shift toward some of the values articulated by the Hutchins Commission, which advanced the "social-responsibility" theory of the press.

Also, French-language journalists in Canada tend to be more willing than their English-Canadian and especially their American counterparts to perceive the press as a public service that can be regulated by the government. As evidence, Langois and Sauvageau found that nearly two-thirds of the French-speaking journalists in their study agreed that the state should intervene in the field of information.

Even before the Kent Commission issued its report and recommendations in 1981, Sauvageau argued that the government might intervene to assure the citizen's right to information, similar to the way it has done in education and health care. More often, though, evidence is used to explain how the traditions and perspectives of journalists in Canada and the United States vary considerably in terms of tolerance for intervention by government and the courts in ways that limit the media and the practice of journalism.

This chapter began with a good example of this variety by comparing reactions to the decision in the United States to publish the Unibomber's manifesto with reaction to CBC cooperation with the RCMP in meeting broadcast demands of a group of renegades in British Columbia.

Another example is reaction to certain recommendations of the Kent Commission on Newspapers. Following the simultaneous sale of newspapers in Winnipeg and Ottawa by two major Canadian newspaper groups, the federal government established the Kent Commission in 1980 and authorized it to study the new newspaper industry and make recommendations to the government.

One of the more controversial recommendations called for the establishment of a Press Rights Panel within the Canadian Human Rights Commission. Response came mainly from representatives and publishers of newspapers owned by large newspaper groups in Canada.

The reaction was tempered and mild compared to what one would expect in the United States if similar recommendations were to come out of a government committee that spent more than $3 million to investigate the daily newspaper industry. Reactions in the United States to any threat of government intervention or control in media affairs tend to be immediate and predictable.

Media owners and spokespersons for associations of journalists, particularly in the print media, are quick to call "infringement" and issue charges of improper violations of cherished First Amendment guarantees of freedom of the press. Still another example has to do with media coverage of criminal trials.

During the months of exhaustive coverage and commentary related to the O.J. Simpson trial in the United States, a trial court judge in Ontario issued a restraining order on the media in the Paul Bernardo murder trial that included, as well, a ban on publication of most information from his wife's trial several months earlier.

Canadian journalists complained but complied with the court order, while American journalists in neighboring border cities did not, continuing what one U.S. newspaper editor had earlier referred to as a "border battle with Canadian law."

These examples help illustrate the differences between Canada and the United States in terms of their legal systems, judicial traditions, and accepted journalistic practice and show a stronger commitment in Canada to the values of community over the individual rights of journalists and the news media.

Important differences in the traditions of law and in the practice of journalism in Canada and the United States result in different approaches to how the rights of the news media are appropriately balanced against the needs of the community and the broader interests of society. To begin with, while the two legal systems share a similar tradition in English Common Law, their judicial and political approaches are different in important ways. As Lipset and Pool explain, while both nations seek to protect the rights of the individual while promoting and protecting the general welfare of the community, they do "strike different balances, with Canada tipping toward the interests of the community, and the United States toward the individual."

This review of the development of media law in the two countries shows that the courts on both sides of the border have expressed a strong commitment to the principle of a free press. However, Canadian courts have been less likely than those in the United States to provide strict protections for the media to publish without government restraint or interference.

This is most obvious in matters related to coverage of the courts, where judicial restraints are more allowable in Canada. Also, Canadian courts have permitted government bans on the publication of truthful information, lawfully obtained, while American courts have held that such bans on the press or punishment for publishing such information is unconstitutional.

Also, media in the United States are allowed greater latitude to criticize public officials than are media in Canada, where the courts have been reluctant to adopt the American approach to civil libel. In other areas, however, involving newsgathering, the duty to testify, and access to information, the courts in both countries have attempted to balance the rights of the news media against the broader interests of society.

Apart from differences in the law are differences in the practice of journalism in Canada and the United States. Journalists in Canada are more inclined toward a "social responsibility" view of the role of the media in society. While this particular perspective was proposed by the prestigious Hutchins Commission on Freedom of the Press in the United States, American journalists have tended not accept its basic premise, which calls for government intervention when and if the media fail to act responsibly.

For the most part, they continue to subscribe to the more libertarian view and its imperative that the media be free from government influence and control. Canadian journalists, however, whether sharing British traditions that allow for more government secrecy and control of information or French traditions that are more accepting of government intervention in media affairs, tend to be more tolerant of government intervention in ways that directly affect the media while serving the broader needs and interests of society.

The most recent national survey of American journalists suggests that there may be some shift toward some of the goals of the Hutchins Commission, which originally proposed the social responsibility model.

SOME FUTURE CONSIDERATIONS

There is, and has been, considerable discussion about the Constitution in Canada since the Charter of Rights and Freedoms was adopted in 1982.

However, little if any of the controversy centres around concerns over government control of the media or court limitations of Charter guarantees of press freedom.

This is not to say that journalists and media owners in Canada do not have concerns about these issues or that they would not prefer greater freedom and less government control. It is just that these are not major concerns, at least not compared to the larger constitutional issues being discussed. This is not the case in the United States, where journalists and media owners have long been eager and vocal critics of any attempts by government or the courts to limit press freedoms and violate their First Amendment guarantees.

However, the growing criticism and concerns about court interpretations of the speech-press clause in the United States are coming from nonmedia sources who are concerned about too much freedom at the expense of other interests, particularly the rights and interests of disadvantaged groups like women and minorities.

In particular, concerns being raised by feminists, critical scholars and, especially, critical legal theorists are that the court's continuing emphasis on protecting press freedoms serves only to advance the status quo and favors the special interests of corporate-owned media conglomerates. These are variations of the same kinds of criticism and concerns expressed by Jerome Barron, who argued nearly thirty years ago that "Our constitutional theory is in the grip of a romantic conception of free expression, a belief that the `marketplace of ideas' is freely accessible.

But if ever there were a self operating marketplace of ideas, it has long ceased to exist." He went on to argue for a legal right of access to the media to provide citizens with the kind of marketplace originally intended by the Founding Fathers. Barron, an American, raises these same concerns over recent developments in media law in Canada, and a growing number of critical theorists and legal scholars in Canada are expressing concerns of their own about constitutional developments related to court interpretations of the Canadian Charter of Rights and Freedoms.

Michael Mandel, for example, frames his criticisms in terms of what he calls "The legalization of politics in Canada," and argues that the representative institutions like Parliament, the legislatures, and municipal councils "are now being pushed from centre stage and told what they can and cannot do by judges elected by and accountable to nobody."

David Schneiderman, in his edited volume on Freedom of Expression and the Charter, explains that critics are not optimistic about the consequences of the constitutionalization of freedom of expression in Canada and are concerned that the Charter favors the value system of liberal individualism over the collectivist aims of the modern welfare state. In the United States, concerns are also being raised in journalistic circles about the status of American journalism, about public criticism of the press, and about the appropriate roles and responsibilities of the media in a free democratic society. One of the best recent books on this subject is by Anderson, Dardenne, and Killenberg, who argue for a more ecumenical, constructive, participative, and democratically responsive role for journalism's institutional future.

Other recent authors like Davis Merritt, Jay Rosen, and James Fallows have called for a revision in journalistic practices in order to promote community through civic or public journalism. This approach has challenged the way responsible media report on and relate to the communities they serve. As Dennis and Merrill put it, "The new communitarians are waging a rhetorical war against Enlightenment liberalism—against individualism and libertarianism."

More specifically, Christians argues that journalists should discard the liberal politics of rights, which "rests on unsupportable foundations," and that such rights should be "given up for a politics of the common good." In response, critics of this approach argue that it "confuses journalism with community organization, a social work concept" and are concerned that if journalists became activists and took positions on community issues, they would lose "any claim to impartiality and would sacrifice credibility."

In summary, what emerges from a review of issues like these is the fact that some of the basic foundations of law and journalistic practice are being challenged in very significant ways by credible practitioners and scholars in Canada and the United States alike. This is all part of the important ongoing discussions about how to appropriately balance the freedoms of the press and other media of communication against the larger interests of society, and about how to frame the practice of journalism in the best way possible to serve the democratic process.

The quality of these discussions on both sides of the border can be enhanced by examining the experiences in both countries and, indeed, in other societies, to see how these issues are being played out against the backdrop of different traditions, practices, values, and beliefs.

Each new technology has brought its share of hype from those who would like to see its use for education. In 1922, Thomas Edison said that the motion picture was destined to revolutionize our educational system. In 1945, William Levenson, director of the Cleveland public schools' radio stations, said that the time might come when a portable radio receiver would be as common in the classroom as the blackboard.

In 1961, the Ford Foundation claimed that educational television promises "a whole treasure-trove of new and stimulating experiences". More recently, at the National Education Computing Conference in June 1997, Bill Gates compared the computer and the Internet revolution with the California gold rush of the mid 1800s.

He exhorted educators to use this new technology in the classroom to give students a better chance at success. Researchers have long been aware of such hype and the often unfulfilled promises that educational technology has brought to education. Few are fully aware of the negative effects that these same technologies can bring to education and to our lives. Television has been in schools and in our homes for nearly half a century.

During that time, extensive studies have been conducted on this medium, with some interesting results. For example, second graders from towns without television score higher on reading fluency and creative ability tests. Non-TV-viewing fourth and eighth graders score higher on basic skills tests. Television viewing is a cause of violent or aggressive behaviour.

It also contributes substantially to obesity. Television can make you dumber, less creative, violent, and obese. What do computers have in store for us? Todd Oppenheimer's article "The Computer Delusion" is highly critical of school districts' cutting programs in art, music, and physical education to add computer programs when "there is no good evidence that most uses of computers significantly improve teaching and learning".

ABC's Nightline with Ted Koppel aired a segment on September 30, 1998 titled "Computers in the Classroom: The $50 Billion Gamble," highlighting the fact that there is little, if any, research to prove that there are any learning benefits to using technology in the classroom. One month before that programme, the front page of the New York Times detailed the startling findings of a $1.5 million, three-year study by Carnegie Mellon researchers.

They found that the longer a person spends online, the more sad, lonely, and depressed he or she becomes. These findings do not surprise critical educators. Every new technology arrives with hype, and years later we find major weaknesses.

Good educational designers should not ignore these findings. They need to find ways to maximize the positive effects of technologies and minimize the weaknesses. Following are three examples of doing just that.

THE NO-SIGNIFICANT-DIFFERENCE EFFECT

One of the most disappointing aspects of using technology in teaching is the so-called no-significant-difference phenomenon. This phenomenon outlines the observation that any technology used in teaching does not make a significant difference in learning.

Statistical comparisons between teaching methodologies, with or without the use of technology, have been made for nearly a century. Researchers have compared how much students learned from a teacher lecturing in a traditional classroom with how much students learned from a traditional correspondence course covering the same material. There was no significant difference. Comparisons have been made between correspondence courses and radio courses, telnet courses and television courses, and traditional lecture courses and online courses, to name a few. The vast majority of the research resulted in no significant difference. In those few cases where a significant difference was found, the most recent technology in the comparison was not always the winner.

Nearly all of the no-significant-difference studies that have been conducted since 1912 have used a model of a traditional classroom with a teacher lecturing to students. Whether it was a teacher in a traditional classroom, on the radio, on television, on telnet, online, or even via correspondence, they all used the lecture format.

Perhaps the hundreds of findings of "no significant difference" really headline the fact that if you use the lecture format, students will learn the material equally well no matter what media are chosen. That being the case, if you are going to lecture, why not use the cheaper format? Why spend thousands of dollars on technology when less expensive printed materials used in a correspondence course will work just as well?

Another alternative is for course designers to think outside the paradigm of the lecture format. Unext.com is creating Cardean, a "no lecture" university. The company contends that learning only happens when students "do," not when they listen passively to a lecture.

The educational content for the courses is being drawn from several eminent institutions, including Stanford and Columbia. Few schools can afford the millions of dollars being spent on developing problem-based learning courses created by expert designers working with Nobel scientists. However, there are a number of practical ways to begin to develop lecture-free courses.

Project-based activities can give students the freedom to apply learning in practical contexts that are personal and relevant to them. Step-by-step tutorials could allow them to work with applicable software tools to develop digital media for their projects. A good place to start would be to use tutorials that are already online for paint programs, Web page editors, or presentation software programs.

Also, teachers could create links to structured tutorials for surfing the Internet to help students find the best "fair-use" digital materials. Other links could provide students with resources that help them learn how to evaluate sites critically to find good sources of legitimate information. Digital projects could be showcased in an online student gallery or in a student portfolio.

Students could provide feedback as they previewed and learned from each other's work. Course readings or activities could be built around real-world or theoretical problems. Teachers could follow these assignments with threaded discussion forums or live chats.

Students would be expected to read and respond to comments made by those in the class. Once this dialogic process was established, students could use this same model for their own project presentations. Similarly, student groups could be assigned topics of importance to research, develop, and teach to the class. Groups could post Web pages with relevant links for class exploration before conducting formal discussions via live chat or threaded forum discussion.

MINIMIZE THE DEPRESSED AND LONELY EFFECT

Want to be depressed and lonely? Spend more time communicating on the Internet. That is the surprising conclusion of the study conducted at Carnegie Mellon University and financed by a number of technology giants including Intel, Hewlett Packard, AT&T Research, and Apple Computer.

Researchers found that people who spent even a few hours per week online experienced higher levels of depression and loneliness than those who used the computer network less frequently.

These results completely surprised the social scientists because participants used social features such as e-mail and Internet chats more than they used passive information gathering resources to read or watch videos. "We were shocked by the findings, because they are counterintuitive to what we know about how socially the Internet is being used," said Robert Kraut, a social psychology professor at Carnegie Mellon's Human Computer Interaction Institute.

"We are not talking here about the extremes. These were normal adults and their families, and on average, for those who used the Internet most, things got worse". Teenagers, unsurprisingly, tended to spend more time online and showed a greater rate of loneliness and depression. What caused this negative side effect? Here is one possibility: Those who participated in the study reported a decline in interaction with family members and friends that directly corresponded to the amount of time they spent online.

A recent study at Stanford University also found that the more time someone spends online, the less time he or she spends with real human beings. Communicating with someone online apparently is not as psychologically fulfilling as is talking to someone you know. Due to the anonymity of the Internet, unless you really know the people you are chatting with, you cannot be sure that they are being honest about their profession or expertise, let alone any of their personal information.

Several things can be done to minimize the effect of student isolation. One idea is to have students and faculty create biographical pages with visual and auditory elements that briefly encapsulate each individual in an interesting way. Everyone in a class or degree programme should have easy access to this password-protected information.

Password protection prevents search engine spiders from cataloging this information in their databases. Without it, students would soon find their bio-pages listed in the directories of major search engines. Another idea is to group students together when they begin to work on a degree online. Students could be grouped by such factors as interests, personal situations, goals, or the pace at which they plan to work through a programme.

If a group of six students with similar interests starts out together in a programme, real friendships may be fostered on the way to a degree. To help forge a connection with the university, graduate assistants or faculty could be assigned to these groups that meet periodically online.

Another way to develop communication avenues that are valuable to students would be to enable students to establish online clubs based on interests. Dating, chess, foreign language, journalism, or even debate clubs are some possibilities. Access to online student lounges could also be valuable.

MINIMIZE THE NUMBER OF DROPOUTS

The Institute for Higher Education Policy conducted a review of the current research on the effectiveness of distance education. Reviewers found that "in a number of studies, there was evidence that a higher percentage of students participating in a distance learning course tended to drop out before the course was completed compared to students in a conventional classroom".

They concluded that the research did "not adequately explain why the drop out rates of distance learners is higher." They also stated that this "subject mortality" was bad because of "negative consequences associated with dropping out" and also because the research was likely "excluding these drop outs—thereby tilting the student outcome findings toward those who are `successful.'.

If the students who had dropped out had remained in the course, the mean score of the achievement test or student survey could be significantly different." The Corporate University Xchange (CUX) is a corporate education research and consulting firm that helps organizations with training. The company says that one of the biggest challenges of online learning programs is to "retain" e-learners.

Their pilot study of e-learners from Fortune 1000 companies revealed that the number one reason that people drop out of online courses was "lack of time." Solutions for this problem were to create courses that give students: (a) the ability to start a course at any time, (b) flexible deadlines, and (c) 24-hour technical support.

Zielinski (2000, 54) describes a number of concerns about the "design and implementation of many self-paced, asynchronous learning courses," including "higher-than-average drop-out rates or disengaged learners who don't receive the level of interaction, personalized feedback, skills practice, managerial oversight or technical support needed for quality learning experiences." It is hard to address these concerns if learning organizations are not tracking students—specifically those who drop out—to find out about their online experiences.

For example, some may be what Zielinski calls "pragmatic learners," who do not finish all the modules of an online course simply because, with "grazing" learning styles, they take only the content they need, leaving superfluous material behind. Without more detailed data like these, it is nearly impossible to address the dropout situation.

Degree programs should be collecting and developing online-accessible databases of this type of information, as well as more personalized information from students including their interests and learning styles. Instructors and developers should have access to this database.

Finalists for the "1998 Outstanding Online Course Award," sponsored by the Paul Allen Virtual Education Foundation, gave presentations at the "Creating Effective Online Instruction" conference in May 1999. Developers of two of the courses stated that the next wave of development for online courses is to make them more personalized for individual students.

Both planned to develop more personalized Web courses with software such as ColdFusion, which allows developers to create database-driven Web sites. When a student accesses one of these course sites, an individualized course Web page can address her by name, and because it has already parsed through her database of interests and learning styles, it can include a quote or story vignette specifically tailored for her. As she works through assignments and online assessments, the database continues to grow.

If she is found to have a weakness in an area, a Web resource can be offered, giving her a chance to review the same material from a more visual perspective if that matches her learning style strength. One way to begin integrating learning styles into online curriculum is to use the sensory styles. Three sensory styles are traditionally associated with academic learning: visual, auditory, and haptic (or kinesthetic).

An excellent way to address the individual differences of sensory learning styles would be to develop courses using the "Universal Design for Learning" framework. In this framework, curricular materials are developed in "many media so that learners can select one or more ways to approach the subject matter. Text, images with no text, images with text, voice, animation, video, or a sequence of sounds can effectively convey a series of events".

Within this framework, students are able to select media in the format in which they learn best. A realistic way to begin this process is by creating multiple sensory options for the most difficult concept that will be covered.

VISUAL LEARNERS

Seeing understands for visual learners. Ross and Schulz state that "online course animations, hypertext, or clickable diagrams and video clips can clarify concepts that a static textbook image simply cannot." They further recommend that instructors maintain online archives of slide presentations to assist these visual learners. Additionally, development of charts, graphs, and any other visual rendition of the information to be covered is preferable for these types of learners.

AUDITORY LEARNERS

Auditory learners tend to benefit most from lectures. Ross and Schulz (1999) recommend that instructors establish audio resources and archive digital audio files of fifteen-minute class summaries on the Web. They can add shorter sound clips of instructor-developed materials to clarify course segments.

They can encourage auditory learners to purchase dictation software that converts their voice to text, These programs can often read the text of online materials and e-mail messages out loud. Some phone companies now offer audio-based e-mail services with which you can send or receive messages over the telephone.

Call up, and a computer dictation device will read your e-mail messages to you over the phone. You can then reply to these messages just as you would leave a message on an answering machine. Your response is saved as a digital audio file, attached to an e-mail message, and sent, all without the use of a computer.

HAPTIC OR KINESTHETIC LEARNERS

Learners who prefer to do something more active to learn course materials are referred to as "haptic" or "kinesthetic" learners. "Practicing problems, doing lab experiments, creating solutions, doing physical activities, engaging in manipulative exercises, and brainstorming ideas are all ways to involve this learner in the classroom".

These learners could print out step-by-step directions for more active course-based experiences that are posted online. Ross and Shultz add that "java-programmed jigsaw puzzles can provide a powerful learning and review tool for students."

Nearly two decades ago, Richard Clark said, "Five decades of research indicate that there are no learning benefits to be gained from applying different media in instruction, regardless of their obviously attractive features or advertised superiority." Clark changes this to "70 years" in his foreword to Russell's The No Significant Difference Phenomenon. Apparently, little has changed in the last twenty years.

Will another twenty years pass us by with the same results? One hope is that designers and teachers will try to use other pedagogies of learning that do not embrace the lecture format. Perhaps new leaders of technology will find ways to tap into individual differences to help create meaningful courses that really make a difference. Additionally, it would be beneficial if students could create real friends and lifelong connections with their peers after experiencing an online degree programme with them. If this hope is realized, two decades from now we may read about online courses encountering the revolutionary "significant difference phenomenon," with students experiencing the "happy and connected" effect.

We might even read articles on the latest methods to stop students from "dropping in" to the class years after they graduate because it was such a life-changing experience.

A PROFILE OF JOURNALISTIC VALUES

The profile of journalists' instrumental values that emerges from the survey places a strong emphasis on a mix of competency-based and morality-oriented concepts, much of which would be expected to describe the professional outlook of journalists. Three respondents did not rank the values but completed other sections of the survey, giving the value rankings a total of 352 valid responses.

An analysis of this journalistic value hierarchy has been reported elsewhere; this study, however, focuses on the value rankings as they are related to journalistic role conceptions. "Honest" was ranked the most important value by far by most journalists; more than one-third of all journalists ranked it first, and another sixty-two journalists ranked it second.

More journalists ranked "Honest" in either one of those positions than all other positions combined. "Honest" was followed by "Fair." Roughly half of all journalists placed this value in one of the top three spots. Those two morally oriented values were followed by two values that Rokeach related to the concept of competency: "Responsible" and "Capable." Nearly one-half of the journalists ranked "Responsible" at positions two through five.

When testing his original list of instrumental values on different populations, Rokeach said the average intercorrelation among the rankings for all the instrumental values was -.06, which suggested that each of the values could be considered discrete, valid measures for different concepts. While several of the original values do significantly correlate with each other due to an intrinsic parallelism of the concepts involved (i.e., "Responsible" and "Self-controlled"), the intercorrelations for the rankings of the original values by journalists in this project mirror intercorrelations that Rokeach found in his general-population studies.

To Rokeach's 18 values, 6 others were added for this study to reflect the most predominant values commonly found in the media ethics literature: "Fair," "Just," "Aboveboard," "Empathetic," "Minimizing harm," and "Civic-minded."

The journalistic-oriented values added by this project also show negligible intercorrelations, with averages ranging from -.03 to -.059, suggesting that each of the added values is in fact measuring additional concepts and not simply other dimensions of values already listed. Among the 18 instrumental values, the highest negative intercorrelation Rokeach found was -.38.

Roles Embraced by Journalists. Responses to 14 journalistic "function" statements generally correspond to what Weaver and Wilhoit found in their survey ten years ago, with some notable differences that may be due to changes in cultural and professional emphases over that time period. The response rate for this final section of the instrument was slightly lower, at 53% (N = 328).

Most of the role-conception items were from Weaver and Wilhoit and can be grouped into the authors' factors of the predominant "interpretive," "disseminator," and "adversarial" functions. Journalists gave "Get information to the public quickly" the highest overall average.

They gave "be less critical of officials during national crisis" the lowest, at 2.3, closely followed by "set the political agenda" at 2.6. This study's three hypotheses predicted that journalists who rank particular values as highly salient also would embrace certain journalistic role conceptions over others. Specifically, Hl predicted that journalists ranking "Courageous," "Independent," and "Just" highly would endorse an adversarial role; H2 predicted that those ranking "Minimizing harm," "Fair," and "Self-controlled" high would endorse a disseminator function; and H3 predicted that those ranking "Civic-minded," "Imaginative," and "Capable" high would endorse an interpretive role.

The predicted relationships did not produce significant Spearman's rho correlations, so data analysis did not show support for Hl and H2. Spearman's correlations also did not appear to provide immediate support for H3.

While the survey included several statements used by Weaver and Wilhoit as indicators of the degree to which journalists embraced the adversarial, disseminator, and interpretive functions of the press, only the two statements associated with the adversarial role ("Be skeptical of public officials" and "Be skeptical of corporations") produced a Cronbach's alpha strong enough to constitute an index.

A linear regression model showed some support for H3 when accounting for the demographic variables. H3 hypothesized that journalists who ranked the values "Civic-minded," "Imaginative," and "Capable" highly also would be more likely to embrace the interpretive function of the press.

In the regression model, the individual values served as the predictor variables and the role-conception statements served as the dependent variables.

For one of the interpretive-function statements, "Influencing public opinion," the value "Civic-minded" proved to be a significant predictor of some of the variance, with a modest yet significant change in the r-square.

Years spent in journalism also were a good predictor in explaining some of the variance in the extent to which journalists embraced the statement, "Influencing public opinion."

The longer journalists were in the profession, the more likely they were to support that statement. The models also showed that the same demographic variables of age and years in journalism produced significant r-square changes for two of the four statements associated with the interpretive function: "Providing analysis and interpretation of complex problems", and "Discussing national policy while it is still being developed".

DISCUSSION

The journalism ethics literature is rich with speculation on the values of journalists, both what people believe they are and what they ought to be; the results of this survey provide a quantitative profile of journalists' actual value systems, which offers a more solid ground on which to theorize about how journalists should conduct themselves. The profile simultaneously points to areas where the theory of media ethics and the practice of newspaper journalism converge as well as to wide gulfs between the hierarchy of values that journalists have and the approach that ethicists say journalists ought to take to their jobs.

Several patterns emerge between the values and journalists' assessments of various roles and functions. The two statements that constitute the adversarial role ("Being constantly skeptical of actions taken by public officials" and "Being constantly skeptical of actions by businesses and corporations") are both positively correlated with "Above-board" and "Broadminded," and negatively correlated with "Polite."

Again, this indicates the immense importance placed on the need for credibility (though not necessarily civility) among those journalists who take the watchdog role as their primary function. A third statement that could be considered a measure of the adversarial-oriented role, "Being less critical of public officials during a national crisis," was negatively correlated with "Fair," "Imaginative," and "Independent," and positively correlated with "Responsible."

The more that journalists indicated that government should be supported in times of national crisis, the less highly they ranked the values of "Fair" and "Independent." While the correlations are relatively weak, they are significant, indicating some relationship.

At the same time, journalists who ranked "Responsible"-as well as "Obedient"-highly appeared to indicate that being less critical during crises was part of what it means to be a responsible journalist. Only one of the two statements ("Getting information to the public quickly") associated with the disseminator role was significantly correlated with any of the values.

Journalists appear to hold a deep ambivalence toward the so-called interpretive function of the press. While the values such as "Broadminded" and "Courageous" are positively correlated with several of the statements ("Providing analysis and interpretation of complex problems" and "Investigating claims and statements made by the government"), "Responsible" is negatively correlated with the first statement, suggesting that journalists remain uncomfortable with being perceived in any way as activists. In addition to these three journalistic role conceptions, the 1992 survey data by Weaver and Wilhoit as well as the 2002 survey data by Weaver, Beam, and colleagues suggested the emergence of a fourth role-that of "populist mobilizer," which "developed and channeled" the public's interest in intellectual and cultural issues after grabbing audience attention. Several statements served to assess support for this role, including "Setting the public agenda," "Developing intellectual and cultural interests of the public," and "Giving ordinary people a chance to express their views on public affairs." Weaver and Wilhoit concluded that the support among journalists for these statements was "tantalizing evidence that the spirit of the 'public journalism' movement may have established a foothold."

Correlations between the mobilizer statements and the value rankings in this project seem to provide qualified confirmation of this. The value "Civic-minded" is positively correlated with the statement, "Developing intellectual and cultural interests of the public."

However, even here journalists appear to shy away from any behaviour that might smack of advocacy: The value "Fair" was negatively correlated with another mobilizer statement, "Setting the public agenda," and none of the values was correlated with a third statement, "Giving ordinary people a chance to express their views on public affairs."

While results yielded little support for the study's specific hypotheses, the data clearly suggest some connection between journalists' value hierarchies and the roles that they embrace. The results also suggest that these two overlapping realms require further research. The survey instrument used here could be applied to broadcast and Internet-based journalists as well, providing potentially valuable comparative profiles. Similar comparisons can be explored regarding journalistic role conceptions among different groups of journalists as well as differences in how these roles are perceived by journalists and the general public.

Several suggestive relationships between journalistic values and roles emerge from this study. But given the research that has explored at length the forces of newsroom socialization, the relationships are surprisingly weak ones.

While previous research has suggested that social control in the newsroom is a strong shaper both of the values that guide their work and how journalists perceive their function in society, this study suggests that newsroom socialization does not exert a strong influence on general values, or vice versa, given the weak correlations between role priorities and the value rankings.

Rather than consider values-whether general or specifically journalistic-as products of a singular newsroom socialization dynamic, research may need to differentiate the various "environments" in which particular values and role conceptions are formed. Values, beliefs, and behaviour interact, as Voakes suggests, in "a dynamic swirl of social factors."

It seems likely that journalistic role priorities are influenced more by the newsroom environment and professional socialization, whereas more general values are shaped by family, religious, and cultural environments. Also, while the value profile of newspaper journalists that emerges is valuable and suggests many different applications, this study also illustrates the difficulty in assigning such broad, generalized values to specific behaviors.

Several associations that emerge in this study are worth considering. The value profile established in this study elaborates upon-and in some cases contradicts-what journalists have reported regarding self-perceptions of their professional roles. Weaver and Wilhoit concluded in their 1992 study that 51% of journalists reported that the disseminator role was "very important," 63% reported that the interpretive role was "very important," and 18% placed a similarly high priority on the adversarial role.

However, just as interesting is the finding that the data showed more correlations among the top six values and the two statements associated with the adversarial role-being skeptical of government and being skeptical of business-than with any other set of role conception statements. And in all, the adversarial role statements were correlated to ten of the values ranked by journalists.

While these correlations are somewhat weak by objective standards, they are among the stronger correlations in the data, and they are statistically significant. They also may reflect the recent findings by Weaver, Beam, and colleagues that more journalists placed importance on the watchdog function of the press in 2002 than in 1992.

The emphasis on the adversarial role also is underscored by the frequency with which five values in particular - "Broadminded," "Fair," "Courageous," "Imaginative," and "Independent" - correlate with various role statements that suggest a watchdog function.

Two of those values rank among the top six. In fact, among the entire list of twenty-four values, the adversarial role is linked to more values than any other role, based on correlations between these values and the two role statements that indicate support for the watchdog function. In total, the adversarial role is linked to five values, while the disseminator role is linked to only three ("Capable," "Fair," and "Responsible").

The interpretive role, which Weaver and Wilhoit found to be most widely endorsed by journalists, is linked to only two values ("Broadminded" and "Courageous"), and both of those are values where the adversarial role also shows strength. In other words, journalists may disavow the public notion of an over-aggressive journalist, yet they consider such a watch-dog function as critical to what constitutes being a credible journalist. However, like the research by Weaver and Wilhoit, this study finds those sometimes contradictory roles that journalists endorse-and the underlying values that are their foundations-can be held simultaneously. The role conceptions research and this value profile both speak to the internal forces that drive journalists. This study reveals some intriguing links between the two approaches. What remains unclear is how the two interact, and to what extent journalists' values and role perceptions influence how they go about the daily job of reporting and presenting the news.

Clarifying these relationships in future research will require revisiting some theoretical constructs used in this study to represent values and roles. It is obvious, for instance, that the "Civic-minded" value triggered possibly negative associations with public journalism in the minds of some journalists, rather than the idea that journalists have a role in the cultivation and maintenance of community. Additionally, the theoretical linkages between some of the findings that were not initially hypothesized should be put to test in future studies. More importantly, however, this study points up the need for more research that brings to bear value theory and social psychology on the profession of journalism and the journalists themselves.

RECENT TRENDS IN JOURNALISTIC AUTONOMY

Random surveys, each of more than a thousand U.S. journalists, con ducted every 10 years since the early 1970s suggest that journalism's century-long ascent toward professionalism has stalled and may, in fact, be reversing. The newsroom surveys show a strong trend toward declining journalistic autonomy. Weaver and Wilhoit, who conducted the last two surveys, wrote:

Compared to the early 1970s, journalists in the 1982 sample reported a significant decline in their freedom to decide news story emphasis and editing. The 1992 interviews suggest that newsroom autonomy has diminished further, and at a startling pace. For the first time in three decades, barely half of reporters see themselves [with] the newsroom clout of their predecessors. And the lessening autonomy is occurring at a time when many in the work force--who entered the profession during a tide of heavy hiring of young staff in the late 1970s and early 1980s--have been in the newsroom long enough to have established their authority. Four of five journalists laid the loss of autonomy to profit-driven management decisions as well as pressure from government, advertisers, or a hostile public. A comment the researchers deemed typical read: "There is increasing pressure from large corporations, including my own, for bottom-line profit and gains at the expense of long-term quality". By contrast, only 8 per cent said they were hindered by professional standards of ethics, good taste, or objectivity.

Other surveys show a similar trend. A 1993 Associated Press Managing Editors survey of 627 newspaper journalists showed rising discontent from a survey 8 years earlier, particularly among the young, minorities, and best educated. Almost half the journalists with graduate degrees counted themselves dissatisfied enough to want to leave their jobs. "About half of these dissatisfied journalists say they do not have sufficient autonomy on the job," the report said, "they lack resources to do their jobs properly and they are not very impressed with the quality of their newspapers".

A 1995 Associated Press Managing Editors study of newsroom managers also showed less autonomy and greater stress than a similar survey in 1983. "Fully 66 per cent of responding editors said their news hole was reduced in the past year. Half reported losing news staffers who were not replaced. Eighty per cent reported that 'there is more work than I can complete in a normal day'". All of these limitations were imposed from above the newsroom.

Summing up these changes for newspapers in an article titled "The Thrill is Gone," Stepp concluded: "In the age-old battle between the editorial side and the business side, the editorialists have lost the upper hand". In local television--the part of the news industry growing A fundamental principle of ethics is that those with greatest power bear the greatest moral accountability.

Fastest over the past several decades in employment, consumer loyalty, and influence over news practice--the outlook for journalistic autonomy is more dismal still. According to Fink, "In television sheer perversity is at work-a sort of Gresham's Law of Journalism: poor quality, low-cost entertainment shows drive out high quality, high-cost news programming". If these assessments are accurate, journalists are more decision takers than decision makers. While they cannot disavow responsibility for their actions so long as they retain the option to quit their jobs, their authority to produce high-quality ethical news reports is circumscribed, tightly for some, loosely for others. A fundamental principle of ethics is that those with the greatest power bear the greatest moral accountability. Journalism's ethical codes have it backward.

A recent text on media ethics concluded: "[I]t's futile to discuss... efforts by individuals to practice ethical journalism without examining the corporate profit motive and its impact on those efforts". Major American journalism ethics codes, however, not only fail to examine the corporate profit motive, most don't even recognize its existence. Difficult structural ethical questions lie at the heart of journalism conducted by profit-seeking businesses.

Particularly in the modern newsroom where barriers between the business side and the news side have been lowered or eliminated, journalism ethics must speak to potential conflicts of interest with powerful news-shapers outside the newsroom. Drawing on theoretical work by Turow, McQuail, and McManus, at least eight such powerful actors can be identified. In each case there should be both a prescription of an optimal relationship and an enforceable ethical proscription to protect the news department's interest in providing news that maximizes public understanding from the media firm's narrow self-interest in serving the following constituencies:

- Shareholders/Owners. If they seek maximum short-term returns on their investment, they may balk at spending what quality journalism requires.

- Rational advertisers seek the largest audience of potential customers in a context that both lends their claims credibility yet encourages consumption, all at the lowest cost. In contrast, quality journalism seeks the largest audience regardless of customer potential--wealth-and freedom from bias toward advertisers and the ethic of consumption.
- Sources may manipulate the supply of raw material for news in order to gain favorable exposure to their ideas and often themselves. In contrast, ethical journalism gathers information without fear or favour and without regard to the information subsidies of public relations.
- Consumers: More people may be attracted to entertainment information. Further, quality journalism that challenges popular myths and prejudices may drive away some consumers.
- Government: In an environment where parent conglomerates of media firms own companies affected by government regulation or government contracts, or simply by government spending, there may be pressure for biased news in return for favors.
- Parent corporations may exert pressure to report favorably or at least not initiate negative coverage of corporate siblings and their business interests.
- Media firms, represented by the newspaper publisher or TV station general manager or network CEO, may not allocate adequate resources to their news departments given the greater profitability of other choices, such as entertainment programming, or entertainment-oriented sections of a newspaper, or other business interests.
- Pressure groups including social institutions may exert influence on the newsroom for content that does not offend the group's sensibilities or that furthers its agenda. Quality journalism, however, is independent, acting in the best interest of the entire community.

The details of such a structural ethics of journalism are beyond the scope of this chapter. Fresh thinking about how to define, measure, and enforce a new moral code for news is urgently needed. Even the most modest proposal is likely to be highly controversial because structural ethics must negotiate the First Amendment, and more importantly, intrude on the "forbidden," realm of ownership prerogatives of private enterprises. My purpose here has been restricted to demonstrating that the current expressions of national codes of ethics ignore or gloss over the most serious moral issues in contemporary journalism. As long as they do, journalism's codes of ethics are themselves suspect ethically. At best, they are incomplete. At worst, they confuse and discourage needed reforms by permitting those who control the news to deflect criticism from themselves onto their employees. In Britain, lone motherhood is not a neutral nor an apolitical status; it evokes strong moral evaluations and therefore easily becomes a political symbol. Although the historical status and treatment of British lone mothers has varied over time, they have almost continually been at the centre of public debates about the state of society in general, but more particularly of 'the family' and the role of women.

Most recently, political and media attention has focused on the doubling of the number of lone parent families in Britain over the past two decades (reaching around 20 per cent of all families with dependent children, over 90 per cent of whom are headed by a lone mother), on the growth of unmarried mothers as a proportion of all lone mothers, and on their increasing reliance on Income Support (the social assistance benefit) rather than on paid work.

Debate has centred around whether lone mothers prefer to live off the state, and may even be created by such policy 'cushioning', or whether they want to be 'self-sufficient' but cannot because welfare policies are unsupportive.

Arguably both views are wide of the mark; research reveals that lone mothers' moral views about 'good' mothering, and how this does or does not combine with paid work, is the crucial issue. Lone mothers received particularly damning attention at the hands of new right politicians and the popular media in 1993, in the context of the then Conservative government's 'back to basics' campaign. Indeed, 1993 has been dubbed 'The year of the lone mother'.

Lone mothers were depicted as a threat to the fabric of society, supposedly rearing delinquent children without the guidance of a proper father, and scrounging benefits and housing off the welfare state. Social policies were called for that would deal with this menace. Lone mothers received further attention in the media as a legitimate cause for social concern during 1996, again functioning as a sort of symbol as part of a national debate about 'moral values', as policies concerning divorce law reform and working mothers were debated.

And towards the end of 1997, lone mothers were once again in the political and media spotlight as a result of the New Labour government's social reforms. Here lone mothers functioned as a symbol in the attempt to restructure social benefits towards welfare-to-work strategies.

Academics have played an important supporting role in media preoccupations with lone mothers. In particular, new right and revisionist/ communitarian academics have gained space in the national media, and have propounded what Judith Stacey calls 'virtual social science'.

Here categorical assertion, anecdote and selective readings of 'facts' are posed as unbiased and fault-free authoritative research, in this case purportedly showing that lone mothers are formative members of a British 'underclass'. The US academic Charles Murray gained particular space in the press in the early-mid 1990s, with Cassandra-like statistical and rhetorical predictions that Britain was heading down the same slippery slope as the US, to extensive urban crime, drug use and disorder-where all this was the result of increasing 'illegitimate' births supported by the benefits system. The answer, in this view, is to stop 'supporting' lone motherhood through social policies and instead support the traditional married family.

Such negative portrayals of lone mothers have not gone unchallenged. Attempts have been made by voluntary pressure groups, such as the National Council for One Parent Families, and liberal left professionals and academics, as well as leading figures in the 'liberal' establishment, such as Church authorities, to reinsert a public image of lone mothers as 'normal' women who are doing their best in externally constrained and unfavourable circumstances. In this view, social policies should be enlarged to properly support such women in bringing up their children.

Consequently, mainstream political and media debates about lone mothers in Britain-and corresponding policy proposals-have become polarised between seeing lone mothers as a threat to society or as victims of social problems. Each of these positions, their propagation in the media, the role of academics within this, and the social policies that accompany them, is reviewed in more detail below: particular attention is focused on the ways in which the media have depicted black lone mothers.

But these polarised positions are not the only ways of understanding lone mothers' situation, or of framing the parameters for social policies in response. Indeed, other views may more accurately reflect how lone mothers themselves understand and experience their lives.

These alternative views of lone motherhood are also discussed albeit more briefly, because they have not gained wider legitimacy or currency in national media and political debates, nor influenced policy frameworks to any great extent. The propagation of particular media images of lone mothers and their accompaniment by recommendations for particular social policies, is posed rather simply above. Clearly, the media increasingly inform public understanding and comprehension of the social world, and play a role in placing issues on the political policy agenda-as this volume attests.

Nevertheless, the relationship between mainstream media presentations of lone motherhood and the actual or possible social policies that address their situation is not a relationship of simple stimulus-response.

As in other policy areas, this relationship is more complex, not least because government and political agendas influence and inform media coverage. It is perhaps more useful to see ideological issues lying at the root of both, which relate to shared social understandings about the relationship between individuals, states, markets and families, and to how 'explanations' are constructed in dominant western and academic categorical modes of thought.

REPRESENTATIONS OF LONE MOTHERS AS A SOCIAL THREAT

One perception of lone mothers expounded in mainstream political and media representations sees them as a social threat: both morally and financially.

They are formative members of an underclass that has no interest in providing for itself in legitimate ways. This position links into the underclass theory that has developed in the USA in particular, but has been imported into, and gained influence in, Britain-although it also has its roots in a longstanding British 'social pathology' view of the poor.

This theory posits that, in spatially segregated areas, there is a developing class that has no stake in, and is hostile to, the social order. Lone mothers are seen as active agents in the creation of this underclass. In Britain, young single (that is, never-married) mothers have been focused on as the central culprits.

Lone mothers allegedly choose to have children outside wedlock to gain welfare and housing benefits, and then, supported by the state, they choose not to get a job. Their sons, assumed to be without male authority or roles, are said to drift into delinquency, crime and the drug culture, while their daughters learn and repeat the cycle of promiscuity and dependency. Popular media depictions of lone mothers as a social threat use emotional symbolism more fully than more 'respectable' academic tracts. Media reports, however, both draw on, and are sometimes written by, academics. The American new right/ republican academic Charles Murray has enjoyed particular prominence in the *Sunday Times,* to purvey his virtual social science.

Andrew Neil, when editor of this paper, claimed that he had introduced Murray to the British public and politicians, and sponsored his 'research' in Britain. During the early 1990s and especially in 1993, the *Sunday Times* and other right-wing broadsheets, along with the tabloid press, devoted considerable and regular editorial attention to stories about single mothers and the underclass. They also displayed some raw prejudice in doing so. An editorial in the *Sunday Times* for example argued that:

It is becoming increasingly clear to all but the most blinkered of social scientists that the disintegration of the nuclear family is the principal source of so much unrest and misery. The creation of an urban underclass, on the margins of society, but doing great damage to itself and the rest of us, is directly linked to the rapid rise in illegitimacy... It is not just a question of a few families without fathers; it is a matter of whole communities with barely a single worthwhile role model.

A headline in the same newspaper queried, 'Wedded to welfare-do they want to marry a man or the state?' The *Daily Mail,* with its ideological and political address to 'middle England', offered a similar viewpoint:

The Willenhall estate, on the outskirts of Coventry, houses a large number of single mothers. There are also a lot of young, single men, many living on the proceeds of either crime or benefit fraud and more or less attached to the young women... It is kept afloat by the niggardly (if costly) charity of the state and the local authority, that is to say the taxes paid by traditional two parent families. The targeting of a particular public housing estate with a supposedly high proportion of young 'underclass' single mothers seems to be a virtual social science technique for delivering messages, and for concretising particular views, as used by Murray and journalists in the popular media. The flagship BBC television current affairs programme, *Panorama,* entitled 'Babies on benefit', broadcast on 20 September 1993, used a similar technique.

In this case it was the St Mellon's council estate in Wales that was portrayed as an underclass breeding ground. This estate had previously received critical attention from the then Conservative Secretary of State for Wales, John Redwood, in a speech arguing for policies that deterred young women from having babies outside marriage and supported by the tax payer. Indeed, the programme makers claimed that they were investigating his contentions. Both Redwood and the *Panorama* programme implied that St Mellon's was typical and could be extrapolated as representative of all lone mothers-despite more considered accounts revealing inaccuracies about the estate and lone mothers generally. Popular media presentations of lone mothers as a social threat link into a conservative new right political view of the state in society, where the welfare provision of housing, benefits and other social provision is castigated as encouraging state dependency, an underclass, and especially single (never-married) motherhood.

Peter Lilley's now infamous 'little list' speech at the 1993 Conservative Party conference, for example, alleged that single mothers were having children to secure welfare benefits and housing, while Stephen Green, Chair of the Conservative Family Campaign, argued that 'Putting girls into council flats and providing taxpayer funded child care is a policy from hell'.

But strands of an underclass discourse are also discernible in the communitarianism underlying the New Labour government's ideas about a 'stakeholder society'. The long-term unemployed, which includes lone mothers, are placed as 'socially excluded'; 'family values' are stressed as the key to a 'decent' and crime-free society, and an element of coercion is required to reintegrate the excluded back into society through paid work. New Labour's view that life in a married two-parent family is better for children and for social cohesion, most notably expounded by Tony Blair and Jack Straw, has been widely reported in the media since 1997.

Media, politicians and academics who promulgate this view of lone motherhood as a threat to society also campaign for social policies that do not reward or encourage such 'self-damaging conduct'.

Consequently, the New Labour government has implemented the previous new right Conservative government's proposal to remove the extra allowances available to (new) lone parents on both the universal child benefit payment and on targeted income-related benefits-with Harriet Harman (then Minister for Social Security and for Women) stating, 'Life is about work, not just about claiming benefit'. Other policy disincentives to lone motherhood advocated by those who hold a social threat view include restrictions on payments to lone mothers who have more children while receiving benefit (as is the practice in some American states). There are also suggestions that young single mothers on benefit should be placed in hostels where their sexual relations and children's upbringing can be supervised. This policy idea has been floated by the New Labour government, in linking hostels with job training-again revisiting proposals of the Conservative government.

Encouragement and reward for traditional male breadwinner/female homemaker couples is also stressed by social threat advocates, with policy proposals to redress the supposed benefit bias towards lone, as opposed to married, parents (another reason given by New Labour for its lone parent benefit cuts). Other policy proposals include a tightening of the divorce law so that fewer lone mother families are created in the first place, as well as advocating 'moral' family and parenting education-the latter being the remit of the government's new National Family and Parenting Institute to be launched in April 1999.

Black Lone Mothers as a Social Threat

Until recently, 'race' and ethnicity were muted features of British social threat representations of lone motherhood. In the wake of the heightened media attention to lone mothers from 1993 onward, however, articles about black lone mothers began increasingly to be reported in the white-dominated media. Under the headline 'The ethnic timebomb', for example, the tabloid *Sunday Express* noted that more than 50 per cent of black families are headed by a lone mother and argued that, 'Almost six in ten black mothers are bringing up children on their own, urged on by the benefit system', implying a direct causal relationship between the incidence of black lone motherhood and the growing social security bill. Such claims ignore the fact that black lone mothers are more likely to be economically active and in full-time employment than their white counterparts; research suggests they also provide healthier lifestyles for their children. The *Sunday Express* article also raises the spectre of 'babyfathers' who-in newspaper accounts-father worryingly large numbers of children with multiple female partners.

Stories about 'babymothers' young black women who are presumed to have children by multiple male partners) also received considerable attention in the broadsheet press. Mainstream radio magazine programmes, such as BBC Radio 4's *The Locker Room* and *Women's Hour,* have also featured discussions about black lone motherhood and its social implications. Much of this coverage has echoed the ongoing debates in black media, especially the tabloid daily, *The Voice*-self-styled 'Britain's best black newspaper'-but there are significant differences between these stories as they are reported in the black press compared with their coverage in the white-dominated media.

First, there are no scare stories about social security bills. Second and importantly, there is a sense of debate in the black press, with the black readership responding to 'personal opinion' columns through the letters page. By contrast, coverage of black lone motherhood in the mainstream press tends to be devoid of vigorous questioning or alternatives, with a flat presentation suggesting that 'this is how it is' in the British black population. It is argued elsewhere that the emergence of a focus on black lone mothers in the British mainstream press is linked to the broader social threat concerns discussed above. It is suggested, moreover, that it is through such 'exotic' media explorations of black family life that white people vicariously play out their fears about social breakdown and relationships between men and women.

REPRESENTATIONS OF LONE MOTHERS AS A SOCIAL PROBLEM

In contrast to the view of lone motherhood as a self-created threat to the social order, a second perception of lone mothers widely reported in mainstream media, presents them as victims of externally created problems and in need of help. Stress is laid on the 'facts': in Britain, the majority of lone mothers (just over 50 per cent) are 'mature' divorced, separated or widowed women, rather than young single mothers (with less than 9 per cent being teenagers). Similarly, there is no underclass in the sense of a self-reproducing distinct part of society which stands outside cultural, political and economic norms.

Rather, there is a growing number of people in poverty, including lone mothers, who have essentially the same ambitions as the rest of society, but who are stigmatised and marginalised. The economic and social causes of this marginalisation are beyond the control of those they affect, while the shrinking welfare state only exacerbates difficulties. According to this perception, lone mothers are seen as social problems. They want paid work to provide for themselves and their children, but are hindered by the structure and nature of the welfare state. From this social problem position, the appropriate policy prescription signals that lone mothers should receive more, not less, state assistance to help them escape poverty and state dependency. By contrast with the social threat perspective discussed above, the social problem framing of lone motherhood is far less common in the tabloid press.

It is mostly limited to broadsheet newspapers with more left wing or 'middle ground' sympathies, such as the *Guardian,* the *Observer* and the *Independent,* which have given a platform to various commentators stressing the poverty and limited options of lone mothers. An article in the *Guardian,* for example, argued that: Reducing the number of single parent families is not an issue about the morality of feckless unmarried women who won't use contraceptives. Two-thirds of single parent families are caused by divorce. What is needed is a genuine political commitment to supporting the family. Better childcare provision for starters.

Despite these broadly sympathetic views, the broadsheets have also published reports by new right/revisionist commentators and, as we noted earlier, they have also been complicit in vicariously playing out social threat views through examinations of black lone motherhood.

Again, academics such as A.H. Halsey and Norman Dennis, taking a revisionist social-problem position, have been given a platform in the mainstream media to advocate a return of the political left to what they call 'ethical socialism', with its 'historic mission to spread the value of the family throughout all the relationships of society'. Indeed, Halsey was one of the commentators featured in the *Panorama* 'Babies-on-benefit' programme. New Labour's commitment to 'the family' as the source of social morality and obligation echoes this ethical socialism. The social problem view of lone motherhood, based on a concern with poverty rather than the fate of 'the family', is dominant among academic social scientists (especially in social policy), however, as well as among welfare practitioners and the British liberal establishment, such as church leaders.

This often reflects a Fabian political inheritance of enlightened state intervention. Jonathan Bradshaw, for example, an academic advisor to the Church of England's commission on the family, supported the Archbishop of Canterbury in arguing that 'lone mothers should be seen primarily as victims and get more help'.

Furthermore, the major lobby group for lone mothers in Britain, the National Council for One Parent Families, has also adopted this view of lone mothers. In contrast with the marginalisation of these arguments during the eighteen years of new right Conservative government, there has been renewed lobbying for intervention with the advent of the New Labour government-some of which was disappointed early on with the continuation of some Conservative policies such as the cutting of lone parent benefit.

In Britain, advocates of the social-problem view argue that day-care costs should be taken into account when calculating in work benefits for lone (and other) mothers. In 1994, under the Conservative government, an earnings disregard for formal day-care costs was indeed made available, although at a niggardly level. This suggests that, despite the prevalence of social threat representations of lone mothers in the media at the time, the social problem approach retained influence in British policy-making circles.

This disregard has since been increased by the New Labour government. Other policy suggestions within the social problem mould which have also been taken up by the New Labour government include measures to encourage lone mothers to pursue training and higher education under the New Deal welfare-to-work strategy.

Since autumn 1998, lone parents on income support with a youngest child over school age have been invited to an interview with a personal advisor in their local job centre to discuss 'upgrading' their job skills and/or finding paid work. An expansion of 'after school' care services for children is also part of this New Labour strategy (although this goes no way to matching the levels of public day-care in most other west European countries).

In championing the two-parent family, New Labour politicians are usually careful to say that they do not intend to demonise lone mothers. Jack Straw, for example, in a speech stating that strengthening the institution of marriage as a basis for bringing up children was a cornerstone of 'modern family policy', added, 'We are not in the business of making the job of lone parents more difficult by blaming them as some have done in the past'.

However, while it might be thought that the social-problem view of lone mothers' position had gained political ascendancy since New Labour's election victory in 1997, another suggestion under this perspective has not had such success in reaching the policy agenda. Rather than increase lone parent 'top up' benefits these have been cut altogether, as we noted above. Indeed, New Labour is effectively combining the social problem view of lone mothers with the social threat view as part of its communitarian approach (a manifestation of its 'third way' between old left and new right). Certainly, lone motherhood continues to be a potent political and media symbol.

There are two alternative views of lone mothers represented in mainstream British media. First, lone motherhood can be seen as part of a general change in family forms and lifestyle patterns, resulting from people's choices about how they live their lives and construct relationships, within a context of overarching economic, social and cultural change. Policies would thus be predicated upon creating better conditions, and reconciling paid work and family life, for all families rather than focusing on lone mothers alone.

This view is strong at the national level in much of continental Europe, where lone motherhood is less commented on and is much less important as a moral or political symbol than it is in Britain and the USA. While such a lifestyle perspective on lone motherhood may be muted within national media discussions in Britain, appeals to such a view can be seen in the launch of the niche monthly glossy magazine *Singled Out* in 1995. This was aimed at the British 'lone parent' market and covered all aspects of lifestyle, from holidays and cookery, through conducting relationships and child rearing, to financial and legal matters. However, the magazine did not survive its first year-signalling either the lack of a large enough audience who saw themselves as living a 'lone parent' lifestyle, or lone mothers' inability to afford the cover price.

Second, lone mothers can be seen as women who are no longer willing to accept control over their lives by individual men and are thus escaping patriarchy, with access to paid work, contraception, divorce and so on giving them the practical means to be independent. Policies should thus support and encourage this autonomy (including, for some, state support through wages for housework). Such a radical feminist perspective is rarely represented in the national press in its own terms (other than in more marginal publications such as the now defunct *Spare Rib*). Rather, it gets caricatured and castigated as part of the social threat view, where feminists (and socialists) are blamed for supporting lone motherhood and thus social breakdown. Other media can portray lone mothers, particularly black lone mothers, as deriving strength from their embeddedness in supportive female networks.

The low budget black-British film *Babymother,* released in September 1998, thus tells the 'ragga to riches story of single mother Anita, bringing up her children on Harlesden's tough Stonebridge estate, and her struggles to make it as a deejay'. But journalists who are committed to a social threat view can take an entirely different perspective on the same story: '*[Babymother's]* aim seems to be to encourage immature black women to behave like aggressive, self-pitying trollops, bring up more and more illegitimate children very badly, with no visible means of finance except the taxpayer'. Bigotry of this calibre seems unmoved by facts such as black lone mothers' high rates of employment.

While alternative views may not have had much influence on mainstream media representations of lone mothers or on policy development, they do hold sway amongst lone mothers themselves. Research conducted by two of us draws on interviews with lone mothers in 1994, just after the furore in the media about the moral and financial threat lone mothers posed to British society.

The research revealed that most lone mothers from all social groups held opinions about their position that were congruent with the (nationally muted) escaping patriarchy position, while aspects of the lifestyle perspective were also much in evidence. They often valued freedom to do what they wanted without having to take account of a male partner and were proud of managing on their own. Some also understood themselves to be just a normal part of the diversity of family forms in contemporary British society, especially younger African-Caribbean and white 'alternative' lone mothers who held a more feminist view of families and society more generally.

Given the plethora of bad press that lone mothers have received, voluntary groups representing lone mothers in Britain-most notably the National Council for One Parent Families (NCOPF) and Gingerbread-have made concerted efforts to counter such negative portrayals. Various forms of media coverage, including both newspapers and television programmes, have been influential in shaping the strategies of such organisations. In fact, the NCOPF has emphasised the importance of negotiating the 'right' image of lone mothers.

While they maintain that they need to make a case for lone mothers' special needs, they stress that they must be careful to avoid potentially incendiary images that emphasise differences rather than commonalities with other families. Thus both lone mother organisations have been prominent in rebutting dominant social threat political and media images.

In particular, the NCOPF evidenced their concern about harmful media portrayals of lone mothers by challenging the content of the *Panorama* 'Babies-on-benefit' programme. This documentary purported to show the reality of lone motherhood, and alleged that feckless, young, single women were having a string of babies, and living off benefits and in council housing. These never-married mothers supposedly saw no point in gaining employment or in having long-term stable relationships with men as providers and active fathers to their children.

The programme also examined the 'effective' policy option of benefit capping to deal with this phenomenon. The NCOPF complained to the Broadcasting Complaints Commission and went to court over this documentary. As is evident from the press release the organisation put out at the time, they did this because of fears that negative media representations might fuel moves towards punitive social policies: 'At the time when Government is investigating ways to reduce the benefit bill, this *Panorama* has been a disastrous intervention into the debate.'

The NCOPF accused the programme makers and the BBC of presenting an 'unfair, misleading and irresponsible' image of lone mothers. Rather, they asserted, for the majority lone parenthood is an unexpected event in people's lives, and the typical lone parent is a responsible, caring, divorced mother struggling to provide for her children. Interestingly, neither the NCOPF nor Gingerbread responded to the treatment of black 'babymothers' in the mainstream press, for fear of promoting racialised debate about lone mothers that would cut across the 'safe' social problem image of their constituency that they wish to portray.

The dominant social threat and social problem views of lone motherhood in Britain, including discussion about black lone mothers, have been articulated strongly in the national media over the past few years. These perspectives, by defining issues and setting agendas around lone motherhood, are significant components in the policy process. They assign meaning and causes to lone motherhood and construct the parameters within which social policies towards lone mothers should be constituted or changed.

But this is not to imply any direct stimulus-response relationship between media representations and policy formulation; the two interact in complex ways. For their part, the media are highly diverse and, as we have seen, there are alternative ways to frame lone motherhood to those which are predominant in mainstream media: and these do find voice in some niche media (as well as amongst lone mothers themselves).

Relations between media and politicians are reciprocal. It is politicians, along with academics who share their political mission, who have provided copy for the media while, in turn, the media have fuelled public opinion and encouraged particular responses from politicians.

At one level, media and policy representations of lone motherhood as interlinked and mutually reinforcing can be seen simply as the result of a small but influential 'chattering class' of media workers and policy makers (and a few academics) who inhabit a restricted social and geographical world, and who define what is important and what is marginal. What happens in the 'real world' becomes little more than symbolic foils for various political groupings and regroupings. However, even if largely correct, this appealing caricature does little to explain why it is that the social threat and social problem views of lone motherhood are promulgated in the media and by politicians, and not alternative perspectives.

The reasons for this dominance are to be found at deeper social levels; first, at the level of shared social understandings about the relationship between individuals, states, markets and families, and second, at the level of how explanations themselves are normally constructed in dominant and 'educated' modes of thought.

On the first level, different welfare state regimes develop different sets of social policy in expressing their particular conceptions of the proper, and gendered, relationship between individuals, families, states and markets, not least with different implications for the position of lone mothers. In Britain, politicians and media workers increasingly seem to share a world view defined in terms of a liberal welfare state regime.

In the liberal welfare state regime (such as the USA) social policy is used to uphold the market and traditional work-ethic norms. Modest and means-tested benefits are aimed at a residualised and stigmatised group of welfare recipients such as lone mothers, and depiction of lone mothers as a social threat more easily attain dominance. Under the conservative welfare regime (with Germany as a type case) states intervene to preserve status difference-including those of traditional gender roles and family forms.

Here lone mothers become peripheralised as mothers without male partners, and the social problem view of lone motherhood more easily gains purchase. In social democratic welfare state regimes (where Sweden is a type case), social policy reforms de-emphasise the market and emphasise equality rather than the meeting of minimal needs. Both men and women-including lone mothers-are seen as independent worker-citizens who support themselves through participation in the labour market, and social problem and lifestyle views of lone motherhood merge.

Within this, Britain presents a complex, hybrid case, where some elements of the social democratic regime (classically in the NHS) have been inserted into a liberal welfare tradition. Thatcherism, however, marked a rapid return towards the liberal model and, whatever its political differences, 'Blairism' seems to share the same liberal assumptions about the proper relationship between states, markets, families and individuals.

It is the USA that is explicitly taken as a policy role model by both media commentators and politicians rather than the increasingly derided 'European model' (other than by marginalised 'Old Labour' politicians or maverick journalists such as Will Hutton, author of the best-selling book *The State of the Nation*).

On the second level, though, why is it that the dominant view of lone mothers is as a trope for welfare dependency, social marginalisation and even hopelessness? After all, people know from both personal experience and research that most lone mothers do not fit this caricature. Partly, this type of image building depends upon a particular method of explanation commonly used in western thought.

When they use the term 'lone mother' (or 'single parent'), politicians, the media and even voluntary organisations representing lone mothers themselves (such as the NCOPF) are attempting to invoke a particular categorical representation of a type of person-a ready-made classificatory package that serves as a short cut to reading off a particular social situation.

'Lone motherhood' is seen to stand for an a priori, unitary, fixed, coherent, inherent and essentialised set of attributes and characteristics-in other words, the category articulates a particular stereotype-which in Britain easily becomes a negative stereotype to fit in with the preconceptions of the liberal welfare state regime.

This short cut in image building, and in explanation more widely, is often completely misleading because it assumes that the taxonomic group accurately delineates a social group. Taxonomic groups, such as lone mothers distinguished as a particular parental family form, are often different from the real substantive social groups that actually carry through social relationships and actions. It is not just that lone mothers are not a homogeneous or unified population, so that different social groups of lone mothers may behave differently.

Rather, it may not be lone motherhood in itself that is substantively or causally most important for their social behaviour. It may, for example, be membership of a particular ethnic or class group, or location in a particular area, that explains why some lone mothers take up paid work and others do not. Underlying social divisions and differences, however, remain unspoken in taxonomic representations. Nevertheless, lone mothers are not the homogenous group, in terms of social characteristics, that media and politicians invoke when they use the term, and it is therefore extremely unlikely that, as a putative categorical group, they will hold similar views and respond to policy development in similar ways, as maintained by media commentators, politicians, and even many academics.

Such categorical thinking, and taxonomic modes of explanation, have their roots in Cartesian thought as a means to produce independent descriptions of social life that are generalisable. This type of conceptualising has received critical attention in a number of ways from philosophers of science such as Wittgenstein to the critical realist, postmodern and feminist theorists of today.

Nonetheless, as a model of understanding and portraying social life (and thus also as a mode of control) it retains enormous purchase and power, underlain as it is by the idea that experts, through their categorisations, have a correct and authoritative access to reality. This is why academics like Murray and Halsey are given media space to confirm stereotypes of lone mothers.

The media and politicians clearly also have greater access to image production and dissemination than most lone mothers. In this way they have the power to impose their categorical version of the reality of lone motherhood-and thus to assert a particular identity of lone mothers, their motivations and behaviour, and the causes of all this-as superordinate and exclusive. A particular image, such as that of lone mothers as a social threat, may be contested by less powerful lobby groups such as the NCOPF. But such attempts to insert an alternative identity for lone mothers into the categorical space still rely on the same unitary and essentialist mode of thought as that dominant in media and political portrayals.

They do not admit, or recognise, diversity within the category, or that the category itself may be cross-cut or even unimportant where other differences (like those of class, ethnicity or location) may be the more influential in explaining motivations, behaviour and causes.

This means, moreover, that the 'categorical identity' that ascribes a particular set of characteristics to the taxonomic group 'lone mothers' is not the same as the various 'ontological identities' of lone mothers themselves-how they think about themselves in relation to others and their situation. These ontological considerations have little authority or power, however, and largely remain invisible unless they are used by the media to support pre-existing categories of lone motherhood as a social threat or a social problem.

9

Technology and Journalism Research

Numerous scholars have recognized the role of communication technologies in shaping newswork, as well as the information that reporters may or may not acquire by using them. The most prominent channel types, mentioned in the literature as tools of sourcing, are new technologies such as the Internet and e-mail.

The other two are non-mediated channels, such as news-scene attendance and face-to-face interviews and more traditional technologies such as landline telephony.The importance of communication channels in journalism lies in their possible impact on news information, enhancing or limiting its scope, quality, diversity, depth, and accuracy, as well as their role in shaping the epistemological qualities of news information.

For example, the face-to-face interview is considered a channel that enables nonverbal information to be obtained, and the telephone interview is one that allows reporters to negotiate source versions and implement interview techniques. E-mail, in turn, is described as a dubious channel that strengthens a source's control over messages and invites untraceable involvement of PR practitioners. The connection between episteme (knowledge) and techne (art) is an ancient concept, dating back to Greek philosophy and addressed by modern thinkers such as Innis and McLuhan.

In this study, however, the concept of epistemological technologies is employed neither as an embodiment of scientific or practical knowledge nor as a tool for shaping the knowledge of media consumers, but rather as the means that media producers use to obtain information.

Not all scholars agree that new technologies necessarily change news practices: "Reformists," probably the largest school of thought, claim that technologies created a significant shift in the work of reporters; "Traditionalists," apparently the smallest group, identified long-range trends in news production methods that may limit the effects of the new technologies significantly; while "Selectivists" assert that journalistic work has changed dramatically for television reporters, whose speed of reaction and ability to gather information have been accelerated by new technologies.

Three shortcomings of the existing body of empirical research may thwart theory-building that would address both journalism and epistemological channels:

- Fragmentation. Most studies focused on a small subset of technologies and sometimes even on one technology only. This fragmented scope limits their generalizability, inviting overestimation or underestimation of the technologies studied. Multi-technology studies were not only scarce but also limited to the public relations field.18 At least one study exhibited a multi-technological and multi-source perspective, but was restricted to print press reporters, who are not necessarily the most advanced among technology users. Moreover, the study was conducted before the new generation of mobile and broadband technologies became popular and possibly revolutionized newswork.
- Non-journalistic Theories. Most studies applied nonjournalistic theories - such as diffusion of innovations or uses and gratifications - that are virtually blind to the specific context of the journalistic field.
- The Novelty Bias. Naturally, new technologies attract extra research attention, especially when perceived as a remedy for the weaknesses of journalism. Nevertheless, exclusive focus on new technologies as "one of the biggest hopes (and hypes)" of journalism, with some studies appearing "upbeat and at times even Utopian in their conclusions," renders all but brand new conduits symbolically extinct.

The current study tries to overcome these shortcomings, supplying a comprehensive picture of old and new channels, both mediated and non-mediated, determining their actual contribution to published news and integrating the results within a broader journalism theory.

Following McManus, the present study distinguishes between two principal stages of the newsmaking process:

- News discovery, during which the reporter becomes acquainted with the existence of a potential new story, and
- News gathering, in which the reporter obtains the building blocks of the news item, as news discovery data is often incomplete and insufficiently substantiated.

Both phases were studied only regarding items that were subsequently published or aired, however. In keeping with its exploratory nature, the study addresses research questions and expectations rather than formal hypotheses.

RQl: What are the relative contributions of the respective communication channels to news published in the three media studied?

With some caution, based on several of the studies mentioned previously, one might expect to find that while most news information is technology-mediated, telephony is still widely used and textual channels serve primarily as news discovery conduits.

RQ2: How often do reporters use the Web as a news source? Do online reporters do so more than their counterparts in other media?

According to several prominent studies, journalists use the Web extensively. Furthermore, online reporters are expected to rely on the Web more often than their counterparts in other media, as they also use it as a vehicle for display and consequently acquire considerable Web savvy.

Traditional methods might prove problematic in examining the journalistic role of technology, as surveys and interviews capture per- ceived functions of the various channels that may differ substantially from their actual use; moreover, observation alone cannot detect the full spectrum of channels operated by different reporters in different settings to obtain information from different sources.

Consequently, the present study uses face-to-face reconstruction interviews, a method that has proven its ability to identify the respective contributions of different entities to the production of news.

The procedure consisted of three steps (prior to the interviews):

- Random Selection of Beats: Ten parallel print press, online, and radio news beats were chosen randomly from nine leading Israeli national news organizations.
- Identification of All Published Items within Beats: The sampling period extended over four weeks (beginning November 15, 2006), reflecting the attempt to achieve a fair balance between variety of stories and use of material still fresh in reporters' memories. News Web sites were visited four times a day.
- Random Sampling of News Items: Ten items per reporter were selected randomly (average monthly output per reporter: fifty-three items) to address the necessities of source confidentiality. The sample is thus large enough to allay any concern that stories could be matched to their descriptions but not so large as to tax reporters' focus and patience.

Further measures to maintain source confidentiality included asking reporters to describe how they obtained each of their sampled items without revealing any identifying details about them, as well as the seating arrangements: the reporter (with a pile of sampled stories) and the interviewer (with a pile of coding sheets) sat on opposite sides of a table with a screen between them.

Reconstruction interviews were conducted during the month following the sampling period, each approximately ninety minutes in duration. Although nearly all interviewees cooperated, the goal of deciphering 300 items per medium was not entirely achieved because of structural constraints applying to the organizations studied, such as insufficient number of business items for one of the radio stations and the need to avoid double-length interviews of Haaretz reporters who work for both print and online media. To preclude the distorting effect that the missing items may exert on comparability, each medium was weighted to 300 items, maintaining the internal proportions of the sampled newsbeats.

For the most part, data were displayed and analysed as percentages, thus presenting an overall picture of the channel mix with each channel displayed in the context of other channels and other media. Because of its exploratory nature, the study uses effect size measures (D-statistic) rather than significance tests. Effect values of 0.20 through 0.49 are customarily considered small, 0.50 through 0.79 medium, and 0.80 and above large.

Obviously, no method is without its shortcomings. The current method's drawback is that data deal very specifically with recollected sources for information subsequently used in published (or broadcast) stories. To compensate for this shortcoming and study the uses of technology beyond the specific item, a supplementary personal interview was introduced.

As these interviews were conducted after the rather long reconstruction interviews, however, only 49-61 reporters out of a total of 80 agreed to respond to them (depending on the specific question). The data display unambiguous differences between common and rare uses of the Web and as such will be used only in the Discussion as a general indicator of Web use for purposes other than news sourcing. The findings supply an initial overview of the ways in which reporters in three different media operate a comprehensive set of epistemological channels to obtain their news.

RELATIVE CONTRIBUTION

The data show that channel use across media is highly homogeneous except for a few aberrations, concentrated in the discovery phase, that may be explained chiefly on organizational grounds.

The greater use of landline telephones among online reporters is not really substantial, as their total use of telephony is very similar to that of their counterparts and the greater use of pager messages among radio reporters is counterbalanced by their limited use of e-mail.

Furthermore, greater use of pagers may reflect the correspondence between the short and instant nature of both pager messages and radio items, as well as the mobility and urgency of radio newswork, at least in the Israeli case.

Similarities across media intensify if the data are clustered according to the three major channel types embodying the epistemological qualities of the interactions they enable:

- Non-mediated channels, involving the reporters' physical presence at news scenes and face to-face interviews, constitute the smallest group: ranging (across media) from 7% to 10% of the contacts in the discovery phase and 15% to 18% in the gathering phase. The remainder consists of technology mediated coverage.

- Oral channels, led by telephony-mediated contacts (landline + cellular), contribute the main course to the news menu: ranging from 46% to 50% in the discovery phase and 54% to 65% in the gathering phase. This cluster's share is actually even greater, as it also includes the non-mediated channels.
- Textual channels comprise a rather formidable cluster, particularly in the news discovery phase, in which it accounts for 39%-43% of the contacts, decreasing to only 18%-29% in the gathering phase.

INTERNET USE

RQ2 focused on the actual contribution of the World Wide Web, the most celebrated technology in journalism literature, across different media. The Web's contribution to published content as a news source was no more than 3%in both phases. Even online reporters do not use their publishing platform as a sourcing tool to any greater extent than their old-media colleagues do.

The Internet's contribution rises substantially if we include e-mail: ranging from 8% to 21% in the discovery phase and 4% to 15% in the gathering phase. This increment is puzzling, however, as reporters play a proactive role when using the Web and generally adopt a passive or reactive one in e-mail use.

DISCUSSION

Four aspects of reporter behaviour are particularly challenging. The discussion begins with the more general aspects, namely the surprisingly modest use of non-mediated coverage and the lack of any substantial differences among the three media. The remaining two aspects are oriented towards specific technologies: the Web's marginal role as a news source and the enduring dominance of telephony. The image of extensive non-mediated coverage is fostered not only by scholars (who contend that such coverage prevails in conjunction with telephone interviews), but also by the traditional ethos that extols "shoeleather reporting" as the supreme news gathering method, as well as by journalists themselves, who do not go out of their way to expose the truth behind a deteriorating work pattern that still establishes their occupational legitimacy and authority. Many have even developed a set of practices to conceal their remote coverage. Although some American reporters declared that face-to-face interviews are their second choice as a newsmaking channel, the current findings indicate that, in practice, non-mediated coverage is far rarer than might be expected, or, as the legendary Jimmy Breslin observed, "in many newsrooms, the shoe-leather reporters are regarded as throwbacks or has-beens."

The overall similarity of channel use across media challenges the widespread belief that at least online reporters embody "new regimes of content creation" with a distinct media logic. Apparently, tendencies toward journalistic "isomorphism" overshadow medium differences, at least insofar as methods used to source information are concerned, reflecting similarities in organization around newsbeats and news sources, perceived newsworthiness, and the inclination towards homogeneous news products.

Two of these relatively homogenous patterns challenge common wisdom regarding specific technologies: the use of telephones and the Web for news sourcing.

QUALITATIVE METHODS MEET JOURNALISM

With each passing decade, journalism training has become more professional to meet whatever challenges are posed by the media environment of the era. Currently, the need exists for specialized skills to discover unreported common problems and context of issues and report them in a way that will help individuals interact with larger networks.

Some journalists are applying the knowledge of qualitative social science research methods to produce verifiable and accurate reports that advance this endeavor.

There is no general epistemology that organizes qualitative methodology, but all qualitative research is based on inductive examination of collected data. To ensure that the research is fair, balanced, accurate, and truthful and to enable the reader or public to evaluate the study, qualitative researchers:

- Conduct their studies in a natural setting,
- Follow strict, multiple protocols for valid and reliable research design and execution,
- Consider the background and perspective of the researcher(s) and the possible effect this might have on the research when designing the research, and
- Include in the written report enough information on the researcher(s), the plan, and the conduct of the study to allow the readers/viewers to decide for themselves the truthfulness and accuracy of the account.

A wide range of qualitative methods exist. Like the many strands of a rope, those methods more often employed make up the wider pieces, and, entwined, the strands together produce a unified and strong methodology. One of the thicker, more prominent strands within qualitative methodology is participant observation.

It is the practice that deals with going into the field, observing or interacting with a group, and then analyzing the situation in order to record commonalities and develop a written report.

To provide some organization for understanding how qualitative research works, the participant observation method can be broken down into three main categories that can then be used as a metaphor to illustrate three elemental processes within qualitative methodology. The categories are not discrete but form a continuum with the prominent reference points providing a vision of what qualitative methodology is (the range of methods involved) and how it is conducted (the protocol and level of involvement of the researcher (s)). The categories are:

What sets observational studies apart is that the researcher does not make contact with the subject (s) of the research.

These researchers investigate artifacts such as pottery, fashion, or popular culture icons.

They use unobtrusive measures to collect data, for example; these researchers may observe the actions of individuals, but at a distance.

Investigative reporters use this technique to monitor and study the coming and going of people and their associations without disturbing the behaviour of those observed.

One of the largest areas of observational study is the examination of texts or written works. Textual, or rhetorical, analysis examines books, movies, and other media. To analyse a text, the researcher "reads between the lines" to interpret underlying meaning.

Morris's chapter explains textual analysis and shows how reporters at *The Washington Post* use it in their work.

PARTICIPANT OBSERVATION

This research happens in the social world. The researcher collects data while observing people interact and by interacting with them. Then the researcher analyzes and writes about themes found in the setting. In order to analyse the setting, the researcher maintains some level of independence in the situation.

That level is dependent on the subjects studied and the purpose of the research. For example, in the focused interview study described by this author in a subsequent chapter, the researchers who conducted a one-time interview with each respondent were more marginal than connected to their subjects.

The reporter who interviewed a young woman to tell the story of her life, entered her world to a limited degree. His work is discussed in the chapter on oral history by Renita Coleman. The community mapping project introduced in Kathryn Campbell's chapter placed the journalists doing the mapping in direct and, in some instances, repeated contact with the individuals and groups from which they wanted to learn.

The case study described in the chapter by Tanni Haas was based largely on participation as well as observation. In that study, journalists at the *Akron Beacon Journal* spent a lengthy time period on the project and worked in partnership with a number of civic groups. In short, participant observers, within predefined limits, engage the daily life of those they study. They do so not just to have an understanding of what is going on, but to provide a systematic report. This is why the researcher must always maintain some distance in his relationship with those he is studying. This level of research is marked by complete immersion into a culture. The researcher who takes this approach may live for extended periods in the same community with those she is studying. The danger, or, to some researchers, the benefit, is that the researcher becomes engulfed in the setting. In those cases, whether by design or chance, the researcher becomes the subjects' advocate.

Since ethnography requires the researcher to enter fully into the life world of the subjects, it is the qualitative technique in which the researcher may be most susceptible to "going native." Not all ethnography is marked by complete assimilation. The student journalists in the chapter by Michael McDevitt and Janet Cramer produced their research and published their stories while retaining an analytic perspective regarding the world of the street people they studied.

On the other hand, Susan Willey's chapter advocates social action theory and shows how news organizations can become directly involved with the public in coming to judgment about an issue. Willey's chapter is devoted to focus group research, a process often associated with quantitative research and, on the qualitative technique continuum, usually found toward the more detached side of the scale.

DOING QUALITATIVE METHOD JOURNALISM

Using qualitative methods in journalism is not difficult. Methods used range from large-scale case studies conducted by multiple teams in converged newsrooms to an oral history interview story conducted by a single reporter for a small town newspaper. The projects can extend over a period of time (creating ethnography, for example) or be done in a series of focus groups conducted in one evening.

Qualitative methods can be used by news organizations as a prereporting tool to identify networks of credible, but nonelite, sources and their relationship to political processes (mapping); or they can be used to identify grassroots issues and inform election coverage (as in the focused interview example) or in many other ways that enhance news coverage. The advantage of qualitative methodology is that it brings the reader and viewer into the story. Knowing how to get in-depth data and first-person insights and what to do with them is the essence of qualitative reporting.

Guidelines for reliable information gathering and valid documentation are detailed for each method in the chapters to follow. The following are general guidelines for applying a qualitative method in a newsroom setting.

- Choose the right story: Not every story is right for qualitative reporting. Enterprise stories are one example of a good fit. Many stories reported with qualitative methods are "bubble up" political issues not found on political party platforms. Some develop from social problems that are being addressed outside governmental processes or are feature stories that exemplify individuals and groups. Part of choosing the right story is creating a "space" for the story—deciding its scope and parameters. It is important to choose the qualitative resources —the method—that will deliver the story best.

- Take it outside: To make the story interactive, go into the "field" with personal/ micro-level qualitative techniques. Plan ways to get input from individuals at more than one point during the story-building process. When useful, offer ways people can connect with the story through Web site, list serve, and other interactive technology. Look for themes that resonate—overlooked or under reported issues common across the general public or those that reflect the concerns of distinct groups of people.
- Bring it home: Above all, build the story from the "ground up. " Keep the focus on an inductive rather than deductive approach. Let the reporting be defined [framed] in the context and perspective of the participants or subjects of the reporting. To guarantee the way that information is collected and reported develops from data that is verifiable and accurate, follow the protocol of the particular method in use and utilize "triangulation" (e.g., more than one method of collecting information) to ensure lack of distortion and freedom from error. Finally, explain the news organization's purposes and the reporter (s) methods and level of involvement prominently in the final coverage that is published or aired.

"We searched hard to find a wide range of people willing to be involved," Winerip said. "Some reporting projects err on the side of over-reporting situations involving the poor. We looked for a variety of experiences.

For example, we wanted to do a story about race relations in the workplace, and we wanted to look at blue-collar workers. I had done some reporting on the steel mills, and someone suggested that we might look there for a story, but I didn't think that would work. For the most part, the men I had interviewed were all middle-aged, and they had substantial salaries.

The industry was declining. They really didn't represent the type of worker we wanted to portray. We wanted something 'rawer. ' We thought of doing the story from a union/non-union perspective. What were the lives of people, black and white, working across those divides? But that didn't seem to be the right vehicle either.

We wanted to have a tough, blue-collar situation, but the point was to capture the workers' relationships, their attitudes and feelings toward each other. We thought of the chicken and pork factories along the Southeast Coast and ended up sending a reporter to live there and work in a pork factory. "

Getting into the field was accomplished by trial and error. "When I went into the precinct to do my work, I met Maria. I knew right off that she was a first-rate police officer. I didn't know if I wanted to do a story about that kind of person or her first-rate squad. I had an opportunity to visit another squad, but they were bland. I decided to go back and stick with Maria."

Getting into the field also took time. "You have to give reporters time to make mistakes. When *[Times* reporter] Amy Harmon was looking for a pair of executives to interview, she was turned down by, probably, 100 companies.

After that it dawned on us that major established corporations wouldn't talk to us without adding so many restrictions, we just wouldn't be able to get the information we needed. But we found people in the dot.com world were independent entrepreneurs and willing to talk to us. That's how we settled on the pair of men to interview who had made millions. "

In retrospect, the criteria for the stories that became part of the series were (a) a mundane situation was the vehicle for each story, (b) the situation provided the opportunity to get people's subjective perceptions, and (c) the people in the situation were willing to talk. "We had to find people willing let you come back again and again, willing to spend the time it takes," Winerip said.

Winerip's work, as the reporting coach for the team, called for him to apply many of the tools used in qualitative research. "Overall, we wanted the reporters to dig in deep and hang in. I coached the team not to take notes at first," he said."

That's an easy way to burn out or scare off the subjects [interviewees]. My counsel to the reporters was to be patient and wait awhile, and then begin taking notes. I also coached them not to get too personal at first. It's like any other relationship. It has to be given time to develop. You can't get too close too soon.

Even though these people have committed to do the interviews, they don't know what they've committed to, so you have to ease into the relationship and the interviewing. " In establishing the relationship, "you walk a fine line," Winerip said. "You end up liking the people. I always do, but it's not friendship. You've got to hold back and learn not to give in to friendship. Your job is not to force anything, just tell the story as it emerges, without drawing conclusions."

As the series went to publication, additional information on the topic, some of it in interactive form, complemented the 15-story series. Some accompanying stories told in first-person voices and question-and-answer stories produced by *Times* magazine correspondents appeared when a special edition of the *Times* magazine published part of the series.

A Web site was created "not to mimic or regurgitate the print series but to be its own iteration of the project," Winerip said. It was a groundbreaking project for the *Times* Web site. An e-mail discussion board was heavily used.

When published in book form, the reporters' first-person impressions of race relations in general and their personal perspectives on racial issues were included. "Overall, the purpose of the series was to get to human beings and to learn from them. The series was a huge commitment. You can't do something like that cavalierly. It takes perseverance. That's the thing, the key to it all. The whole idea was to let the people talk for themselves and let the reader put it into the larger context," Winerip concluded.

The reporters at *The New York Times* did not set out to do qualitative method journalism. Certainly, many on the team, including Winerip, were not even aware of the term. The reporting that resulted did, however, correspond closely with the purposes and principles of qualitative research.

The conceptualization of individuals' personal circumstances as newsworthy and important to the understanding of larger social issues of the day is indicative of the qualitative approach.

From the initial desire to do in-depth, in-the-field reporting to the use of multiple settings and multiple opportunities to gather personal insights all the way to the presentation of the findings in stories that included the role of the reporters and the *Times,* the process was an unambiguous approximation of thorough qualitative research.

The qualitative method provides an avenue for reporting that reaches the individual and brings the common concerns of everyday people into the public sphere. Using qualitative research techniques in journalism is not a new idea. However, until recently, the qualitative method has not been given much attention by journalists. Changing conditions, both institutionally and technologically, now encourage this specialized training for journalists.

The very term "qualitative research" implies that it is something set apart, defined by certain methods or approaches—that is, by particular "qualities. " By implication, "qualitative research" is done in contrast to "quantitative research, " which has its own rules for summing up social, psychological, and political life in numbers and equations.

These assertions are more or less true, but they are also more or less beside the main point, at least the one we want to make in this chapter. Qualitative research, as practiced in the founding traditions of sociology at the University of Chicago, is defined not so much by how it goes about knowing, but how it defines what it wants to know about.

That is to say, the goal of research in the Chicago tradition is to get as complete as possible an understanding of what is being studied, and that means always trying to understand the larger picture, or context.

Research in this tradition, called the Chicago School of sociology, often tries to look at whole communities—neighborhoods, social groups, or even big cities; occasionally, it tries to look at all of these at once in relation to each other. It is a kind of research that tries to understand people, their actions, and institutions in all of their complicated interactions with each other. This emphasis on the whole community does not necessarily make qualitative research better than variables-based, quantitative research, but it does make it different—even when, as was often the case in the larger Chicago School studies, statistical and other data also were used to understand how the complicated parts of a large community fit together.

So, more than anything else, qualitative research as we will use the term is holistic, meaning that it tries to situate the things it studies in their broadest possible context. There are many ways to do this, and most of them rely on various forms and combinations of interviews and observation. The largest possible picture of some group of social phenomena is the goal.

Qualitative research can be described in a number of ways, and each has a different shade of meaning. "Ethnography" is literally writing about people or culture. It grew from the writings of the early anthropologists who lived with tribal cultures outside of the United States and wrote up everything possible (or at least everything they could see) about the way the people lived and worked together.

The hallmark of this work was the anthropologists' close contact with people—their research "subjects"—over a period of time. Their research methods included both "participant observation, " meaning that they watched their research subjects while doing things with them; and "depth interviews, " meaning that they participated in extended conversations over time, asking people about what they were doing and what it meant.

The term "fieldwork" grew to mean just this kind of research: going out into the "field, " that is, the places where people conduct their daily lives. This remains a defining element of all qualitative research. At about the time that early anthropologists were visiting countries beyond the borders of their homelands, sociologists at the University of Chicago were asking the same kinds of questions about life in the United States.

The shape and size of the city of Chicago was changing quickly in the early part of the 20th century under the pressures of urban industrialization and massive immigration. Understanding these changes—and the social problems that accompanied them—posed a huge challenge for researchers. In some ways, the communities that sociologists wanted to investigate were much more complex than the societies studied by the anthropologists.

Textual analysis is sometimes called careful reading, and it is as important to a journalist as good listening. Textual analysis is a method that communication researchers use to describe, interpret, and evaluate the characteristics of a recorded message.

This type of qualitative research and analysis focuses on a particular text to determine its characteristics and place it in a category shared by other similar texts for comparison and contrast purposes. Qualitative textual analysis can lead to quantitative research methods such as content analysis or Q methodology, which can be used to analyze publications or opinions about texts.

For example, researchers might categorize the types of message strategies that politicians use in public campaign speeches as fear-appeals and reward-appeals by studying individual texts, and then conduct a quantitative study. This research project might study how the *New York Times* and the Los *Angeles Times* covered campaign speeches over the period of a year by focusing on the textual attributes of each paper's campaign coverage.

Reporters who write the news stories also use some level of textual analysis to compare and contrast oral and written language. Reporters at the *Washington Post* use personal computers to search for key words in bills and legislation that indicate stakeholders—winners and losers—in the documents.

Mass media textual analysis is closely related to literary criticism, which, broadly used today, encompasses any discourse on any literature, including three distinguishable but overlapping areas: history, theory, and evaluation.

Many scholars view literature as part of an historical process, a phenomenon that can be described by internal principles such as types, techniques, and functions, or as objects to be studied, analyzed, and judged. Several methods and approaches to criticism fiercely compete for attention in the field. Wellek commented on this new age of criticism:

The variety of voices today is so great that the situation has been compared to the Tower of Babel, with its mutually incompatible languages.

Never before has there been such a ferment in criticism, and critics have never before attracted so much attention and fervent loyalty ... Indeed some scholars argue that this is the age of criticism, since literary critics now often function not only as specialists in literature, but also as general critics of society and civilization.

This chapter focuses on only the most common terms of textual analysis that are used by journalists. It addresses how journalists read, analyze, categorize, describe, and evaluate their own writing as well as the writing and oral language of others.

There are two basic uses of textual analysis for practicing journalists. The first is to study the language of their sources for specific stories; the second is to study the language of journalism to refine their art of writing.

This broad approach to criticism is relatively new; it has been advanced in recent decades by critiques of English composition and rhetorical analyses of speech communication. In their 1991 book, Investigating Communication, Frey and colleagues explained that textual analysis stems from a systematic attempt to understand how meaning moves from author to audience and how the text is related to other variables that precede it.

Ultimately, textual analysis is a scientific attempt to evaluate a text based on a set of established standards or criteria. Several organizations and publications have begun criticizing the content of the news media on a regular basis for the general public. They include *News Watch, MediaChannel, Brill's Content, Fairness & Accuracy in Reporting, CounterSpin, Medianews,* and *Media Watch*.

Textual analysis can be applied to any communications medium because photos, illustrations, graphics, and video images can be reduced to textual summaries before analysis. Some language theorists claim that history in general consists of texts to be analyzed.

Scripts of radio and television news and entertainment are more readily available than ever, and they often can be secured over the Internet for textual analysis.

Five types of media criticism use textual analysis: Aristotelian, genre, historical, dramatic, and fantasy theme. The first is a return to Aristotle's judicial, logical, and formal analysis centered on the work itself rather than its historical, moral or religious context.

Genre critics group texts that are similar in function, purpose, and form, and then evaluate each text based on the established attributes of the genre. An example of genre criticism is Cawelti's *Adventure, Mystery, and Romance: Formula Stories as Art and Popular Culture,* published by the University of Chicago Press in 1976.

Historical criticism consists of oral histories, case studies, bibliographical studies and social movement studies. The historical critic attempts to evaluate the influence of events on the creation of the text. Dramatic critics study principles drawn from theater—act, purpose, agent, agency, and scene—to evaluate texts.

Finally, fantasy theme critics focus on stories with characters that symbolize cultural moral principles or philosophies. Examples of this type of criticism include Chance's *The Lord of the Rings: The Mythology of Power,* published by Twayne Publishers of New York in 1992.

Each of these critical approaches used to study journalism and media share a common list of textual attributes that can be identified and then described, analyzed, and evaluated by a community of readers.

Careful and comparative reading and analysis by knowledgeable critics help to create a richer understanding of the function and value of any single text, and such case studies contribute to the general knowledge in the field. While some media criticism attempts to measure the influence of the mass media on society, in general, textual analysis attempts to categorize, analyze, and evaluate one particular text.

Visual forms such as the inverted pyramid are tools of textual analysis that critics use to classify one piece of writing as a report, another as a story, and still another as an essay. Careless use of these forms contribute to confusion and imprecision in the profession.

Thus, textual analysis is an activity that reporters, editors, publishers, news directors, producers, media critics, and researchers use on a daily basis. For example, a reporter writes a 25-inch news story on Afghanistan, but how good is it?

How can working journalists evaluate the quality of the texts they receive and create on a daily basis? Textual analysis can help. Attributes of nonfiction prose, including journalism, can be used to categorize, analyze, and evaluate any news report or feature story.

Many of these textual attributes can be applied to texts of sources, too, but some other specialization, including terminology from a field other than journalism, may be required for such an analysis.

Evan Mahoney, a reporter for the Fund for Investigative Reporting and a professor at University of North Carolina at Asheville, uses the following terms when teaching, analyzing, and evaluating news writing (personal communication, February 21, 2002): abstraction, attribution, connotation, denotation, contrast, lead, nut graph, narration, exposition, form, induction, deduction, tone, voice, mood, style, thesis, quotation, and metaphor.

Consistently careful use of such attributes of language can enrich the experience of reading in addition to simply informing the public. For example, smell and fragrance have the same denotative (literal) meaning, but one has a positive connotative (suggestive) meaning while the other is negative. A quick reading, without textual analysis, can miss connotations.

Exposition is logical explanation, and form is the overall structure of an article. Induction is reasoning that moves from specific details to a generalization, while deduction moves from a generalization to specifics. Tone and mood refer to word choices that indicate seriousness, humor, glee or depression, to name only a few emotions.

Paying careful attention to these attributes of language can lead to an enriched understanding of a text. Mahoney urged writers to check for these attributes when revising their texts to enrich their writing and make it more engaging.

Diana Fishlock, diversity reporter for the Harrison (Penn.) *Patriot-News,* considered brainstorming, ambiguity, cliches, character, close-ups (concrete, sensory details), and editorializing when evaluating her own writing and the writing of others. Brainstorming is a method for analyzing topics or ideas for a news story.

It ranges from making simple lists of ideas and ranking them in importance to semantic webbing, in which the writer begins with a key word and diagrammatically connects it to another word, whatever comes to mind, and so on, through lines and circles. New connections are made in this playful act of discovery, and the process helps the writer see new possibilities for the article. Fishlock explains:

Brainstorming often is extremely useful. Brainstorming and simply having time to let a concept percolate in my mind help me to explore more facets of the idea. Is there a historical context? What about religion? Given the time (or brainstorming input from other people) the story becomes much more complete.

Often character makes or breaks a story. If the character is compelling and the writer is able to show that, I'll read about someone doing almost anything—even something I may have no interest in.

Media criticism is growing as a classroom and newsroom practice, so news writers must become more sophisticated about their use of language. Textual analysis is a qualitative method that can be used to create, defend, and improve writing skills. "Making meaning clear does not mean making the copy tedious," Peter Jacobi explained during the Association for Education in Journalism and Mass Communication's Gannett Teaching Fellows Workshop at Indiana University. "Exposition [information delivery] must go beyond a dictionary definition and be as bright and intriguing as narration [story telling]."

THE WEB AS A NEWS SOURCE

The limited use of the Web observed in this study appears to challenge findings suggesting that the Web had become a "dominant" and "indispensable" newsgathering tool that had changed the face - if not the soul - of journalism. Interestingly, the Web's contribution as a source for published news is not only marginal but also stagnant, having displayed no growth over time - at least with regard to the Israeli print press, studied in 2001 using the same method and research tools as the present study.

However, in contrast to its limited use for sourcing, the Web is widely used for more general newswork functions. Personal interviews with reporters show that they use the Web for two hours and fifty minutes a day for journalistic purposes, plus one hour and twelve minutes for personal matters - about four times more than the average Israeli citizen and about an hour less per day than American computer reporters, who are probably among the most intensive Web users.

During those long hours, reporters were using the Web for the functions. The rich assortment of Web functions used by reporters may be categorized into three basic types:

- Productive: These include core journalistic functions directly involved in sourcing publishable news materials, such as discovering and gathering news information, followed by two types of auxiliary functions that exert less direct impact on news products and more on news processes and news environments.
- Referential: Including self-updates, monitoring other publications, fact checking, locating potential news sources, and finding background material.

- Communicative Functions: Communicating with different stakeholders-superiors, news sources, counterparts, and competitors, mostly via e-mail.

Functions performed routinely (i.e., on a daily basis by at least half the reporters) are mostly referential. The only exception is the highly frequent use of e-mail for receipt of press releases. This still does not guarantee an impact on publications, however, as many if not most press releases are discarded during the selection process.

The highly infrequent use of e-mail for interviews may surprise scholars who described e-mail as "the killer [Internet] application" for journalists. On the other hand, it will relieve those who condemn e-mail interviews as a "method of last resort for conducting anything approaching a candid interview" because it avoids real interaction and invites hoaxes and "canned" PR responses.

Journalists' paradoxical use of the Web - seldom for sourcing and often for more general newswork assignments - suggests that although journalists enjoy "cutting edge gizmos," they are choosier about using them for core journalistic assignments such as sourcing.

Hence, until another study refutes the current findings by taking the exhausting route of investigating - source by source - a sample of published items outside Israel, using the current method and research tools, one cannot rule out that limited use of the Web for sourcing, together with extensive use for more general newswork assignments, extends beyond the case at hand and may even be a relatively universal phenomenon.

It is definitely not an Israeli peculiarity, as shown by initial findings of another study employing the same method and research tool to study Chilean national press reporters in the summer of 2007. Those reporters used the Web for only 5% of discovery contacts and 7% of gathering contacts. There is some indication that figures for the United States, Portugal, and Greece do not differ dramatically.

At least part of the difference between the current study and those claiming vast use of the Web may thus be rooted in method (reconstructions of specific published items versus general estimations of technology use in surveys and interviews) and research focus (specific uses for sourcing of published items versus more auxiliary uses for reporting).

This line of reasoning is supported by current findings reflecting heavy daily use of the Web, mostly for functions other than sourcing. Some American scholars agree that the Web has not become a major news source despite its numerous advantages. According to one observation, American newsroom adoption of computer-assisted reporting yielded mixed results.

Another opinion maintains that the journalistic advantages of the Internet "are counterbalanced by a number of inherent weaknesses," some of which have already been mentioned in the relevant literature: poor quality of information; limited reliability, believability, and accuracy; as well as time constraints, lack of training and navigation and design faults.

The following drawbacks should be considered as well:

- The Proactive Role: While most other textual channels, including e-mail, assign reporters a passive or reactive role, the Web calls for their proactive performance in such tasks as database analysis or investigation - demands that go against the grain of mainstream news reporting, which is reactive in nature.
- Impersonal Data: While other channels enable and improve communication with human agents, the Web usually bypasses them in favour of largely impersonal data. Hence those who perceived the Web as a promising news source were not wrong about the technology, only about its users. Journalists, it turns out, are not in the general information business but rather supply information originating among human agents.
- The Extra Burden of Corroboration: Constant suspicions concerning the trustworthiness of Web materials could have been resolved by crosschecking with additional sources. As their time frame shrinks, however, reporters may wonder why they ought to use a news source that requires additional sources a priori instead of simply contacting these sources themselves.
- Unqualified Material: Apparently, the Web's marginal contribution to published news (and that of other mass media) contradicts the nature of news producers as heavy news consumers above all, who start each day by reading one another's publications. Media consumption does not necessarily contribute directly to specific news items that are subsequently published, however, but rather informs reporters about current events in general and the output of competitors and counterparts. Furthermore, the Web offers "too much information or [.] too little information" and is loaded with previously published items that are useless to reporters who refrain from plagiarism unless they find their own angle or follow-up, employing an independent sourcing process.

Some of these weaknesses are the strengths of a much older technology, whose contribution to the public news menu tends to be overlooked.

THE ENDURING DOMINANCE OF THE TELEPHONE

The enduring dominance of telephony challenges the assertion that newsmaking was conquered by new technologies, especially when combined with insistence that the golden age of the telephone in journalism ended during the 1950s. Some scholars have mentioned the ongoing prominence of telephony together with face-to-face interviews but did not specify the respective contributions of each. The continuing dominance of the telephone in the new technology-saturated news environment, after a hundred years of service and despite more sophisticated alternatives, can no longer be explained in simple terms such as the immediacy and efficiency of the given technology.

At first glance, it may appear that numerous factors motivate reporter and source alike to avoid oral communication. Why should reporters trap themselves between oral input and textual output, adding the burden of translating vocal utterances into written stories?

Why would they work with loosely structured, ephemeral raw material that leaves no paper trail and is replete with redundancies, inconsistencies, and multiple, interwoven threads of thought?

And why would news sources, in turn, use channels that impede realization of a speaker's full potential and downgrade control over verbalization, precision of expression, lexical richness, and grammatical sophistication, thereby forgoing the advantage of imperceptible emendation and rendering themselves vulnerable to audible self-correction that sounds like "denial and patchwork"?

Several considerations may explain the persistence of the present situation:

- *Naturalness:* Oral channels are a "primary form of communication for humans." They are "addressed by a real, living person [.] at a specific time in a real setting" and are more "natural to thought and speech" than writing, more spontaneous and more dynamic and vivid, as vocal expression is itself a live event in space and time, anchored in the "life-worlds" of real people.
- *Informativeness:* Oral communication always includes "much more than mere words." Even telephone conversations retain many attributes of face-to-face interactions, including "use of language [.] the way words are pronounced, elements of intonation or prosody, syntax and semantics [.] variations of loudness and pitch beyond that involved in intonation, tempo, resonance, pauses and nonfluencies, as well as nonlanguage sounds such as laughing and sighing."
- *Unavailability of Suitable Texts:* Journalists generally search for news within a narrow time slot once a new event or story begins to unfold and before others cover them - at least in the same news market. During this short period, texts may be unavailable, unsuitable, already published, or authored by PR professionals.
- *Participatory Role:* Oral channels are actually the only conduit through which reporters may play a participatory role in shaping the raw materials of news.

This role corresponds with four aspects of newswork:

- As a "negotiated phenomenon" (i.e., an output of bargaining between reporters and sources), news tends to flow through channels such as the telephone, that enable negotiations between the parties.

- As news constitutes a co-production by reporters and their sources, the former perceive their authorship as including mandatory participation in the formation of raw news material and not only post hoc reduction of source-initiated texts.
- Oral channels increase reporters' control over their raw material, whereas written versions accord their writers the advantage, giving them more leeway to hide, slant or frame information as they see fit.

Oral channels enable interview techniques that may not only improve source accountability but also reinforce the status and legitimacy of reporters as trustees of the public who pose questions on its behalf.

- *Competitive Advantage:* While many written materials are distributed to or may be approached by numerous journalists, oral channels give reporters a chance at exclusivity. Most of the time, such exclusivity does not apply to the items as a whole, that are shared by their counterparts and competitors, but rather to certain details thereof.
- *Smaller (Perceived) Risk:* When leaks are involved, both sources and reporters are especially careful to avoid textual channels, as they may leave clear traces in case of investigation. Although they cannot promise full protection, oral channels are perceived as safer than others except in cases of serial leaks, such as the Pentagon Papers, in which randomly chosen pay phones were the instrument of choice.

Epistemological channels, a collection of communication technologies and non-mediated conduits of news coverage, are probably the keystone of technology and journalism theorization, thanks to their crucial role in shaping the scope and quality of information that subsequently becomes the public news diet. The current study suggests an initial theoretical outline for the role of these channels in news sourcing, based on a careful analysis of their contribution to a random sample of about 850 stories from three different media.

Just as a hierarchy of credibility prevails in the realm of sourcing, according precedence to certain informants over others, a technological hierarchy governs the world of communication channels that echo the logic of sourcing, determining which conduits are to be given priority.

The subordination of these channels to a higher order of sourcing considerations is observed both in the combined tendency of the reporters studied to rely on human agents (in 87% of their contacts in the discovery phase and 92% in the gathering phase) and to communicate with them orally (57% and 75%, respectively). Heavy reliance on technology-mediated coverage suggests that reporters accord much lower priority to the demands of space than to those of time. Hence the basic role of communication technologies is to release reporters from spatial constraints, thereby enabling them to meet temporal demands. According to the findings, reporters sourcing their published news prefer various remote data excavation technologies to first-hand witnessing, and prefer reliance on human agents to technological sources such as the Web and oral communication to textual. Hence the principal role of epistemological technologies is to enable remote coverage while keeping close to human informants. The methods journalists employ to obtain published news indicate that news is a social product, fabricated chiefly through interpersonal reporter-source contact. As such, news is more a matter of trust between humans than of independent witnessing, fact finding, or fact checking.

This process is none too compliant with "foundationalist epistemology" that expects validation of facts by empirical findings or rational substantiation, but rather conforms with social epistemology that makes do with facts established by communal agreement within "specific epistemic communities."

Furthermore, news is a textual product of oral processes. This "oral culture" allows reporters to omit, edit, select excerpts, and "tidy up" quotes in a manner that often bears the seeds of tension between parties. To a certain extent, this may explain the vast quantities of journalistic errors, misunderstandings, misquotes, and source statements taken out of context.

As one Wall Street Journal reporter put it, "It's your notes against their word." This study focuses on the most substantial role of communication channels as conduits for generating the public news diet. Despite the meticulous methods employed, however, it is not free of weaknesses and blind spots, as it addresses involvement of different channels only in items that were subsequently published or aired, relying on the recollection of reporters themselves. Hence, the current study sets a broad agenda for further studies, especially those considering other types of reporters who probably employ different patterns of channel use, particularly TV reporters, investigative reporters, citizen journalists, multimedia and multi-skilled reporters, and so on. Subsequent studies should focus on other news cultures especially that of the United States, testing the hypothesis of limited use of the Web as a news source and extensive use for other newswork functions. Newsroom observations may contribute another missing link by mapping the inevitable gaps between reported and actual uses of communication channels.

These may also focus on the oral culture that associates reporters and sources, the patterns in which oral raw materials are transformed into final news texts and the extent to which this transformation is susceptible to errors, misunderstandings, and disputes between the parties.

HYPOTHESES AND RESEARCH QUESTIONS

Web news editors use links in stories to point readers to additional material. If Web pages about news follow the growth patterns of the Web as a whole we should expect to find evidence of Barabasi and Albert's two principles, growth and preferred attachment. Therefore: H1: The number of links in news stories will increase over time.

As news sites' digital archives grow (stories, maps, photos, graphics, etc.), there are more opportunities for linking. While growth in the use of linking within news stories should rise across the board, preferential attachment predicts that some stories will grow at a faster rate than others.

There are a number of factors that might explain which stories are "preferred." One is context. Recall the findings of Barnhurst and Mutz concerning the use of context and interpretation in newspaper stories. They documented a century-long upward trend. Their study concerned news stories on three topics: jobs, crime, and accidents. Each type of story lengthened, but accident stories were the shortest and job stories the longest.

This makes sense if one considers the possible context a journalist could include in different stories. Many accidents will lack obvious historical, geographic, economic, social, or political context.

And consequences may not be known at press time. Stories concerning jobs, however, are likely to involve economic and political context and may also have historical and geographic aspects. If the choices Web editors make concerning linked material are driven by contextual possibilities then we can predict that some types of stories will benefit from preferred attachment. This proposition was tested by selecting categories of news that would logically require a great deal, or very little, context. First: H2: Stories about international relations will be more heavily linked than other stories.

Stories involving negotiation or conflict between two or more countries present numerous possibilities for geographical, historical, and political context and in some cases economic and social context. Contrast this with another category used by journalism professionals: spot news. As this label implies, these are stories concerning discrete events such as accidents and crimes.

While adding context to these types of stories occurs, the possibilities may be fewer than for other news stories. Therefore: H3: Spot news stories will be less heavily linked than other stories. The power law distribution is believed to result from the interaction of growth and preferred attachment. If this is the case, then not only should story types differ in the quantity of links but also in their respective rates of increase. Therefore: H4: The gap in the number of links used between spot news and international relations should widen over time. Media type may also affect linking practices. When compared to print news, television news has been labeled event-driven or episodic. If this is the case we might expect Web news stories produced by television-affiliated companies to use fewer links than those produced by print-affiliated companies. However, television-based Web sites may be more likely to link to audio or video material because of its availability. Rather than a hypothesis, the following research question is explored: RQ1: Do print- or broadcast-affiliated Web sites make greater use of hyperlinks in news stories? Other variables that might play into preferred attachment for Web news are considered in the conclusion.

Ten U.S. national news Web sites were examined for a period of five years, from 1997 to 2001. At the beginning of this period, the 10 were the news organizations with the largest viewing audiences or circulations that had a Web news presence. Five are the Web counterparts of newspapers or magazines.

Answering the research questions required a content analysis of the Web sites. An after-the-fact data collection scheme, such as one that might be conducted for a newspaper content analysis, would not be practical for the ever-changing Web. Instead, a sample of Web news content was created by periodically recording the home pages of the 10 sites. A systematic sample was recorded using the following scheme. In March of each year the 10 Web sites were visited every four days, with a random start for a total of seven days each year. Main page stories appearing on the screen of a standard-sized monitor were coded. This process yielded 1,493 stories or about 300 a year.

CODING AND RELIABILITY

Over the course of the project a number of variables were measured including topic, links per story, node modality (audio, video, text, etc.), internal versus external links, etc. Two of these are of interest here: topic and links per story. Hyperlinks were initially defined as any clickable text or graphic that leads to additional material related directly to the story. What constituted "related" was left to the coders but specifically excluded standard site navigation icons and advertising links. Also excluded were next-page links and those beyond the first level. Following a hypertext story beyond the main page is problematic for coders if the story is hierarchically constructed and/or circular.

Limiting the coding to the main page is also consistent with the standard industry practice of using one primary story page and linking from it to prior and related stories as well as, in some cases, multimedia elements. Rarely do Web editors require lengthy scrolls by the user. This coding procedure thus provided some control for story length, although variance in the primary text was observed. Coding occurred at two points. In the first year of the study, testing the reliability of the links variable was logistically cumbersome due to the ever-changing nature of the Web, a fact that has been noted by others. It was accomplished by having two coders access, on computers in separate rooms, two stories on each of the seven coding days. The 10 Web sites were sampled in alphabetical order; each was represented by one or two stories in the reliability sample. These 14 stories represented 5% of the total sample that year. Reliability on links per story was very high by Krippendorf's alpha. In 1999 the definition of hyperlink was expanded to include material obtained by placing the cursor on, but not clicking, certain Web elements (rollover graphics). By this time Web news stories had become more sophisticated, but software made it easier to preserve digital copies of hypermedia stories. Another test of reliability was conducted, using a simple random sample of 100 cases.

To these 100 cases, 66 more from the first two years of data were selected following the same method. Each story was coded for topic using the headline and sub-head. There were twelve categories including the two of interest here, spot news and international relations. Spot news was any story about a crime or an accident posted within one day of the incident. International relations stories involved conflict or cooperation between two or more countries. When two or more news categories applied, the coder was instructed to select the one considered primary. Coder agreement on story topic was by Krippendorf's alpha.

RESULTS

The links variable is heavily skewed as a result of a high number of stories (29%) having no links at all and cannot be normalized by data transformation. Use of ANOVA is not recommended for data that are skewed because results can be unreliable and statistical power forfeited, especially for smaller sample sizes. Because the sample here is large accurate p values are likely; these analyses are presented here. Nonparametric tests, which do not rely on normality, are also presented. The first hypothesis concerns a test of trend in the use of hyperlinks in Web news stories. In 1997 the average main-page story on a U.S. national-news Web site had three links to related material. By 2000 that number more than tripled. A Kruskal-Wallis test was performed to confirm significant differences among groups. Additionally, a test of linear trend using two-way ANOVA was conducted. The growth hypothesis was confirmed.

The remaining hypotheses concern preferred attachment and were tested using a sub-sample of the Web news data which included 398 spot news and international relations stories. Those news categories were selected to test the idea that context would drive preferred attachment.

The second hypothesis predicts that stories about international relations will be more heavily linked than other stories. A Mann-Whitney U test confirmed this hypothesis. International relations stories had almost three more links than other stories during the five-year period. This gap was not consistent over time, but grew from only 0.5 (not significant) the first year to 5.5 by the final year. The third hypothesis predicts the opposite result for spot news stories and is also confirmed by a Mann-Whitney U test. Spot news had three fewer links than other stories during the period of study. The gap was more consistent than the one observed for international relations, growing from about 2.5 in the first year to 4 in the final year. H4 concerns the relative rates of growth between spot news stories and international relations stories. Specifically, it proposes a linear interaction between the growth and preferred attachment concepts proposed by Barabasi and Albert. If true, the gap between spot news and international relations stories should widen over time.

There is no procedure for testing a two-way linear interaction (with unequal cell sizes) with nonparametric statistics, but ANOVA can provide a conservative p value for reasons described above. The p value is not large but the limitations of ANOVA for nonnormally distributed data may be preventing a significant result. With a Type 1 error held to 5%, the fourth hypothesis is not supported.

The research question requires a comparison of Web news stories produced by print and broadcast companies. A two-tailed Mann-Whitney U test confirms what is apparent in the figure: stories on Web sites affiliated with broadcast outlets are considerably more "linked" than stories on sites associated with print publications. Broadcast Web stories had more than twice the number of links. Initially, only a small difference was apparent, but the gap widened to 7 links by 2000. A narrowing of the gap was observed for 2001.

ALTERNATIVE EXPLANATIONS

The data suggest an increased use of hyperlinks over time and a statistically significant variance by topic. Alternatively, story length could be driving both trends. If news stories on the Web are getting longer, the opportunities for linking might likewise increase. An extensive literature citing Web news professionals suggests otherwise, but a test for this possibility is worthwhile.

Word counts were not recorded during the live coding done in the 1990s, but by the final year a complete digital record was preserved. This year of cases (n=241) was used to test the relationship between links and topic while controlling for story length. In addition, one site in the sample, CNN.com, maintains a Web archive of stories which was utilized to attach word counts to the existing data for CNN (n=157). Unlike many of the 10 sites studied, this site has never limited page lengths by breaking the primary text into sequential chunks, so variance in words per main story page is substantial; CNN is an ideal test of the notion that story length and links may co-vary. Using these two sources of data, we can explore the effect of story length on the identified relationships. During the five-year period, CNN.com stories did not vary significantly from a mean length of 647 words. That word count is consistent with the optimum page length recommended by Web professionals. There is a significant correlation between length and links. Longer stories did have more links. By dividing links by words, a composite variable was created to test the trend over time. ANOVA revealed a significant linear contrast. Controlling for story length, the number of links increased over time; the growth hypothesis (H1) was confirmed for the sub-sample.

The second and third hypotheses were retested to control for length using the 2001 sub-sample. A links-per-word composite variable was computed for each case and normalized using a log transformation. Spot news did not differ significantly from other topics when controlling for story length.

International relations did differ significantly from other topics. For this sub-sample, the second hypothesis was rejected and the third confirmed. In 2001, stories from broadcast sites were shorter (763 words) than stories from print media sites (909 words) but used more links (11.6 compared to 6.6). Controlling for story length, broadcast stories had more links.

Previous studies on the increased use of context and interpretation in journalism and new theories about how networks grow led to the hypotheses and research question explored here. The growth effect of Hl was tested and confirmed. Two instances of preferential attachment were also discovered. Story topic (H2 and H3) affected the amount of linking in the predicted manner, although H2 was not supported when controlling for story length. Medium also made a statistically significant difference (RQ1).

Stories on Web sites of television companies were more heavily linked than on Web sites of print companies. This supports a recent study by Lin and Jeffres that found greater use of linking on local television Web sites than newspaper sites, although this study used the site rather than the story unit of analysis. The additional linking on national broadcast sites is not attributable to a significantly greater use of audio and video clips. That difference accounts for only 0.28 links per story while the overall gap between print and broadcast sites is 4.4 links per story. More likely, the difference stems from national broadcast outlets writing Web stories from scratch, while print sites can rely more on shovelware.

More than 400 stories (28.6%) contain no links at all, but 5 stories have more than 60 links. As a result, stories with the mean of 6 links cannot be convincingly described as "typical." The curve is very similar in shape to one depicting the Web as a whole although somewhat more gentle. Rather than following the 80/20 rule, this one follows an 80/31 distribution. That is, 31% of the stories in the sample accounted for 80% of the links.

Why is the curve more gentle? The purpose of journalism may limit the number of links a news story will offer on its main page. The story with the most links in this sample had 81, a relatively small number compared to the most-linked pages on the Web. Stories that offered more links than this would fail at one of journalism's primary missions: providing the reader with a clear view of what really matters. Adherence to this mission may cap the effects of growth and preferred attachment and limits the length of the tail on the distribution. This may also explain why the growing gap between spot news and international relations failed to reach statistical significance.

An examination of the most linked stories is useful. The number-one story was from 28 March 1999 and appeared on CNN.com. This was the fifth day of NATO bombing during the Kosovo conflict that had been in the news for two years and was heavily covered in the preceding weeks. This provided editors with ample historical context and recently produced material.

The result: links to 37 internal pages of text, 18 other Web sites, 10 video clips, 8 photos, 6 maps, 1 audio clip, and 1 discussion forum. Although not investigated in this study, it is reasonable to conclude that the time a reader spends on such a presentation would, on average, exceed the time spent on a story that did not provide any linked material. In this way the technical characteristics of the Web could drive coverage the way television's news is driven, in part, by its technology. The next 5 most-linked stories shared the same topic: the stock market. This may be an example of the interaction between growth and preferred attachment.

The business audience was among the first to take advantage of the new medium. If Web editors targeted this audience then stories of this type would have received preferred attachment early on and would have grown at a faster rate than other stories. During the five years investigated, financial stories were more heavily linked than stories about international relations. The sample for this study has some limitations which affect generalizability. For each of the five years, systematic sampling occurred in March rather than throughout the year. Only the top stories for each sampling day were recorded; stories further down on a news Web site are likely less "linked." And because story length was not recorded until the final year, a more detailed examination of that variable is warranted. This chapter addressed the increased use of hyperlinking but did not examine where those links lead. Are the points of view available to readers being broadened by linking, or are the same types of sources being used on the Web as in traditional journalism? When news organizations link to other Web sites, which ones are linked to and which are not? Are there trends already discernable that allow us to predict which kinds of ideas become "hubs" in the electronic network and which become isolated pockets?

Does the linking of news stories to discussion forums, a common practice on the Web sites examined here, affect the pattern of discourse surrounding current events? Two types of preferential attachment were confirmed in this study. Stories produced by broadcast companies were more heavily linked, and story topic also had a statistically significant effect on linking practice.

Another bias of Web editors that may affect link usage is commercial. If television news favors good pictures to hold an audience, we might expect Web editors to use links strategically to keep readers on their sites. The special characteristics of the Web could be changing the way news stories are crafted.

By linking to contextual material instead of including it in the primary text, a separation may be occurring between "events" and "context." In this scenario individual stories may become at once more event-driven and more contextual (through the use of links). If this is the case, an examination of linking patterns becomes critical if we are to understand the way stories are framed in the Web of context.

LIMITATIONS AND FUTURE RESEARCH

The results of this chapter are based on a single study in one community, thus restricting any inferential claims based on an assumption of external validity. But the findings reflect a certain degree of construct validity given our emphasis on autonomy as a professional value that should dampen support for civic journalism. Students who work for a campus newspaper should be moving closer to professionals and away from fellow students; the data consistently fit this pattern across various measures of civic journalism support.

Future research would ideally incorporate a panel design of at least two years' duration, with a larger and broader sample of respondents, to track the development of journalistic values as students enter the initial stage of their professional careers. Studies should also incorporate direct attitudinal measures of autonomy as a professional value to supplement the attitudinal and experiential measures used in this study. We suggest a framework for field research based on the development of operational measures that represent the twentieth-century ethos of professional journalism (e.g., detachment, free press, watchdog role, people's right to know, criticizing institutions) alongside the civic journalism approach (e.g., social responsibility, community building, self-criticizing press institutions, problem-solving).

This approach might generate insight that can be used for the reform of journalism instruction as educators promote autonomy in service to democracy. Public journalism began as a series of experiments in the late 1980s and early 1990s, and soon developed into what Schudson has called "the most impressive critique of journalistic practice inside journalism in a generation" and "the best organized social movement inside journalism in the history of the American press."

Also known as civic journalism, the movement arose in response to a perceived crisis in the role of the press in constituting a public sphere in which citizens could understand and engage productively with the issues of the day. During the first decade, the movement generated an array of innovative practices in newsrooms and communities, as well as an extensive network of journalism practitioners and educators committed to reshaping professional and institutional norms. The primary philosophical emphasis of public journalism, as manifest in the writings of its leading theorists and practitioners, is on the relationship between the practice of journalism and the democratic work of citizens in a self-governing republic, and suggests journalists are ideally suited to help constitute vital "publics" to deliberate complex issues and engage in collective problem-solving activities. Public journalism, thus, has set out to help members of the public come to see themselves as citizens, and hold them accountable for grappling with the full complexity of issues and become participants in civil society rather than mere spectators of it.

Still, after more than a decade of practice of public journalism, empirical knowledge of whether and how public journalism has met these goals remains largely based on in-depth case studies. Early literature focused on cases generally acknowledged as the seed-beds of the public journalism movement.

Subsequent comparative research examined other best cases, focusing on changes in newsroom reporting and editing practices, community recognition of public journalism efforts, and shifts in community problem-solving and public deliberation. While researchers found positive evidence in each area, elements were not disaggregated and case studies were often idiosyncratic, making it difficult to measure impact or establish clear relationships among elements.

In their critical review of forty-seven evaluative studies of public journalism, Massey and Haas found that public journalism practices have had limited effects on the attitudes, beliefs, and behaviours of news audiences. They criticize existing research for focusing on "a handful of showcase public-journalism news organizations and projects."

In doing so, they highlight the methodological shortcomings of many of the efforts to assess public journalism, and recommend that future research capture a wider array of experiments and trace the effects of these efforts on community life. With prior research lacking a broad, systematic assessment of public journalism efforts, we set out to provide a holistic analysis of the movement, shedding light on participating organizations, practices, and effects.

An inventory of the archives of the Pew Centre for Civic Journalism found 651 public journalism projects conducted from 1994 to 20027 Our research analyses the inventory using hierarchical regression analysis to trace the effects of organizational factors, project features, story frames, and efforts to involve community members and assess public opinion on three civil society goals:

- Improving citizens' civic competencies,
- Influencing policymaking processes, and
- Increasing civic volunteerism.

The literature on public journalism is extensive, but extracting clear empirical propositions is challenging. First, much of the best literature is normative, advocating a role of the press in improving public life, and tends to draw case-based observations about changes public journalism creates in news organizations.

Second, the large body of case literature is very uneven, ranging from anecdotal and polemic to qualitative and comparative case observation. While it is difficult to untangle the effects of public journalism on civil society given these inconsistencies, there are important insights to be gained from the extant research. Public journalism research has primarily concentrated on several flagship public journalism newsrooms and projects. Additionally, there are numerous case studies of other cities and regions. These cases, however, have not been analysed using a systematic empirical-quantitative framework.

Here, we consider the scholarship in three domains of public journalism:

- Organization of newsrooms and their effects on individual journalists' values, norms, and behaviour;
- Links between public journalism efforts and changes in news content, framing, and sourcing; and

- Public journalism's impact on electoral knowledge and behaviour, and on citizen participation in public life.

MEDIA ORGANIZATIONS AND NEWS VALUES

There are two broad types of newsroom studies: (1) of news organizations; and (2) of journalists' beliefs and attitudes. While there are no inherent methodological contradictions between them, each tends to have its own understandings of how public journalism is established in newsrooms.

Organizational studies see the adoption of public journalism from the top down, with publisher and editor orientations as the important predictors of public journalism practice. An investment by news organizations in public journalism shapes reporting routines and story content, and accounts for the adoption of the practice over longer periods of time.

This approach posits institutionalization as a property of the organization, with organizational decisions molding the actions and routines, if not beliefs, of individuals within them. Evidence suggests that newsrooms institutionalizing public journalism (i.e., commitments to partnerships with other community organizations and lengthy projects) produce stronger public effects.

A second approach looks at the effect of values of journalists on attitudes and behaviour. Here, the adoption of public journalism values is a prerequisite for genuine individual transformation that leads to newsroom change. Proponents of this approach hold that positive attitudes toward public journalism should precede behavioural change."

This values approach, then, sees change in beliefs and attitudes as generating new public reporting behaviour that underlies the transformation of news organizations. From their review of public journalism studies, Massey and Haas found that journalists are most comfortable with the more "traditional" shadings of public journalism, though some support for more "activist" roles exists. These mixed results indicate traditional and public journalism beliefs seem to coexist in many newsrooms and within individual journalists, suggesting an "occupational pragmatism." Not surprisingly, "mixed-change" characterizes virtually every case of public journalism, positing a kind of "tipping point" within newsrooms and individuals.

If newsrooms have not tipped, public journalism practice should be weak. As this suggests, both the organizational approach and the news values approach ultimately focus on the degree to which newsrooms have adopted and integrated public journalism practices into the newsroom culture, regardless of whether the spur of this transformation is from the top down or the bottom up.

NEWS COVERAGE AND CONTENT

Research on changes in reporting spurred by public journalism is sparse, with little attention to whether certain topics or frames of reporting are particularly suited to public journalism. Although public journalism often implicitly focuses on community, efforts have addressed a plethora of issues confronting localities, including crime, diversity, education, environment, health, poverty, and, of course, elections and government. Public journalists have utilized a range of issue frames to structure their reporting, from established conflict and human-interest frames to more novel problem-solving and historical frames. However, little is known about the potency of these framing devices for civil society outcomes or whether certain topics lend themselves to successful public journalism as defined by increases in civic competence and volunteerism.

Instead, most coverage studies focus on the type of content and sources used in public journalism stories, with inconsistent evidence. Some indicate little difference in content, while others have found that public journalism efforts have a greater focus on local concerns and help citizens engage in civic activities.

There is also inconsistent evidence on sourcing. Thus, it remains unclear whether certain public journalism tools, such as encouraging citizen involvement or giving citizen voices greater prominence, improves civil society outcomes.

EFFECTS OF PUBLIC JOURNALISM

The evidence for public journalism effects on civic and public life is partial and incomplete. Studies divide broadly into those investigating the effect of public journalism on electoral outcomes and those addressing civic and public problem solving.

First, there is evidence supporting a positive relationship between citizenfocused journalism and knowledge, trust, and civic participation in elections. There is, however, some evidence to the contrary. Thus, on the whole, studies support a moderate effect of civic electoral coverage in the areas of voter awareness of issues and traditional forms of political participation.

Although untangling political cause and effect is difficult, there is a case for public journalism efforts and broader public engagement. Studies have found an increase in political participation. There is also some evidence that public journalism increases public deliberation and civic problem solving. Moreover, Friedland's study of the "We the People" project in Madison, Wisconsin, found project longevity to have substantial cumulative impact on opinion leaders, media cooperation, and institutional effectiveness, with mixed effects on citizen engagement. If there is episodic coverage with little follow-up, however, a project's cumulative problem-solving effects were attenuated.

In sum, the case-based evidence shows effects of increased civic and public problem solving in limited areas. Past theorizing and case studies concerning the practices and effects of public journalism do not present a clear picture of the consequences of this shift in coverage for civil society. Scholars have focused on different levels of analysis-organization, newsroom, story, and citizens-and attended to a wide range of outcome variables.

Results have not been consistent, though this inconsistency may be a function of community and organizational factors that are not the focus of a particular case study. After a decade of broad practice, it is unclear which organizational factors beyond length of adoption and integration of public journalism contribute to the success of public journalism efforts.

Likewise, beyond attention to certain patterns of sourcing and shifts in content, it is not known whether the success of public journalism efforts is connected with attention to certain topics-such as poverty or crime-and particular frames of reference - such as human interest or problem-solving.

On a more basic level, evidence is lacking on whether particular ways of giving voice to the perspectives of citizens improve civil society in the ways that theorists of public journalism attest. Accordingly, we examine here the effects of a wide range of potentially explanatory variables on assessments of the outcomes of a wide cross-section of public journalism efforts between 1994 and 2002. This study attempts to answer how the influence of organizational factors, project features, story frames, and efforts to involve community members and assess public opinion uniquely contribute to three broad goals of public journalism: (1) improving civic skills among citizens; (2) influencing the policymaking process; and (3) increasing levels of civic volunteerism.

Accordingly, we offer the following research questions to guide our analysis:

- RQ1: What features of news organizations involved in public journalism projects appear to influence whether sponsored efforts increase civic skills of citizens, public input on policymaking, and levels of civic volunteerism?
- RQ2: What features of public journalism projects appear to influence whether sponsored efforts increase civic skills of citizens, public input on policymaking, and levels of civic volunteerism?
- RQ3: What types of story frames used by journalists involved in public journalism projects appear to influence whether sponsored efforts increase civic skills of citizens, public input on policymaking, and levels of civic volunteerism?
- RQ4: What types of efforts to involve community members and assess public opinion appear to influence whether sponsored efforts increase civic skills of citizens, public input on policymaking, and levels of civic volunteerism?

METHODS

Data3

This study is based on data collected at the University of Wisconsin-Madison from the archives of the Pew Centre for Civic Journalism. During its ten years of operation as the principle incubator for the movement, between 1993 and 2003, the Pew Centre collected examples of public journalism projects submitted by U.S. newsrooms seeking funding, competing for awards, and/or seeking informal recognition and advice.

Between January 2000 and May 2001, this archive was systematically examined for all evidence of public journalism experiments, with the archive structured into a set of cases organized by discrete projects and publication dates.

A qualitative coding scheme was developed to capture a descriptive account of project attributes, including, but not limited to: the news organization (circulation, population served, partnerships); the project (topic, publication dates, presentation format); the news frames, sources, and civic linkages used in news construction; and the civic practices, polls, and public deliberative events used to give citizens a voice.

In addition, outcomes such as improved civic and deliberative skills, increased public funding and volunteerism, and improved public policy processes were gauged from these reports.

A quantitative coding guide was developed so that statistical tools could be used to more systematically analyse these data. The final inventory of the archive contained a total of 651 cases of public journalism completed between 1994 and 2002. Although the study sample is limited to public journalism projects in the Pew Centre's archive and undercounts the full range of public journalism work conducted by U.S. newsrooms during this period, it captures public journalism as practiced by the most dedicated of self-identified public journalism practitioners.

Thus, the sample, while biased in favour of best practices, provides a solid foundation upon which to assess a broad range of public journalism practices and evaluate the movement's reach and impact on community life.

Measures

Items coded from the public journalism projects were used to operationalize six general clusters of variables: (1) outcomes of the public journalism project, (2) features of the news organization, (3) features of the project, (4) features of the stories, particularly story frames, (5) citizen involvement, and (6) public assessment.

In the analyses reported in this chapter, the outcomes of public journalism were used as dependent variables predicted by the other five sets of variables.

Bibliography

Ajay Dash: *Basic Concept of Journalism*, Discovery Publishing House, Delhi, 2007.

Ajay Dash: *Broadcasting Journalism*, Discovery Publishing House, Delhi, 2007.

Arun Bhatia: *Impact of Internet on Journalism*, Akansha Publication, Delhi, 2005.

B.N. Tripathi: *Handbook of Journalism and Mass Media*, Saurabh Publishing House, Delhi, 2001.

Balai Lal Jana and Kanai Prasad Mitra: *Farm Journalism*, Agrotech Publishing Academy, Delhi, 2013.

D.V.R. Murthy: *Developmental Journalism*, Dominant Publication, Delhi, 2012.

Deepak Kumar: *Citizen and Community Journalism*, Aarti Prakashan, Delhi, 2011.

Dhawal Paramjeet Singh: *Community Journalism*, Anmol Publication, Delhi, 2011.

G.C. Kundra: *History of Journalism in India*, ALP Books, Delhi, 2011.

Gaurav Oberoi: *Electronic Media And Journalism*, Murari Lal and Sons, Delhi, 2009.

Hari Mohan Agarwal: *Journalism in Practice*, Reference Press, Delhi, 2005.

Jitendra Kumar Sharma: *Ethics of Journalism in Transition*, Authors Press, Delhi, 2002.

Kewal Anand: *Dynamics of Journalism : In Historical Perspective*, Swastik Publication, Delhi, 2008.

M.S. Bisht: *Journalism, Advertisement and Public Relations*, Cyber Tech Publications, New Delhi, 2011.

Nalini Rajan: *21st Century Journalism in India*, Sage Publication, Delhi, 2007.

Om Gupta and Ajay S. Jasra: *Information Technology in Journalism*, Kanishka Publication, Delhi, 2002.

P.K. Ravindranath: *Contemporary Issues : For Students of Journalism*, Authorspress, Delhi, 2008.

P.K. Sinha: *Global Journalism in Digital Age*, ALP Books, Delhi, 2009.

Priyanka Wadhwa: *History of Journalism*, Murari Lal and Sons, Delhi, 2007.

R. Choudhary: *Journalism Ethics*, Centrum Press, Delhi, 2010.

Rabindra K Mahapatra and Krushna C Panda: *Information Science and Journalism : A Symbiosis*, Rawat Publication, Delhi, 2004.

Rahul Mudgal: *Journalism and Law*, Sarup & Sons, Delhi, 2009.

Rahul Singhai: *Computer Applications for Journalism*, Reference Press, Delhi, 2006.

Rajesh K Singh: *Broadcast Journalism : Techniques of News Writing Reporting and Production*, Manglam Publications, Delhi, 2009.

Rajiv Saxena: *Computer Application for Journalism*, Centrum Press, Delhi, 2010.

Rajnish: *History and Development of Responsible Journalism*, Sumit Enterprises, Delhi, 2007.

S Kumar: *Encyclopaedia of Journalism and Mass Communication (6 Vols-Set)*, Shubhi Publication, Delhi, 2005.

S N Das Gupta: *Journalism : A Digital Literacy Guide*, ALP Books, Delhi, 2009.

Sanjay Gaur: *e-Journalism*, Yking Books, Delhi, 2011.

Shekhar Verma: *Journalism and Mass Communication*, Sonali Publications, Delhi, 2011.

Shyam Nath: *Assessing the State of Web Journalism*, Authors Press, Delhi, 2002.

Stuart Allan: *Journalism : Critical Issues*, Rawat Publication, Delhi, 2008.

Subhesh Chand Sharma and Sweta Bakshi: *Development Communication and Journalism*, A.K. Publications, Delhi, 2009.

Swati Chauhan and Navin Chandra: *Foundations of News and Journalism*, Kanishka Publication, Delhi, 2011.

T C Verma: *Dimensions of Modern Journalism*, ABD Publishers, Delhi, 2006.

Tony Harcup: *Journalism : Principles and Practice*, Sage Publication, Delhi, 2009.

Studies, International Book Dist, Delhi, 2009.

Veena Sharma: *Journalism with New Challenge*, ALP Books, Delhi, 2012.

Vir Bala Aggarwal: *Essentials of Practical Journalism*, Concept Publication, New Delhi, 2006.

Y. D'Souza: *Functions and Areas of Journalism*, Wisdom Press, Delhi, 2012.

Index